Reason in Controversy

REASON IN CONTROVERSY

An Introduction

to General Argumentation

GLEN E. MILLS

NORTHWESTERN UNIVERSITY

ALLYN AND BACON, INC.   Boston

First printing ....April, 1964
Second printing ....January, 1966

PREFACE

In this time of numerous and serious controversies, which mass persuaders and censors hope to settle *for* us, many thoughtful persons of all ages are feeling a need for some help in meeting the challenge. What they need is systematic instruction in the analysis of controversial statements, the accumulation and the testing of evidence, the drawing and the criticism of inferences, the questions of logical and ethical responsibility, the procedures of attack and defense, the logical arrangement of materials, the social import of advocacy in a free society, and the effective presentation of their views.

This application of the principles of primarily reasoned discourse to the everyday experience of speakers, listeners, writers, and readers can be stimulating and rewarding. It can be pursued by college and university students, by adults, and by more mature high school students. As an offering under general or liberal education, this work can be treated either as a separate subject (general argumentation) or as part of a course in communication arts, English composition, editorial writing, critical thinking, public speaking, or contemporary problems.

For these various interests the author hopes to provide sound, up-to-date doctrine and tested assignments. The principles have come from many sources, ranging from ancient rhetoric and dialectic to the contributions of speech, philosophy, and psychology in the nineteen-sixties. The professionals in this field will notice some points at which this book differs more or less from some others: definitions of argumentation, correction of misconceptions concerning the subject, interpretations of presumption and burden of proof, kinds of debate, classes of propositions, analysis of nonpolicy propositions, use of evidence, definition of proof, and especially the kinds of reasoning and the relation of dialectic to cross-examination. Six specimens in the Appendixes will be found useful for descriptive and critical analysis.

G.E.M.

[v]

CONTENTS

[vii]

Reason in Controversy

CHAPTER I

INTRODUCTION

TO ARGUMENTATION

CONTROVERSY, WHICH IS THE EXCHANGE OF OPPOSING VIEWS ON PROBLEMS of mutual interest to the contending parties, is an ancient and yet a vital activity in an open society. Its competitive communication may involve many combinations of rational, nonrational, and irrational appeals. However, the study of argumentation stresses the values of reasoned discourse; hence the title, *Reason in Controversy*.

DEFINITIONS OF ARGUMENTATION

As a Form of Discourse

Traditionally, four forms of discourse have been discussed in textbooks on composition. It may be helpful to review briefly the meaning of argumentation in this context.

After the cause of death was found to have been homicide by person or persons unknown, the officers of the law continued their investigation until they found a suspect who was subsequently tried for first degree murder. The proof was such that the jury brought in a verdict of guilty, and the judge sentenced the convict to death in the electric chair.

[1]

This specimen of discourse is mostly narration; it relates a series of events as in a story. In a fictional work, the plot is developed by narration. In ancient times narration meant the statement of facts in a given case, but today we think of narration as a compositional element which can be used in speech or writing for the purpose of relating a succession of events. Illustrations are probably the most familiar narrative materials in speeches and essays.

The sound of footsteps outside his cell made him feel certain that his time had come. Though dazed by fear, he sat up on his bunk as the guards and other prison officials came to escort him to the execution chamber. Down the long, gray corridor he moved as if in a dream.

Description, which predominates in the foregoing paragraph, involves the recording of sensory impressions. We say "predominates" because one kind of discourse rarely occurs in pure form. For example, description is often combined with narration to make more interesting composition. Speakers and writers use description to reveal the appearance, attributes, or the nature of objects, scenes, persons, and experiences of many sorts.

What is capital punishment? It is the legal application of the death penalty for certain serious crimes. Historically it has taken several forms, including electrocution, hanging, shooting, gassing, decapitation, and burning.

Exposition, in this case by definition, appears in the preceding paragraph. This third traditional form of discourse explains or informs, yet it often appears in persuasive communication, as do narration and description. Exposition is used to achieve clarity by explaining, defining, and perhaps evaluating. It is concerned with the nature, the scope and the relations, but not the truth or falsity, of ideas. When exposition is associated with things rather than with abstract ideas, it relates to processes, functions, and parts.

Capital punishment should be abolished wherever it exists, because it is based upon the discredited notion of retribution and because it is ineffective as a deterrent to crime.

Clearly this is a specimen of argumentation, though it is too sketchy to qualify as one worthy of emulation. Its weakness is its incompleteness, not its purpose or form. Sometimes a message of this sort includes narration, description, and exposition in the interest of effective style, but it is definable as argumentation if the central purpose is the advocacy of a controversial conclusion or the criticism of ideas. For the present we shall consider only the first purpose, that of advocacy, when defining argumentation as a form of discourse or communication. In this sense it is purposeful in terms of audience reaction, i.e., behavior in the form of attitude, belief, or overt action.

Used in this broad sense as one of the four traditional forms of discourse, argumentation would include what we know as persuasion. However, our professional usage has narrowed the concept of argumentation so that it covers that part of persuasive communication which employs reasoned discourse as its principal form of support. This means that even though some emotional and personal proofs are used, they are set in logical frameworks which impose at least a modicum of rigor upon the arguments. In other words, through argumentation we solve problems with a deliberative method. In saying this we imply the assumption that man is a rational creature, despite his lapses into superstition, mass hysteria, the following of pied pipers, rumor mongering, witch hunting, and the like. Perhaps all we are saying is that man reacts emotionally as well as intellectually, but that the primarily emotional "thinking" is much more likely to be "crooked thinking." Thus the preferred form of proof among thoughtful persons is the kind we have labeled reasoned discourse.

As a Critical Apparatus

When we wish to make a critical analysis of argumentative discourse, what tools do we employ? Many persons appear to be limited to an unorganized assortment of items including "correct" grammar, pronunciation, paragraphing, and punctuation, and outward signs of sincerity, enthusiasm, and so forth. These criteria are not completely irrelevant, but they do not enable us to evaluate the intellectual merit of the presentation.

The more sophisticated kind of evaluation involves us as critics in asking discerning questions about what the arguer is trying to prove, what he must do to prove it, and how well or ill he fares in his attempt. Concepts such as probability, presumption, burden of proof, burden of rebuttal, analysis, evidence, and others which will be explained in the following chapters comprise the critical apparatus which should be brought to bear in the sort of evaluation we are discussing.

Frequently a critic of an argument will compose his comment in argumentative form, because there is probably no better way to marshal reasons for a critical position. Some of George Bernard Shaw's essays in criticism are cases in point.

This critical apparatus is intended not only to evaluate the discourses of others but also to test our own arguments during the compositional process. It often helps to imagine yourself on the opposing side, looking for flaws in your intended case. More will be said of this critical function in Chapter X.

As an Academic Discipline

As it is understood today, argumentation is probably not much more than a century old. Among the earliest specialized textbooks or manuals were Rowton's *How To Conduct a Debate* (c. 1840), Holyoake's *Public Speaking and Debate* (1853), and McElligott's *The American Debater* (1855). Probably the most influential in terms of defining the scope of the subject was George P. Baker's *Principles of Argumentation* (1895) which he developed while teaching a pioneer course at Harvard.

Some of the early credit-bearing courses in argumentation were brought into college curricula in response to requests by intercollegiate debaters for systematic faculty assistance in preparing for contests. Thus the close linkage of argumentation and debate came about quite naturally. This circumstance plus the early popularity of the course with prelegal students may explain why so many courses and textbooks in argumentation have stressed the applications of the subject to school debating and courtroom pleading.

Although argumentation as a distinct subject is comparatively new, its parent disciplines, rhetoric and dialectic, date back at least twenty-four centuries. According to Aristotle, whose *Rhetoric* has been placed at 330–322 B.C., rhetoric was concerned with persuasive discourse, usually in the form of oratory. According to Cooper's translation, Aristotle defined rhetoric as the faculty or power of discovering in the particular case what are the available means of persuasion. The principles of this ancient liberal art were generalized by observing and analyzing the persuasive oratory of the popular speakers in the legislative and judicial assemblies of that time.

Classical rhetoric embodied a broad range of advice, only a part of which has central relevance to argumentation. One of the distinctive categories of advice concerned the modes of proof, which Aristotle divided into *logos*, *ethos*, and *pathos*. Logical proof (*logos*) included the materials which would induce a commitment based upon reflection. These materials typically took the form of probability and signs expressed in enthymemes (conclusions and reasons); the known and the certainly knowable were excluded. In short, argumentation has derived much of its doctrine on analysis, evidence, and reasoning from rhetoric.

Ethical (*ethos*) and emotional (*pathos*) forms of support are not core concepts in argumentation as they are in the broader field of persuasion in general; but when argumentation is viewed as a part of persuasion, these forms of support must be considered. Ethical proof originally meant the persuasive impact of the speaker's personality, i.e., the impressions of character, intelligence, and good will which the listeners received during the speaker's presentation. Now, one's status or prior reputation is included among the constituents of ethical proof. Emotional proof, including appeals to values and goals as well as to the familiar emotional states, is likewise more clearly identified with the theory of persuasion than with that of argumentation.

However, these three modes of proof (logical, ethical, emotional) are not discrete in real life. In fact, they were not so conceived by Aristotle. Thought and emotion were not completely separated; he used the enthymeme mainly for logical argument, but in treating emotional argument he wrote of discovering materials for enthymemes which would put listeners into a receptive state of feeling. An example of an argument embodying all three forms of support would be one which is perceived as being substantively sound, emotionally satisfying, and coming from a credible source.

Having sketchily treated rhetoric as one of the parent disciplines of argumentation, we can next consider another, which is dialectic. This tool of intellectual criticism has been called the counterpart of rhetoric, because rhetoric deals with the art of public speaking, while dialectic deals with the art of logical discussion. Although its origin is unknown, we know that Socrates used it for inquiry and for teaching, and that Plato immortalized its literary form in his *Dialogues*. In brief, dialectic originally was the art of disputation by question and answer. Socrates used it to reveal the inadequacy of popular beliefs. He did so, not by stating a contention supported by evidence, as in rhetoric, but by asking a series of questions in which each successive one was based upon the respondent's reply to the preceding question. Thus, the answers served as evidence or as logical premises for the questioner's next step. Like rhetoric, this procedure attains only probability, but it uses formal logic as it deals in universals; it admits the debatable only in the assumption of its premises. Obviously the discipline of argumentation is indebted to ancient dialectic for some principles of argumentative conversation and of cross-examination. These will be explained and illustrated in a later chapter.

As an academic discipline, therefore, argumentation is a branch of communication theory which deals with the analysis, synthesis, and criticism of primarily reasoned discourse about controversial ideas. The principles of this subject are applied in order to discover the proof requirements of an assertion or to make a case for or against an assertion. Argumentation is concerned mainly with advocacy and, to a lesser degree, with inquiry. In this latter sense, it teaches analysis for one's own understanding, whether or not he advocates or perceives advocacy. This conception of its scope is indicated by the listing of its major topics: proof requirements of a thesis, propositions, analysis, investigation, evidence, reasoning, cases, attack and defense, and cross-examination.

In Relation to Discussion, Debate, and Persuasion

Argumentation is related in various respects and degrees to the communicative forms and the school subjects known as discussion, debate, and persuasion. These three have in common the fact that they are possible routes between problems and decisions. Perhaps the similarities and the interrelationships among these processes have accounted for some of the misconceptions which have become widespread in recent decades.

Some discussion enthusiasts in the early thirties, for instance, maintained that discussing and arguing were antithetical processes and that they represented good and evil, respectively. Occasionally these discussants-turned-advocates would debate on the affirmative side of the proposition that debate was educationally undesirable. Later the prevailing view came to be that argumentation (or debate) and discussion were complementary processes whose differences could be visualized on several continua. On the inquiry-advocacy continuum, the reflective thinking-intentional reasoning continuum, and the cooperation-competition continuum, discussion would be placed nearer the first term in each pair, and debate would be placed nearer the second. These differences in degree and kind were not intended to express a preference for either discussion or debate.[1]

Actually, the theorists who formulated the foregoing doctrine had observed that in many real-life situations one cannot draw a sharp distinction between discussion and debate. A situation which begins as a discussion can become a debate if an issue divides the group into irreconcilable sides. Conversely two sides which start to debate can sometimes be brought together through a reflective thinking process. Even when the pattern and the spirit of the group communication are clearly definable as inquiry rather than advocacy, there are or should be some applications of argumentation within that framework, particularly in the testing of the proposed solutions. More will be said of this in a later chapter on investigation.

This leads to the point that in the utilization of oral communication for problem solving, discussion must sometimes give way to debate or possibly persuasion. Occasions for this shift include the following: when an honest disagreement cannot be resolved by the discussion method, when some persons either cannot or will not discuss, when a large assembly has to act, and when time is short.

Although the relationships between argumentation and discussion have produced some serious confusion, the same can hardly be said of the relationships between argumentation and debate. Only two minor difficulties occur with any significant frequency here: either the two terms are erroneously treated as synonyms, or debate is narrowly defined as formal, oral controversy.

It is a mistake to treat argumentation and debate as synonyms, because the former is the theoretical field or the body of principles, while the latter is a specialized application of the former. It is equally wrong, in the view of this writer, to limit the definition of debate to the oral practice of argumentation by two or more persons who are physically present in one place at the same time. In this book, debate is defined as competitive advocacy, either oral or written, between pro and con sides of a proposition, and taking place with or without limitations of time, place, or form. A debate may be formally structured, as in a school contest or in some parliamentary proceedings, or it may be as informal as casual conversation. Thus we may say that speakers and writers have been debating the states' rights proposition since 1787.

[1] J. H. McBurney and K. G. Hance, *The Principles and Methods of Discussion* (New York: Harper and Bros., 1939).

Some relationships between argumentation and persuasion were discussed in an earlier paragraph which treated rhetoric as one of the sources of argumentation theory. Since argumentation has drawn its principles from dialectic as well as from rhetoric, and since argumentation serves analytical and critical functions which are not used to effect persuasion, we should conclude that argumentation is something more than the logical part of persuasion. In fact, if argumentation were defined as persuasion, its "logic" would have to be judged in terms of its persuasive effect instead of some external standard of reasonableness. But when argumentation is taken to be a kind of "science of proof," it can be used to test the reasoning in a persuasive communication, because, as we saw earlier in this chapter, it has objective standards of critical analysis.

Debate, which is an applied form of argumentation, differs from persuasion in at least one important respect; *it requires competition* between rival ideas, while persuasion may mean one-sided advocacy which typically avoids deliberative thinking by the listeners or readers. Thus persuasion can become propaganda, but debate cannot.

THE SOCIAL CONTEXT OF THIS SUBJECT

Ideals of a Democracy

What they are. Before we can relate the principles of argumentation to the philosophical tenets of our social order, we must state what we believe to be the relevant ideals of our democracy. One is that individuals will participate in making decisions. This is the essence of self-government. Another is the faith that man, if sufficiently well informed and in communication with his fellows, can solve social problems. Thus education and communication are of great importance, because if one cannot hear or understand what others say, or if they cannot hear or understand him, there can be no dialogue, and democracy loses its meaning, as Robert M. Hutchins has said.[2] A third ideal is that the dialogue will not cease. As Alexander Meiklejohn put it,[3]

[2] "Is Democracy Possible?," *Saturday Review*, February 21, 1959.
[3] "Everything Worth Saying Should Be Said," New York *Times* Magazine, July 18, 1948.

the basic need of free discussion is not that everyone shall speak but that everything worth saying shall be said. Another ideal is that we can have majority rule coupled with a respect for minority views, even though some persons argue that the two are mutually exclusive. The hard fact is that the persons on the winning side who try to silence the minority are revealing their contempt for the democratic ideal. This thought suggests the fifth ideal, the right of dissent. But this implies more than protection against arbitrary power; it means that no one may be barred from expressing views which some say are false or unwise. When people govern themselves, it is they alone who must judge falsehood or folly. In Judge Learned Hand's view, the privilege of free speech rests upon the assumption that there is no proposition so uniformly believed that it is beyond challenge or debate. In other words, in the end it is "worse to suppress dissent than to run the risk of heresy." [4]

Some threats they face. Though these ideals sound familiar and are subject to much lip-service, they constantly face serious threats. One of these threats stems from the failures of education and of communication on some occasions to achieve the ideal expressed above. Germany under the Weimar Republic, for instance, had a high literacy rate, ample publication, a tradition of scholarship, and a scheme of proportional representation, but these could not prevail against the emergent dictatorship of Hitler. And this can happen elsewhere. Education can become trivial, and the communication media can become exclusively purveyors of entertainment or of propaganda. The dialogue which is the essence of a free society may practically cease because the citizens either have nothing to say or have no place to say it.

Another threat, probably a consequence of the first, involves the development of authoritarian leadership behind a democratic disguise consisting of the forms, rituals, slogans, and other symbols of a free society. At all levels of human organization, from a small, local group to a major nation-state, we have seen leaders make a mockery of parliamentary procedure, the ballot, constitutions, and labels such as "democratic," "people's," and "peace-loving."

A third threat to our cherished ideals comes about through the desire for "efficiency" in the face of the amazing complexity and number of problems which citizens are expected to solve. One is

[4] *Saturday Review*, March 15, 1958, p. 17.

sorely tempted to give up and turn the whole business over to administrators and bureaucrats. This attitude of resignation becomes understandable when we realize that the mass of technical information on many public problems makes it unlikely that there can be a fully informed citizen. Because thorough debating takes much time, because none can become fully informed, and because the analogy of the New England town meeting cannot apply to our large, heterogeneous, industrial, bureacratic society, it is argued that the most we should hope for is a condition of order, efficiency, and some semblance of civil rights.

Fourth in our list of threats is the widespread fear of unpopular opinions and the resulting temptation to deny them a forum. A case in point was the reaction to a paid advertisement in the Chicago *Daily News* which sought support for the defense of a man who had been indicted under the Smith Act. A letter writer contended that the accused should have his hearing in court but not in "an American newspaper worthy of the name." The editor replied that his paper did not favor jailing people solely for their ideas, however perverted, and that the issue of civil liberty was so fundamental that the defense was entitled to appeal for public support. Perhaps the most familiar type of case is that of the school and college teachers who have been reprimanded or discharged for exposing young minds to "controversial subjects." This verbal subterfuge scarcely conceals the fact that the real objection is to the disclosure that there is a view other than the prevailing opinion. One is reminded of the futile attempt which was made to prohibit intercollegiate debating of the recognition of Red China a few years ago. As if these instances were insufficient to make the point, we can recall local, state-wide, and nation-wide agitations to ban allegedly "subversive" books or authors such as Carl Sandburg, Archibald MacLeish, and "Robin Hood." As several interpreters of the First Amendment have pointed out, we will be fit to govern ourselves only if we have faced everything that can be said in favor of or against our institutions. Unabridged freedom of public discussion and debate on public policy has been called the rock on which our government stands.

The fifth and last threat to democratic ideals is the fear of community decision. It is fomented by those who seek sources of wisdom other than the people of the community debating and deciding together. Some would limit the area in which the citizens have the right to choose what is to be preserved, changed, or abolished. There are individuals and groups that seek the uncritical preservation of their cherished values, institutions, activities, and ideas. They try to prevent the critical scrutiny of the status quo by limiting the authority of the community.

Relevance of Argumentation to Democratic Ideals

In perpetuating and improving the dialogue. Little needs to be said to the point that the study and practice of argumentation can contribute to the perpetuation and improvement of the dialogue. As we increase the understanding of and the enthusiasm for discussion and debate, we stimulate the exercise of free speech. This is the best way to prevent the triumph of censors and propagandists.

But mere freedom of speech is not enough; there must be thoughtful and responsible speech. Widespread indulgence in irrational or unethical communication cannot measure up to our democratic ideals. This points up the importance of critical thinking and the ethics of advocacy which are expounded in this book.

A significant part of this thoughtful and responsible speech occurs in the expression of dissenting opinions. These expressions are essential to the continued existence of a free society, and argumentation serves to instruct persons in formulating them or in replying to them.

In the instance of political debating, which increased in popularity during the presidential campaign of 1960, there is an opportunity for argumentation to play a part in civic education. This means that when the voters learn to demand competent argument from campaigners, the political debates will help to clarify positions, reveal issues, arouse interest, provide opportunities to evaluate candidates, and reduce the amount of "hot air." However, as we observed in the 1960 Kennedy-Nixon campaign, merely calling a televised joint appearance a "debate" does not produce these desirable outcomes.

The importance of educating the young people in particular for democratic participation has been mentioned by Aristotle ("the fate of empires depends upon it"), Thomas Jefferson, and many others. As Admiral Rickover argued, public debate is needed to clarify issues, but this contest will often deteriorate into mere quarreling when the uneducated confront the educated, because the former cannot argue on the level of facts and ideas, so they stoop to personal vilification instead.[5]

[5] "The World of the Uneducated," *Saturday Evening Post*, November 28, 1959.

Assumptions on which this relevance is based. For the doctrine of argumentation to be meaningful in the social context described above, it must be predicated upon certain assumptions. The first of these four is that a case can be made for either side of a controversial judgment. Proof in this context means adducing evidence and reasoning sufficient to establish a reasonable degree of probability in favor of the position taken.

It is assumed, secondly, that ". . . truth and justice are by nature more powerful than their opposites . . . ," as Aristotle put it. Elaborating on this notion, he continued, ". . . speaking broadly, what is true and preferable is by nature always easier to prove, and more convincing" (*Rhetoric*, 1355a). A more familiar version of the indestructibility of right ideas is to be found in Goethe's statement that nothing is so powerful as an idea whose time has come. Similarly comforting is Bryant's line, "Truth crushed to earth shall rise again." [6] In some specific cases, this idea is scarcely reassuring, because the individuals concerned are afraid they won't live to see the day. Aristotle did not set a time limit or give any other qualifications which life's experiences have taught us to add. We know that despots have ruled for decades, that some murderers are never caught, that innocent men have been imprisoned or executed, and that some wrongs have been righted only after long delay. However, Aristotle did not say that truth could be counted on to win by itself; he explained that one function of rhetoric was to prevent the triumph of fraud and injustice. But in order for debate or persuasion to perform this function, the society must be one which permits free competition among ideas.

A third assumption is that deliberative decisions are preferable to emotional reactions, impulsive snap judgments, and trial-and-error procedures. Commitments which develop from rational, logical thought are ethically defensible and generally are more enduring. Obviously this assumption, like most of the doctrine of argumentation, is predicated upon the prior assumption that man is a rational being, at least potentially. This reservation is suggested by the statement that often in times past men have preferred fighting for freedom to thinking about it. There may be better ways to establish good on earth than by fighting for it, but they can be found only by making rational decisions.

Even if it is deemed necessary, in the interest of persuasion, to motivate the acceptance of a decision, it is better to begin with a logi-

---

[6] William Cullen Bryant, "The Battle Field," Stanza 9.

cally adequate case and then to add the so-called emotional appeals. This is the meaning of the fourth assumption, which is that affective appeals work best when they supplement the logical ones which were discussed under the third assumption. To omit the rational element of persuasion is to violate the ethical principle which holds that an appeal should not circumvent the critical thinking process. That would, by definition, result in propaganda.

MISCONCEPTIONS CONCERNING ARGUMENTATION

That It Is Indistinguishable From Discussion and Inquiry

Earlier in this chapter, when argumentation was defined in relation to discussion, debate, and persuasion, we noted the misconception of polarity and incompatibility between discussion and debate. Now we move to the opposite extreme to consider the notion that discussion is a form of debate, or vice versa. This view ignores the significant difference in the thought processes which are involved. Discussion requires reflective thinking, which means working from a question to a solution which is not known in advance. The process is inquiry. Argumentation, which includes debate, requires intentional thinking, which proceeds from a solution (proposition) to the evidence and reasons which support it. This process is advocacy. Even though inquiry and advocacy are not strictly dichotomous, their differences are worthy of note. But these differences appear to be ignored by the few persons who write of debate as bilateral reflective thinking and of discussion as multilateral. True, debate is bilateral (two-sided), but it is not reflective in process or intent; it is competitive.

This notion that debate is a form of inquiry and is therefore basically cooperative is sometimes true but oftentimes false. When a local unit of the League of Women Voters invites rival candidates for mayor to debate in their meeting, the confrontation may be for the League members a form of inquiry, but for the candidates it is mainly competitive advocacy. The cooperation between the rivals is only procedural; they agree on the ground rules of the occasion. The same is true of prizefighters: they cooperate in the sense that they appear at the same place, comply with a commission's rules, obey a referee's orders, and provide entertainment for spectators; however, if they cooperate beyond that level, they are likely to be charged with "fixing" the fight.

In this connection it may be helpful to think of several levels of cooperation and competition on a sort of continuum, ranging from perfect cooperation through independent action to extreme competition. The phenomenon we label "discussion, inquiry, and cooperation" and the one we call "debate, advocacy, and competition" will not always occupy the fixed places on that continuum. Each can be moved toward one end or the other in terms of the goals, attitudes, and procedures that are dominant at any given instant. How we label the discourse when it is finished should depend upon the central tendency in respect to the goals sought, the attitudes of the participants, and the procedures followed.

That All Pro-Con Material Is Debate

Sometimes a newspaper, a magazine, or a broadcaster will present what purports to be an impartial, "both sides" feature on public issues, but in some cases the content has been slanted in favor of one side. In short, that which is called a free debate in good faith may be disguised propaganda.[7]

That It Is Useless

Several versions of this position have been expressed. One is that we cannot resolve any problems by means of advocacy. As one television viewer complained, "The debates didn't help me. They were always contradicting each other." This would be distressing news if it were not for the fact that one can cite countless controversies that have been adjudicated or have been settled by parliamentary debate.

Competitive advocacy is occasionally decried on the ground that it does not discover truth. Even if we assume for the moment that our critic could recognize a discovered truth if it were revealed to him, we must insist that discovery is not the main purpose of argumentation.

[7] See "Facts-Forum Facts," *Time*, January 11, 1954.

Writers as far back as Aristotle have distinguished between inquiry, or the ascertainment of truth, and the advocacy or proof of that truth to the satisfaction of others. Inquiry should precede advocacy, but the two processes need not be performed by the same person. An advocate may do his own research, or he may use the findings of others.

A third reason for the alleged futility of argumentative communication is the belief that "facts speak for themselves." The folly of this notion was pointed up by a newspaper feature story titled "Great Health Discoveries Wasted." It cited five widely known facts about life-and-death matters which have not spoken effectively on their own behalf: after the Salk polio vaccine had been widely available for six years, at least half of our children under five years of age had not been immunized; antibiotic treatment can often prevent the recurrence of rheumatic fever, yet thousands of cases are not so treated and hence recur; simple tests for certain diseases which produce forty per cent of the cases of blindness could practically eliminate those sources, but thousands are blinded yearly by cataracts, glaucoma, and diabetes; automobile seat belts could save an estimated 5,500 lives annually, yet only a few motorists use them; fluoridation of city water is a demonstrated success in reducing tooth decay by two-thirds in young people, but only one-third of the persons using central water sources have been afforded this boon. Obviously these facts need some help in reaching and influencing people.

That It Should Be Used Vigorously in All Differences of Opinion

William Hazlitt, the essayist, explained the error in this opinion when he said that the main purposes of conversation among friends are to learn the views of others and to see what they think of yours. These ends are thwarted by contentious persons who "get up a thesis upon every topic" as if they were in a debating society. Indulging in vigorous argument is equally unwise when one is in the presence of a closed mind. "It is impossible," said Dean Swift, "to reason a man out of something he has not been reasoned into." The trouble is that a dogmatist when opposed grows more extreme, more heated, and increasingly abusive. Finally, there is the problem of when and how to argue with your boss. Many professional personnel advisers caution us to exercise tact when we feel a compulsion to dispute with our superiors, but usually they conclude with the warning to avoid disagreement altogether unless the difference is of such importance that it is worth the risk.

That Disagreement Requires Disagreeableness

Unsophisticated disputants often behave as if they believe it is necessary to become disagreeable when they disagree with someone. G. K. Chesterton put it this way: "People generally quarrel because they cannot argue." Another man said to his opponent in debate, "Sir, you raise your voice when you should reinforce your argument." The point, of course, is that one should be able to disagree without being disagreeable. But this, too, can be carried to such an extreme that competent spokesmen for opposing sides of controversial questions are sometimes asked by moderators to act as if their differences were slight and easily smoothed over. Both extremes, belligerency and pseudo-agreement, are inimical to worthwhile debating.

That Opposing Debaters Usually Try to Convince Each Other

For years we have heard the complaint that, since school debaters can't convince each other, the activity is unrealistic. The implicit assumption is that competing advocates should try to change each other's minds. A recent book on group dynamics [8] echoes this notion by stating that people do not ordinarily engage in serious debate on a direct clash of interests unless they hope to exert influence upon the other side. And Anatol Rapoport, in his *Fights, Games, and Debates,* prefers to define debate as a clash which cannot be resolved rationally but in which the object is to convince your opponent. Rapoport acknowledges reality for a moment when he concedes that the more common objective of debate is the influencing of "some bystander." In a political campaign debate, this so-called "bystander" may be millions of voters. A few questions will point up this misconception: Did Webster try to convince Hayne? Did Lincoln try to convince Douglas? Did Darrow try to convince Bryan? Did Kennedy try to convince Nixon?

In answer to the question, "Do debaters try to convince each other?," the best answer is "Sometimes." When two persons dispute

[8] D. C. Barnlund and F. S. Haiman, *The Dynamics of Discussion* (Boston: Houghton Mifflin Co., 1960), p. 49.

without an audience, presumably they hope to influence each other. In terms of its impact upon events, however, this kind of controversy is of lesser significance than the kind in which rival advocates complete for the approval of an audience.

ARGUMENTATION IN GENERAL EDUCATION

Specific Topics Involved

It is assumed to be self-evident that there is a place in the general education of most college students for an academic experience which includes systematic instruction in the analysis of controversial statements, the accumulation and the testing of evidence, the making and the criticism of inferences, the questions of logical responsibility, the making of value judgments, the application of ethical standards to decisions, the procedures of intellectual attack and defense, the logical marshaling of ideas, the social import of advocacy, and the effective communication of one's views. This is what argumentation is about.

Some Essential Attitudes and Beliefs

Our notions about the ethics of advocacy are of basic importance; they influence much of what we think or do as students, teachers, and practitioners of the art. This book supports the view that free competition among ideas should take place in order to facilitate an honest search for wise conclusions. Putting the idea negatively, one might say that the central purpose of argumentation is *not* to teach persons how to get ahead of their fellows in the struggle for personal gain. Nor is it to sanction the catering to ignorance, bias, or irrationality by stressing audience acceptability of evidence and reasoning at the expense of logical adequacy or substantive accuracy!

This ethical commitment implies an attitude of openmindedness at least to the point of being tolerant toward different ideas and objective enough to admit the possibility of one's own error. One who has this attitude will try to analyze why he thinks as he does and what makes the other fellow think differently about a controversial subject.

He would not say, "I may have my faults, but being wrong isn't one of them." Nor would he retort, "I didn't say there aren't two sides to every dispute; I merely said I wouldn't listen to yours."

A belief in the constructive uses of disagreement is an obvious corollary of the preceding point. Intelligently expressed disagreement can often move us to re-examine our beliefs and feelings. This is a symptom of growth; we don't learn from sycophants. Today this advice applies to both men and women, but it was not always so. In the early days of Radcliffe, when Professor Copeland of Harvard was asked if he would teach argumentation to the young ladies, he is reported to have answered, "How deplorable for women to become apt in argument. We can't obliterate a natural tendency, but why cultivate it?"

Finally, a reasonable confidence in his ability to think is an essential attitude for one to develop. But this is difficult in our time, as Albert Schweitzer has explained.[9] The influences of what one hears and reads, the examples of his associates, and the pressures from the organizations which claim his loyalty tend to make him doubt his own thinking ability and thereby make him receptive to the "truth" which a so-called "authority" hands down. One who would be a truly educated person must successfully resist this erosion of the self.

When argumentation is so taught and learned that it contributes to the development of these attitudes and beliefs, its claim to a place in general education cannot be denied.

QUESTIONS

1. Explain what is meant by "argumentation as a critical apparatus."
2. In what respect are rhetoric and dialectic the parent disciplines of argumentation? Why are logic and psychology not so treated here?
3. What might be the consequences of defining argumentation as merely a part of persuasion? Or as a form of cooperative inquiry?
4. In what circumstances might real-life debaters reasonably expect to convince each other?

[9] Charles R. Joy, ed., Albert Schweitzer: An Anthology (Boston: Beacon Press, 1947).

5. What is meant by "general education," and what is the relevance of argumentation to it?

6. For what reasons might one call argumentation and debate "techniques of a free society"?

7. Comment upon this statement: Some people might contend, however, that persuasion involves a degree of polarity in that it presumes a change from an existing condition, either reinforcing or changing direction.

EXERCISES

1. Give an example of the placing of emotional or personal proofs into a logical framework for the purpose of imposing some rigor upon the arguments.

2. Select a short specimen of argumentative discourse such as an editorial, a letter to the editor, or a printed speech. Apply as best you can at this stage the evaluative criteria listed under "Critical Apparatus" in this chapter.

3. Discuss, or prepare oral reports on, the implications of the John Stuart Mill "Essay on Liberty" in relation to this chapter. For instance, dare we go as far with freedom of speech as he proposes?

4. Report on the following article in relation to the idea that persuasion can become propaganda much more easily than debate can: T. R. Nilsen, "Free Speech, Persuasion, and the Democratic Process," *Quarterly Journal of Speech*, XLIV, No. 3 (1958), 235–243.

5. Report in class on your observation of argumentation in use in a city council meeting, a legislature, or a business meeting of an organization.

6. Do you think John Milton, in *Areopagitica* (1644), placed too much value upon certain liberties when he wrote: "Give me the liberty to know, to utter, and to argue freely according to conscience, above all liberties."?

7. Is debating in the U.S. Senate declining? If so, why? How does this relate to the section of this chapter titled "The Social Context of This Subject"? (See "Debate's Decline," *Wall Street Journal*, February 7, 1963, p. 12.)

CHAPTER II

ETHICAL AND LOGICAL

RESPONSIBILITIES

FREEDOM OF SPEECH, WHICH HAS BEEN SHOWN IN THE PRECEDING CHAPTER to be of central importance to our study, involves equally vital *responsibilities* to be informed, to be thoughtful, to be socially conscious, and to be ethical. Let us start with the last of these.

ETHICAL RESPONSIBILITY OF AN ADVOCATE

Whether an advocate communicates in a political campaign, a deliberative assembly, a philosophical dispute, a courtroom, or a school debate—or whether he seeks a critical decision or a popular vote—he has an ethical responsibility to give the cause the representation it deserves. This means that once he espouses the cause, he is under a moral obligation to make the best case he can in terms of the assumptions, evidence, and reasoning which are both available and legitimate.

Obviously this principle rules out the philosophy of "win at any cost" or "victory by fair means or foul." The use of fallacious strategems, lies, misquotations, and the suppression of evidence is reprehensible, according to this view, and letting someone "get away with" such behavior is deplorable. Debate is designed to expose such deficiencies in proof, as we shall see in the materials on the tests of evidence, the tests of reasoning, and the tactics of attack and defense.

Much of what is said about the ethical responsibility to represent a cause competently stems from the adversary system which characterizes trial procedures in the Western world. The prosecutor or the lawyer for the plaintiff is supposed to try his best, and so is his opponent. From this clash we expect justice to emerge.[1] So important is this clash situation deemed to be that the court will appoint counsel if someone cannot pay for his own, and any case, however unpopular in the community, is supposedly assured of representation. This latter point was forcefully illustrated by the efforts of Robert Servatius to defend Adolph Eichmann in an Israeli court against charges of responsibility for the massacre of millions of Jews during Hitler's regime.

But our system doesn't always work this way. Some legal scholars have pointed out that occasional cases go unrepresented or poorly represented either because of the poverty of the defendant or the unpopularity of his side. Unpopular cases sometimes fail to attract lawyers at any price because of the fear of social and economic reprisals stemming from the typical citizen's inability to distinguish between the offense charged and the constitutional guaranty of defense. Thus we may conclude that society, as well as the advocate, has an ethical responsibility here.

This ethical responsibility of an advocate to represent his cause the best he can is similar to his logical responsibility, which is to secure a commitment based upon intellectually defensible grounds. Even though he starts with emotionally toned assumptions and value judgments, he should expound their logical consequences. That is a form of proof, as we shall see below.

PROBABILITY

Degrees of proof may be thought about in terms of objective verifiability and in terms of belief. The crucial difference between these two

[1] See Joseph N. Welch, "Should a Lawyer Defend a Guilty Man?," *This Week Magazine*, December 6, 1959, p. 9.

is that the former is by far the better source of reliable knowledge. It is more nearly free of the biasing effects of human frailties such as ignorance and wishful thinking.

Perhaps this difference can be shown in relation to the vernacular words for the degrees of proof: possible, plausible, probable, and certain. *Possible* usually means "it could be." One would, at most, accept a possibly valid statement as a tentative hypothesis subject to further scrutiny. A possibility is reliably so if objectively verified, but not if belief by the gullible is the standard. *Plausible* conveys some likelihood of credibility. Its lowest level is characterized by what the gullible will accept. Plausibility is a matter of belief, not verification. *Probable*, in a nonmathematical sense, means more likely true than false. Probability can be established by objective methods, but when it is thought of in terms of belief, it means little more than plausibility. *Certain* designates the highest degree of proof when objectively verified; but when certainty is strictly a function of belief, its reliability may vary from nil to considerable. In a closed system of discourse such as plane geometry or formal logic, a kind of certainty can be achieved. However, in the so-called exact sciences, certainty is not generally asserted today. Heisenberg's uncertainty principle, which came from a physical finding of quantum mechanics, implies that a physicist cannot show by experiment any more than a probable prediction, because the improbable may still happen.[2]

In the study of argumentation we are concerned with probability as a rhetorical concept. In this setting the standards are less exacting than they are in science. For example, probability in science does not bear upon one case. The word has no operational meaning except in relation to frequency of occurrence in numerous situations. But as a *minimal* rhetorical goal, probability may mean as little as plausibility and bear upon a single case. The position of this book is that an intelligent person should demand something better than the minimum.

Some level of probability is all we can hope to achieve, because the human behavior about which we deliberate belongs in the class of uncertainties. We argue about matters which appear to admit of two possibilities: expedient or inexpedient, just or unjust, wise or foolish, etc. In each case we advocate a view which we think is true for the most part or as a general rule. If we think of probability as meaning more than mere plausibility to the gullible, we must offer proof suffi-

[2] D. Bergamini, "The Language of Science," *The Reporter*, March 31, 1960, p. 38.

cient to satisfy a critical thinker that our view is the preferable one.

Probability in argumentation is rarely mathematical; it is expressed in the somewhat vague language of relations. Words such as *probably, likely, highly probable,* and their antonyms are typical choices. Fractions or percentages are, of course, more precise than adverbs, but they are less often applicable. In view of these observations, a student of argumentation should heed these hints: (1) Express the claimed degree of probability candidly, avoiding extravagances such as "beyond a shadow of doubt"; (2) Do enough research so that the highest potential degree of proof can be asserted; (3) Whenever feasible, express the degree of probability as a numerical estimate. The establishment of probability, as defined above, in favor of one's position on a controversial matter is both an ethical and a logical responsibility.

PRESUMPTION

More than twenty-three centuries ago, Corax of Syracuse defined rhetoric as the art of persuasion and wrote some principles of successful pleading, including his formulation of the "probability" argument.[3] This ancient bit of empirical psychology was based on the idea that a person will accept a proposition without having certain knowledge if that conclusion conforms with his own experience or the testimony of credible sources. In practice it meant more nearly what we would call plausibility, or likeness to be true and wise. Aristotle's *Rhetoric* renounced this as sophistic for "making the worse appear the better reason," yet in Book I, Chapter 2 we read how either a strong or a weak defendant charged with assault can argue the improbability of his risking such an act.

As a legal convention, presumption is extremely important in the Anglo-American tradition. Even though the legal usage is not our main concern here, it does help us to appreciate the significance of presumption. The law presumes certain things to be true until evidence and argument sufficient to overcome the presumption are introduced. Presumptions vary in strength, as we can see in these examples: innocence of the accused until guilt is proved, sanity until otherwise

[3] B. Smith, "Corax and Probability," *Quarterly Journal of Speech,* VII (1921), pp. 13–42.

is proved, ownership implied by possession, validity of a will, survivorship of someone in a common disaster, and presumption of death after a certain period of absence.

There have been violations of this principle in "trial by mass media" (newspaper, radio, television), because this treatment creates a presumption of guilt before a hearing or a trial. Branding a person "questionable" or "controversial" has led to lawsuits over loss of employment stemming from such branding. Some businessmen have found themselves without the benefit of presumption in their dealings with regulatory agencies. Processed food containing additives to color, flavor, or preserve it is no longer presumed to be safe; it must be proved to be so. On some occasions when firms are charged with criminal offenses in the regulatory field, the traditional presumption of innocence is replaced by the doctrine of absolute criminal liability.[4]

As a modern rhetorical convention, which is our main concern here, presumption means "a pre-occupation of the ground," as Whately so aptly put it.[5] But a presumption in favor of what exists or is believed to be does not imply that the status quo is true or good or desirable. It does imply that the existing situation must stand until sufficient proof is offered to rebut that presumption. For example, if it is proposed that a college now on the quarterly calendar should adopt a trimester plan, the presumption favors the quarterly arrangement at that institution. If the proponents of change merely say, "Let's change to the trimester plan," the defenders of the quarterly system need not reply, because the presumption in their favor has not been overcome by that unsupported assertion. A reply in defense of the status quo is called for only after the advocates of change have made a case. What this entails will be explained later.

In a situation involving a contest between two ways of doing something, as in the quarterly vs. trimester case, it is easy to see which party has the presumption at the outset. But in controversies about what is true and what is good, the placement of presumption is less clear. The traditional doctrine holds that presumption favors prevailing belief at the beginning of the controversy. If one asserted that the earth was round when all about him believed it was flat, the presumption favored the "flat" side. If a minority in a materialistic society asserts that mate-

---

[4] G. O. W. Mueller, "Ambushed Businessmen," *Wall Street Journal*, October 23, 1961.

[5] Richard Whately, *Elements of Rhetoric* (Cambridge: Jas. Munroe and Co., 1834), p. 74.

rialism is an unworthy philosophy of life, the presumption favors the materialists in the beginning. In these examples we can observe that a presumption is an advanced starting point or a procedural convention which identifies the party which occupies the disputed ground at the outset and therefore does not have to make the first move.

Is presumption a logical constant or a psychological variable? To put it another way, do impersonal factors determine the placement of presumption, or does audience opinion determine who has the initial benefit of presumption? We can discern three views on this problem. One is the Whately position which holds that a general presumption is placed without regard for audience opinion. Thus the status quo would be given the initial benefit of presumption even if the audience were opposed to it. As long as unregulated child labor was the status quo, it enjoyed a presumption despite any unfavorable public opinion which may have existed. A second view is that a general presumption is determined by a favorable public opinion. According to this interpretation, there is a presumption in favor of the majority opinion on a given question. This is not as simple as it seems, because majority opinion varies enormously among audiences, and the measurements of range and intensity are difficult to perform. Finally, there is the notion that specific presumptions are determined in relation to individual opinions in specific audiences. Thus some listeners or readers would entertain a presumption in favor of the status quo, while others would initially favor a change. This view is geared directly to the business of persuading individuals.

The difficulty in these disparate views results from a confusion of a procedural convention and the tactics of popular persuasion. The latter interpretation has not prevailed because it is less dependable and is potentially more troublesome. It is better to have a nonevaluative convention which enables the parties to determine what ground is in dispute. This is the reason for defining presumption as the initial advantage enjoyed by the side which defends existing institutions, prevailing values, or the innocence of the accused. This last item, "the accused," differs from the other two in that it involves an assigned, rather than a natural or existential, presumption.

BURDEN OF PROOF

As a *legal* convention, burden of proof means the responsibility of the prosecution or the plaintiff to proceed first and make a case. That burden in a criminal case is "proof beyond reasonable doubt," while in a civil action it is "proof by mere preponderance of evidence." In a larger sense, burden of proof is more than a procedural rule; it is a time-tested device to protect the integrity of the individual. Were it not for this protection, anyone might be continually harassed and called upon to answer irresponsible and unsupported accusations. Under this protection, the accused may stand upon his presumption and say to the accuser, "Prove it."

Burden of proof means the risk of the proposition, and it entails on the part of the affirmative the duty to affirm the issues. This is another way of saying that the affirmative has the responsibility to submit a prima facie case. Failure to affirm *one* contested issue usually means defeat for the prosecution or the plaintiff, especially in a trial before a judge or judges. For instance, the Justice Department lawyers tried for nearly three years to prove seventeen investment banks guilty of a conspiracy to monopolize the securities business, but all they could show was some parallel behavior. When a deliberate conspiracy could not be proved, Judge Medina ruled that the defense did not have to present its side. Similarly, in the DuPont-General Motors case, Judge La Buy ruled that the government failed to prove conspiracy to restrain trade. Finally, in the Crest Theater case, Justice Clark spoke for the majority in ruling that proof of parallel business behavior does not also prove conspiratorial agreement. Thus the affirmative failed on *one* issue.

The legal concept of burden of proof is sometimes hard for laymen to understand. For instance, there was the case of a juror in a murder trial who, despite the judge's instructions to vote "not guilty" or "guilty of first-degree murder," voted "second-degree murder" because she had some doubts about the prisoner's guilt. In effect this juror gave the affirmative a partial victory for proving part of its case. Her confusion about burden of proof becomes more comprehensible when we observe how it operates in the regulatory field. After six airlines made a mutual-aid pact to minimize losses due to strikes, the

Civil Aeronautics Board challenged them to prove that their pact would not reduce competition in that industry. Most of us would assume that the burden of proof belonged on the accuser's side.

Perhaps it is just as well that our main concern is with burden of proof as a *rhetorical* convention. In this context the meaning is different, although there are five similarities: the extent of the burden is variable; in a counterproposition debate, each side must try to prove its own case; the negative needs only to balance the affirmative, but the affirmative must preponderate in order to win; each side in turn must maintain the burden of proceeding, as explained below; the burden is on the affirmative, and it does not shift.

To place the burden of proof on the affirmative is not to relieve the negative of responsibility. The opponents of the proposition have several strategic options, as we shall see under "Cases," but each kind of negative case entails some responsibility to make arguments. A given negative may have to show why the present situation is not as bad as the affirmative alleges, or it may have to show that the affirmative plan is faulty, or it may choose to support an alternative proposal, or it may prefer to argue that the affirmative's criteria are unsatisfactory. When a negative offers a counterproposition, it has as much burden as the affirmative, but it is not called *the* burden of proof, because it is not on the original proposition.

In general argumentation, burden of proof has traditionally meant the risk of the proposition, or the responsibility of the party who will be dissatisfied if the present situation remains unchanged. He has the job of making good on his controversial charge that something will happen, that an action should be taken, that an idea is worthy, that an assertion is true. In all of these situations the affirmative would have the burden of proof because it would oppose an existing institution, a prevalent belief, a cultural norm, or some other kind of status quo. This will be illustrated in relation to phrasing each kind of proposition in Chapter III. Whether burden of proof in general argumentation should be defined as a logical constant or as a psychological variable will now be discussed.

If we call it a psychological variable, we mean that the burden of proof is the task of persuading our listeners or readers, whoever they may be. Then the doctrine on burden of proof must be more practical than ideal, because its focus is upon audience analysis and adaptation. As it often happens in real life, this pragmatic standard, also known as the "results" criterion, may lead to demagoguery. It does so because, if one says "proof means belief," he must reckon with the fact that some persons will believe almost anything. He must also reckon with the opposite of gullibility—pigheadedness—which means refusal to believe an argument despite an avalanche of proof. In this situation the psychological criterion of burden of proof would give the affirmative an unreasonable responsibility. Thus it seems wise to apply a separate term such as "burden of persuasion" to this psychological problem of influencing popular belief.

There is some oversimplification in using "logical constant" to describe burden of proof in nonlegal situations, but at least it rules out popular belief as the standard. It is a way of saying that an affirmative case should meet certain theoretical, ideal proof requirements, achieve logical cogency, or at least satisfy some qualified critics of argumentation. This is to be done by answering all issues with affirmative arguments as explained in the chapters on Analysis (IV) and Cases (VIII). It must be admitted, however, that the number, quality, and composition of said affirmative arguments cannot be *precisely* stipulated in the form of a general rule.

As in the case of presumption, it is a matter of importance to understand what the burden of proof means and to know who has it. The sides in a controversy and their responsibilities for the conduct of the exchange are determined by the burden of proof. In a properly worded proposition, as we shall see in the next chapter, the affirmative has that burden and responsibility, while the negative has the presumption. That is why, in debates which are conducted with regard for logical sequence, fairness, and economy of time, the affirmative must make the first move. Referring back to the illustrations under "Presumption," we note that the proponents of a trimester calendar for a quarterly system school would have the burden of proof and should expect to argue first. Likewise, anyone who alleges that Mr. X is a Communist or a crook, unless these facts have been established, has the burden of proof. Suspicion does not relieve him of this logical and ethical responsibility to prove his charge; saying "where there's smoke there's fire" does not suffice. Similarly, a person in the United States would have the burden of proof if he argued that installment buying is economically harmful to the country generally.

BURDEN OF PROCEEDING

Last among the responsibilities to be discussed is the burden of proceeding, otherwise known as the burden of going forward with the argument, or as the burden of rebuttal. In judicial proceedings this responsibility can be enforced by the presiding judge, while in general argumentation it is done less formally and sometimes less strictly by adversaries or by listeners and readers. An example will show how the burden of proceeding appeared in a public controversy over the charge that the management of a county hospital was poor. The complainant (affirmative) made a case by arguing: (1) That poor hospital management could be measured by certain criteria such as research activities of the staff, training facilities, range of services, reputation among physicians, and overcrowding, and (2) That the hospital in question deserved a poor rating on those counts. Since these matters were developed by evidence and reasoning, we should say that the affirmative met its responsibility known as the burden of proof, thereby undermining the presumption which favored the negative before the dispute began. At this juncture the burden of proceeding has been shifted to the negative side. Now suppose the negative replies by showing that the criteria are improper, or, even if they are proper, that the hospital does not rate poorly in terms of them. At this point the burden of proceeding has been shifted back upon the affirmative.

This exchange could go on indefinitely, but enough has been reported to warrant some generalizations about the burden of proceeding. One is that this responsibility can shift and does so in a good debate. As we saw above, after an affirmative has discharged its burden of proof by giving a logically adequate case, the negative is under obligation to reply in an attempt to balance the affirmative case or possibly to outweigh it. If it succeeds in doing either, the burden of proceeding shifts to the affirmative. Then the affirmative has to overpower the negative rejoinder or fall behind at this point. A second observation is that the number of shifts of this responsibility is limited only by existing rules, the persistence of the contestants, the resolution of the problem, or the patience of those who could stop the exchange. We know that the number of "turns" is arbitrarily determined by rules in some legislative assemblies and in most judicial and school debates.

In many nonlegal contexts, especially school debates, the shifts occur point by point instead of after a completed case.

KINDS OF DEBATE

It will be recalled that debate was defined as competitive advocacy, oral or written, between pro and con sides of a proposition, and taking place with or without limitations of time, place, or form. This type of discourse occurs in a variety of settings, each of which affects the procedures, goals, and responsibilities of the parties in discernible ways; therefore, it seems useful to classify debates as political, legislative, philosophical, judicial, and school. These class names are useful but not necessarily mutually exclusive or all-inclusive. Even so, one can explain each kind and particularize the ethical and logical responsibilities of the participants. But first it is worth noting that all five kinds involve the ethical responsibility to make the best case one can in terms of available and legitimate assumptions, evidence, and reasoning.

Political Debate

Political or campaign debate takes place when rival candidates contend for nomination or election, and when controversial public questions are referred to the citizenry for decision. In this kind there are the fewest procedural regulations. What few limitations there are can be seen in the laws relating to elections and libel and slander.

Often the demands in terms of probability, presumption, burden of proof, and burden of proceeding are less rigorous than they are in the other kinds of debate. True, the objective is a decision, but it is typically sought with the use of popular persuasion rather than rigorous argumentation. When rival spokesmen do not confront each other on the same platform or in the same publication, there are only some listeners' or readers' critical faculties to satisfy. There is nothing so salutary as the presence of a competent adversary. When a confrontation of peers occurs, the ethical and logical responsibilities are more likely to be met, because each rival fears the exposure of his weakness.

Legislative Debate

Deliberative assemblies use this kind in reaching decisions on matters of policy concerning which motions are made. Many think of Congress as the place where legislative debating goes on. They are correct, but they would be equally right in naming countless other situations, down to the lowliest local committee meeting. One relationship between this kind of debate and the first one can be a source of embarrassment to a politician; he may make a promise while campaigning, but after election he may not be able to make good on it.

While it is true that some legislative debating is incredibly poor according to our critical standards, the fact is that parliamentary procedure makes it more difficult for speakers to ignore the burden of proof and the burden of proceeding than it is in those political debates which involve no confrontation.

Philosophical Debate

Most of us will agree, once we think about it, that there are many informal, decisionless controversies in real life which cannot be classified as political, legislative, judicial, or school debates. Every college generation as far back as we have heard of has engaged in informal discussions and debates about more or less philosophical questions such as "Is politics a worthwhile career?," "Are grades over-rated?," "Is the administration paternalistic?," and the old stand-bys, religion and sex. Frequently the controversies deal with value judgments, and understanding more often than victory is the goal.

Strictly speaking, philosophical argumentation is more closely related to dialectic than it is to the persuasive applications of argumentation.[6] The use of "philosophical debate" to classify the many miscellaneous controversies which would not be so considered by a philosopher is justified on the ground that it meets a need and apparently does no harm.

When a dialectical give-and-take involves good minds, there is a testing of the consequences of premises which might profitably take place more often in the other four kinds of debate. From this observa-

[6] M. Natanson, "Rhetoric and Philosophical Argumentation," *Quarterly Journal of Speech*, XLVIII (1962), pp. 24–30.

tion we may readily infer that the burden of proceeding is well taken care of, even though the placement of presumption and burden of proof may not be clear to the participants.

Judicial Debate

This is what the ancients called forensic speaking, and it takes place in courts of law. Contrary to the impression gained by many "who-dunit" addicts, this kind of debating, which takes a small fraction of the time of the typical law firm, is concerned with facts, laws, decisions, and such matters.

Of all the kinds of debate, this one is the most demanding with respect to evidence, presumption, burden of proof, and burden of proceeding. There are rules governing all of these matters, and judges are expected to enforce them. It is unfortunate that many persons think these rules apply in the same way to the other four kinds of debate. We hear them say, "You couldn't prove that in court." The obvious reply is that we aren't in court when we participate in nonlegal debates.

Most legal controversies are on so-called questions of fact, but there are some on value judgments and policy decisions. The two sides in this adversary situation are, as previously stated, the plaintiff (in civil actions) or the prosecution (in criminal actions) and the defendant. These correspond to affirmative and negative, respectively. Decisions are rendered by judges or juries.

School Debate

If a pollster were to ask hundreds of college students which of the five kinds of debate they should expect to study the most in an argumentation course, it is likely that school debate would "win." The fact is that almost all college textbooks in this field pay most attention to this kind. They do so because traditionally most of the students have been debaters, and their teachers have been debate directors. This book is an exception, but its concepts are as valid and essential in the preparation of school debaters as they are to the other four kinds.

School debates can be structured so as to simulate any of the other four kinds. In fact, the educational version is intended to prepare students for participation in the real-life kinds of debate. However, because of this educational aim, the canons of criticism and the type of decision rendered are unlike those in real-life situations. More will be said of this later, but for the present it is well to know that school debates are often judged by critics who apply criteria of excellence instead of voting for the side they agree with.

As we should expect, the presence of a critic-judge and presumably skilled opponents tends to make the participants more careful in their handling of the ethical and logical responsibilities which have been discussed in this chapter. Perhaps the similarity to judicial debate is exaggerated in current practice,[7] but that can be corrected in time.

QUESTIONS

1. What is involved when one says, "A lawyer should not defend a guilty person"?

   What if he has been found guilty in court, or what if his so-called "guilt" is merely a public opinion?

   What if the defense counsel tries to prove innocence? Or what if he only *tests* the prosecutor's case?

2. What went wrong with the probability inferences in this anecdote? When Joe and Bill came back to school after Christmas, each noticed that the other was wearing a new watch. They fell to guessing and arguing about the comparative prices of their gifts, and they agreed to settle the dispute by checking prices at a local store. They agreed that the man who "won," i.e., had the more expensive watch, would give his to the "loser." Both men reasoned thus: "My chances of winning or of losing are even. If I win, I shall be poorer by the price of my watch; but if I lose, I am certain to gain a more expensive watch. Hence the bet is advantageous to me."

3. An article in the April, 1960 *Reader's Digest* urged the abolition of professional boxing, alleging that fights are "fixed" and that unsavory characters actually control the business behind "front men." The Illinois Athletic Commission subpoenaed the author to substantiate his allegations. Was that action proper in relation to the doctrine of presumption and burden of proof?

[7] J. L. Robinson, "Are We 'Overlegalizing' School Debate?" *The Speech Teacher*, IX (1960), pp. 109–115.

4. Suppose that the proponents of fluoridation of the water supply in Bumpkin Center argue that the natural fluoride in the local water is insufficient to retard tooth decay in children, and that the artificial fluoridation of that water supply would reduce decay and introduce no harmful side-effects. They quote endorsements by the American Dental Association, the American Medical Association, and the U.S. Public Health Service. They also cite the studies conducted in Grand Rapids, Newburgh, Brantford, Jacksonville, Evanston, and elsewhere. In fact, they refer to 8,500 separate research reports which support the belief that fluoridation can prevent tooth decay and is harmless to public health. Should this suffice to discharge the burden of proof for the time being? If so, what must the opposition do to discharge its burden of proceeding? However, if the affirmative case above is judged to be logically inadequate, what more is needed to make it adequate?

EXERCISES

1. Read "Trial By Newspaper" in the February, 1949, *Scientific American*. Discuss its implications for the concepts treated in this chapter (ethical responsibility, probability, presumption, burden of proof, etc.).

2. Select for comment a current controversy or one in the Appendixes. How well do the advocates meet their ethical responsibilities?

3. Choose a controversy as in Exercise 2 above. Who had the presumption and who had the burden of proof at the outset? Evaluate the work of the two sides in terms of discharging the burden of proof and the burden of proceeding. If the last speaker or writer in your specimen debate could be followed by a new opponent, what would you have that new opponent say?

4. One or more students might be assigned to read one of the Lincoln-Douglas debates in P. M. Angle, ed., *Created Equal?* (Chicago: University of Chicago Press, 1958). Others might be assigned to read some of the four Kennedy-Nixon encounters in S. Kraus, ed., *The Great Debates* (Bloomington: Indiana University Press, 1962). After the reviews have been heard, the class might profitably discuss the comparative merits of these specimens of political debate.

5. Read the Welch item cited in footnote #1, if available, and compare his view of the adversary system with that of D. Dressler, "Trial by Combat in American Courts," *Harper's Magazine*, Vol. 222, No. 1331 (1961), pp. 31–36.

THE BASIS OF

CONTROVERSY

ANY CONTROVERSY, DISPUTE, CLASH OF OPINION, DEBATE, OR WHATEVER else we call this phenomenon must be *about* something if it is to be worthy of study. Persons who are not acquainted with the theory of argumentation are likely to express the basis of a controversy with this kind of remark: "The Student Senate is arguing about an honor system." This is sufficient for casual readers and listeners, but it is insufficient for the disputants, thoughtful voters, and critics of argumentation. These more demanding persons prefer that the basis of the controversy be clearly stated in one of the accepted forms which will now be named and defined.

ITS NAMES AND DEFINITIONS

Forms of Statement

In political or campaign debating, the subject or the basis of the controversy is usually implied; it can be inferred from the nature of the speaking or writing. Typically it is something like one of these: "Mr.

X should be nominated (or elected)," or "Vote 'yes' on the bond issue." In court (judicial) proceedings, the basis of the controversy is usually stated in the form of the prosecutor's charge or the plaintiff's complaint. In school debates, the basis is almost always given explicit statement in the form of a resolution which has for more than sixty years been called a proposition: "Resolved, That the school-attendance requirement in Illinois should be raised to age seventeen." In philosophical debates, the bases are not always exactly verbalized, but when they are, they are likely to be statements of opinion, questions, or phrases: "Self-reliance is an antiquated notion"; "Should one practice Emerson's idea of self-reliance?"; "Self-reliance as a personal philosophy." Finally, in legislative debates, the bases may be expressed in motions, bills, ordinances, and resolutions.

MOTION
     Mr. Chairman, I move that the report of the nominating committee be accepted.

BILL
     Be it enacted by the Senate and the House of Representatives of the United States of America in Congress assembled, That . . .

ORDINANCE
     It shall be unlawful for any person to show or exhibit, or cause to be shown or exhibited, any moving picture which is immoral or obscene, salacious or teaches false ethics, or which contains nakedness or suggestive dress, prolonged passionate love scenes, or scenes making crime, drunkenness or the use of narcotics attractive, or which depicts the commission of crime, the white-slave traffic or resistance to police authority, or scenes that are unduly horrible.

RESOLUTION (long form)
     WHEREAS, The membership of the Association is confident that federal support, through the School Assistance Act of 1961, can be provided without federal control; and
     WHEREAS, The survival and growth of our democratic way of life depend upon the quality of public education, and the people of this country desire and deserve high quality education for all children and youth consistent with the enduring ideals and aspirations of our nation; and
     WHEREAS, The unprecedented increases in enrollment have created urgent needs for more classrooms, facilities and an increasing supply of qualified teachers; and
     WHEREAS, Only four per cent of the gross national product is now being spent for education; and

WHEREAS, The Association recognizes the imperative need for additional finances for research and experimentation in education at the federal, state, and local levels; and

WHEREAS, Many states and local school districts have reached the point of saturation in financing public education; and

WHEREAS, We believe that this bill is sound and strong because it is only a money bill and does not attempt to settle other issues such as desegregation and the place of financial aid for parochial and other private schools; therefore,

BE IT RESOLVED, That the Association go on record as strongly supporting the School Assistance Act of 1961 (HR4970) and make its support known to the President of the United States, the Secretary of Health, Education and Welfare, and to other appropriate persons.

Proposition Defined

"Proposition" has several meanings, as a quick reference to a dictionary will show: colloquially, an indecent proposal; in logic, a sentence in which the predicate affirms or denies something concerning the subject; in mathematics, a problem to be solved; in rhetoric, a statement to be supported. Despite these variations in usage, the writers on argumentation have agreed that the assertion which expresses the basis of a controversy shall be called a proposition. It may take any of the forms mentioned above.

It has been suggested that a statement embodying a controversial judgment is not a proposition in a logical or a grammatical sense, which is true. From this it is inferred that the tests of factual or logical truth do not apply, and that a debate resolution must, therefore, be a sort of hypothesis.[1] Granted, it would be simpler for us if the "founding fathers" of argumentation had devised a wholly new set of names for their concepts. Instead, they borrowed and modified some terms from logic, law, rhetoric, dialectic, pedagogy, and other disciplines. The result, as viewed over a span of more than half a century, has been quite satisfactory. It could be even better if all who communicate about argumentation would use the word "proposition" in the sense that it is defined here, rather than vainly urging upon one discipline the lexicon of another. It would also be helpful if writers and speakers

[1] D. W. Shepard, "Logical Propositions and Debate Resolutions," *Central States Speech Journal*, XI (1960), 186–190.

on argumentation and debate would resist the temptation to use "topic" and "question" as precise equivalents of "proposition."

IMPORTANCE OF ISOLATING
PROPOSITIONS

Essential in Analysis

While preparing to advocate, either orally or in writing, one needs to isolate the essence of the controversy and to state it in a proposition. If the statement is only a catch phrase instead of a complete thought, he cannot satisfactorily define the terms, find the issues, determine his side and his proof responsibilities, or select his evidence and arguments. In sum, he cannot realistically expect to make the best possible case for his side if he hasn't clearly formulated the basis of the controversy.

When evaluating the advocacy of others, which is one of the principal uses of argumentation, it is again necessary to express the basis of the controversy in a complete sentence rather than a phrase. Before this can be done, it is necessary to ask whether the communicator would be dissatisfied if no change occurred. If the answer is "yes," that party is on the affirmative side, and the proposition should express his view. Occasionally this determination is hard to make, because the author was not clear, or he argued more than one proposition, or the exact nature of the status quo is in doubt. The specimen below will serve as a model for analysis.

POLICE IN HIDING [2]
Police Commissioner O'Connor has threatened to suspend any policeman who waits in hiding and then pounces upon the unsuspecting speeder. Franklin M. Kreml, director of the Northwestern University Traffic Institute, spoke up in favor of "hiding."

There is little doubt that Commissioner O'Connor is on the popular side of the issue. Motorists are jealous of their rights and privileges. They want no policeman popping out from a side street when they think the coast is clear.

This debate has no reference to "speed-traps," which nobody defends.

[2] Chicago *Daily News*, December 22, 1954, p. 10.

Speed traps result from overzealous enforcement of unrealistic regulations. Both O'Connor and Kreml desire to promote safe driving, not primarily to make arrests.

But is a motorist guilty of a traffic violation only if he is caught at it? Is traffic enforcement to be some kind of a game, in which the driver who can outwit the police deserves immunity? Or is it a deadly serious business demanding the most rigorous measures consistent with civil rights?

If the 440 dead and 27,797 injured in Chicago last year were playing a game, it is a cruel one that must not be allowed to continue.

Mr. Kreml says it would cost an extra $30 million to put enough police on the streets to maintain an adequate patrol. The alternative is to spot them in places where accidents are most likely to occur. But if motorists know that unless there is a policeman in plain sight there is no possibility of arrest, even this system breaks down.

The only really effective way to enforce traffic laws is to convince the motorist that violations will be punished. Given a sound set of traffic rules and police who are sincerely interested in preventing accidents by enforcing those rules, there is nothing basically wrong in allowing the police to "hide," because the only people affected will be violators who deserve to be caught.

Assuming that "hiding" was the status quo and that the Commissioner was the affirmative urging a change, one would infer the proposition to be: "Chicago traffic policemen must enforce the laws without 'hiding'." Stated in question form, this becomes: "Should traffic cops 'hide'?" Since the editorial is in defense of the status quo, namely, "hiding," it is on the negative side.

But suppose we assume that the Commissioner's ban on "hiding" was in effect when the editorial was written, and that enforcement without "hiding" was the status quo. Then the writer would have been the dissatisfied party if no change occurred, and he would have been the affirmative on this proposition: "Chicago traffic policemen should be permitted to 'hide' in the performance of their duties." However, the nature of the writing in the editorial is such that the implied proposition is more nearly a value judgment: ". . . there is nothing basically wrong in allowing the police to 'hide' . . ."

Other Functions of Propositions

The importance of identifying or stating a proposition is attributable to the significant functions which it serves. These are not discrete or mutually exclusive functions, but each has enough meaning to justify its inclusion. First among these is to verbalize explicitly the basis of the controversy, be it a conviction or merely a kind of hypothesis offered for testing. A proposition should serve this purpose regardless of the formality or the informality of its statement. Thus a speaker or a writer is well advised to state the proposition for his own use, even if he does not announce it, because without it an intelligent discourse is unlikely. An explicit statement is even more necessary when both sides are to be represented on the same occasion; a controversy can rarely be kept on the point otherwise.

Another function of a proposition is to express the affirmative stand, thereby naming the sides and placing the presumption and the burden of proof. (The reader is referred to "presumption" and "burden of proof" in Chapter II and to a section on "Wording a proposition" near the end of this chapter.)

Finally, and this may be another way of expressing the preceding function, a proposition asserts a claim for acceptance. Anyone who offers a motion or a hypothesis for debate may phrase it, but he has a responsibility to make it clear. Should he fail to state his claim clearly, fairly, and reasonably, the negative may raise an objection, and this is not quibbling. This and the other functions of a proposition are closely related to the problems of wording which will be discussed a few pages hence.

KINDS OF PROPOSITIONS

Importance of Classification

One might guess that the naming and classifying of propositions is a mere technicality the purpose of which is to increase the students' burden. He might also conclude, after consulting several textbooks, that the names were chosen for reasons of personal taste rather than function. These are a few of the class names for propositions which he could find: fact, value, policy, belief, explanation, definition, and theoretically sound. Both views are mistaken; classification is no mere technicality, and the names have more substantial bases than whimsy. In practice, the classification of a given proposition is an almost indispensable step in analyzing it, because each kind of proposition has distinctive proof requirements. If this were not true, it would be pointless to discuss the kinds of propositions.

Propositions of Definition and Classification

Another name for this category could be "criteria and application." It is the first of two main types, and it has at least five distinguishable subtypes, the first of which is the so-called proposition of fact in legal proceedings. Strictly speaking, "fact" implies objective verifiability as in the instance of the charge that A's wound was made by B's gun. But when it is contended that a committed act is definable as a felony, we have the additional problem of definition and classification, which involves inference beyond raw fact. If the proposition asserts that the committed act was justified, we have added a value dimension. Finally, if the case turns upon the question of whether capital punishment should be employed, a policy dimension has been added. Returning to the simplest form of the legal proposition of fact, we can observe that definition and classification (or criteria and application) are involved. In each case there are two basic questions: What did the party in question do? Is it definable as loitering, slander, or whatever the allegation stated?

Sam is guilty of loitering.
Z Company is engaging in an unfair labor practice.
John Dough's Bakery is violating the health ordinance.
X injured Y's professional reputation by slandering him.

A second subtype is the proposition of past fact. It asserts a controversial claim concerning a past event. Its analysis involves two questions similar to those immediately above: What would be required to establish the alleged fact? Do our available data meet this requirement?

President Lincoln's party was split over the purpose of the war.
Bacon wrote some of the literature attributed to Shakespeare.
Columbus never reached America.
A Russian invented the airplane.

Third among the subcategories of definition and classification is the proposition of present fact. It makes a controversial claim concerning a current situation. Here we would ask the same preliminary, analytical questions that are given for the past-fact propositions above.

Amateur investors are making money in the stock market.
"Obscene" in the municipal censorship ordinance means "immoral in the opinion of the ordinary person."
The Monroe Doctrine is dead.
The party in power is responsible for the farm problem.

A fourth subtype is the proposition of future fact, better known as a prediction. Again we would ask what evidence would be necessary to make the prediction probably true, and whether we have such evidence. These are specimen predictions:

Deficit financing will result in an accelerated growth rate in our economy.
Extensive broadening of the Social Security system will socialize the United States.
Mass education at the collegiate level will reduce the quality of higher education.
The current trend in the financial support of science and technology by government and foundations will retard the comparative growth of the other disciplines.

The last of the five subtypes of definition-and-classification propositions is familiarly known as the proposition of value. It is more aptly characterized as a criteria-and-application proposition. This is so because the appropriate analytical questions ask what criteria or standards apply, and whether the matter in question meets these criteria. In this kind of proposition, as distinguished from most of those above, the criteria are subjectively determined.

In this treatment of propositions we are grouping factual claims and evaluative claims under one heading because of their similarity in relation to analysis. But there is another reason for this grouping; we can sometimes, but not always, distinguish between statements of fact and statements of evaluation. Some statements are both descriptive and evaluative.[3] The following are mainly evaluative:

Materialism is an unworthy philosophy of life.
British schools prepare for college better than ours do.
Our foreign economic aid is wrong in principle.
No-money-down house buying is economically unsound.
Big-time football is out of place on a university campus.

[3] M. White, "New Horizons in Philosophy," *Central States Speech Journal,* XII (1961), 192.

Propositions of Policy

In legislative and school debating, and perhaps in political debating, this kind of proposition predominates. It calls for a change of policy; it proposes some action. Typically the word "should" is used, as we see in the specimens below. This word implies that the action *could* be taken, but not that it will be taken.

A proposition of policy is, generally speaking, more complex than one of definition and classification. The simplest, but not necessarily the easiest, involves the proof of a factual claim. Above this in complexity is the subtype which involves not only facts but also standards of judgment. The proposition of policy involves facts and values, but it extends into expediency, practicality, and action. These are typical specimens:

The Federal Government should subsidize the higher education of superior students.

Fraternity pledging should be deferred until the sophomore year throughout the U.S.A.

Photography should be permitted in court.

The U.S.A. should quit competing in the Olympic Games.

Athletic grants-in-aid should be abolished.

School marks should be "pass" and "fail."

SOURCES OF PROPOSITIONS

Obviously, propositions are formulated and expressed by persons who wish either to advocate a controversial point of view or to set it out as a kind of hypothesis to be tested. The question of source actually asks under what circumstances a person or a group becomes identified with a proposition.

One is the situation in which a problem gives rise to one or more proposed solutions in a group meeting. When this happens, motions or their equivalents are debated. This is true whether the problem comes up in a regular meeting, or whether the group has been formed ad hoc in response to the problem. Some years ago a science teacher entered her junior-high classroom, noticed an odor, and demanded: "What jackass turned on the gas?" Whereupon some irate parents complained to the school board, and that group conducted a hearing for four and one-half days. Several charges and proposals were offered, but the final proposition came in the form of a charge of misconduct. This proposition was defeated, but unresolved was the original question: What jackass *did* turn on the gas? [4]

Another source of a proposition might be an individual's reaction to a disturbance of his equilibrium, so to speak. A citizen might be so irritated by a sound truck during a political campaign that he would attend the local council meeting and demand the passage of an ordinance to ban such advertising. Of course, he might change his stand if he became intensely involved in a campaign sometime. Such was the experience of a farmer who was circulating handbills opposing a law to curb livestock on highways. He joined the opposite side after his car was smashed in a collision with a stray bull.

A third source might be the circumstances of employment or one's involvement in some activity. In this situation the proposition, and perhaps even one's side, would probably be assigned. When an advertising agent or a lawyer is retained by a client, the proposition and the side are not matters of independent choice; they are imposed by circumstances. Both the proposition and the side are likewise imposed upon anyone who is made a defendant in a legal action. In school debating, the propositions are in most situations selected by national committees. The individual director may cast one of hundreds of votes, but his student debaters have no direct voice in the selection process.

SELECTION OF A PROPOSITION

Whenever a person has a choice of problem areas or of stated propositions, he has at his disposal several criteria to guide his choice. At this stage, before the wording of propositions has been discussed, the selection of a proposition refers in the main to the business of selecting a problem area in which a resolution will be framed. For our present purpose, four broadly stated criteria will suffice.

One is that the problem should be worthy of debate, i.e., controversial and significant or interesting. It is not worthwhile to select a problem which is likely to produce emotional ravings or shallow specu-

[4] "The Teacher and the Jackass," *Time*, March 17, 1958.

lations. More satisfaction stems from a controversy which calls forth the best efforts of the participants.

Another criterion is that the problem be suited to the advocate's interests, information, and convictions. A speaker or a writer is well advised to select a problem area or a stated proposition from the fields in which his background enables him to communicate something worthy of attention. School debaters, of course, have to develop a specific background *after* the proposition has been given to them. If the "official" proposition doesn't suit a student, and if there is no alternative, he may drop out of the activity.

The third standard is that the problem or the proposition be potentially interesting to the intended audience. This implies audience analysis and adaptation to discover what is timely, ego-involving, and comprehensible. In addition, the affirmation of one of these questions is likely to indicate the interest value of a proposition: Is it possible to solve? Is it possible to convince some persons of this? Is it possible to stimulate critical thinking about this? The last question is especially relevant in the instance of a philosophical proposition.

Finally, the problem or proposition should be adaptable to the occasion. As is the case with any subject for whatever purpose, there are common-sense criteria of appropriateness. While it is possible that the same problem area or specific proposition would be adaptable to a classroom exercise, an intercollegiate debate, or a public lecture, it is probable that one choice would not be equally wise in all three situations. Then too, some kinds of propositions (policy, etc.) are better suited than others to certain kinds of debates (philosophical, political, etc.). As we noted earlier, the legislative context typically calls for a policy proposition, the judicial calls most often for a factual determination, the philosophical calls for a debate on values, and the school debate is almost always based upon a proposition of policy. If the speaking time or the space in print is limited, the scope of the proposition has to be considered, too.

WORDING A PROPOSITION

When one has an opportunity to verbalize the proposition to which he expects to address himself, he is well advised to observe several principles which have been grouped under four headings: clarity of language, correct placement of burden of proof, limited scope, and the effect of amendment.

Clarity of language means that the locution avoids vague or ambiguous terms, has no question-begging words, indicates the kind of proposition, and achieves plainness without the loss of accuracy. A vague term has many meanings, while an ambiguous one has two. Note the lack of clarity in this proposition from an editorial: "What our colleges need is more emphasis upon the laboratory and the library rather than intercollegiate athletics." Another violation of clarity consists of the use of a question-begging term as in this specimen: "The unfair income tax law should be repealed." Something ("unfair") which should be proved by the affirmative is assumed to have been proved. Clarity is also served by phrasing a proposition so as to indicate its kind and consequently the appropriate analysis. Note the difficulty in classifying this proposition: "America needs men like Robinson Crusoe." Are these two statements the same kind of proposition: "Teacher May *is* guilty of misconduct," and "Teacher May *should be declared* guilty of misconduct"? Finally, there is the problem of achieving plainness without losing accuracy. In the following propositions we have apparent plainness which is actually vagueness: "The U.S.A. needs her allies more than they need her"; "Washington was greater than Lincoln." Although perfect clarity is seldom if ever achieved, it is reasonably approximated in this statement: "The membership dues of this club should be increased from the current two dollars per month to three dollars per month."

Correct placement of burden of proof is, as we have seen before, a matter of immense importance in the conduct of a controversy. Since the affirmative speaks in the proposition, this statement must clearly express the affirmative's claim and thereby define its responsibility for proof. But merely calling one side "affirmative" does not make it so; it may be merely the *nominal* affirmative as distinguished from the *actual* affirmative. Referring back to Chapter II, we recall that the actual affirmative is the party that will be dissatisfied if the situation in question remains as it is. Thus the proposition must express the actual affirmative's view by calling for a change in belief or action. If the proposition says we should retain the Social Security system, the side saying "yes" is merely the nominal affirmative, because it is not calling for a change. These propositions involve improper or highly questionable placement of burden of proof: "Socialism and democracy are incompatible," and "Monogamy is natural and desirable."

They are wrong because the nominal affirmative is the actual negative, i.e., the side saying "yes" has no burden of proof. No change from the prevailing belief or the cultural norm in our society is being urged. The proposition about socialism would place the burden of proof upon the affirmative (both nominal and actual) if the wording were something like this: "America could realize her democratic ideals through socialism." The proposition about monogamy should, for the same reason, be changed to something like this: "Monogamy is an unnatural (or undesirable) custom." Note the option of either of two single ideas.

This comment about a single idea leads us to a third general principle of correct phrasing, which is that a proposition should be limited in scope. Undoubtedly the best general rule is to express one idea in a simple sentence. Imagine the difficulties you would face in arguing either side of this two-ideas proposition: "Ivy College should adopt an honor system and a trimester calendar." A certain editorial gave a student some trouble when he was attempting to isolate the proposition. He justifiably thought the proposition was calling for the passage of a bill to ban "mail-order filth" from the mails when he read: "Give the Post Office Department the legal weapon with which to fight those vile creatures. . . ." However, the bulk of the editorial argued that parents should take more notice of what their children read. Two propositions were being argued at once. The legal remedy and parental vigilance could have been made major points under a definitely phrased, but rather broad, proposition such as: "Parents and the Congress should join forces in combatting mail-order filth."

Lastly, on this matter of wording, there is the question of the status of a proposition which has been changed by amendment. In parliamentary deliberations this is done by adding, deleting, substituting, and the like. The result is a *new* proposition, regardless of how much or how little it resembles the original motion. A slight change will not affect the sides, but a major one might. Take the case of Magnolia Normal which is on the semester calendar. If the proposition called for a change to the trimester calendar, an amendment substituting "quarter" for "trimester" would make a real difference in the choice of sides and in the nature of their cases.

QUESTIONS

1. Evaluate these propositions as worded:
   a. The United Nations is an ineffective agency for maintaining collective security.
   b. Marriage is undesirable for undergraduates.
   c. The price of the affluent society is not worth paying.
   d. Good government is better than self-government.
   e. Democratic socialism is the best answer to communism.
   f. Evanston should legalize 3.2 beer and off-track betting.

2. Carlyle (*On Heroes, Hero-Worship, and the Heroic in History*) said that men of genius played causative roles in history, while Tolstoy (*War and Peace*) argued that leaders of men did not really have free will to influence events. What is the proposition here? What kind is it? What kind or kinds of debate could be held on it?

3. On the matter of military examination of the Civil War, Roland wrote, in *Albert Sidney Johnston and the Shiloh Campaign*: "Many historians have attempted to expurgate Grant for the cardinal sin of permitting himself to be out-generaled and surprised by his opponent at Shiloh. They point out that Grant had recommended . . . a bolder strategy which, if adopted, would have made impossible the Battle of Shiloh. This does not, however, excuse Grant for the gross misjudgment as to Confederate capabilities and intentions, nor relieve him of the responsibility of protecting his command against surprise . . ." Catton, in *Grant Moves South*, however, wrote: "General Buell remarks that Grant is very seldom seen in reports of the Shiloh fight, and implies broadly that the Army commander was very inert. Actually, there are few Civil War battles in which one gets so many glimpses of a commanding general going about his business so energetically and competently." What is the proposition? What kind is it? What kind or kinds of debate could be held on it?

4. What proposition or propositions come to mind when you observe on one page of a metropolitan daily newspaper at least ten advertisements containing captions such as these: "Short on Cash? Bankrupt? Bad Credit? Just Turned 21? Try Our Credit Plan"; "Bad Credit Our Specialty"; "Repossessed? Short on Cash? We Finance You on Premises"; "Bankrupt? We Finance Anyone!"

5. Discuss some of the above propositions (Questions 1–4) in terms of (a) the functions served, (b) their likely sources, (c) their suitability as measured by the four criteria of selection, and (d) the suitability of their wording.

EXERCISES

1. Select an editorial, a letter to the editor, or a short printed speech. State its proposition. What kind is it? Evaluate the composition on the basis of the ease or difficulty in isolating the proposition and in classifying it.

2. On a specified number of these general subjects, compose one proposition for each of four out of five subcategories of propositions of definition and classification (or criteria and application):
   a. Labor-management relations
   b. International relations
   c. Intercollegiate athletics
   d. Cheating in school

3. Compose one proposition of policy on each of the four subjects above.

4. The class (or each subgroup thereof) will select a problem and word a proposition on it for use in later exercises. In this way the exercises will build toward something more meaningful than would result from unrelated assignments.

5. Report critically on one or more items in the Appendixes, using topics similar to those in Question 5 in the preceding section. In addition, word the proposition if it isn't stated in print, and classify it.

ANALYSIS:

A CRUCIAL PROCESS

WHENEVER A PROCESS IS CHARACTERIZED AS BEING CRITICAL, DECISIVE, OR of supreme importance, there is ample reason to ask what the process is and why it is so rated. In the next two paragraphs more will be said on these topics, but for the moment a high-level abstraction in the form of a value judgment will be offered: Analysis is probably the most intellectual of the processes studied in argumentation, and it is one of the two or three most essential. In this book, therefore, analysis is treated as a central or core concept in the theory of argumentation.

In this subject, analysis is the process of determining what a proposition means and what are the controversial questions which must be answered if the deliberation is to be critical and thorough. Speakers and writers, some of whom do this better than others, analyze their propositions in order to determine what their lines of argument shall be. At the receiving end of the communication, listeners and readers use analysis, too, if they are intelligently critical. In other words, analysis plays a vital role in constructing a case, in attacking a case, in defending a case, and in evaluating or criticizing a case.

It will be recalled that in Chapter II we stated that anyone who espouses a cause has an ethical obligation to make the best case he can in terms of the assumptions, evidence, and reasoning which are both available and legitimate. This necessitates his knowing what must be argued if he is to meet his responsibilities in terms of probability and presumption or burden of proof. Only through competent analysis can he reliably determine what must be argued.

There are several important, specific benefits of such analysis: the saving of time because of spending it only on essentials, the prevention of surprise attacks by an opponent, the guidance of one's preparation, the providing of questions to evaluate the relevance of one's materials, and the clarification of the basis of the controversy for all interested parties. In terms of strictly logical considerations, an advocate would confine himself to the controversial topics within his subject, but in the interest of popular persuasion he would discover and make use of the points of agreement as well. For example, most questions of public policy in this country must be considered on two levels: one is what would be best under ideal conditions; the other is what is expedient in relation to the voting interests involved.

Thus far we have considered the uses of analysis in case construction, attack, and defense. However, analysis is a crucial process in the arbitration or in the evaluation of a dispute. For instance, in a labor-management dispute it is necessary to isolate the issues before any fruitful bargaining can take place. The chairman of a fact-finding panel in a lengthy steel strike once remarked that the mediators could not work effectively until the issues were etched out, and he complained that this process could take many days.

POSSIBLE STEPS INVOLVED

Determination of the Kind of Proposition

Perhaps the first analytical step should be the determination of the kind of proposition one is dealing with. If one is a speaker or a writer, he should verbalize and classify his proposition in order that he can estimate the nature of his responsibilities. If, on the other hand, one is a listener or a reader, he should perform the same process for the purpose of estimating the demands he will make upon the advocate who seeks his vote. The kinds of propositions were explained in Chapter III, and the methods of analyzing them will be discussed later in this chapter.

For the presen.   .il note that the classification of a proposition provides a guide ⟍ its proof requirements; each kind has its characteristic issues, as we shall see. It is useful to think of the kinds of propositions in terms of degrees of complexity. For instance, the allegation of a fact is the simplest, the urging of a value judgment is more complicated, and the advocacy of a policy is the most complex. A value judgment involves facts plus criteria and their application, while a proposition of policy involves facts and values plus considerations of practicality, expediency, and action.

Definition and Interpretation

What does the proposition mean? If you originate a proposition, try to make it convey your intent to those to whom it is addressed. If you are given the proposition, try to interpret the intent of its source. The reason for giving this apparently obvious advice is that some writers and teachers say that an affirmative spokesman may interpret a proposition however he wishes. This is only partly true, because we should not expect any fruitful deliberation to take place on a proposition interpreted in "Alice in Wonderland" language. Unless an advocate is practicing intentional ambiguity, which this book treats as "crooked thinking," he has an obligation to use language which facilitates understanding.

Think before "looking it up" in a dictionary. Your own background is a resource which may easily be overlooked. It is wise to begin with a mental inventory of what one knows and thinks about a problem. For instance, a person might begin by ascertaining the context of his proposition: Social Security? International politics? Medical economics? Labor-management relations? Race relations? Other? Definitions drawn from dictionaries and encyclopedias are not helpful unless the terms are treated in relation to the context in question. "Condominium" does not have identical meanings in international law and in real estate transactions, for example.

This leads us to a consideration of the other major methods of definition, some of which may in certain propositions reveal the issues. The familiar methods include synonym, classification, etymology, illustration, and negation. A synonym is a word or phrase whose meaning approximates that of the word being defined, as in using "disengage" for "extricate." Definition by classification is accomplished by showing how the item to be defined belongs to a larger class of related items. Thus an atomic device would be classified as weaponry, and its differences from conventional weapons would be pointed out. Sometimes the etymology of a term throws some light on its meaning, but the dynamic character of a living language renders the historical approach a bit risky. "Parlay" may have come from *paro*, meaning "pair," but not all pairs are parlays. Occasionally terms are defined by negation, which involves stating what they are not: "When I speak of courage, I don't mean foolhardiness." Finally, when a case in point is cited, the definition is by illustration: "If you seek the meaning of humility, consider the life of Lincoln."

Perhaps the most often ignored of the procedures of definition and interpretation is the statement of philosophical positions and their assumptions. Suppose you are urging that Congress expand the coverage of Social Security to include many more aspects of health, education, and general welfare. Do you favor or oppose the *direction* of the on-going social change in relation to Social Security? Do you favor or oppose only the *rate* of that change? Do you oppose the value assumptions underlying the proposal, or do you favor them? One such value assumption might be that the achievement of a higher minimum standard of health, education, and general welfare for citizens of the U.S.A. is more important than any considerations of financial cost, bureaucracy, impairment of self-reliance, etc. On the opposite side might be value assumptions which hold that the preservation of self-reliance, a balanced federal budget, and a minimum of governmental control over local matters are the most important considerations.

When the contending sides in a controversy fail to state their philosophical positions or to reveal their assumptions, the debate is not likely to be intellectually satisfying. Some say that Republicans and Democrats are often indistinguishable and that their political debates are consequently dull. The reason is that they dispute about tactics instead of getting to the roots of the problems. Perhaps they do so because most of their listeners and readers do not demand better of them.

Sketching of History of Problem

This step and the next one are both analytical and investigative, i.e., they could be explained in this chapter on analysis or in the following one on investigation. They are discussed here because the nature of a controversy depends in a large measure upon the circumstances of its origin and the reasons for its present importance. These matters of origin and development assist one in interpreting a proposition, and this is an essential part of analysis.

Suppose you are going to participate in a debate on the proposal to adopt the city manager form of government in your home town. You will want to learn what kinds of local government have been tried in times past and what some qualified observers have said about their virtues and faults. In particular you will be well advised to examine most carefully the experiences of your town and many others with the mayor-and-council format, which is the most common in this country. Then you will trace the origin and development of the manager form of government, paying particular attention to the experiences of towns similar to yours which have this arrangement. Finally, you will want to study the history of this problem in order to observe trends. Is the manager form of government the coming thing, or is it a passing fad?

Citation of Reasons for Present Controversy

In this step we have essentially a continuation of the preceding one. We bring the background survey right down to the present and ask what are the immediate causes of the controversy. Typically we find a situation which is sufficiently disturbing to prompt someone to challenge a prevailing belief, a current practice, an existing institution, or some other status quo. The disclosure of gross mismanagement of a city's finances may lead to the demand for a professional city manager. Deaths in the ring or on the field often prompt individuals or groups to urge the abolition or the closer regulation of contact sports. Disclosures of greedy behavior have been known to give rise to propositions calling for a change in our values. An examination of precipitating causes such as these may help one to locate the issues. At the very least it will provide an advocate with some attention-getting material.

Finding Issues

If any one part of the analytical process accounts for its being crucial, this is it. From the definition of issues in the next paragraph one can judge that the finding of issues in a proposition is the most important step in the preparation of a case or in the critical analysis of someone else's case. When one is preparing a case, his preliminary analysis yields only tentative issues which he subsequently refines through further investigation and analysis. The number of issues thereby arrived at will vary among propositions; some will have one or two, while others will have three, four, five, or more. In the following quotations General Eisenhower says there is one issue in the 1952 campaign, while Governor Stevenson says there are three: [1]

> "The basic long-term issue of this campaign is between two totally different concepts of America and two totally different estimates of the American people.
> "On the one hand, there is that school of thought whose spokesmen regard America as finished: a 'mature economy'; a land of closed frontiers . . .
> "There is another and opposite school of thought and of action. This school of thought regards America as more, much more, than the sum total of the things that are wrong with it. It regards America not as a dead end but still at its beginning; and the American nation as still in its youth . . ." (Eisenhower)

> "There are three great issues before the country.
>
> The first is how to stop Communist aggression, prevent a third World War, and achieve peace with freedom and justice.
> "The second is how to foster continued economic growth and a steadily rising standard of living for all our people.
> "The third is how to build an even more decent and rational democracy in a free society . . ." (Stevenson)

NATURE AND KINDS OF ISSUES

Issues Defined

Some writers say an issue is any question the affirmative must affirm. This definition doesn't explain *why* a certain question must be affirmed, and it doesn't stipulate any *negative* obligation. Others say issues

---

[1] *The New York Times Magazine*, November 2, 1952, p. 9. Copyright by the New York *Times*. Reprinted by permission.

are points of disagreement between persuader and persuadee, but what if argumentation is used without persuasive intent? Still others, who are more numerous, define issues as points of clash between affirmative and negative cases, or as questions which express differences of opinion between the two sides. Generally speaking, this is a usable definition, except that is presupposes the existence of cases on both sides. What if someone is going to *originate* a controversy? He needs a method of finding the potential points of clash before they become actual. Or what if one wishes to analyze critically a debate which has taken place, and it turns out that the participants did not meet their logical responsibilities? If the critic considers as issues only those points on which a clash occurred, he will of necessity ignore any potential issues which did not become actual, and he cannot judge whether a case is prima facie or logically adequate. More will be said about the kinds of issues in the next section.

In view of these considerations, it seems advisable to define issues in more detail. One part of this definition states that an issue is an inherent and vital question within a proposition: inherent because it exists inseparably and inevitably within a proposition, and vital because it is crucial or essential to the meaning of that proposition. A second part of this definition follows in consequence of the first: each issue must be affirmed unless it is waived or admitted by the negative, and at least one issue must be denied by the negative. The imperative *must* is not an overstatement if we assume that each side will be held to its logical and ethical responsibilities.

Two uses of the word *issues* in the mass media of communication will illustrate the difference between the meaning intended here and a confusion of it. The first use occurred in an editorial (on Title Seven of the Taft-Hartley Act amendments) [2] which answered three issues: Will it handle "no-man's-land" labor cases? Will it bar secondary boycotts? Will it ban organizational picketing? These areas were said to be "of vital concern," which is one way to characterize issues. A less helpful usage occurred on the evening of July 28, 1960 when candidate Nixon told an interviewer that he hoped the televised debates between himself and candidate Kennedy would not merely show who was the better debater but would show who could better handle the issues. In the context of this course, the better debater *is* the one who better handles the issues.

[2] *Salt Lake City Tribune,* August 26, 1959, p. 16.

Kinds of Issues

Issues are often classified as potential, stock, waived or admitted, and actual. Potential issues are all of the issues which are possible in a given proposition. They are to be found, not selected, and they are the same for both sides of the controversy. However, the affirmative can be held responsible for every one, while the negative may limit its own responsibility to as few as one if it chooses, according to the standard of logical responsibility. If the standard of popular persuasion were applied here, we should have to say that the listeners or readers would determine the number of issues which either side would have to answer.

Benjamin Franklin and several authors of argumentation textbooks have advised us to locate potential issues by listing all of the affirmative points we can find, doing likewise with negative points, and then observing where the lists clash. This will reveal the actual issues in a controversy which has taken place, but it is less reliable as a method of finding potential issues before a controversy begins. For example, suppose we wanted to find the potential issues in a Senate debate on a bill to increase the regulation of the securities markets. If some potential issues were not brought up, our lists of pro and con points would not reveal them. In this particular controversy nobody raised the potential issue concerning the wisdom of checking the sharp increase in consumer debt.

Stock issues are potential issues in a preliminary, generalized form. They are preliminary in that they are used early in the analytical process, and they are general in statement because they are intended to apply to all propositions of a given type. Thus at the beginning of his analysis of a proposition of policy, an advocate might use stock issues such as these: Are there serious, inherent evils in the status quo? Is the affirmative plan the best solution? Stock issues would be worded differently for other kinds of propositions.

Although this "formula" approach to analysis is in some ways convenient, there are limitations which should be noted.[3] It is stereotyped or "cut-and-dried," and hence it does not say anything about the subject matter of the particular proposition. Suppose the proposition calls for an honor system at Igloo U. We don't say anything specific

[3] R. P. Newman, "Analysis and Issues—A Study of Doctrine," *Central States Speech Journal*, XIII, No. 1 (1961), 43.

about the system or the school when we ask a stock question about "serious, inherent evils in the status quo," but we do get some guidance in framing the desired, specific questions about the proposition. Perhaps the greatest risk in using stock-issue analysis is that it will become a poor substitute for original thinking.

These objections have been answered by several explanations,[4] one of which is that stock issues are intended to be used only as broad questions which serve as guide lines to suggest areas for further study. Thus they are not the end of analysis. They don't commit anyone to a position before he has studied the proposition thoroughly. The fact that not all stock issues become actual issues is not remarkable; that is to be expected of potential issues, whether stated in stock form or otherwise. Also, in the later stages of analysis, the stock issues take on qualifiers such as the degree of need, the details of a plan, the nature of benefits, etc. Finally, the "need-plan-benefits" matters need not be handled in three separate units; they may be developed in a series of "need-plan-benefit" topics, as we shall see in the discussion of Cases.

Waived or admitted issues are those which are subtracted from the list of potential issues by action of the negative side. This necessarily follows from the fact that the negative *may* require the affirmative to affirm every potential issue. In practice, though, the negative side often contests fewer than all of the potential issues. Considerations of time, interest, and vulnerability account for this. Perhaps the most familiar instance of admission occurs when the negative side on a proposition of policy concedes some cause for action ("need") but offers a rival solution (counter-proposition). Once an issue is waived or admitted, it ceases to be an issue in that particular debate.

Actual issues are, as explained above, those which remain in contention after waivers and admissions have been subtracted from the list of potential issues. Actual issues are also called "ultimate," "real," and "issues of the debate." They are the key questions on which the sides clash. In fact, the best way to find the points of clash in an actual controversy which has taken place or is going on is to make parallel outlines of the two sides, placing opposing points directly opposite each other, and leaving blank spaces opposite those points which are not attacked. Critic judges of school debates typically do this. However, as was argued earlier, this method is less useful in the analysis of a proposition which has not yet been debated. Below is a specimen of

---

[4] R. Nadeau, "In Defense of Deliberative Stock Issues," *Central States Speech Journal*, XIII, No. 2 (1962), 142.

the clash-outline method of locating the actual issues in a debate that has been going on. The proposition, as of 1961, called for the amendment of the Illinois Banking Act to allow banks to open branches in their own trade areas.

AFFIRMATIVE POINTS	NEGATIVE POINTS
Business development is retarded by inadequate banking facilities.	Chicago is a net exporter of bank loans.
Individuals are inconvenienced by a shortage of banks.	Very few communities are more than a few minutes from a bank.
Only large banks can provide specialized services.	
	Branches cost more than independent local units to operate.
Chicago banks are losing business because of having no branches.	
It would not lead to monopoly.	It would create a monopoly.

The actual issues were: (1) Is the present arrangement of banks in the Chicago area unable to render satisfactory service? (2) Would branch banking avoid the danger of monopoly?

ISSUES IN NONPOLICY PROPOSITIONS

In this section we shall consider by means of definition and illustration the analytical process of finding issues in propositions of definition and classification or of criteria and application. These five kinds or subtypes of propositions have in common two analytical steps: the definition of the predicate term and the application of criteria to the subject term.

Propositions of Legal Fact

As we noted in Chapter III, there are two basic questions which need to be asked in order to get at the issues in this kind of proposition: What did the party in question do? Is it definable as the offense which is charged? Suppose the proposition is *Sam is guilty of loitering*. The potential issues would be worded as questions to which the affirmative would have to answer "yes": (1) Did Sam spend a considerable amount of time aimlessly leaning against a downtown building? (2) Is this classifiable as loitering as defined in the statutes? Obviously something more than simple fact is involved here.

Propositions of Past Fact

Again we would raise two exploratory questions: What would be required to establish the alleged fact? Do our available data meet this requirement? Suppose the proposition is *President Lincoln's party was split over the purpose of the war.* Again the potential issues would appear as questions which the affirmative must affirm: (1) Were there in the Republican Party in 1864 two or more views of the purpose of the war? (2) Were these differences serious enough to be called a "split"?

Propositions of Present Fact

Preliminary, analytical questions the same as those at the beginning of the preceding paragraph are applicable here, too. Thus these exploratory questions are, in a way, similar to stock issues. Suppose the proposition is *The Monroe Doctrine is dead.* The potential issues which probably would be found as a result of asking the exploratory questions are: (1) Did the Monroe Doctrine promise to resist European incursions into the Western Hemisphere? (2) Have some such activities gone unopposed? (3) Do these circumstances warrant our declaring the Monroe Doctrine dead?

Propositions of Prediction

These might be called propositions of future fact, except that "prediction" is the more familiar word. Their preliminary analysis can be accomplished by asking the same two questions that were used in the three preceding subtypes of nonpolicy propositions. Suppose the proposition is *Mass education at the collegiate level will reduce the quality of higher education.* After asking the preliminary questions mentioned above, one would arrive at tentative statements of potential issues somewhat like these: (1) Must standards be lowered for some when larger numbers are admitted to college? (2) Will the lowering of standards for some students result in the reduction in the quality of higher education?

Before leaving the so-called factual subtypes of nonpolicy propositions and moving on to those of evaluation, it might be prudent to observe that facts and values are sometimes closely interrelated. This is true, contrary to popular belief, even in science, as Dr. Conant points out.[5] He explains that science is not neutral in regard to value judgments. For instance, researchers and practitioners in the medical sciences operate on the basis of these values: that life is preferable to death, that good health is important, and that each person has a kind of sanctity which requires that life be saved whenever possible. These value judgments serve as implied premises in medical discourse.

Propositions of Value

The preliminary, analytical questions which would be useful in the search for potential issues in a proposition of value might be phrased this way: Upon what criteria should the evaluation be based? How well does the matter to be evaluated measure up to these criteria? Suppose the proposition is *Resolved, That big-time football is out of place on a university campus.* The analytical questions can now be phrased more specifically: Under what conditions might we decide that an activity is out of place on a campus? Does big-time football qualify under these criteria? In the next analytical stage one would state pairs of criteria-and-application questions somewhat like these: (1) Is an activity out of place on a campus if it is not academically oriented? (1′) Does big-time football lack an academic orientation? (2) Is it out of place if it becomes an end in itself? (2′) Is big-time football an end in itself? (3) Is it out of place if it exploits the participants? (3′) Does big-time football exploit its players? Further study, as explained in the next chapter, may lead to a further refinement of the potential issues.

Before leaving the propositions of value we might at least raise a few relevant, philosophical questions: What are the human values? Where do we get them? Why are they believed to be good? There are many values, the highest of which are love, truth, beauty, self-realization, etc., in *our* culture. We get our values through our cultural heri-

[5] J. B. Conant, "The Scientist in Our Unique Society," *Atlantic*, 181, No. 3 (1948), p. 49.

tage. They became a part of the cultural heritage because of the social good which they served. Through the centuries man learned to value good relations within his social units, because he perceived the unpleasant effects of dissention, disruption, and the like. But the reasons *why* certain values are believed in are in dispute. Some say that values are not rationally derived; they are arbitrary postulates. Others contend that human nature determines the norms, i.e., that the pursuit of certain values is conducive to psychological well-being. Finally, there is a metaphysical view which is that the highest values are inherent in the character of being.

When analyzing a problem in which two or more values are in conflict, it might be well to determine which values are operating, in what rank order the persons concerned seem to hold them, and why the parties hold certain values. This procedure has obvious uses in persuasion, but it also serves in the reasoned development of the implications or consequences of any value judgments which are used as postulates or premises for argument. In philosophical debates we should expect to use this sort of analysis, but we should find it useful also in a proposition like the one above on big-time football.

ISSUES IN POLICY PROPOSITIONS

While it is true that the literature of argumentation has not been particularly helpful in past years with respect to the analysis of propositions of definition and classification or of criteria and application, the same cannot be said of propositions of policy. There have been several contributing causes, one of which is the almost exclusive use of propositions of policy in school debating. Thus it is not surprising that the articles and textbooks on argumentation and debate, being oriented toward the school activity, heavily emphasized the analysis of propositions of policy. It was in this setting that the stock-issue formula, which has been described above (under "Kinds of Issues"), was elaborated.

Stock-Issue Formulas

Although the elaboration of stereotyped formulas for use by school debaters is a twentieth-century phenomenon, the roots of such procedures have been traced back to *stasis* and *status* in ancient Greek and Roman rhetoric, respectively. Some influence from this tradition can be seen in the Baker-Huntington *Principles of Argumentation* in 1905, but the most extensive elaboration of the idea appeared in Shaw's *Art of Debate* in 1922. As recently as 1958 a laborious attempt was made to adapt the ancient doctrine of *status* to the analysis of propositions of policy. More will be said of this later.

Using Edmund Burke's speech, "Conciliation with the American Colonies," as a specimen for analysis, Shaw [6] located four issues: (1) Is some change from the present policy of taxation necessary to restore peace in America? (2) Would Burke's policy of conciliation restore peace in America? (3) Would Burke's policy of conciliation introduce new and worse evils? (4) Would any other policy be more satisfactory than Burke's policy of conciliation?

Before coming to these issues, which resemble the stock issues we have discussed, Shaw diagrammed under "Surveying the Proof" a fifteen-step procedure (including negative counter-proposition) for use with a proposition of policy:

Phases 1–4 represent the affirmative constructive case. Phases 5–7 represent a negative case of attacking the affirmative's plan. Phases 8–11 represent a negative counter-proposition case. Phases 12–15 represent the affirmative attack upon the counterproposition. Dotted lines represent comparisons such as "better than" or "worse than."

A more recent adaptation of the ancient method [7] features four stock issues and ten subissues: ill (apparent evil, real evil), blame (scapegoat, remediable), cure (remove causes, apparent benefits, real benefits), and cost (alleged evils, real evils, better remedy).

Analysis Illustrated

Nowadays the stock-issue analysis of a proposition of policy typically begins with questions such as these: Is there a need for a fundamental change from the present policy? Would the affirmative's plan remedy the serious, inherent difficulties in the status quo? Would the new plan avoid new and worse problems? Sometimes, in order to cope with

---

[6] W. C. Shaw, *The Art of Debate* (Boston: Allyn and Bacon, 1922), pp. 201–202.

[7] L. S. Hultzén, "Status in Deliberative Analysis," in *The Rhetorical Idiom*, ed. D. C. Bryant (Ithaca, N. Y.: Cornell University Press, 1958), pp. 97–123.

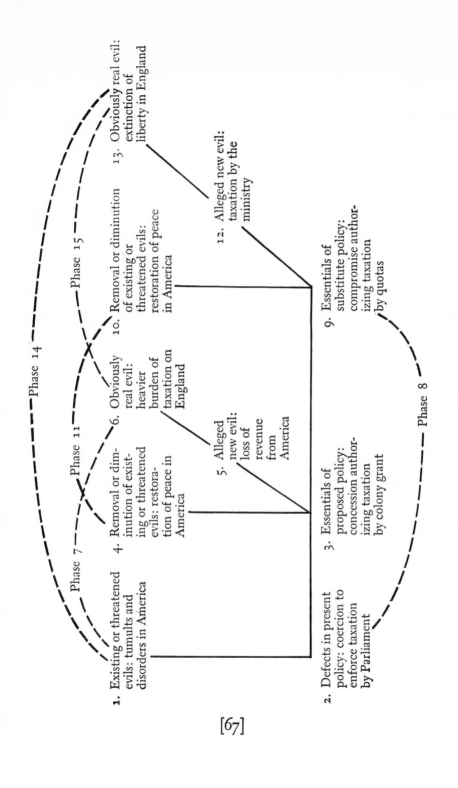

1. Existing or threatened evils: tumults and disorders in America

2. Defects in present policy: coercion to enforce taxation by Parliament

3. Essentials of proposed policy: concession taxation authorizing taxation by colony grant

4. Removal or diminution of existing or threatened evils: restoration of peace in America

5. Alleged new evil: loss of revenue from America

6. Obviously real evil: heavier burden of taxation on England

9. Essentials of substitute policy: compromise authorizing taxation by quotas

10. Removal or diminution of existing or threatened evils: restoration of peace in America

12. Alleged new evil: taxation by the ministry

13. Obviously real evil: extinction of liberty in England

Phase 7
Phase 8
Phase 11
Phase 14
Phase 15

possible counterpropositions, the third stock issue is changed to this: Is the affirmative plan the best answer to the problem? Details of wording will vary in terms of the subtype of proposition of policy one is dealing with—a whole new policy, a substitution of one for another, or the cessation of a current policy. The first might call for the establishment of a community college where no college has existed; the second might call for a change from the quarterly calendar to the semester; the third might call for the abolishment of capital punishment where it now exists.

Let us analyze the second proposition of policy by modifying the stock issues into more meaningful potential issues and by stating some potential subissues which our research has turned up:

    I. Are there important shortcomings in the quarterly division of the academic year?
       A. Do quarter-length courses sacrifice some comprehensiveness in the students' grasp of the subjects?
       B. Do they give too little opportunity for independent study between meetings?
       C. Do they aggravate the problems of academic adjustment?
       D. Do the frequent starts and stops break the continuity of learning?
    II. Would the change to a semester calendar remedy these shortcomings?
       A. Would semester courses provide more comprehensive treatment of each subject?
       B. Would they allow for more independent work?
       C. Would they give more time for academic adjustment?
       D. Would they provide more continuity of study?
    III. Would the semester plan be the best solution?
       A. Would it suit our purposes better than some trimester plan?
       B. Would it be better than some other alternative?
       C. Could it be adopted without serious inconvenience?

When the shortcomings of the status quo are not serious, and when only modest claims can be made for the benefits of the proposed change, we can use the comparative-advantages approach instead of the outline above. Actually, an advocate who would try to make a "crying shame" argument about the "evils" of the quarterly calendar would be suspected of exaggerating. More will be said of this in the chapter on "Cases."

EFFECTS OF SPECIAL SITUATIONS

In this section we shall consider the relationships between issues and each of three special situations: a negative counterproposition case, a choice between a critical and a popular decision, and the partitioning of a case.

Negative Counterproposition

Let us suppose that our proposition calls for statehood for Puerto Rico. If the negative concedes that the present status is not the best but urges a substitute solution in the form of national independence for Puerto Rico, we have a counterproposition. Each side in this situation has a responsibility to prove its own case. The affirmative has *the* burden of proof on the statehood proposal, but the negative has what we could call *a* burden of proof on national independence.

Does this change the issues? It does not; the counterplan fits under the issue which asks whether the affirmative proposal is the best answer to the problem. Instead of saying, "No, because of its drawbacks," the negative says, "No, because our plan is better." Thus the substitute acts as an obstacle to the affirmation on at least one issue. If this obstacle blocks the affirmative on one issue, that is enough to defeat the affirmative case, at least insofar as the logic of the controversy is concerned.

Does this imply that the negative counterplan should be adopted? It does not, because the alternative was advanced merely to challenge the affirmative's claim that statehood would be the best solution. We should expect to debate a proposition calling for national independence before there would be ample grounds for adopting that solution. Something like this occurs in a criminal trial when the defense contends that someone other than the accused did the deed. The new suspect is not thereby proved guilty; he is entitled to his own trial, and he goes into it with a presumption of innocence.

Popular vs. Critical Decision

The kind of decision an advocate seeks will affect his analysis in one major respect: it will prompt him to emphasize either the analysis of the audience or the analysis of the subject. A writer on legal evidence was getting at a point like this when he wrote, "The risk of not having persuaded the jury is one thing; the duty of producing evidence sufficient to cause the court to submit the case to the jury is a very different matter." [8] A practical politician is thinking of audience analysis and a popular decision when he advises, "You can talk all campaign long on an issue, but if the public isn't interested in it, you've wasted your time." But an idealist in politics would insist upon trying to *educate* the voters on issues which he thought were important, even if initial public interest were lacking.

Two modern textbooks epitomize the difference between these two views on analysis. The first [9] says an advocate analyzes the audience as well as the proposition for the purpose of discovering persuasive points. Applying this doctrine to rhetorical criticism, one writer [10] explained that spokesmen for political protest movements have been generally unsuccessful because they failed adequately to adapt to specific desires and experiences of the voters. Instead, they dealt in abstract, theoretical terms of the federal deficit while the voters wanted jobs, better prices, etc. The second of the modern textbooks [11] espouses the nearly opposite view, namely, that analysis should disregard the beliefs of the debaters and the audience. The latter of these two conceptions of analysis is much more likely to result in logically adequate cases, or proof which is not equated with belief.

Partitioning a Case

Analysis has presumably been completed when an advocate sets down his points in partition. These are the main "talking points" which will

[8] H. W. Humble, *Principles of the Law of Evidence with Cases for Discussion* (Chicago: Callaghan and Co., 1934), p. 25.

[9] C. S. Mudd and M. O. Sillars, *Speech Content and Communication* (San Francisco: Chandler Publishing Co., 1962), p. 42.

[10] H. P. Kerr, "The Rhetoric of Political Protest," *Quarterly Journal of Speech*, XLV, No. 2 (1959), 146.

[11] D. Ehninger and W. Brockriede, *Decision by Debate* (New York: Dodd, Mead and Co., 1963), p. 233.

be treated later under "Cases." The reason for mentioning the partitioning of a case at this juncture is that the relationships between issues and points in partition are frequently misunderstood.

It will be recalled that issues are inherent, vital questions, *all* of which the affirmative must be prepared to affirm, and *some* of which the negative must negate. Points in partition are declarative sentences which answer issues affirmatively or negatively. These points may closely resemble the issues in number and form, but they may also differ widely. An issue is vital, but a point in partition is not that important unless it is the only answer which one side gives to an actual issue.

Take this proposition: Dean Doe destroyed student government at Flywheel Tech. Potential issues might be these: (1) Did student government function at F.T. prior to the alleged action? (2) Did Dean Doe do something which terminated student government there? (3) Did he do it alone or principally? (4) Did this act result in the termination of student government at F.T.? (5) Was this act the main cause? Note that the points in partition can be fewer: (1) Dean Doe suspended the constitution of student government at F.T. (2) This action made it impossible for the active organization to continue. These two main points plus their supporting subpoints could be made to answer all five issues.

Or consider this proposition: Installment buying is harmful to the public interest. These might be potential issues: (1) Is a system of consumer finance harmful if it contributes to inflation? (1′) Does installment buying contribute to inflation? (2) Is a system of consumer finance harmful if it encourages many persons to live beyond their means? (2′) Does installment buying encourage many persons to live beyond their means? (3) Do the faults of this system outweigh its benefits? There might be as many as five points in partition, each one in the form of a declarative sentence to answer an issue. It is more likely, however, that subpoints would be used to cover some issues and that three points in partition would suffice: (1) Installment buying harmfully contributes to inflation; (2) It harmfully encourages many of us to live beyond our means; (3) These faults outweigh any claimed advantages.

QUESTIONS

1. Comment upon the conception of analysis which this statement implies: "Debaters in this generation must measure ideas in terms of the needs and values of the next generation as opposed to the present desire for lower taxes, etc."

2. A proposed amendment which would extend Swiss female suffrage to the federal level stirred up a lively controversy. The affirmative points were: (a) Progress demands that Switzerland not lag behind the rest of the world; (b) The traditional rule discriminates unfairly against women; (c) Swiss women are politically mature. The negative points were: (a) Swiss women have not voted in the past; (b) Women are emotional; (c) Women are not interested in politics; (d) They don't understand complex Swiss politics; (e) Disunity in the home might ensue; (f) Loss of femininity might result.

   What actual issue or issues does the "clash" technique yield? Which of the above points are main points, and which are subordinate? Which are required for a critical decision, and which for a popular one?

3. Analysis has been explained as a process which is essential to any advocate who wishes to meet his ethical and logical responsibilities. Discuss that view in relation to this statement attributed to a campus politician: "When you go to a house to speak, don't talk about issues, especially if they are controversial [What other kind is there?], or even yourself. Concentrate on complimenting someone outstanding in the house. They'll remember you because they'll think you're interested in them."

4. The *Saturday Review* of February 22, 1958 gave this summary of "clash points" between the pro's and con's of "Pay TV":

   a) The minority should have the opportunity to decide what it is willing to pay for.

   b) Free TV will still have the bulk of viewing time.

   c) Nobody can determine what the outcome might be without trial.

   d) Pay TV would provide a source of competition from which everybody would benefit.

   a) Presentation of programs for which a charge is made would be "fencing off the best for the carriage trade."

   b) Pay TV can succeed only by "cannibalizing free television."

   c) Trial performances would give "pay interests a golden opportunity to infiltrate."

   d) The "best programs would inevitably go over to pay television, should a successful nationwide system be established."

What actual issues are involved here? Are any potential issues not used?

5. Why doesn't the negative have to negate as many issues as the affirmative has to affirm?

EXERCISES

1. Analyze a printed argument such as a speech or an essay selected from an Appendix or elsewhere. Report in outline form on these topics: (a) Statement of proposition, (b) Kind of proposition, (c) Side taken by author, (d) Whether he had presumption or burden of proof, (e) Evaluation of proposition in terms of the criteria of selection and of phrasing, (f) Potential issues, (g) Issue or issues treated here, (h) Expressed or implied assumptions, and (i) Point or points in partition.

2. Analyze a proposition for use in your own future oral or written discourses. Report in topical form your analytical steps such as these: (a) Statement of proposition, (b) Classification of proposition, (c) Choice of side, (d) Obligation in terms of presumption or of burden of proof, (e) Evaluation of proposition in relation to criteria of selection and of phrasing, (f) Define and interpret it, (g) Sketch its history, (h) Cite reason for present controversy, (i) List potential issues, (j) State admissions or waivers if you are negative and wish to omit anything, (k) List any expressed or implied assumptions, and (l) Set out your intended points in partition.

3. Prepare an oral or a written report on the debate on stock issues which can be located through footnotes 3 and 4 in this chapter.

4. Apply the Shaw diagram, or as much of it as is applicable, to a debate in an Appendix or in a collection of school debates. See footnote 6.

5. Criticize the analysis which is apparent in this segment of a college oration: [12]

One University group could do much to develop thinking, responsible men who could help save America from world hate and intolerance. But this organization is a breeding ground for conformity, intellectual nihilism and adolescent superficiality. I refer to college fraternities. . . . Two and one-half years ago I was proud I was a fraternity man. Today, I am not. Why? . . . First, because our

[12] D. Croessmann, "Whatsoever Things Are True . . . ," *Winning Orations of the Northern Oratorical League* (Minneapolis: The Northwestern Press, 1940), pp. 10–12.

fraternities are not living up to their obligation to produce intelligent leaders. . . . Secondly, America needs men with a spiritual and cultural outlook on life, with a feeling for the beauty of the universe, with a love and appreciation for the arts. . . . And finally, America needs men imbued with the philosophy of tolerance and understanding, which they should preach to an intolerant world—a world salaaming to the doctrines of Nordic superiority, class hatred, racial discrimination.

CHAPTER V

INVESTIGATION

IN THE CONTEXT OF ARGUMENTATION, INVESTIGATION IS THE PROCESS OF accumulating information about a proposition. Sometimes it involves no more than looking up a few magazine articles or conversing with some friends, but it may be a long and arduous inquiry which can properly be called research. Within this broad range there are several investigative procedures, including thinking, observing, reading, listening, discussion, interviewing, corresponding, and recording the results of these activities. Directions on the utilization of these procedures will be given shortly.

When should investigation take place? Is it not the same process as analysis? These related questions can be answered by saying that analysis is the process of determining the meaning of a proposition and discovering its issues, while investigation is the closely related process of finding materials with which to develop the points which will answer those issues. Thus it follows that a studious advocate typically alternates between analysis and investigation. When he already has his proposition, he begins with a preliminary analysis which will direct his study, next he seeks material on the tentative issues, then he sharpens the issues in the light of greater knowledge, and finally he continues his investigation as guided by these more specifically worded issues. In other words, analysis tells him what he must be prepared to argue, and investigation provides the material with which to do it.

The importance of investigation is obvious, or at least it should be. Readers and listeners who have any claim to rationality expect an advocate to know what he is arguing about. When he does not, he

[75]

risks exposure. Such was the experience of a letter writer who attacked the scientists who helped with the American missile program and then praised "scientists like Einstein who refuse to prostitute their genius to perfecting methods of exterminating life . . ." The editor's reply reminded the writer that Einstein signed the letter that persuaded President Franklin Roosevelt to order top priority for the development of the first A-bomb.

It is useful to distinguish between original and unoriginal investigation. The former is first-hand inquiry as in the personal observation discussed below. Unoriginal investigation is by far the more popular with students who prepare arguments. It means the use of reports made by others who did the research. On subjects other than strictly local or personal matters it is usually wise to concentrate on unoriginal investigation after the preliminary stages.

Investigation may also be classified as direct or indirect. Direct preparation is the kind most of us think of; it is the thought and study which an advocate undertakes after he knows what his proposition is and perhaps when he will argue it. Students who "go out for debate" and lawyers who accept cases are obliged to do direct preparation. Indirect investigation may take place over a long period of time and without reference to a specific use. It actually means one's background of knowledge and experience. The value of this kind of investigation is pointed out in a later section, "Following Current Affairs."

Thorough investigation means work, which is to say that it requires time, energy, skill, patience, and, in a word, self-discipline. Consequently it is to be expected that some persons will try the easy shortcuts. But when they do, they fall short of meeting their ethical and logical responsibilities. The harm may be slight when a student does inadequate investigation for one classroom exercise, but it is a cause for alarm when police detectives detain a suspect for prolonged "grilling" which is an undisciplined, sloppy substitute for efficient criminal investigation. This point about taking time for research calls to mind the remark attributed to Warden Duffy of San Quentin: "Our debating teams go against the colleges and usually win. Why do they? Well, I always say, they have more time for research."

THINKING AND OBSERVING

Start With Self-Inventory

A speaker's or a writer's own background may be his best potential resource, but it is often overlooked. To prevent this mistake, an advocate should begin his investigation with a mental inventory of what he knows and thinks about the proposition. It is wise to take ample time to survey one's own knowledge and ideas before rushing to a library. These are some of the general hints which experienced persons have given: ask guiding questions like those in the study outline below; recall pertinent experiences; determine meanings of words and ideas; set up tests and classifications of material.

Observe When Feasible

If, as is often the case, previous personal experience is not enough, it may be supplemented with original investigation. This is first-hand inquiry which may include field trips and experiments. A newspaper feature writer who planned a series on the sharp practices of some used-car dealers and their finance companies sent some assistants out to make deals at some suspected lots. Through this procedure he turned up some cases in which the interest on installment contracts ranged between 139 and 275 per cent. Not only did he obtain striking evidence; it is doubtful that he could have found it by other means. In a quite different area of human concern there are cases of certain state legislators being moved from indifference to advocacy by a tour of a substandard state mental hospital. The point is that, however useful reading is, it is no substitute for thinking and first-hand observation.

Be Systematic

In all phases of investigation—thinking, observing, reading, interviewing, discussing, and the like—a guiding plan is at least useful if not indispensable. When surveying his own ideas or making observations, one should ask analytical questions, record his impressions, and make allowances for his own limitations in terms of selective perception, imperfect recall, and amateurishness in general. The first major step in the making of a guiding plan is taken when one performs the preliminary analysis as explained in Chapter IV. Once he defines the proposition and discovers the potential issues, he has some guidelines to follow. From this stage he can move on to the construction of a study guide or discussion outline of the sort illustrated in the final section of this chapter.

A true story of scholarly sleuthing will serve to illustrate the importance of systematic questioning and observing. For more than a half century some Viking lore enthusiasts had accepted as authentic the Kensington stone which a Minnesota farmer allegedly found in 1898. The stone bore runic inscriptions relating the adventures of a band of Norsemen in 1362. It could not be a fake, the believers said, because the farmer was almost unlettered and had no books to guide him. However, one scholar in Germanic languages, sensing some peculiarities in the inscription, determined to test his hypothesis that the late farmer had perpetrated a hoax. He engaged a professor of Norse from a nearby college to visit the farm, then occupied by the "discoverer's" sons. This visit yielded the contents of the old farmer's scrapbook and the knowledge that he owned a Swedish encyclopedia. Next it was learned by interviewing old neighbors that the uneducated farmer was considered to be intelligent and had often expressed his wish to fool the experts. In the four pages on runes in the encyclopedia there was enough information to enable one to compose the Kensington stone inscription. The characters on the stone were exact copies of those in the book; in fact, the farmer had even copied the mistakes. His old scrapbook revealed the practice exercises which he worked on while perfecting his technique.

FOLLOWING CURRENT AFFAIRS

Adopt a Program

Students who try to keep up on current affairs read with some regularity a few representative samples of daily newspapers, weekly news summaries, and monthly or quarterly journals of opinion. Three newspapers among the many possible choices are noteworthy in their categories: *New York Times, Christian Science Monitor,* and *Wall Street Journal.* Most familiar of the weekly publications are *Time, Newsweek, U.S. News and World Report,* and *Facts on File.* Depending upon his specific research interest, a student would be likely to use some of these periodical publications as well: *Reporter, Business Week, Congressional Record, Harper's, Atlantic, New Republic, Nation, Fortune, Monthly Labor Review, Congressional Digest, American Economic Review, Foreign Affairs, Editorial Research Reports,* and *Annals of the American Academy of Political and Social Science.*

How To Read

Suppose that you are working on the general subject of wage and price controls administered by the national government. Before getting down to particulars, read for general background in the main subject and in the bordering subjects as well. One of the first lessons a novice has to learn—often the hard way—is that an advocate has to read more than the minimum material for one speech or essay. On the economic-controls proposition, begin by looking up the topic in an encyclopedia, some economics books, the periodical indexes, and the general guides (especially Winchell's) in the following section. Find out what the controls are, how they work, when they originated, what they have accomplished, and what people have said about them. Look into bordering subjects such as the economic philosophies (R. L. Heilbroner, *The Worldly Philosophers*), public administration, supply and demand, and the like. Seek out some critical articles in journals of opinion and the professional journals in economics and political science.

When you progress beyond these preliminaries, go to the primary sources of information. It is better, for example, to quote from the opinion of the Supreme Court than to rely solely upon a newspaper columnist's version of that decision. If you want to cite what Senator X said about economic controls during the debate on a bill, look it up in the *Congressional Record.* Experienced scholars know the hazards of relying upon secondary sources such as newspapers, magazines, biographies, textbooks, and handbooks. Particular care must be exercised when quoting from condensations in popular magazines. They are the most likely to distort the original, however honest the editors' intentions may be.

This comment suggests the further advice to read with an alert, open, and inquiring mind. Analyze and evaluate the purported facts and the opinions. Systematic instructions on this process are given under "Tests of Evidence" in the next chapter. Perhaps the hardest advice to follow concerns the keeping of an open mind. This does not mean a state of indecision; it implies that an advocate will consider views in addition to the one he favors at the outset. The practical value of this attitude stems from the fact that a debater who is broadly prepared is better able to conduct attack and defense. He knows what to expect.

USING LIBRARY RESOURCES [1]

Reference Works

Until library resources become extensively automated, and perhaps even afterward, any student who investigates a proposition with sufficient thoroughness will need to know how to find what he needs in a library. The research tools and procedures explained here will not soon be rendered obsolete by microfilm cameras, computers, and mechanical selection devices combined into information retrieval systems.

General guides to reference works are designed to help the investigator to locate the more specific reference works. The first choice should be Constance Winchell's Guide to Reference Books, with its supplements, to answer the question, "Where can I find something on . . . ?" It also gives helpful hints on how to look up information. Three other guides are Subject Guide to Reference Books by Herbert Hirshberg, Basic Reference Sources by Louis Shores, and Guide to Reference Material by Arthur J. Walford.

Guides to newspapers and periodicals include British Union—Catalogue of Periodicals, N. W. Ayer and Son's Directory of Newspapers and Periodicals (by state, city, and title in the United States, Canada, and territories), Ulrich's Periodical Directory (world-wide and by subject), and the Union List of Serials (kept up to date by New Serial Titles).

Periodical indexes, including Readers' Guide, are numerous and

[1] The author gratefully acknowledges the professional advice given by George M. Bailey, Executive Secretary, Association of College and Research Libraries. Information Leaflets prepared by the Deering Library staff have been used extensively here.

cover a wide variety of interests. The standard items are listed here alphabetically.

> An Index to Book Reviews in the Humanities
> Art Index (1929—date)
> Bibliographie der Deutschen Zeitschriften-literatur (1876—date; German index to German periodicals)
> Bibliographie der Fremdsprachigen Zeitschriften-literatur (1911—date; a German index to non-German periodicals)
> Biography Index (1946—date; biographical material in books and magazines)
> Book Review Digest (1910—date; an index to book reviews)
> Canadian Index (1931—date; for Canadian periodicals)
> Cumulative Book Index (1898—date; for books in English)
> Education Index (1929—date)
> Essay and General Literature Index (1900—date; for essays in collections, book chapters, etc.)
> International Index (1920—date; humanities and social sciences)
> Magazine Subject Index and Dramatic Index (1907–49; American and British)
> Pais (1915—date; economics, political science, public administration)
> Poole's Index (1802–1906; general)
> Publishers' Weekly (1872—date; for new U.S. books)
> Readers' Guide to Periodical Literature (1900—date; general)
> Subject Index to Periodicals (1915–16, 1926—date; British)

Newspaper indexes enable one to locate newspaper materials on specific subjects and by names of writers. After locating the date of a story in the New York Times, one could consult other papers of the same or approximate dates. The four principal newspaper indexes are those of the New York Times (1913—date), London Times (1790—date), Christian Science Monitor, and Wall Street Journal (December, 1957—date).

Bibliographies are lists of source materials on specific subjects. Such lists may be classified according to types of material such as books, periodicals, documents, recordings, etc. They may also be annotated, which means that the nature of the contents is indicated under each entry. The two most important bibliographies of bibliography are Besterman's World Bibliography of Bibliographies and the Bibliographic Index. There are many specialized subject bibliographies such as The Cambridge Bibliography of English Literature, "American Bibliography" in PMLA, Writings in American History, Year's Work in Modern Language Studies, and The International Bibliography of Political Science. National and trade bibliographies such as the Cumulative Book Index and the British National Bibliography, the National Union

Catalogue of the Library of Congress, the catalogs of the British Museum and the Bibliothèque Nationale, and the later edition of the British Museum catalog are available in the larger libraries. See also Winchell's *Guide to Reference Books*, 19 ff.

Biographical reference works will be useful to students of argumentation when they need to look up the qualifications of experts whom they intend to quote. The following are the most widely known:

Allgemeine Deutsche Biographie (Germans no longer living)
Biographie Universelle (universal)
Contemporary Authors
Current Biographies (universal)
Dictionary of American Biography (Americans no longer living)
Dictionnaire de Biographie Francaise (Frenchmen no longer living)
Dictionary of National Biography (Englishmen no longer living)
Neue Deutsche Biographie (Germans no longer living)
Nouvelle Biographie Generale (universal)
Who's Who (living Englishmen)
Who Was Who (Englishmen no longer living)
Who Was Who in America (Americans no longer living)
Who's Who in America (living Americans)

In addition to the above, there are biographical references for other nationalities, regions of the United States, and subject specialties. Among these are *Who's Who in the Midwest, Who's Who in American Education, Directory of American Scholars, American Men of Science,* and *Who Knows—and What.*

Encyclopedias, yearbooks, dictionaries, directories, and statistical compilations are numerous and cover most subjects, countries, and languages. Encyclopedias are good for general background. Best known among the general encyclopedias used by college people are the *Britannica,* the *Americana,* the *New International,* and *Colliers'.* Specialized encyclopedias are available in social sciences, education, government, social reform, and other fields of interest. Yearbooks containing information on events in specific years include *World Almanac, Statesman's Yearbook, Information Please Almanac, American Yearbook, New International Yearbook, Statistical Abstract of the United States, Commerce Yearbook, Statistical Yearbook of the United Nations,* and *Demographic Yearbook of the United Nations.* General dictionaries, especially the unabridged, contain information on usage, derivation, pronunciation, place geography, weights and measures, colleges, holidays, etc. The data on postal rates and foreign exchange are likely to be out of date. *Webster's, Funk and Wagnalls, American College Dic-*

tionary, and *Oxford* are the best known. Law, medicine, and other specialized fields have their own dictionaries.

Government documents contain important source material for many propositions. The *Congressional Record* and records of committee hearings are perhaps the best known. Publications of foreign, state, and local governments are also included in this category of government documents, as are the many items issued by the United Nations and its specialized agencies. Guides to U.S. government publications include *United States Government Publications* by Boyd and Rips and *Manual of Government Publications* by E. S. Brown. The U.S. Government Printing Office is the source of the *Documents Catalogue* and the *U.S. Government Publications: Monthly Catalogue*.

Pamphlets on a vast number of subjects are available in the larger collections, some of which have upwards of forty thousand items. Two guides to consult are the *Vertical File Index* and *Public Affairs Pamphlets*. Since much of this kind of material is issued by interest groups, it is useful to know that the names and addresses of organizations can be found in *Guide to Public Affairs Organizations*, *World Almanac*, and the U.S. Chamber of Commerce *Trade and Professional Associations of the United States*. A critical reader will make allowance for the fact that a pamphlet or a leaflet issued by an interest group may be intended to promote that interest.

Theses and dissertations are not often used by persons who are developing arguments, but this does not imply that they should not be included as potential sources of evidence. *Dissertation Abstracts*, a monthly publication, is the best current listing in abstract form of the dissertations of 117 universities. *Index to American Doctoral Dissertations* serves as an annual index to *Dissertation Abstracts* and as a continuation of *Doctoral Dissertations Accepted by American Universities*.

Interlibrary loan and microfilm have expanded the resources of individual libraries without adding much bulk to any one. Some years ago a researcher had to travel to a library which held something he wished to consult, but interlibrary loan enabled him to borrow such things by paying the postage. Today, thanks to regional library associations and the development of copying machines which reduce the size of the material, the distant resources can be brought to the investigator. Microfilm, microprint, microcards, and photocopy are familiar to most scholars and librarians. Guides to this sort of material include the *Union List of Microfilms* and the *Guide to Microfilms in Print*. Dissertations are available through University Microfilms.

Card Catalogs

In the libraries which will be used by many students of this subject, each card catalog is divided into a general catalog and a serial catalog. Cards are filed alphabetically in the sliding trays according to the system explained below.

General catalog books will be found under their authors' names, or, when no author is given, under the title. The author may be a person (Milton, John), a society or institution (Speech Association of America), or a branch of government (Department of Labor). In addition to the author card there are entries for titles, subjects, and secondary authors. These are interfiled with the author cards.

Subject headings appear at the top of a card in red, or in black underlined in red. A subject will be put under the most specific term applying to it, that is, the subject "oak trees" will be under "Oak," not "Trees." Proper names may also appear as subjects (Lee, Robert E.). Cross references are used when it is necessary to refer from a variant form of a subject to the form used in the catalog (Organic chemistry, see Chemistry, organic), and when referring from one subject heading to other headings under which related material may be found (Architecture, see also Building). Cross references are filed at the end of a subject. A list of subject headings with the appropriate cross references may be found in the U.S. Library of Congress, Subject Cataloging Division, Subject Headings. . . .

Titles appear on title cards which are made for works having distinctive titles, such as belles-lettres, anonymous works, and collections. They are generally not made for biographical works which have as their title the subject of the biography, or for works with commonly used phrases such as "A history of . . ." or "A study of . . . ." Look under the subject heading when neither the author nor the title of a book is known.

Cross references, such as those used with subjects, are often necessary to refer from variant forms of an author's name, editions of a work, titles, and translations of a work, to the form used in the catalog. Cross references also are used to refer the user of the general catalog to the serial catalog for fuller information concerning the library's holdings of a particular series or serial. In case there are branch or cooperating libraries, there will be cross-reference cards for items in those places. Special cards are inserted for new accessions, removals, and new orders.

The following are specimens of cards in general card catalogs: the first five are for personal authors; the last five are for corporate bodies as authors.

Serial catalogs contain cards for bound periodicals and society publications which are issued in numbered series. Magazines are generally found under their titles, such as *Atlantic Monthly* or *Journal of Higher Education.* Many serials, however, can be found only by looking under the name of the issuing organization, as in the case of the *Proceedings* of the National Education Association. Cards in this catalog indicate which volumes and numbers of a given serial are held by the library. In most cases the recent issues are shelved in a periodical room, but they are listed in the serial catalog. There are no subject cards in this catalog. Below are five specimens of serial catalog cards.

INTERVIEWS AND CORRESPONDENCE

An advocate who is in the investigative stage of his preparation may find it useful to consult with experts in person or by correspondence. We shall consider first the interview in some detail and then apply many of the principles to correspondence as well.

Interviews are used for the purpose of asking knowledgeable persons what they know or think about specific matters in relation to the interviewer's proposition. Students often consult professors, government officials, commentators, and others who seem to qualify either as sources of evidence or as guides to research. Thus it should be obvious that an interview requires more purpose and plan than a social conversation does. But when it is well managed, an interview may yield expert opinion, new facts, different insights, and hints on further research. One step in good management is advance preparation in the form of composing some opening questions, making an appointment, and keeping it promptly. Next, the interviewer should avoid imposing upon the interviewee. This involves investigating elsewhere first so that naive questions will not be asked, and it means that the interrogation will be brief, to the point, and courteous. Finally, before the interview takes place, it is wise to learn about the interviewee. This includes reading what he has written on the subject.

When the conversation gets under way, focus upon his area of

CROSS REFERENCE TO RELATED SUBJECT

Literature, Modern. History and criticism see also

Baroque literature

TITLE ADDED ENTRY

809
B163i
Ishmael
Baird, James.
Ishmael. Baltimore, Johns Hopkins
Press, 1956.
xxviii,445p. 24cm.

Bibliographical footnotes.

SUBJECT ADDED ENTRY, PERSON AS SUBJECT

809
B163i
Melville, Herman, 1819–1891
Baird, James.
Ishmael. Baltimore, Johns Hopkins
Press, 1956.
xxviii,445p. 24cm.

Bibliographical footnotes.

SUBJECT ADDED ENTRY, IN RED OR UNDERLINED IN RED

809
B163i
Literature, Modern. History and criticism Baird, James.
Ishmael. Baltimore, Johns Hopkins
Press, 1956.
xxviii,445p. 24cm.

Bibliographical footnotes.

MAIN ENTRY

809
B163i
Baird, James.
Ishmael. Baltimore, Johns Hopkins
Press, 1956.
xxviii,445p. 24cm.

Bibliographical footnotes.

1. Literature, Modern. Hist. & crit.
2. Primitivism in literature. 3. Symbolism in literature. 4. Melville, Herman,
1819–1891. 5. Religion, Primitive. I.
Title.

CROSS REFERENCE FROM ALTERNATE
FORM OF AUTHOR
Museum of Fine Arts, Boston
see
Boston. Museum of Fine Arts.

TITLE ADDED ENTRY
L741.64   The artist & the book, 1860–1960
B747a   Boston. Museum of Fine Arts.
          The artist & the book, 1860–1960,
in western Europe and the United
States. Boston, Museum of Fine Arts;
[Cambridge] Harvard College Library,
Dept. of Printing and Graphic Arts
[1961]
          232p. illus.(part col.) 29cm.

AUTHOR ADDED ENTRY
L741.64   Harvard University. Library. Dept. of
B747a   Graphic Arts
          Boston. Museum of Fine Arts.
          The artist & the book, 1860–1960,
in western Europe and the United
States. Boston, Museum of Fine Arts;
[Cambridge] Harvard College Library,
Dept. of Printing and Graphic Arts
[1961]
          232p. illus.(part col.) 29cm.

SUBJECT ADDED ENTRY, IN RED
OR UNDERLINED IN RED
L741.64   Illustrated books. Exhibitions
B747a   Boston. Museum of Fine Arts.
          The artist & the book, 1860–1960,
in western Europe and the United
States. Boston, Museum of Fine Arts;
[Cambridge] Harvard College Library,
Dept. of Printing and Graphic Arts
[1961]
          232p. illus.(part col.) 29cm.

MAIN ENTRY
L741.64
B747a   Boston. Museum of Fine Arts.
          The artist & the book, 1860–1960,
in western Europe and the United
States. Boston, Museum of Fine Arts;
[Cambridge] Harvard College Library,
Dept. of Printing and Graphic Arts
[1961]
          232p. illus.(part col.) 29cm.
          "Exhibition held at the Museum of
Fine Arts, Boston, May 4–July 16, 1961."
          Bibliography: p.222–227.
          1.   Illustrated books. Exhibitions.
I. Harvard University. Library. Dept.
of Graphic Arts. II. Title.

CROSS REFERENCE TO SERIAL CATALOG
FROM GENERAL CATALOG

AFRICANA
960.5   Northwestern University, Evanston,
N879   Ill. African studies.

               For full record see Serial catalog
               at beginning of Main catalog.

CARD 2 FOR SERIES SHOWING CONTENTS

AFRICANA   Northwestern University, Evanston,
960.5   Ill. African studies . . . (Card
N879   2)
                       Contents.
               no.1. Herskovits, M.J. Dahomean
                      narrative. [1958]
               no.2. Cohen, A. British policy in
                      changing

MAIN ENTRY FOR SERIES

AFRICANA
960.5   Northwestern University, Evanston,
N879   Ill. African studies. no.1—
               [1958]—
               Evanston.

CROSS REFERENCE TO SERIAL CATALOG
FROM GENERAL CATALOG

Lo51   New statesman; the week-end re-
N553   view.

               For full record see Serial catalog
               at beginning of Main catalog.

MAIN ENTRY FOR PERIODICAL

Lo51   New statesman; the week-end re-
N553   view. v.1–36, Apr.12, 1913–Feb.
               21, 1931; new ser., v.1–Feb.28,
               1931—
               London.

               Title varies: Apr.12, 1913–Feb.
               21, 1931, The New statesman; a
               weekly review of politics and liter-
               ature; Feb.28, 1931–June29, 1957,
               The New statesman and nation.

                            See next card

special competence; presumably that is the reason for the visit. Get him to talk while you listen. Avoid the temptation to debate with him or to press him for a conclusion on the whole proposition. Finally, take notes and ask permission to quote, if that is what you intend to do with his testimony.

Much the same advice applies to correspondence, including questionnaires. This procedure is actually a substitute for interviewing. Probably the best advice is that letters and questionnaires should be used sparingly if at all. If they are used, they should ask about specific evidence, sources, and the like. Use library sources first, and above all, don't reveal your ignorance with a request like this: "Please send me everything you have about speech."

Sometimes a well-designed survey questionnaire is the only feasible instrument. When the General Faculty Committee of Northwestern University was discussing the probable faculty preference for fringe benefits as opposed to the equivalent in take-home pay, there seemed to be no other suitable way to find the answer. Accordingly a questionnaire was carefully designed and administered, and the results were analyzed and interpreted. The finding was in favor of increased fringe benefits, and the administration acted accordingly.

RECORDING NOTES

General Hints

While there is little doubt about the desirability of recording some sort of notes, there is some question about which system is best. Perhaps there is no single, best system, but there is a worst one which we shall call the makeshift or casual system. This judgment stems from the observation that there are distinct advantages in the systematic recording of research notes: it assembles in usable form the materials for essays, speeches, and debates; it facilitates the exchange of information; it prevents the loss of ideas and sources.

Assuming that the systematic recording of *some* notes is desirable, there is still the question of *what* or *how much* to record. A few students record too much—or at least too much that will be practically useless.

They need to develop more discrimination. Others, and they seem to be the more numerous, record too little. Precisely how much is enough one cannot say in advance. The nature and the amount of the notes will vary in relation to the complexity of the subject, the investigator's acquaintance with it, the time available for study, and the importance of the occasion for which he is preparing. A survey of the advice on logical responsibility (Chapter II), analysis (Chapter IV), and evidence (Chapter VI) will provide guidance on what and how much to study and record.

File cards and loose-leaf notebooks are by far the most satisfactory for the storage of notes. Among school debaters and many other library researchers, the 4 x 6 cards seem to be the most popular. They can be moved about easily as the need arises. Of course this advantage holds only if the investigator places just one item on a card and includes enough information about it. This information, in the instance of an evidence card, includes the topic involved, the authority and his qualifications (for opinion evidence), the quotation or paraphrase, and the documentation which would enable any interested person to look up the citation. Ideally, each card should contain enough information to defend its evidence against the likely attacks. See "Types of Notes" below.

Accuracy in recording is of prime importance. If a reader or a listener finds out that someone's words have been misquoted or that a figure is wrong, he is likely to discount everything else that advocate says. Use quotation marks for direct quotations, and plainly identify omissions, condensations, and paraphrases. Copyreading for accuracy can best be done by two persons, one to read aloud from the card and the other to follow the original.

As soon as one accumulates a few cards he is likely to sense the need for a filing system. Suppose he has a box of 4 x 6 cards with raised dividers and a table of contents inside the lid. If he groups his cards by topics or likely points of clash, and if he writes key words and documentation at the top of each card, he can easily find what he wants. These evidence cards are to be used in building a case, in attacking a case, and in defending a case. Variations of this filing system have stood the test of countless school debates in which the speakers needed to select the right cards in a hurry.

Cost	Red-tape	Graft	Unfair

Types of Notes

Bibliography cards or sheets, preferably the former during the investigative stage, are useful in keeping a record of the worthwhile sources. To this end the following items are included: identification of the reference (person's name, title of article and magazine or book, publication date, pages used), place of storage (general library, law library, closed reserve, stacks, reference room, etc.), and annotation (what is in it, and of what use to one side or both sides). The identification of the reference comes first.

Geo. L. Bach, Prof. & Head, Econ. Dept., Carnegie Tech.

Economics: An Intro. to Analysis & Policy
N.Y., Prentice-Hall, 1954

Business Reading Room

Book VII, pp. 547–617.
   Ch. 31—Monetary Policy . . .
   Ch. 32—Fiscal Policy . . .
   Ch. 33—Anti-Monopoly Measures . . .

Affirmative on liberal, planned fiscal policy.

Evidence cards, including those which contain ideas for attack and defense, are often drawn from the sources recorded on bibliography cards. Since the "General Hints" above cover all but the illustration of evidence cards, the following specimens will suffice. The first is for a direct quotation, and the second is for a paraphrase or a précis:

Increased industrial output of CM nations.

Robert L. Heilbroner, *The Making of Economic Society*, p. 191

Ed. at Harvard and New School for Social Research; author of economic history, *The Worldly Philosophers*.

"The Common Market is still in the process of achieving many of these goals, although it is well ahead of its timetable. Already, however, it has led to a remarkable increase in European production. By the early 1960's, industrial production has more than doubled, and agricultural output has risen by a third. Over the entire decade, Western Europe's rate of growth has exceeded by 50% that of the United States, and most important of all, for the first time the standard of living for the middle and working classes of Europe has begun to resemble that of America."

Food pollution from testing

"Iodine-131 in Fallout: a Public Health Problem," *Consumer's Reports*, XVII (September, 1962), p. 447.

A leading periodical devoted to making available objective research data. Completely unbiased politically.

(Précis)

No. of micromicrocuries per liter of milk: The Radiation Protection Guide for Iodine-131 for children is 100 micromicrocuries per day over a year's time. Yet, in May of 1962 Wichita, Kansas, averaged 220 micromicrocuries per day; Kansas City, 200 per day; Minneapolis, 120 per day. In June, 1962, Kansas City was up to 240 per day; Wichita was still above safe levels with 130 per day. In the same month Spokane, Washington, averaged 350 micromicrocuries per day and in July, 1962, Salt Lake City averaged 650 micromicrocuries per day. If these present high levels continue, our milk supply will actually endanger our children's health.

DISCUSSION

To Develop a Proposition

In the preceding sections of this chapter it has been assumed that the investigator has a stated proposition with which to work. But now let us suppose a situation in which some persons discover a common interest in a problem which has not yet been verbalized. What can they do? Where should they begin? Their investigative problem can be handled by means of the Dewey formulation of reflective thinking.[2] But before they can use this procedure they must express their problem in question form. It could be something like this: What should be done to provide a higher minimum of educational opportunity in this country? Then they can develop an expanded version of this sketchy outline:

    I. Define and delimit the problem
       A. What is the general problem?
       B. How much of it will we consider?
       C. What do the terms mean?
    II. Analyze the problem
       A. What are signs of problem?
       B. Why do these signs exist?
       C. By what criteria should proposals be judged?
   III. Offer solutions
       A. Explain solution "A."
       B. Explain solution "B," etc.

By the time the discussants have moved through the third of the five possible steps, they are likely to choose either of two courses: to continue the reflective deliberation until one solution is agreed upon, or to move into a parliamentary context and reach a decision through debating. The latter has often occurred with the question of how to improve educational opportunity. Federal aid in some form usually comes into contention. In this kind of situation we see how discussion can serve to develop a proposition. This is obviously one of the investigative functions of discussion.

  [2] See J. H. McBurney and K. G. Hance, *Discussion in Human Affairs* (New York: Harper and Brothers, 1950), pp. 65–80.

To Plan a Case

The second investigative function of discussion is to assist in planning a case. In this setting, however, discussion undergoes changes in attitude, purpose, and possibly method. Here the idea changes from "What should be done to provide a higher minimum of educational opportunity in this country?" to "How can we prove that our scheme of federal aid is the best solution?" Even so, the individual contributions need not be advanced in the spirit of controversy; they can be expressed in explanatory form. If each speaker in the conference, "skull session," or "brainstorming" period explains what arguments he thinks would be good and how he so decided, then the colleagues can understand him and in turn explain why and how they agree or disagree with him. In this way some of the valuable features of reflective group deliberation are preserved. This outcome is even more likely if each contributed idea for the case is advanced as a hypothesis without personal commitment or ego involvement.

QUESTIONS

1. Define these terms so as to distinguish among them: investigation, research, analysis.
2. Why start with a self-inventory and possibly observation? Illustrate with a proposition.
3. What about the widespread claim that undergraduates have no time to read newspapers or magazines?
4. In order to locate newspaper accounts of the NATO conference held on a certain date, which reference work should be consulted first?
5. What if "magazine" were substituted for "newspaper" in item 2?
6. Is it not a contradiction in terms to speak of a group of advocates discussing ways to prove a predetermined proposition?
7. With how much confidence can one assert that the printed record in the *Congressional Record* is an exact report of what a member of Congress said?

EXERCISES

(Covering investigation plus a review of analysis)

1. As a *speaker*, report orally for three to four minutes on these items:
   A. Statement of a controversial problem
   B. Statement of your proposition based upon "A"
   C. Classification of that proposition
   D. List of potential issues in question form
   E. Stipulation of any waived or admitted issues
   F. Issues on which you would contend
   G. Point or points in partition on which you would build your case
   H. Kinds of material needed to support "G"
   I. Where would you seek it? Sketch an investigative procedure.

2. As a *writer*, submit the equivalent of Exercise 1 in outline form.

3. As a *reader or a listener*, submit this version of Exercise 1 in outline form, except that you will use the text of someone else's argument (in Appendix or elsewhere):
   A. State his proposition.
   B. Classify it.
   C. List his actual issues.
   D. List any potential issues not used.
   E. State his points in partition.
   F. Are these points, if well supported, sufficient to discharge the advocate's ethical and logical responsibilities?
   G. How thoroughly did the advocate apparently conduct his investigation? Did he seem to know enough about his proposition? Explain your evaluation.

4. This is an assignment in the investigation of a proposition of one type. Either an oral or a written composition may be based upon this exercise on a later occasion. First, you will think through the steps of Exercise 2 at the end of Chapter IV as they apply to your proposition for this lesson. That analysis will guide your reading. Second, you will prepare five cards for bibliography. Third, you will prepare twenty evidence cards which will be used in the next oral or written lesson. Finally, you will hand in the cards, but some students will be asked to demonstrate by reading some cards or copying one or two on the board.

CHAPTER VI

EVIDENCE

IN THE NORMAL ORDER OF EVENTS, ANALYSIS AND INVESTIGATION LEAD TO the accumulation and the testing of evidence. But before explaining these processes, let us define evidence as the term is used here. A typical dictionary definition is inadequate; it broadly characterizes evidence as that which tends to prove or that which serves as a ground for belief. Legal definitions are functional in the judicial context, but they leave something to be desired in the setting of general argumentation. Evidence in court consists of testimony, documents, and things which, if found admissible by the judge, are presented to support a point in question. In other words, legal evidence is informative material, acceptable to those who are to judge, which is offered by an advocate to buttress his own inferences. It is often called the raw material of proof in the sense that evidence plus inference equals proof. These two major ingredients of proof differ in that evidence is independent of and external to the advocate; it is not of his own invention. Under what circumstances his persuadees or his critics will or should accept his evidence will be treated under "Tests."

For the purposes of general argumentation, let us define evidence as factual statements, objects not created by the advocate, and opinions of persons other than the advocate which are offered in support of his claims. Factual statements or empirical data consist of presumably verifiable information on the occurrence, existence, classification, or character of phenomena. These data are sometimes statistically expressed and sometimes not. Opinions of persons other than the advocate will be discussed under "Legal Classification" and "Tests," wherein a distinction between ordinary and expert opinion will be drawn. In this category we should also place the admissions of a respondent in a dialectical (cross-examination) situation. Our present distinction between factual statements and statements of opinion is neat and convenient, but it is not universally applicable. Allegedly factual statements sometimes turn out to be expressions of opinion, and misguided ones at that. Objects not created by the speaker or writer will be defined in more detail under "real evidence." For the present we shall merely mention that material things such as weapons, burglar tools, ladders, eye glasses, and articles of clothing have often been offered as real evidence.

THEORETICAL IMPORTANCE

In rhetorical theory there are three main reasons given for the use of evidence in argumentative discourse: it adds probative force; it tends to increase the credibility of the communicator; it may add emotional impact. Evidence is part of what the ancients called *logos*, or the logical part of the argument. The importance of evidence to logical adequacy can be seen in the fact that a controversial statement which is not evidenced is potentially a fallacy of unsupported assertion. When we say that the use of evidence enhances the credibility (*ethos*) of the communicator, we mean that a writer or a speaker in a controversial situation makes his statements more believable when he supports them with material other than his own. If the advocate is not a high-prestige source in his own right, he may improve his acceptability by quoting approvingly from esteemed sources. Thus a student speaking on the need for a common market in a certain region would be well advised to use the opinions of acknowledged experts in international trade and finance. This bolstering of *ethos* is actually a by-product of the addition of probative force. In saying that evidence may add emotional impact to the advocate's persuasive message, we mean that a quoted, vivid description or a photograph of a policeman setting a dog to biting a man is likely to add force to the advocate's assertion that we have an unsolved problem in human relations.

But not all factual statements and inferences require evidence. Matters of common notoriety (those which are commonly known by a group or a community) need not be proved. This is analogous to judicial notice in law, but the critical listener or reader would do well to test any statement prefaced by "We all know that . . ." or some beguiling equivalent. Finally, waived or admitted matters need not be proved either in court or elsewhere.

In the last segment of this chapter, "How To Use It," we shall review some findings of research which raise serious doubts about the *practical* importance of evidence in discourse that is intended to persuade.

COMMON FORMS

Witnesses

Evidence appears in a variety of forms, one of which is the testimony of witnesses. Personal testimony is given under oath in legal and quasi-legal cases, but it also appears in the form of reports in nonlegal meetings. The distinguishing characteristic of this form of evidence is the physical presence of the source before the audience. This makes cross-examination possible. We are familiar with the situation in which a witness is called to the stand to testify in a trial. In general argumentation we find more relevance in the description of a public meeting on campus during Parents' Day when a dean, who was arguing that students have more serious interests than their parents' student generation had, called upon several students, faculty men, and personnel administrators to report their impressions and to answer questions from the floor.

Documents

Material written by someone other than the advocatory speaker or writer is classified as documentary. More is said of this in Chapter V and in the next major division ("Legal Classification") of this chapter. One class of document is the deposition, which is a sworn statement taken by a court stenographer from a witness who will not appear in court. The obvious weakness of this form of evidence is the impossibility of cross-examination. A second class of documentary evidence is the public record which includes statute books, ordinances, minutes, the *Congressional Record*, deeds, vital statistics, and the like. Public records usually contain accurate factual matter, but all sorts of personal remarks appear in some of these sources. Public written material is a third class of documentary evidence. It includes books, newspapers, magazines, and similar materials which were listed under "How to Read." Finally, there is private written matter which was originally for private use but which may be made public later as in the instances of wills, contracts, diaries, correspondence, and company records.

Recordings

Evidence in this form is more likely to be used in nonlegal situations which are not covered by the rules of evidence. At present most courts do not admit, and most states do not allow, wiretapping or other kinds of electronic eavesdropping. But there are nonjudicial situations in which recorded sounds are the best evidence that the sounds were made. Tape recordings of business conferences and interviews are cases in point. The extent to which the presence of the recorder causes speakers to modify their remarks is, of course, a question of some importance.

Graphics

Pictorial representations are typically referred to as visual aids rather than a form of evidence. Still photographs, movies, video tape, charts, diagrams, graphs, drawings, and mock-ups are familiar varieties of the graphic form of evidence. With the growth of television has come an increasing awareness of the part that visual aids can play in entertaining and persuading vast audiences. In the absence of precise measurement of this effectiveness there has been substituted an abundance of guesswork which has resulted in a flood of apparently ridiculous visual commercials. On the other side it must be conceded that some psychological studies have indicated the persuasive superiority of a verbal message which is visually augmented. The risks of "doctored" evidence apply to the visual form as well as the others.

Objects

Concreteness can be achieved through the use of real things far better than by any other means. This is true by definition. In the legal classification this form of evidence is known as real, demonstrative, or of inspection. More will be said of real evidence later, but for the present we shall discuss the other two names for it. Demonstrative evidence involves someone's showing how something works, while evidence of inspection means that the speaker gives the listeners something to look over. From the fundamentalist-modernist religious debate of the 1920's we get an interesting specimen of the object as a form of evidence. According to an article titled, "Monkey in Pulpit—Which?," a fundamentalist preacher in Montana brought into his pulpit a chattering monkey in support of his argument against evolution. "The presence of the monkey in the pulpit is supposed to have proved something, and it did, but possibly not what the Rev. Mr. _____ anticipated." [1]

LEGAL CLASSIFICATION

Although most students of general argumentation will not have occasion to use all of these distinctions which are important in judicial settings, there are two reasons for presenting a brief exposition here: modifications of some of these categories will be serviceable, and pre-law students will find the introduction instructive.

Admissible or Inadmissible

In one sense this dichotomy has a null class; if some material is not admitted in evidence, it is actually not evidence in that case. If it is not admitted, it need not be classified in terms of the following pairs of categories. The general reason for rules on this point is to screen potential evidence so as to exclude that which would not aid in the decision-making process. There are two broad rules of exclusion: ob-

---

[1] *Christian Century*, XLI, 39 (1924), 1245.

jections to the form in which a question is put to a witness (coaching or leading), and objections to the substance of the evidence sought (irrelevant, immaterial, and incompetent). In addition to the one general reason for rules of exclusion there are four particular reasons: they make for a more orderly presentation of cases; they save time by allowing only that evidence which bears upon the issues before the court; they aim to have evidence authenticated before the jury is permitted to ponder it; they preserve the privileged status of some communications, such as those between physician and patient, priest and penitent, lawyer and client, and husband and wife.

Rules of evidence exist only in judicial settings except as "ground rules" may be established by assemblies, debate leagues, and the like. Legal rules are obviously too complex for other situations. However, a person of integrity, judgment, and taste can profitably apply some of these standards to his own evidence and to that of others who seek his approval.

Original or Hearsay

In nonlegal usage these might be named primary and secondary, respectively. Original evidence comes directly from the primary source: the eyewitness himself, the researcher who made the finding, the expert who looked into the matter, or the document in question. Hearsay, on the other hand, is secondary and somewhat suspect, although it is under certain conditions admissible. Sometimes it is the only evidence available. An oral report of the contents of a document or a senator's version of the President's opinion on a pending bill would be classified as hearsay.

For purposes of general argumentation, five principles will serve to guide our use of hearsay evidence: its use is entirely proper if it is the best available; reliable hearsay should not be stigmatized because of the shoddy hearsay which some persons use; the intermediary should be checked for reliability; public records and public written material which students use extensively are acceptable because their public nature stands in lieu of cross-examination; hearsay testimony given before the controversy arose is generally given more credence than that which is given during the debate. When these principles are followed, the use of hearsay evidence or secondary sources need not be a cause of embarrassment.

Direct or Circumstantial

Direct evidence applies, without the need of any mediating inference, to the precise point in issue. Circumstantial evidence involves a set of facts other than those in issue which, when coupled with an inference, tend to support the point in issue. Statistical data on employment, production, consumer spending, bank deposits, consumer debt, and interest rates, for instance, would approximate direct evidence on the health of the economy. A more obvious instance of direct evidence is the testimony of an eyewitness who reports that Mr. X was standing on the sidewalk when Mr. Y's car struck him. The point in issue was the whereabouts of the victim at the moment of impact. Circumstantial evidence abounds in criminal trials because wrongdoers rarely invite witnesses. Also, on the suspected connection between cigarette smoking and lung cancer and heart disease, the evidence is thus far circumstantial.

Although direct evidence in often preferable, we should recognize that it may be unreliable because of faulty perception by a witness, inaccurate reporting by him, or intentional misrepresentation. And, as one should expect, circumstantial evidence may be misleading because of fallacious inferences which may be drawn from it. For these reasons it is advisable, whenever possible, to use the two kinds in combination. If they corroborate each other, the result is a stronger argument.

Ordinary or Expert

When classified by source, evidence may be termed ordinary or expert. According to law, an ordinary witness may testify to facts, not opinions. This rule stems from the fact that an ordinary witness is, by definition, without qualifications in the disputed matter. He is supposed to report observation rather than inference, but these are easily confused. A cross-examining lawyer had this in mind when he admonished a witness to tell what he saw and omit what he thought. "I can't talk without thinking," replied the witness, "I'm not a lawyer."

In general argumentation, opinions of laymen, as in opinion polls, are often cited. Ordinary evidence may also be seen in the testimony of a student who testifies before the Discipline Committee that he saw another student copying someone's paper. When an ordinary witness is quoted, one should ask whether he is giving a fact or an opinion, and whether it meets the appropriate tests as explained below.

Expert opinion evidence is, as the name indicates, an expression of a judgment by one whose training and experience qualify him as an authority on the subject at hand. Social science testimony was used by both sides in the public school segregation cases before the Supreme Court.[2] Experts in this field include specialists in sociology, psychology, anthropology, political science, economics, psychiatry, history, and law. Experts disagree on bygone events as well as on current controversies, as we see in this century-old topic. "Almost from the day when armed conflict began," wrote T. Harry Williams in *Lincoln and the Radicals,* "the Radical and Conservative factions of the Republican Party clashed over the purpose of the War. Lincoln and the moderates attempted to make the restoration of the union the sole objective . . . against this mild program the radicals inveighed, ranted and sneered." In *Lincoln Reconsidered,* however, Ronald states: "To picture Lincoln at swords' points with the Radical leaders of his own party . . . is an error. It is also a reflection of the naive view of the nature of American politics."

Since qualified experts disagree, and since self-styled "authorities" exist in profusion, what is a student to do? Unfortunately there are too few persons like Mr. A. P. Herbert who once stood for Parliament. He stated his platform on several leading issues of the day, but under Agriculture he confessed, "I know nothing whatsoever about agriculture." Have we heard any of our politicians disclaiming expertness on any subjects lately? Specific tests for ordinary and expert evidence, as well as for other kinds, will be set out in the next main division of this chapter.

Written or Unwritten

These categories of evidence are based upon form. In court the unwritten evidence is mostly the oral testimony of witnesses, and it is often the larger part of the total evidence. In the other formal situations such as legislative and school debate, most advocates use written evidence, while in the countless, informal advocatory situations the

2 D. B. Strother, "Polemics and the Reversal of the 'Separate But Equal' Doctrine," *Quarterly Journal of Speech,* XLIX, No. 1 (1963), 50–56.

use of experts' oral comments in hearsay form is commonplace. For purposes of general argumentation we may conclude that written evidence can be authenticated more easily and is generally preferable in nonlegal situations.

Real or Personal

Needless repetition can be avoided here if we refer back to "Witnesses" and "Objects" under "Common Forms" in this chapter. It will suffice to say that real evidence includes tangible objects, while personal evidence means information given by a person or persons. An interesting but inconclusive use of real evidence occurred in a school debate on the detrimental character of chain stores. A student shopped an independent store and a chain store for identical lists of groceries and displayed the two market baskets with their respective sales slips for the purpose of demonstrating a price differential. This would have been personal evidence if the shopper had reported his experience without bringing the groceries. Some of the tests explained below might well be applied to real evidence as well as to the personal evidence to which they so clearly apply.

Preappointed or Casual

Material which is created and kept for future use in proving something is called preappointed evidence. Most of us have or will have first-hand acquaintance with contracts, deeds, notes, and wills, all of which are preappointed and stand ready to be used as evidence if the need arises. If a student asks the manager of a local television station what he thinks of a particular regulation by the Federal Communications Commission, and if that student plans to quote the source in a speech against that regulation, he is dealing with preappointed evidence.

A comment which is spoken or written without intending it for use as evidence in the future is called casual evidence when it is subsequently employed in proof. Thus if a student were to describe to his roommate the appearance of a man he had seen emerging from a darkened store, that testimony would become casual evidence if it were later used in a burglary trial. One is tempted to place greater trust in this kind because there is less suspicion of bias or self-serving intent. However, this kind of remark may have been made in an off-hand, careless manner. For these reasons evaluation should involve more than a snap judgment; it calls for the careful application of the appropriate tests of evidence.

Willing or Reluctant

A distinction similar to the one immediately above is occasionally made between the willing or eager and the reluctant or unwilling witness. This is akin to the test of moral qualification for the reason that the motivation of the witness has a considerable bearing upon the reliability of his evidence. Someone who dislikes college students in general is likely to testify willingly against one who is charged with a traffic violation. However, a friend of the accused is likely to be reluctant in that situation. A reluctant witness may not be hiding anything; he may simply be timid. At the other extreme, a willing witness may be pleasantly cooperative, but he may be acting out of self-interest, such as the desire for vengeance. As a classification this has little usefulness, and as a test it is less significant than several others.

Positive or Negative

Negative evidence is the name given to the so-called testimony of silence, which means a significant absence of evidence to the contrary. It implies that a statement is true because it cannot be proved false. Failure to find cheaters on a relief roll would be negative evidence of graft. Similarly one might conclude that a library does not own a specific book if there is no entry for it in the card catalog. Potential weaknesses of this kind of evidence, if we may call it such, are apparent.

Most of what we have treated as evidence is positive, i.e., it directly supports a contention. Since all evidence, strictly speaking, is positive, we rarely use the name. When, in a rare circumstance, the absence of contrary evidence is used as proof, we use the adjective "negative." In all other cases neither of these two modifiers is used; we simply use the word "evidence" alone or modify it with "hearsay," "circumstantial," or some other class name.

TESTS

If we assume the importance of evidence in most argumentation, our next concern should be with the dependability of that evidence. Whether we speak, write, listen, or read, we have a stake in the quality of the evidence used. If we wish to behave as rationally as we can, we will demand that the evidence approximate the probable truth, which implies the achievement of as much verifiability as possible. To this end the following tests of evidence are named and explained. The two major classes of tests are those of substance and of sources, while the three lesser classes are those of reporting, of documentation, and (except in popular persuasion, where it is a major test) of audience acceptability. Obviously there is overlapping, especially between audience acceptability and many of the other tests of evidence.

Of Substance

Honesty has not heretofore been given as a test of the substance of evidence, although several of the traditional tests imply it. The honesty criterion is specifically stated and placed in first position for two reasons: wise decisions cannot be based upon falsehood, and lying is sufficiently widespread to warrant specific attention. Two cases will illustrate this principle. One is from the United States, the other from Communist Poland. The Federal Trade Commission has charged that a televised commercial purporting to prove the clearness of one brand of automobile glass was actually filmed through an open window. In a desperate attempt to cope with a meat shortage late in 1959, the Communist government of Poland launched a massive propaganda campaign to persuade its people to eat horsemeat. "Many doctors recommend eating horseflesh, since it has great curative powers. It helps relieve pains of older people. The meat, though sweet, tastes not unlike beef," according to Radio Warsaw.

Recency of evidence is not always important, but at times it is crucial. When one is dealing with current, changing events, he must be alert to the risks of outdated evidence. Last year's fact may be this year's fiction. Old statistics and quoted opinions from persons who have since changed their minds have embarrassed many an advocate. The unkindest cut of all occurs when, in reply to your evidence, your opponent quotes substantially different information given by your own source at a later date.

Relevance may be either legal or logical. Legal relevance is a test which excludes some logically relevant evidence which might mislead a jury or unduly complicate the case. But in general argumentation our greater concern is for logical relevance, which means that evidence is supposed to support the point in connection with which it is used. This test is intended to discourage the raising of side issues like those which muddied the Army-McCarthy hearings in 1954.[3] Practically no tests were applied there; the committee admitted nearly all of the evidence and entertained all issues which anyone chose to raise. The result was a mixture of show, inquiry, trial, and policy debate.

Internal consistency as a test of the substance of the evidence means that one asks, "Is the evidence consistent within itself?" Evidence that is self-contradictory would seem to be the weakest kind imaginable, but it sometimes goes undetected, probably because of a complicated message and uncritical listening or reading. The following are three shortened versions of internally inconsistent evidential statements which were not detected by college students: [4] (1) Non-Jewish teachers have never properly taught Jewish children the fundamentals of their religion, but proper instruction of this sort has been found in a few cases; (2) All students received religious instruction, but some, including those who were opposed to it, did not; (3) The program was discontinued in 1956, but it is still being conducted. No doubt these flaws would have been noticed by most of the experimental subjects if the above statements had been taken from context and listed under the caption, "Is there anything wrong with these statements?" But propagandists do not give us this much help.

External consistency of evidence is determined by comparing the item in question with similar material from another source. Is the evidence in question consistent with known fact? Is it consistent with human experience? In other words, is it verifiable in terms of outside criteria? Consider the case of the female worker in a workshop for

[3] F. W. Haberman, *et al.*, "Views on the Army-McCarthy Hearings," *Quarterly Journal of Speech*, XLI, No. 1 (1955), 1–18.

[4] W. R. Dresser, "Studies of the Effects of 'Satisfactory' and 'Unsatisfactory' Evidence in a Speech of Advocacy" (Ph.D. dissertation, Northwestern University, 1962).

the blind who testified that a male fellow worker had window-peeped at her. In a more serious vein were the McCarthy charges of communism in the State Department, which Professor Hart found to be at variance with the facts in fifty specific instances.[5]

Sufficiency of evidence is such a variable test that only a few, broad comments can be made about it. Some claims are acceptable without evidence, some require only a little, and still others require an abundance of evidence. Then too, the quality of evidence is more important than mere quantity. Let it suffice to generalize that multiple sources tend to be better than single ones, that the selection ought to be representative, and that "card stacking" should be avoided. To take a specific example, should we conclude that a "drunkometer" test administered by highway police is sufficient evidence to convict a motorist of drunken driving? The criterion is a certain concentration of alcohol in the breath or the blood, despite the fact that persons vary enormously in their tolerance levels. Our second case is one of too much evidence. It concerns a young Englishman who vowed that he loved his girl so much he could not live without her. Apparently she did not believe him, because he took his life after writing a note which said in part, "She will believe me now, but it's a hard way of proving my love, don't you think?"

Comparative quality as a test of evidence includes what lawyers know as the "best evidence rule." Without going into technicalities, let us interpret this rule to mean that one is under obligation to bring the best evidence he can—not merely whatever happens to be easily accessible. For instance, secondary evidence is acceptable if primary evidence is not available, admissions against self-interest are usually valued, casual evidence is generally preferable to preappointed, negative evidence is free from contrivance, real evidence is stronger than a hearsay description, and factual statements often carry more weight than opinions.

In the following narrative, the salesman jumped to a conclusion on the basis of a little circumstantial evidence which proved to be completely misleading. At noon on a rainy day an absent-minded judge who was leaving a restaurant paused to take an umbrella from the rack. He was observed by the owner of the umbrella, a salesman, who retrieved the article and accepted the judge's apology. Before leaving for home in the afternoon, the judge decided to take some of his

[5] H. Hart, "McCarthyism versus Democracy," *New Republic*, CXXVI (1952), 12.

family's umbrellas which had been accumulating in his office. At the train station the salesman chanced to see him again and remarked, "You had a good day, didn't you?"

Special tests of statistics apply to the procedures employed in obtaining and presenting them, not to the reasoning based upon them. A few suggestive questions will be raised here, but for fuller exposition the reader is referred to books and articles on statistics. Is the level of statistical significance given? If not, the result may be no better than a chance occurrence. Then too, a statistically significant figure may be inconsequential in practical affairs. Is the correlation partial, simple, or multiple? The weakest is the partial, as in connecting housing conditions and crime. What does "average" mean, or what does "mean" mean, for that matter? Actually, median or mode would be more meaningful in some cases. Averages, if unspecified, are questionable at best. Have the influential variables been considered? This is where predictions of voting behavior have come to grief. Is it safe to predict the future in terms of a trend line established up to now? Pertinent factors may not stay in their present relationships. Can the phenomenon in question be quantified, i.e., expressed in numbers? It is not meaningful to assert that beauty queens are fifty per cent prettier than they were in mother's day. Are the data relatively free from sampling error? This problem has plagued opinion pollsters, television audience measurers, and market researchers who want to get a representative sample of the universe that interests them. Has the base of the percentage computation remained constant during the figuring? Suppose a registrar announces that the enrollment in 1962 was 5,000, that it rose four per cent in 1963, and then it declined four per cent in 1964. It is important to ask whether the 1964 figure was based upon 5,000 or 5,200. Are compared figures based upon the same definitions and unit values? When an "old-timer" tells how he once bought a new car for five hundred dollars, he may neglect to add that it was a much simpler machine and that five dollars was a good day's pay.

Of Sources

Ordinary witnesses need to be tested as a group as well as individually, because the value of their testimony is primarily corroborative rather than designative or demonstrative. Thus we need to ask whether we have enough of them and whether they contradict each other. Testing may be worth the effort, because ordinary witnesses are often useful and occasionally necessary in general argumentation. An apt example of contradiction appeared in two letters to an editor on the same day: one lauded the admirable job of snow removal by the city crew, saying that even the side streets were something to be proud of after the heavy snowfall; the second writer charged that the city did not make a reasonable effort to clear the streets, adding that it "doesn't even remove the snow on the business streets which have parking meters." [6]

Integrity stands in a pre-eminent position among the tests of an individual, ordinary witness. Is he impartial in this matter, or does he have a stake in the outcome? Does he have a reputation for veracity, or has he been impeached by his own previous, inconsistent testimony? Doubtful character, which sometimes is taken to include the lack of religious belief, is a basis for the impeachment of a witness. Sometimes the testing is done rigorously, especially when a witness behaves in a suspicious manner, that is to say, with hesitation or with assertiveness.

Opportunity to observe what he is commenting upon is a second, individual test. Credibility is bound to be undermined by the disclosure that the witness was not present when the event in question took place, or that he was there too little time, or that there was some obstacle to clear perception. If someone starts telling us what goes on in a meeting of the University Discipline Committee, let us ask him when he was there.

Mental qualifications, broadly defined, comprise a third test. Intelligence, education, memory, perceptiveness, verbal ability, and psychological condition are the familiar components. Under psychological condition we should place "expectancy set," which refers to the readiness of the nervous system to respond to a given stimulus in a specific manner. Some persons expect to see certain things before they look; others expect to hear ghostly sounds in an empty house.[7] The other mental qualifications are perhaps more familiar, as the following case will illustrate. During a controversy over the teaching of American history in a community high school, the local editor observed that ". . . those who talk loudest and most violently will be those who have never read any of the history texts in question and who haven't any standards for judging them if they did."

Finally, physical qualifications, including vision, hearing, smell,

[6] "Review Forum," *Evanston Review*, January 29, 1959.

[7] A. Hastings and S. Krippner, "Expectancy Set and 'Poltergeist' Phenomena," *ETC: A Review of General Semantics*, XVIII, No. 3 (1961), 349–360.

taste, touch, and equilibrium, are subjected to testing when the senses of a witness are involved. This class of tests is typically less important in general argumentation than it is in judicial argumentation.

Expert witnesses have been facetiously characterized as persons who can make something we already know sound confusing. Our penchant for paying more attention to persons from distant places has prompted the cynical observation that an expert is an average person far from home. Despite these quips, expertness is recognizable and testable. The first question might well be, "Is opinion evidence the best kind to use here?" If the point concerns the volume of foreign steel coming into the United States annually, facts are preferable to opinions; but if quantitative data are too difficult to obtain, expert opinions are better than unsupported assertions.

Does the source qualify as an expert in the field about which he speaks or writes? This is the essential, general test which includes many subsidiary questions, two of which are: (1) Has the field developed to the point that an expert therein can provide reliable knowledge on the point in issue? (2) Does this person have the credentials (trustworthiness, experience, etc.) of an authority in that field? [8] In court an opposing attorney will occasionally make disparaging insinuations to discredit an expert witness in the minds of the laymen in the jury. Remarks about race, religion, name, and reputations of relatives are made. Although factually irrelevant, such jibes are often persuasive and, in the view of this writer, unethical. They are in many textbooks classified as fallacies of "poisoning the well." Thus they have no legitimate place in general argumentation or in school debate. One last thought to consider is that, even if the particular field of knowledge is reputable, and even if one has several acknowledged experts from it, future developments may prove them wrong. However, there is some comfort in knowing that numerous factual statements have been proven as wrong as the statements of opinion.

Of Reporting

Tests of reporting are not necessarily the same as tests of sources, because the media of transmission and the character of the reporting may

[8] It is hard to disentangle the effects of trustworthiness and expertness as factors of credibility, according to C. I. Hovland *et al.*, *Communication and Persuasion* (New Haven: Yale University Press, 1953), p. 35.

be beyond the control or the responsibility of the human source of the evidence. Five questions, some of which partially overlap, are recommended as tests: Is the reporting clear? Is it accurate as far as it goes? Is an ample context provided? If there is interpretation, is it fair? Is the medium itself reputable?

In asking that the reporting be clear, one means that several persons who are presumably qualified to understand the content should derive essentially the same message from what was reported. The second question, namely, the one on accuracy as far as the report goes, raises a related question concerning the possibility of reporting without selectivity. Even if some selection is inevitable, a critical listener or reader may properly ask whether unfavorable information was omitted, whether important words or figures were left out, whether there was needless delay in giving some vital information, or whether the reporter was lying. Adequacy of context includes the giving of attendant circumstances, dates, sources, and enough of the quotation in question to indicate its tone and intent. Quoting out of context is a familiar violation of this test. Fairness of interpretation becomes increasingly important as the nature of the report shifts from straight reporting to commenting. Some publications mix reports and commentary in a misleading fashion. This is still worse when irrelevant emotionalism is added to one side of the story for "slanting" effect. Finally, with respect to the reputation of the medium itself, it is thought that we are more likely to believe an otherwise doubtful story if we get the report through a reputable medium like the *Christian Science Monitor* as opposed to a sensational tabloid. The credibility of an advertisement, too, seems to be related to the reputation of the magazine in which it appears.[9] One of the exercises will give the reader a functional review of these tests.

Of Documentation

Listeners and readers have the right to know the date and the source of any evidence offered in support of a claim on their belief. Ideally, the documentation should be such as to enable an interested person to authenticate the evidence if he so desired. In the absence of any real risk of exposure, some advocates will cite nonexistent documents or will

[9] D. B. Lucas and S. H. Britt, *Advertising Psychology and Research* (N.Y.: McGraw-Hill, 1950), p. 660.

misrepresent the contents of existing materials. For instance, two atheists who were seeking an injunction against the issuance of postage
stamps carrying the motto, "In God We Trust," quoted George Washington as having said, "The Government of the United States of America is not, in any sense, founded on the Christian religion." A "quote
detective" traced the quotation to an old English translation of a treaty
between the United States and Tripoli in 1797 and signed by President
John Adams. The quotation was not part of the official text but apparently was written into the translation by Joel Barlow, the United
States Consul General in Algiers at the time.[10]

More notorious was the McCarthy charge that a Justice Department report dated July 28, 1952 showed there were Communists in
the State Department. True, the report was dated in 1952, but it
reported testimony on an *unsuccessful* plot during the Coolidge administration in 1928. The content of the so-called evidence was misrepre-
sented, and the dating of the source was off the mark by twenty-four
years.

Under "How To Use It" we shall see whether, in terms of experimental findings and surveys of actual practice, it is necessary to document evidence as thoroughly as the foregoing paragraphs advise.

Of Audience Acceptability

Under this topic we need not repeat any of the above tests which affect
the acceptability of the evidence to the audience. Now we are concerned with the credibility of evidence as it is related to the attitudes
and beliefs of readers or listeners toward points which the evidence is
used to support. For instance, before a young Republican Club audience, one student gave an anti-New Deal speech without any evidence,
while another gave a pro-New Deal speech with every point evidenced.
At the end a vote by ballot was taken on this question: "Which speaker
made the better use of evidence?" A majority voted for the speech
with no evidence. A month later the same procedure was followed in
a young Democrat Club meeting, and again evidence was "observed"
where none existed.

The distressing implication is that we often see and hear what
we want to rather than what is actually said. Perhaps this is why

[10] "Precis," *Presbyterian Life*, September 17, 1955, p. 29.

myths and symbols frequently outlast facts. It also reveals the folly of taking audience acceptability as the supreme test of evidence. It is supreme only in terms of the "results" criterion of popular persuasion; most of the other tests of evidence are superior in terms of critical standards which stress ethical and logical values. This point harks back to the distinctions between argumentation and persuasion and between proof and belief in Chapter I.

HOW TO USE IT

In view of what has been said of proof in general and of evidence in particular, what should teachers and students of general argumentation conclude is the proper use of evidence? Whatever they conclude must be applicable to speaking, listening, writing, and reading. It should also take into account the differences between the necessities of popular persuasion and the demands of rationality in terms of ethical and logical responsibilities. Whatever evidence is used fits under either "data" or "backing" in the Toulmin layout in Chapter VII. Finally, a decision on the proper use of evidence might be influenced by the results of descriptive studies, the data from experimental research, and the prescriptive advice from teachers.

According To Empirical Studies

Using the method of content analysis, several investigators have dis covered what the actual practices of some advocates have been. These scholars described their categories such as "complete documentation," "no documentation," etc., and then they tabulated the occurrences of such phenomena in selected specimens of argumentative discourse. A graduate student in the author's seminar applied this method to the texts of two annual, final debates from the West Point tournament. In one of the debates the affirmative gave complete documentation (source, date, qualification) for fifty per cent of its evidence, partial documentation for forty-four per cent, and no documentation for only six per cent. The negative in the same debate provided complete documentation for sixteen per cent, partial documentation for twenty-nine per cent, and no documentation for fifty-five per cent. In the second debate the scores were almost even: the two teams scored twenty-two and twenty-five per cent on complete documentation, and twenty-three and thirty per cent on no documentation. It is safe to say that the score of fifty per cent on complete documentation is relatively high for school debates. This prompts one to ask how he can judge whether the evidence is the best available if he can verify less than half of it.

Could a similar question be raised against real-life debates? A comparative analysis of four school debates and four real-life debates revealed that the latter used more cited evidence per one hundred words of discourse, but that the school debates had better documentation.[11] These data are, of course, insufficient for a generalization. A more extensive survey of intercollegiate debates found that evidence of some sort was submitted for fifty-three per cent of the contentions and that it generally met the tests of evidence.[12] In contrast to this, a study of the evidence used in four major speeches by Dean Acheson and Robert Taft turned up only five items.[13] A comparably low rating for real-life advocates was found in a comparative study of evidence used by "high-ranking" and "low-ranking" United States senators. Neither group used very much.[14] On the basis of limited empirical data, we may tentatively conclude that current practice does not measure up to the standards expressed by teachers and textbooks.

According To Experimental Research

Instead of surveying what happens in actual advocacy, the experimenter contrives situations which will enable him to measure objectively the difference which a given variable such as evidence makes in the persuasive impact of a message. One experiment compared the persuasiveness of Speech 1 and Speech 2, both of which contained six quotations of expert opinion evidence; however, Speech 1 included names and

[11] John Jellicorse, "Measures of Factual Evidence and Its Documentation in Selected 'Real' and 'School' Debates" (Seminar paper, Northwestern University, 1962), pp. 22–25.

[12] P. R. McKee, "An Analysis of the Use of Evidence in Ten Intercollegiate Debates" (Master's thesis, University of Kansas, 1959).

[13] C. S. Goetzinger, Jr., "An Analysis of the 'Validity' of Reasoning and Evidence in Four Major Foreign Policy Speeches, 1950–51" (Master's thesis, Purdue University, 1952).

[14] P. D. Brandes, "Evidence and Its Use by Selected United States Senators" (Doctoral dissertation, University of Wisconsin, 1953).

credentials, while Speech 2 omitted the sources and qualifying phrases. No significant difference in effectiveness was found.[15] Four methods of handling evidence were compared in an experimental dissertation: no evidence, adequate evidence but no documentation, adequate evidence and documentation, and adequate evidence and documentation plus laudatory comments to add weight to the authority. The second and the fourth methods proved to be the most persuasive, showing that it paid to use evidence but that documentation did not help unless it included a "build-up" for the source.[16] In a somewhat similar study three ways of handling evidence were compared: no outside authority used, seven quotations used and authors' names given, and documented quotations plus a "build-up" for each source. There was no advantage for any of the three in respect to persuasiveness, but the third imparted information more successfully.[17] At least the familiar advice on the presentation of statistical evidence has been supported by an experiment. Three versions of a speech of advocacy were used: in one, statistics were compared with quantities which were familiar to the audience; in the second, only statistics appeared; in the third, generalized statements replaced the statistical evidence. The first form worked best.[18]

Possibly the most disturbing findings, at least to anyone who values critical thinking, are that unsound evidence proved to be as persuasive as the sound evidence, and that the college students who heard the speeches did not detect the flaws (internal inconsistencies) in the unsound evidence.[19] The four versions which were equally persuasive were distinguished as follows: one used evidence rated satisfactory by experts; the second used questionable sources; the third used irrelevant materials in lieu of evidence; the fourth used internally inconsistent evidence.

[15] H. Gilkinson, S. F. Paulson, and D. E. Sikkink, "Effects of Order and Authority in an Argumentative Speech," *Quarterly Journal of Speech*, XL (1954), 183–192.

[16] R. S. Cathcart, "An Experimental Study of the Relative Effectiveness of Four Methods of Presenting Evidence," *Speech Monographs*, XXII (1955), 227–233.

[17] D. C. Anderson, "The Effect of Various Uses of Authoritative Testimony in Persuasive Speaking" (Master's thesis, Ohio State University, 1958).

[18] D. L. Costley, "An Experimental Study of the Effectiveness of Quantitative Evidence in Speeches of Advocacy" (Master's thesis, University of Oklahoma, 1958).

[19] W. R. Dresser, "Studies of the Effects of Evidence: Implications for Forensics," *Register* of American Forensic Association, X, No. 3 (1962), 14–19.

According To Prescriptive Advice

After consulting these findings, what shall we say about the use of evidence in advoctory discourse? One might counsel "realism," saying that a clever persuader can make a little material go a long way, or one might stand fast for the ideals of ethical and logical responsibility in all situations, or he might approve some compromises between these extremes in certain situations. On pragmatic grounds, evidence is more important in school debate and in law than it is in popular persuasion. The obvious reason is that those who do the judging are more demanding in the forensic situations. In the analytical and critical applications of argumentation, evidence is important indeed. In preparation for their frequent experiences as listeners and readers, students need to form the habit of demanding the best of the available evidence. When they do, the future research will turn out differently, and so will human affairs in general—we hope.

There are, in addition to these broad principles, several specific recommendations relating to the use of evidence. They will be stated briefly in question-and-answer form.

1. Is the quoted source reporting a factual statement or expressing his personal opinion? The advocate should tell us which.

2. If it is opinion evidence, does the source give any factual basis for it? This could be done more often than it has been.

3. If it is opinion evidence, have the qualifications of the source been stated? Some indications of study, training, or other experience will improve both the logical adequacy and the audience acceptability of that evidence.

4. How much documentation is provided? For substantive adequacy as in making a critical judgment, the documentation should enable a listener or a reader to authenticate the reference if he desires. For purposes of persuasion, even if the criterion is what the advocate can "get away with," the attitudes in the audience will make a difference. In the face of hostility, an advocate will need to do all he can to bolster his credibility.

5. Is it ever proper to use secondary evidence, circumstantial evidence, or evidence from a prejudiced source? Here an approximation of the "best evidence rule" applies. If any one of these three kinds of evidence happens to be the best that can reasonably be expected in

the situation, it should not be disqualified summarily. Other tests should be applied.

6. Is it better to vary the kinds of evidence which one uses in arguments? Variety for its own sake is a stylistic matter, but it may appeal to audience interest. In terms of ethical and logical responsibilities, though, the kinds of evidence should be considered only for the purpose of choosing the *best* evidence.

7. Can the audience understand the evidence? In one sense, proof can be made from evidence which most persons do not understand. However, when comprehension is desired, an advocate can facilitate it by explaining, repeating, or using a visual aid.

8. Can the audience evaluate the evidence? A communicator can aid his listeners or readers by presenting his evidence specifically (verbatim) instead of paraphrasing, and by adding the qualifications of his sources.

9. How can evidence from someone else be made to fit smoothly into the advocate's speech or essay? No doubt this is one of the troublesome stylistic problems, but it is basically a thought problem. We do not think enough about the relationship between a piece of evidence and the inference it supports. Too often we state a point and then, without making any linkage, say, "And now permit me to quote . . . ." It is much better to weave evidence and one's own inference together into a consistent style so that each part complements the other without any jerkiness or abruptness. Some of the language of the quotation might be picked up in the interpretative statement before or after the citation. Evidence is important, but it is less so in educational exercises than is the expression of the advocate's own thinking about that evidence.

10. Finally, how much evidence is enough? A blanket answer cannot be given except in the most abstract terms. In academic exercises such as case outlining, the preparation of single speeches or essays of advocacy, or school debating, it is customary to advise that each unit of proof must rest either upon evidence or upon a premise that is admitted or assumed. The following is the most likely arrangement:

> I. Point in partition
> A. Principal sub-point
> 1. Evidence or premise.

QUESTIONS

1. Explain the differences between the definitions of evidence in law and its definition in general argumentation.
2. Compare the theoretical importance of evidence with the findings of empirical and experimental research with regard to the importance of evidence. In what circumstances might one be wise to give precedence to one or the other?
3. When might some of the legal classifications of evidence be useful in general argumentation?
4. Why test the source of evidence? Is not the substance of the evidence all that really should concern us?
5. When, if ever, should an advocate use second-best or third-best evidence in order to secure audience acceptance of his proof?
6. What research is still needed in the field of the persuasiveness of evidence?
7. At the 1929 peak, the Dow-Jones average was approximately 380, and for comparative purposes the dollar was worth 100 cents in buying power. Early in March of 1959, the D-J average reached 610 in terms of sixty-two-cent dollars. Which peak was really the higher?

EXERCISES

1. Using a selected or an assigned essay, speech, or debate from the Appendixes, list and count the points that are evidenced and those that are not. Which of the latter needed evidence, in your judgment? Which kinds of evidence were used? Evaluate the instances of evidence in terms of the appropriate tests of substance, of sources, and of documentation.
2. Using the proposition which served for the oral or written exercise on analysis (Chapter IV) or investigation (Chapter V), prepare a five-minute argumentative speech in which evidence appears as needed and is the best you can obtain in the available time. Quote the evidence and its documentation, and give qualifications of any experts you use. Follow

the speeches with critiques, preferably oral if time permits, using some topics from sections IV (Tests) and V-C (Prescriptive Advice). Specific topics might be assigned to individuals. This part is a lesson in critical listening.

3. Write an argumentative essay in the form of an editorial or a letter to the editor. Try to balance the sometimes conflicting demands of space, popular persuasion, and logical adequacy.

4. Apply the tests of reporting to these two accounts of the same event, President Eisenhower's press conference in which he spoke on military policy: [20]

As Lawrence Sees It

BY DAVID LAWRENCE

Mr. Eisenhower has been accused of being more interested in budget balancing than in national safety—a foolish, partisan and silly charge. He answered bluntly at his news conference Wednesday that, even if the federal government were operating at a surplus, he wouldn't spend more than is currently being recommended in the budget for the armed forces. Instead, he would use that surplus for such things as improving education.

But it was in dealing with the possibility of a ground war, instead of a nuclear war, that President Eisenhower gave at his news conference an impressive example of statesmanship. This is what really makes America so strong in the eyes of clear-thinking people everywhere.

The President has been urged to increase the ground forces because of the possibility that the crisis in Berlin might lead to a ground war. But he declined to make this an excuse for augmenting the budget for ground troops.

In fact, he issued what must certainly be viewed in Moscow as a stern warning when he remarked that he did not intend to see the Allies fight a ground war in Europe. He left the implication that the use of nuclear weapons would be seriously considered.

This is laying it on the line to Moscow, where there should not be the slightest doubt now that America is in earnest about resisting any attempt to force Western troops out of Berlin.

Mr. Eisenhower says that the West doesn't intend to start any war and that only if the Soviets start pushing Western troops out of their positions, or start denying them access to West Berlin, will there be any force used in defense.

But even as he utters these unmistakable words of warning, the President urges people not to get hysterical. He doesn't want to see any general mobilization measures taken.

They are unnecessary for many reasons, not the least of which is the needless excitement they induce.

[20] *The Chicago Daily News,* March 13, 1959, p. 18.

Nikita Khrushchev may hem and haw and even hedge on his threats of war, but the fact remains that, as long as the President of the United States—leader of the free world and commander of the most powerful armed forces the West has ever assembled—stands firm, the Soviets will not take a chance on war.

Mr. Eisenhower says significantly that the American people must learn to live in a long period of tension. To unbalance the budget unnecessarily can weaken the national economy and give the enemy a victory without firing a shot. The American people should be grateful that there's a steady hand at the helm of our Ship of State today.

The Fleeson Viewpoint

BY DORIS FLEESON

President Eisenhower's comments on military policy at his press conference were a model of confusion. If they were calculated to obfuscate the issue for the Russians, the performance was a notable success. It left reporters dazed.

The President ruled out a ground war in Europe in defense of Berlin. What good would it do to send a few more thousands of troops or even several divisions to Europe? he asked. As against the 175 or so divisions the Soviets and East Germans might muster, why would anybody dream of fighting a ground war, he wanted to know.

Yet when he was asked later whether the United States was prepared to use nuclear warfare, if necessary, to defend free Berlin, the President replied that he didn't know how you could free anything with nuclear weapons.

When toward the end of the press conference a reporter asked him to reconcile these views, he declared that nuclear war was not a complete impossibility but that nuclear warfare seemed to him a self-defeating thing.

What we need to do, he declared, is to stand right and ready, do what is necessary to protect ourselves, and never go back on responsibilities.

If any threat or any thrust in the direction of genuine hostilities comes over Berlin, it will have to come from the side of the Soviets, the President said.

He indicated that he did not believe it would happen, but if it did, then it would be time to decide what the Allies would expect to do.

This statement few of his hearers could credit. Congress, in its doubtful mood about the wisdom of reducing the armed forces at this time, fretful at the decision not to close the missile gap between the United States and the Soviet Union, will not credit it.

Press conferences, and particularly those of Mr. Eisenhower, are likely to give imprecise impressions.

It will certainly be true that when the Allies reach any truly crucial points in the forthcoming conferences with the Soviet Union over the future of Berlin, they will know what they are capable of doing and must do in any of the possible eventualities.

The President, of course, was right in emphasizing the fact that our military policy should be based on the long pull rather than on the excitements of various crises.

He has seen numbers of them fade away.

But even if the crisis fades, as it gives at the moment no sign of doing, the problem will remain. And both Congress and the country will expect us to be ready with guns cocked and loaded if the real thing comes.

5. Describe and criticize the use of evidence in one of the Lincoln-Douglas debates in P. M. Angle, *Created Equal? The Complete Lincoln-Douglas Debates of 1858* (Chicago: University of Chicago Press, 1958).

6. After surveying the accounts of President Kennedy's assassination in newspapers and magazines beginning with November 22, 1963, compile the circumstantial evidence of Lee Harvey Oswald's guilt. What grounds might there be for any other hypothesis? Or do you believe the evidence of guilt, although it was not offered in court, was conclusive?

CHAPTER VII

REASONING PROCESSES

By Arthur Hastings, Stanford University

PROOF IS AN INHERENT PART OF EVERY STEP IN ADVOCACY. THE SUBPOINTS or contentions prove the points in partition which in turn prove the proposition. This chapter describes the basic reasoning processes by which contentions are proved from premises such as facts or other statements. The basic unit of reasoning is an argument, which is a statement asserted to follow from other statements, a conclusion supported by premises. There are several different ways that premises lead to conclusions, and these processes are the subject of this chapter.

RHETORICAL REASONING

We are dealing exclusively with rhetorical reasoning,[1] arguments that appear in oral or written discourse, not the logical processes used by the formal logician or the scientist, although there are obvious relationships among rhetoric, logic, and scientific method. The processes described here are those which people use for proof in advocacy and they have certain important characteristics. The first characteristic is that rhetor-

[1] Also known as enthymematic reasoning.

ical proof is less demanding than scientific proof or the proof of formal logic. In scientific experiments or formal logic each variable or each step must be carefully analyzed, and the conclusion is tested by established criteria. In rhetorical reasoning the advocate may report less of the probative process, ignoring some factors and presenting only minimal evidence. Secondly, most rhetorical reasoning leads to probable rather than certain conclusions as in logic. Causal relations are probable, definitions may be challenged, events may be interpreted variously, and standards may be questioned. Thus the conclusions can be considered only probable, rather than certain. A third aspect of rhetorical reasoning is that, if persuasion is intended, the premises or assumptions in the proof must be drawn from the beliefs of the audience. Obviously to prove anything to the satisfaction of an audience, the advocate must begin from premises which will be accepted as true. These may be definitions, facts, general principles or standards, and on these the advocate builds the proof for his conclusions. However, as we noted in Chapter I, argumentation is not always used for persuasion. When it is used as a critical apparatus, the requirement of audience acceptability should be replaced by one of rationality.

THE STRUCTURE OF AN ARGUMENT

To analyze an argument it should be broken down into elements more specific than the gross parts of premises and conclusion. The most practical structural analysis is one devised by the British philosopher Stephen Toulmin, which identifies six elements in an argument: [2]

1. Conclusion (C).
2. Data (D). The evidence or premises.
3. Warrant (W). This is a statement which asserts that the conclusion follows from the data. It is the reasoning process which leads to the conclusion. In some arguments it may not be stated explicitly, but only implied.
4. Backing (B). Evidence or reasoning which explains why the warrant is true.

[2] This structural layout for arguments is described in Toulmin's book, *The Uses of Argument* (Cambridge; University Press, 1954), Chapter III. One application of this pattern to the analysis of rhetorical arguments appeared in "Toulmin on Argument: An Interpretation and Application," Wayne Brockriede and Douglas Ehninger, *Quarterly Journal of Speech*, XLIV, No. 1 (February, 1960).

5. Qualifier (Q). This states how probable or certain is the conclusion. In rhetoric, most conclusions are probable, not certain.

6. Rebuttal (R). This element is the reservations or possible refutations of the conclusion.

This is a diagram of the relations among these six elements:

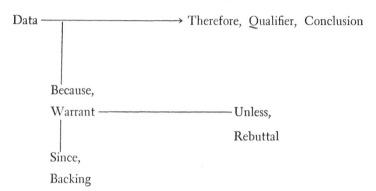

To illustrate these elements in the context of an argument, consider this proof that the inhabitants of Grubnia do not like their government.

It is reliably reported that large numbers of Grubnian citizens are crossing the border daily and asking for asylum. We know from past experience that this is a good indication of domestic trouble in the political life of the country, so we can conclude that the Grubnian citizens are displeased and fearful of their government, unless, of course, those leaving are members of some minority faction.

CONCLUSION: Grubnian citizens are displeased with and fearful of their government.

DATA: Large numbers of Grubnian citizens are crossing the border daily and asking political asylum.

WARRANT: When citizens leave the country and ask for asylum there is usually dissatisfaction with the government and fear of the government.

BACKING: This has been the case when such situations occurred in the past.

QUALIFIER: "Probably." The qualification of the strength of the conclusion is implied, and the argument is clearly one of probability because a reservation is stated.

REBUTTAL: Those leaving may be a minority faction, which is not representative of the entire populace.

In this argument it will be observed that all of the elements are not made explicit, and those which are stated are not stated fully at times. This will be found true of most arguments used in advocacy. It will be necessary for the critic to supply missing elements and to restate elements to obtain a picture of the entire argument. This is one advantage of this structural approach to arguments: it provides a pattern for locating or discovering the vital elements in reasoning.

The methods of proof in this chapter will be described in terms of this pattern, with the principal emphasis on the data, warrant, and conclusion. The five major methods of proof, which make up more than three-fourths of the arguments studied,[3] are described first. And when the demands of persuasion (as in the case of audience acceptance of evidence) differ from those of pure rationality, the *former* are explained.

MAJOR METHODS OF PROOF

Argument from Example to a Descriptive Generalization

In this process of reasoning the conclusion is a general pattern or characteristic which is inferred from one or more examples. The conclusion is a description of what is observed in the data and it is asserted to be true for all similar examples or situations, not just the ones presented as data.

There is general misadministration in the system of unemployment compensation (C). In California, according to state officials, one out of every five dollars paid last year in unemployment compensation has gone to workers with no legal right to the money (D). In New York false claims make up over forty per cent of the claims (D). What is true of the system in these two states should be true of the same program in many other states (W).[4]

Data. The above example demonstrates that the process is one of accurately describing a pattern or characteristic and then asserting it

[3] The nine modes of reasoning described in this chapter were derived from the study and analysis of more than 250 sample arguments taken from speeches, debates, discussions, and written discourse. Therefore these processes should be the ones of most use to the advocate, both in constructing his own proof and in analyzing the proof of others. For a more detailed description and analysis of each form of argument, see Arthur Hastings, "A Reformulation of the Modes of Reasoning in Argumentation" (Ph.D. Dissertation, Northwestern University, 1962).

[4] The examples used to illustrate each type of argument are based on actual arguments from oral or written discourse, although they have been rephrased for purposes of clarity and illustration.

applies to all similar situations. The evidence usually consists of examples, instances, or descriptions of events. The situations must be described in enough detail to allow the generalization to be drawn. In the above argument the data could be challenged on the grounds that they do not clearly indicate misadministration of funds.

Warrant. The warrant must assert that what is true of the examples in the data is true of all similar examples, i.e., the examples are typical of the field. Only if the audience will accept the evidence as typical, representative instances will they accept the conclusion as a valid one. In the sample argument on unemployment compensation it might be asserted that New York and California are atypical because of their size, and so the speaker should present examples of large states, small states, and states with varying incomes to show that the generalization can be made. This is one way of demonstrating typicality, that of giving examples which vary in several aspects, but not in their common characteristic which is to be generalized. Another method of proving typicality is by giving a large number of examples. For some conclusions the audience will accept one example carefully explained, while other conclusions will require many examples for their support. Here is an argument in which one example is used to support a generalization.

In the seven-months' period that followed the beginning of the Korean war, prices and inflation so rose in the United States that the government lost four billion dollars in defense expenditures alone, and the consuming public lost some twenty billion dollars in purchasing power (D). Clearly, the effects of inflation are harmful and detrimental to the economy (C).

Conclusion. The conclusion is a descriptive generalization, which means it is a statement describing a general pattern, an attempt to make an accurate statement about a type of situation. The generalization may be about a characteristic or pattern, e.g., Russian satellites follow the party line, the city manager form of government is generally efficient. Or the conclusion may be a causal relation or correlation of events, e.g., state income is correlated with quantity and quality of medical facilities in the state, foreign aid produces internal inflation. Care must be taken that the conclusion accurately describes the examples. A common fault of speakers and writers using this type of reasoning is to present examples which are not accurately described by the generalization. For example, cases of misadministration of United States' foreign economic aid do not lead to the conclusion that such foreign aid does not help the receiving nations.

Rebuttal. From the preceding description of the requirements of argument from example, these points of rebuttal can be summarized.

1. Does the generalization accurately describe the pattern found in the examples? The data must be detailed enough for the conclusion to be accurately formulated, and the generalization must not go beyond a description of the actual pattern.

2. Are the examples typical of their class? Are the relationships true most of the time or are they due to unusual or atypical factors? Are the examples typical and are they consistent with other information or experience?

Argument from Criteria to a Verbal Classification

Many arguments attempt to classify, categorize, or label a situation. An action may be classified as a robbery. A corporation is labeled a monopoly. A newspaper is asserted to be a good newspaper. Narcotic addiction may be classed as a harm to society. These conclusions are reached by the application of criteria to the characteristics of a situation. To prove a corporation is a monopoly, the advocate proves that the characteristics of the corporation satisfy the criteria for a monopoly, *viz.*, exclusive control over the supply of a product, or control sufficient to determine the market price. If the corporation has these characteristics then it is a monopoly, because this is what is meant by the term "monopoly." To classify a business as "efficient" or "inefficient" one must apply criteria of efficient business operation to the operations of the firm and observe how well it meets those standards. Thus in argument from criteria, characteristics of an event are presented to show that it fits the criteria for a category or an evaluative label.[5]

On individual health insurance policies, Company Z spends for overhead and profits about sixty per cent of what you pay them and only about forty cents of each premium dollar goes for benefits to policyholders (D). Obviously such insurance is a poor economic investment (C).

[5] This process of reasoning has not been recognized as an independent mode of argument in earlier argumentation texts. Nevertheless, it is one of the major methods of proving conclusions. It was used twenty per cent of the time in the 250 arguments analyzed by the author.

Data. The data are the characteristics or attributes of the event or situation. The exact nature and number of them is determined by the criteria, which are expressed in the warrant. As with all data, they should be accurate, verifiable facts.

Warrant. The warrant states the criteria for the use of the classification or label in the conclusion. These criteria can be stated explicitly in the argument or only implied. In either case the warrant is the vital premise in the process and should be carefully analyzed. Two general types of warrants occur in this mode of reasoning. The first is illustrated by the argument on health insurance policies in which the criteria are value standards, criteria of good and bad. The criteria for evaluating a play or novel or painting, the criteria for testing cars or appliances, and the criteria for labeling political platforms or economic programs are all criteria of value judgments. In the argument on health insurance, the criteria are standards which our society has set up for what is and what is not a good return on a financial investment. In asserting that a newspaper is good because it has accurate reporting, thorough coverage, and good makeup, an argument is using standards derived from our experience with the functions of newspapers.

The criteria for this warrant are located in the knowledge and experience of the audience, which determines how values are to be assigned. The advocate must prove the conclusion on the basis of criteria which the audience will accept. If the criteria are value standards, the principal question to be asked in evaluation is whether they are acceptable standards for judgment. These standards must be in terms of the particular field of the subject matter, whether economics, politics, city government, personal adjustment, etc., and the criteria may be grounded in authorities, generally accepted principles, or personal experience. It may be found that additional criteria are necessary for a fair evaluation, e.g., perhaps other aspects of health insurance are just as important as the monetary value returned.

Another type of criterion is that of "defining characteristics," in which the characteristics in the data comprise the definition of the classification: an aardvark has the characteristic of a backbone (D), therefore it is a vertebrate (C). The warrant states the definition of the category and the characteristics are presented to show the situation fits the definition.

The United States Congress is not representative of the people (C). If policy is to be made by a majority of the people, then the congressional majority is not representative (W). Consider these statistics. Two-fifths of the population elect three-fifths of the representatives to the House, and the majority of the senators are elected by only nineteen per cent of the population (D).

The conclusion of the sample argument depends upon the definition of the term "representative." As with value criteria, to evaluate the argument the defining characteristics should be first explicitly stated. They should be adequate and complete as an acceptable definition of the terms of the conclusion. The definition should be one that is understood and accepted by the audience, and it may be backed by reference to authorities, dictionaries, or technical references in the particular field. Once the criteria of the warrant are established the characteristics must be shown to satisfy them.

The warrants for persuasive arguments from criteria lie in the knowledge and experience of the audience, and the advocate must prove the conclusion on the basis of criteria which are agreeable to the beliefs of the audience. Explicit statement of the warrant may increase the strength of the proof, but this is not always necessary, since there may be an implicit understanding of the standards concerned. Nevertheless, it is important for the advocate to realize his argument must be built on criteria which the audience holds or which it can be persuaded to adopt.

Conclusion. The conclusion is always a classification or labeling of the situation described in the data and is always concerned with only the situation described. The conclusion does not extend its coverage to situations outside the data as does the conclusion in argument from example to a descriptive generalization. That is, the label is applied to the situation described, but not to others of the same nature. The conclusion in the health insurance argument applies only to the policies described and not to other health insurance policies. It should also be noted that the conclusion need not be one word, but can be a phrase or a clause, e.g., the state of X has violated citizen K's civil rights, where the conclusion is that an action is to be classified as a "violation of civil rights."

Rebuttal. These tests apply both to value standards and defining characteristics.

1. Are the criteria satisfactory? The definition or standards must be adequate, comprehensive, and acceptable to the audience. There should be no significant exceptions or qualifications.

2. Do the characteristics satisfy the criteria? The data should be true, the characteristics should correspond to the criteria, and sufficient data should be presented to satisfy the warrant.

Argument from Cause to Effect

Often it is necessary to analyze the effects of events, plans, policies, or actions. In predicting consequences the advocate must use reasoning from cause to effect. He may predict that a diplomatic treaty will be broken, that a new missile will require a shift in defense strategy, or that a new sewer tax will provide a certain amount of revenue. In all of these arguments, the first event is a cause and on the basis of known causal relations, its effects are predicted. Two forms of this process occur. The first is a prediction on the basis of existing conditions. The second form is hypothetical: *if* we adopt your membership policy, *then* we will lose members. In this second form the causal conditions are not in existence but they are assumed and their implications predicted.

Recognition of Communist China (D) would harm our relations in Asia (C) simply because we would be retreating once more from the Communists (W). We have said we are going to defend Formosa against Communist Chinese attack, but if we abandon the island of Formosa, the effect on the Asians would be that we were afraid (W).

Data. The evidence is always events—situations that are in existence or that could be in existence. If the events exist they can be described with enough actual detail to demonstrate their causal properties, i.e., that they fit the pattern of the causal generalization. Such situations might be current inflation, consumer purchases, military defenses, or any type of policy or condition. On the other hand, if the premises are hypothetical their description must be based on assumptions, blueprints, suggested policies, legislative descriptions, or other descriptions of nonexistent events.

Warrant. The prediction of effects is always on the basis of causal generalizations. These assert that certain events are usually followed by certain other events, e.g., when nations do not maintain consistent policies other nations do not respect them; wars can be stopped in the beginning more easily than later; in Western culture economic competition results in productive efficiency; representatives who vote against their constituents' interests are often defeated; rejection in childhood results in neurotic adulthood; tariffs between nations reduce the volume of trade. These statements are descriptive generalizations which assert causal relations: X events are followed by Y events.[6] In reasoning from cause to effect, the generalization is applied to a specific case which fits the pattern. The data correspond to the first type of event and the generalization asserts that the second event will follow, e.g., in recognizing Communist China the United States would be inconsistent in its policy, and therefore the United States would lose other nations' respect.

In the phrasing of the argument the warrant may not be stated, but the relations stated by the warrant must be believed by the audience if the argument is to be accepted. If the warrant is already accepted as true there is no need for elaborate support of it. For example, a majority of Americans would believe that free enterprise produces economic incentive. On the other hand, it may be necessary for the speaker to prove the causal relation to the audience. One method of proof is to break down the causal generalization into component causal relations which contribute to the overall relation. In arguing that government ownership of a business results in inefficient operation, an advocate may break this down into component causal generalizations: government ownership involves more red tape and more administration; government ownership removes the business from competition; government ownership allows operation at a loss, etc. These component generalizations must all support the major warrant that government operation causes inefficient operation. Once this is established the advocate can argue that this will apply to a particular business under consideration. These component generalizations must be acceptable to the audience, and when the advocate analyzes a causal generalization into components and these components into more specific causal relations, he must at some point rest his reasoning upon generalizations which are believed by the audience.

A second method of supporting a causal generalization is through reasoning from example to a descriptive generalization. This is direct support of the correlation, since examples are given from which the pattern of the generalization can be derived. In supporting the generalization that government operation results in inefficient operation,

---

[6] I am making no distinction between a causal relation and a correlation. The cautious reader should feel free to translate my term "causal relation" into "correlative relation."

the advocate would present actual instances where this has occurred, e.g., the post office. Since there may be examples which contradict the generalization (e.g., government operated businesses which are efficiently operated) the advocate should be able to analyze the causal factors in the examples he presents. These two methods of supporting the warrant are quite different. The first method, that of separating the warrant into component relations, is based on cause to effect reasoning on a more specific level. The second method of proof, the presentation of examples to prove the correlation, is not causal reasoning, but argument from example to a descriptive causal generalization.[7] Whichever method is used to back the warrant, the advocate should explain the process as specifically and comprehensively as possible, because it is on the strength of the warrant that the argument rests.

Conclusion. The conclusion is the assertion of another event: a prediction of a condition, state, fact, attitude, or other phenomena. It is an event of the type specified in the warrant.

Rebuttal. Evaluating the argument from cause to effect requires the testing first of the warrant, and second the application of the warrant to the situation.

1. Is the causal generalization of the warrant probable on the basis of its component relations? That is, can the warrant be broken down into component generalizations which confirm it, or are some important relations contradictory?

2. Do examples confirm or disconfirm the warrant? Both of these first two tests are concerned with the backing of the warrant.

3. Does the situation in the data contain the causal factors asserted in the warrant, i.e., is the situation the type described by the warrant? For example, government regulation of utilities such as the telephone utility is not the same as government ownership of utilities, and generalizations about the first will not apply to the second. Not only should the case be of the type covered, but the complex causal components of the warrant should be present.

4. Are there any factors present which would interfere with the effect? Although the necessary causes may exist, other factors may also exist which will alter the overall result. The possible use of nuclear

---

[7] Some textbooks are unaware of this distinction and assume that every argument which contains a causal generalization has a causal warrant, and is thus causal reasoning. This is not the case.

weapons may alter the effects of a "minor" war, or government subsidies may change the effects of lowered tariff barriers on formerly protected industries.

Argument from Comparison [8]

This process of reasoning draws conclusions by comparing one situation with another. Event A is shown to be similar to event B, and conclusions drawn about the first event are then applied to the second. The items compared between the two events are facts and actual characteristics, and the conclusion for event A is based on these facts. Since the same facts are found in event B, the same conclusion is asserted to apply there also. This type of argument can prove that a plan of city government will work well in Cleveland because it worked well in Cincinnati, that one organization should be classified as subversive because an organization with similar characteristics was so classified, or that the 1969 model of an automobile will be trouble free because the 1960 model was trouble free (although the astute reader will detect differences in the degree of probability possessed by each argument).

If the government were to enact national health insurance, doctors would have no additional problems with red tape or bureaucratic requirements (C). Today under private health insurance doctors have the same problems regarding reports, hypochondriacs, arrangement for payments, and fees as they would under national health insurance. The only difference in the two programs would be that the check would be paid from a national insurance fund instead of a private insurance fund (D).

Data. There are three aspects to the data: (1) The characteristics of situation A, (2) conclusions about situation A, (3) characteristics of situation B. The data must show that the characteristics of the two situations are similar, and these facts must be the ones which lead to the conclusion about A which is to be applied to B. To determine the relevant characteristics it is necessary to consider the conclusion to be drawn. The conclusion may be either one of classification or an assertion of the existence of characteristics or effects. The conclusion is first drawn about situation A, and this is an internal

---

[8] Often referred to as "literal analogy" by current textbooks. This process is called comparison here because it should not be confused with argument from analogy, which requires different data and a different method of evaluation.

argument in the premises. If the internal conclusion is one of classification it is derived by reasoning from criteria to classification, and it must satisfy the requirements for that mode of reasoning. Therefore situations A and B must be shown similar in the characteristics which satisfy the criteria.

If the conclusion about situation A is the assertion of effects or characteristics, there is a causal or correlative relationship involved. If a causal relation is apparent in situation A, then the second situation must be shown to contain the same causal factors. If a correlation or association is asserted, enough similar characteristics must be cited to show that the pattern is present.

Warrant. There may be two warrants in this process. One is the major warrant which allows you to assert that statements about situation A can be made about situation B. There may be another warrant allowing the conclusion about situation A. These warrants may be evaluated with the usual tests for argument from cause or argument from criteria. The major warrant is grounded in the experience of the audience which tells them that similar assertions can be made about similar situations. The validity of this warrant depends upon what types of situations this relationship applies to, and these are the ones that have been described (classifications, predictions, characteristics). The movement from data to conclusion depends on how relevantly similar situations A and B are.[9] This the advocate must demonstrate.

Rebuttal. The rebuttal of this argument hinges on two aspects: the validity of the assertions about situation A and the similarities between the two situations.

1. Is the conclusion or assertion acceptable for situation A? Consider this argument against an international economic organization.

We find, as we look at the League of Nations, that you do not have to kill an organization directly to make it ineffective. Just amend it to death

---

[9] Some textbooks assert there is an implicit generalization in argument from comparison: Situation A leads to a generalization which is then applied to situation B. In a sense this is true, but there is no attempt to assert a generalization even as a way station. Because of the specificity of the situations which are used as data, any generalization would be in terms of the very specific characteristics present, usually a complex of facts and relations. Thus any generalizations involved would be complex also, and so apply to a narrow range of situations, indeed perhaps only two situations. Thus, it seems unnecessary to be concerned with an implicit generalization in this process of reasoning.

as was done to the League (D). In the same way this international economic agency will be rendered incapable of action (C).

The assertion that the League was killed by amendment is not justifiable, since there were many more important factors. The conclusion about situation A must be valid, else it can not be applied to situation B. It is also clear that the more probable the conclusion and the more typical the situation, the more it is possible to transfer the same assertions to the second situation.

2. How similar are the two situations? To answer this question involves several considerations. First, are the characteristics of each situation actually similar? In this argument they are not.

In Berlin and in Korea the Communists retreated when we showed that we were going to stand up and fight (D). So if we stand up in Cuba they will back down (C).

But in Berlin, when the Communists blocked road transportation to the city, and in Korea, where there was armed attack, different characteristics were present which cannot be specifically compared to the attempt to move forces into a willing nation. Only the very general characteristics are similar.

Further, the characteristics which are compared must be the essential elements. They must be those which lead causally to the conclusion or which allow a verbal classification or which are sufficient to determine a pattern. An adequate number of essential elements must be presented and there should be no significant difference in these elements.

More than one situation may be used as data, as in the argument on Cuba, and each is subject to the same tests for internal adequacy and for similarities. In legal advocacy similar cases may be cited to establish precedent for the case under consideration; this is argument from comparison. In all fields of subject matter, the more cases that can be compared, the stronger is the conclusion.[10]

Argument from Testimony

One of the most common ways of supporting a conclusion is by quoting a person, hopefully an authority, who says that the conclusion is true.

[10] For an excellent discussion of this mode of reasoning (labeled as analogy) see Irving M. Copi, *Introduction to Logic*, 2nd Edition (New York: Macmillan,

The reasoning is "A, who ought to know, says this is true, or advisable, etc., and therefore we can conclude that it *is* true, or advisable, etc." The fact that A asserts the conclusion is taken to be a sign that the conclusion is true (this is a form of effect to cause, or sign, reasoning, but it is of a particular kind, and so is discussed here).

To prove that the Soviet Union can now fight an all-out nuclear war (D) I refer to William Smith, military editor of the Z newspaper, who wrote on December 15, 1963, "The Soviet armed forces, capable fifteen years ago of fighting a conventional war with conventional arms, now have developed a vast nuclear capability as well. Today the Kremlin can engage in an unlimited as well as a limited nuclear or nonnuclear war." (D).

Data. The source of the statement cited may be either a person or an institution. Usually the quotation is from written material, but this is not essential, although for purposes of verification this is most practical. The specificity of the statement may vary. The argument cited refers in general to nuclear capability, but the actual weapons or destructive power might have been given by another authority. Since the content of the statement determines the content of the conclusion, the specificity or precision of the quotation is important. Further, the advocate may be more or less precise in presenting the data. He may quote literally and accurately or he may paraphrase and quote indirectly. Unless the content is already well known, the more direct and complete the quotation, the stronger and less open to attack will be the argument.

The qualification of the source of the testimony is an important part of the data. Why are we justified in accepting as true the statements of the London Disarmament Conference, or Dwight Eisenhower, or Leo Szilard? The answer is that these authorities have certain qualifications which make it likely that their statements will be accurate descriptions or valid opinions in certain fields. Therefore, part of the data of the argument from testimony should be the presentation of these qualifications, if they are not already known. The source may be qualified because of his position, because of special research, because of previous experience, because of recognition or success in his field, because of a previous reputation for accuracy or honesty, or because of other reasons which make a person an authority. These are signs of reliability, and the advocate should use them to validate his source of testimony. For well-known authorities, little more than the name may be necessary, but for sources not well known to the audience the advocate may have to present substantial backing to establish their authority.

The same requirements hold for impersonal testimony, such as that from newsmagazines or newspapers. For these the reputation for accuracy and unbiased reporting is important.

One further characteristic of the quoted material in the data should be noted. The statement may be a flat assertion of a conclusion or it may also contain internal reasoning supporting that conclusion.

The defense of Europe is essential for the survival of both Europe and the United States (C). General George Spelvin, commander of NATO's military force, says, "Western Europe has the largest pool of skilled labor in the world and an industrial capacity second only to the United States. If we take that complex with its military potential and shift it from the side of the Free World to the other side, the balance of power would be greatly shifted, and the safety of the United States would be imperiled." (D)

If the testimony contains internal explanation or reasoning, that reasoning can be tested by itself to add support to the conclusion.

Warrant. The question answered by the warrant is: How likely is statement S to be true, considering it has been made by A who has these qualifications? The warrant passes on the reliability of the source and allows us to accept his assertion as a basis for the conclusion. The qualifications of the source are indications of authority which warrant the conclusion. These indications are backing for the warrant, and were discussed under the data. They are based on what our society or culture considers necessary for a person to be an authority. They may be drawn from professional standards or general opinion.

Conclusion. The conclusion is the meaning of the testimony itself, which may be a factual description, classification, generalization, effect, characteristics, or hypothesis. This is a "free floating" argument, in the sense that it can be used to support any type of conclusion. It is important to distinguish between the premises and the conclusion. The premises or data include the statement, the source of the statement, and the qualifications of that source. The conclusion is what the statement says.

Rebuttal. In citing testimony as proof, this process is assumed to occur: a situation exists, the source comes in contact with it, he makes statements or opinions from his knowledge about it, and we accept his statements as reliable. Given this chain of events, there are several tests which can be applied.

1. Did the source observe the situation? Was the observation direct or through other reports or secondary sources? The closer the person is to the actual situation, the more reliable can be his testimony. For example, a report of the level of employment by the government Bureau of Labor Statistics would be more reliable than one by an economist in a private corporation, because the government has best access to reliable information on this matter.

2. Is the person competent in this field? To be considered an authority in the field he must have some of the characteristics already mentioned, and these should be relevant to the field of the subject. This does not mean that an authority on insurance may not also be an authority on linguistics, but this fact must be established.

3. Is the source motivated to be accurate? One of the requirements is that the authority is motivated to be honest, or at least not dishonest, in his reports or opinions. This requires an evaluation of moral reliability, integrity, commitments, associations, biases, prejudices, objectivity, and conscientiousness of the person.

Is there internal evidence of the conclusion? Is the testimony internally consistent; is there logical support for the statement?

4. Does the testimony have factors which are correlated with reliability? How trustworthy has this person been in the past on these matters? Primary sources are more reliable than secondary sources because of the danger of misquotation or distortion in the latter. Testimony against the interests of the source is considered more significant than testimony in conformity with his interests. Publication in an independent, highly regarded magazine is more highly correlated with reliability than publication in a magazine with known biases. For further details, see "Tests of Evidence."

FURTHER METHODS OF PROOF

Now we turn to processes of reasoning which are important, but which are used less frequently or which are less useful than the five methods just described. Still they are necessary to prove certain conclusions and the advocate should understand them in order both to build and to attack arguments. Taken together, the nine methods of reasoning described in this chapter cover over 95 per cent of the arguments found in discourse.[11]

Argument from an Observed Effect to an Unobserved Cause

Sometimes called argument from sign, this process uses one event as an indication of the presence of another event. An event is observed and therefore its cause is asserted to exist, though unobserved.

The existence of a police state would make it impossible to have a free election (W), so the fact that the elections of 1960 and 1962 in Grubnia were found to be fair and free by the United Nations commission (D) should indicate to us that there is no police state in that country (C).

The data for this argument are always events, states, or conditions which are known to exist. Obviously these signs must be located in the present or past, and the argument cannot predict what will happen in the future (although a hypothetical argument from effect to cause can be laid in the future: if country Z mobilizes its troops, it will be preparing for war). The warrant states that the event in the data is caused by an event, condition, or state, and that when the data are present, their cause is probably present or was present, because the two events are highly correlated. That is, they occur together with high frequency. The conclusion asserts the existence of an event or condition, although that condition has not been observed.

The event claimed by the conclusion may be either a direct cause of the sign or it may be an event correlated with the sign, without a direct causal relation being present. For example, a police state could exist and still have free elections, because several factors could modify the causal relation stated in the warrant. The conclusion may also be a sufficient or a necessary cause. If it is a sufficient cause, it alone is enough to produce the data. If it is a necessary cause, its presence is required or necessary, though other conditions must also occur, i.e., it

---

[11] The study from which this chapter was derived found the frequency of the nine forms of reasoning as follows: Argument from example, 26 per cent; criteria, 20 per cent; cause, 10 per cent; comparison, 3 per cent; testimony, 18 per cent; effect, 5 per cent; circumstantial evidence, 6 per cent; definition, 7 per cent; and analogy, 2 per cent.

is necessary that a person be at least age 35 to be President of the United States, therefore if a person is President, it is a sign that he is at least age 35.

Two basic questions should be asked in evaluating argument from effect. First, what is the correlation of the effect with the cause? This evaluates the strength of the association between the two events. Since there is usually a complex causal relation involved, the warrant is one of probability, and the stronger the association of the two events, the stronger is the argument. For example, the argument that we should not recognize the Communist Chinese government because the recognition of a foreign government is a sign of approval, is one based on a weak relation between the two events, at least on the basis of past political behavior. The second question is whether there are other events which would more reliably account for the data. In other words, are there more likely causes for the effect? The Soviet Union once accused Britain of being against peace because they rejected a Soviet proposal for disarmament, but there are many other more likely causes for the data, causes based on warrants with higher probability.

Argument from Circumstantial Evidence to a Hypothesis

Several facts are presented as data and their existence is explained by a pattern, event, or fact which accounts for them, as in a trial for burglary the guilt of the accused is based on the circumstantial evidence of his fingerprints, his business card, and his automobile all being found at the scene of the crime (an additional hypothesis might be that he also must be insane or feeble minded). The hypothetical fact that he committed the crime would explain the existence of the other facts. This mode of reasoning is an important method of proof in scientific investigation, where a scientist formulates a theory (C) to account for or organize facts (D).[12] The connection between the facts of the conclusion and the facts of the data is usually one of cause to effect.

A steel price increase was first announced by the X steel corporation. Y corporation and Z corporation, as well as other large companies, increased their prices without hesitation. By a remarkable coincidence these com-

---

[12] This is also the method of reasoning most used by that ace detective, Sherlock Holmes. For an interesting discussion of Holmes' use of reasoning from circumstantial evidence, see Lionel Ruby, The Art of Making Sense (Philadelphia: J. B. Lippincott Co., 1954), ch. 13.

panies were inspired to achieve this increase by switching their quotation base from gross tons to net tons (D). Does not that look as if there was a definite oligopolic agreement for the control of prices (C)?

The data may be two or three facts or more, and the conclusion is an event or pattern which would explain or account for those facts. If the conclusion is a formulation of a pattern or descriptive hypothesis (e.g., the earth is round) then the data are related to it because they correspond to the pattern; without the condition of the pattern they would not occur. This is a causal relation, but less clearly than the causal hypothesis, which postulates an event which produces the data (e.g., Senator G is a secret Communist, and that is why he voted the way he did on those bills). The warrant in argument from circumstantial evidence asserts that the data can be accounted for by the conclusion and so the conclusion is probably true.[13]

In rebuttal, the first question is to ask whether the hypothesis does explain or account for the evidence: assuming the conclusion is true, does it explain the existence of the data? Secondly, enough evidence must be presented to justify the hypothesis. Deriving a complex hypothesis from one fact is not normally justified. For example, the one fact that France rejected disarmament proposal K is insufficient evidence for the broad conclusion that France is a warlike nation, even though the hypothesis would explain the fact. A final important point to consider in testing this type of reasoning is whether there are other hypotheses which would be equally or more probable, i.e., are there alternative hypotheses which would also explain the data? In the sample argument on the existence of an oligopoly, an alternative explanation might be that there is a natural tendency for steel companies to follow the lead of a major firm as the result of the highly competitive field.

Reasoning from a Definition to Characteristics

A condition or situation is defined and then attributes of that definition are asserted to apply to the situation. For example, an argument

---

[13] This argument is similar to the argument from effect to cause (argument from sign) in that the data are caused by the conclusion. However, in sign reasoning an individual sign is correlated highly with the event it indicates; in reasoning from circumstantial evidence, any one fact in the data has a low correlation with the cause, and it is only when several facts are considered together that the conclusion may be asserted. Reasoning from effect to cause uses warrants which are already accepted, but in argument from circumstantial evidence, the warrant is accepted on the basis of how well the conclusion explains the facts.

against capital punishment is that the U. S. is a country with Judeo-Christian beliefs, including the commandment not to kill; therefore capital punishment should not be allowed.

This is a Christian country (D). The message of Christ calls us to good will, to the love of our neighbor, to humility, and to the forgiveness, not the slaughter, of our enemies (W). It hardly follows that we should kill Communists because they are atheists and we are Christians; rather, we should not kill them (C).

The datum is the definition of the situation. This definition is asserted by the speaker, and therefore it must be one which the audience will accept as reasonable. This definition may be a classification of the situation into an already established category of situations (U. S. values are Judeo-Christian) or it may be an application of a new definition. An illustration of the second type is Abraham Lincoln's argument that the South was still a part of the Union even in Civil War (C), because the Union was a contract (D), and a contract can not be broken save by the consent of all parties (W).[14]

The conclusion of this mode of reasoning is a characteristic that follows from the definition, and the warrant states that relationship. The basis of this argument is semantic in nature, since the application of definitions and the implied attributes are determined by the meanings of the words used. It is important in this reasoning process, as with argument from criteria to a classification, to use warrants which will be accepted by the audience.

Three lines of rebuttal are possible. First, is the definition an accurate or agreed-upon definition? If the audience will not accept the definition, the rest of the argument is blocked, e.g., if the Union is not considered a contract, then the seceding states are an enemy nation. The second test is of the warrant: do the implications or characteristics follow from the definition? If the conclusion is not implied by the definition, the argument is invalid. Finally, are there any qualifications or superseding principles which might negate the conclusion by modifying the warrant? For example, there are those who contend that we should normally maintain the principle and right of free speech, but that this right should be curtailed in times of war or national emergency.

---

[14] Lincoln used argument from definition extensively. See Richard Weaver, "Lincoln and the Argument from Definition," in *The Ethics of Rhetoric* (Chicago: Henry Regnery Company, 1953).

Argument from Analogy

In this process, often called figurative analogy, the abstract relationships of two events are compared, and conclusions drawn about the first situation are asserted to apply to the second situation, even though the situations are not factually similar, e.g., a war is like a fire: the best time to stop it is in the beginning while it is small. The characteristics which are compared are not facts (as in the argument from comparison) but abstract patterns, and conclusions about one pattern are extended to the other pattern.

It is not possible to halt price increases immediately with a price freeze (C). You must realize that the brakes can not be applied suddenly to a truck going seventy miles an hour without a smash-up. The brakes must be applied gradually (D). In the same way, we must apply the controls to the economy gradually (C).

Argument from analogy is a weak method of reasoning and many textbooks do not consider it valid. It is more valuable as psychological proof because it stimulates the audience to supply their own proof to fill out the principles involved. It should be used as supplementary proof or illustration rather than primary logical support. The data are the two situations and the abstract relations they hold in common. The conclusion applies known relationships from the first situation to the second situation on the basis of the warrant. The warrant is drawn from an understanding of the situations and the recognition that the relationships from situation A may be extended meaningfully to situation B. Here lies the weakness of this reasoning process: it is difficult to find comparable abstract relationships which will allow sound conclusions.

Since the argument hinges on patterns as they imply facts, both aspects must be considered in rebuttal. First, is the analogy a valid comparison of relations; are the two patterns actually similar? There may be a lack of correspondence or there may be differences which are ignored. Second, do the factual characteristics implied by the pattern carry out the relationships, e.g., the asserted patterns may be similar, but they may not apply to the facts of the situations. Finally, the entire argument should be evaluated on the basis of its suggested proof to discover how well it conforms with other experience with the subject.

General Analysis of Proof

There are modes of reasoning other than those described in this chapter, and the advocate must learn how to analyze their nature when they occur or how to construct them when needed. An argument occurs whenever one statement is asserted to follow from another statement or a fact, and the first step is to identify the argument and isolate it from the surrounding discourse. Once this is done, the data and the conclusion should be located. These may occur in any order in the presentation of the argument. Then the warrant must be formulated if it is not explicit. Since the warrant states how the conclusion is derived from the data, the critic must decide exactly what process of reasoning is required, and the statement of that relation is the warrant. This may correspond with one of the nine forms of argument or a combination of them, and the argument can be tested appropriately. If it is of a different type from those described in this chapter, the critic must analyze for himself in fear and trembling the logical requirements of proof.

The construction of an argument is more difficult than the analysis of an existent argument. The usual task of the advocate in this case is to support conclusions which are already determined, and his search is for data and warrants which will lead to those conclusions. The first step is to formulate carefully the desired conclusion and analyze its nature. Is it a classification, an effect, a cause, or a characteristic, etc.? Once the type of conclusion is determined, the advocate can examine methods of argument to discover which ones will lead to that conclusion. For example, a classification can be supported by argument from criteria, from comparison, from testimony, and from analogy. A descriptive generalization can be proved by argument from example, from cause, and from testimony. Once the possible methods of reasoning are found, the data should be examined to discover what can be used in any of the processes. It may be discovered that the tentative conclusions cannot be supported with the data which are available, in which case different conclusions must be drawn. Or it may be that none of the nine described forms of reasoning will lead to the conclusion, in which case the advocate must attempt to discover a warrant which, with the data, will lead to the conclusion.

QUESTIONS

1. If the standards of rhetorical proof are less demanding than those of science or of logic, how should we interpret the claim that an advocate's main job is to discover truth?
2. Some writers define an argument (meaning the smallest unit of a sense-making argument) as a conclusion and a reason. This seems to resemble the Data and Conclusion of the Toulmin layout. If we extend this argument through all six steps of the layout, do we still have one argument, or do we have a series of interrelated arguments?
3. In "Rebuttal" at the end of the section on "Argument from Example to a Descriptive Generalization," nothing was said about the importance of having *enough* examples. Why was the quantitative test omitted? Should it have been?
4. Which of the major methods of proof is likely to be of central importance in a main point on a proposition of value?
5. Which method of proof is likely to be used on a proposition of prediction (future fact)?

EXERCISES

1. Select from Appendixes a specimen of argument for each of the five major methods of proof and diagram each with the Toulmin structural layout. Add parenthetically any missing elements.
2. Evaluate the strength of each of the five arguments above in terms of the principles described under "rebuttal" for the appropriate process.
3. Write four short paragraphs of original argument—one for each of the "further methods of proof." Use the proposition you have been working with for earlier exercises.
4. In class discussion, evaluate some of the arguments which are read aloud for Exercise 3. Apply the "rebuttal" principles as directed in Exercise 2.
5. Have a page or two of argumentative discourse read aloud to the class. During a brief pause at the end of each unit of argument, ask students to identify the method or methods of proof being used.

CHAPTER VIII

ANCILLARY FORMS

OF SUPPORT

IF, AS IN CHAPTER I, WE DEFINE ARGUMENTATION AS A CRITICAL APPARATUS and as a deliberative method which employs primarily reasoned discourse, we should place in subordinate positions those forms of support known as explanation, ethos, and motivation. In terms of this definition, these forms of support are judged to be generally auxiliary to the essential forms of support known as evidence and reasoning. In other words, when popular persuasion is not our main concern, we de-emphasize its characteristic materials and methods, and the practical justifications are those of pedagogical focus and the limitations of space.

E X P L A N A T I O N

As Incidental Material

When explanation is used as incidental material in argumentative discourse, it includes description, narration, and exposition. These supporting materials in various proportions are used to supplement the evidence and the reasoning in ways which will be explained in the next paragraph.

Of what importance is explanation as incidental material in an advocatory speech or essay? We know that explanation is of primary importance in a discourse to inform, but in advocacy it serves to improve understanding and interest. The reason is that listeners and readers tend to grow bored with prosaic, bare, or abstract ideas. They want details and particulars such as definitions, examples, figures, and sensory impressions which will clarify and enliven the ideas. Exposition, for instance, brings the unfamiliar into the understanding by associating it with the knowledge and experience of the listeners or readers. Description adds sensory imagery to the message, and narration lends action or a story line.

Applications of these principles may be seen in editorials, advertising, judicial opinions, philosophical arguments, school debates, and other forms of argumentative discourse. For example, the proposition of an editorial was that any decision on the nature of future space explorations should be based upon the criterion of efficient advancement of knowledge rather than an emotional flush over successful competition with a rival country. The paragraphs which led to this conclusion were in part explanatory: they reported and sketched the backgrounds of the competing views on the comparative advantages of continuing the Mercury-Atlas flights as opposed to proceeding at once to the Gemini series. Explanation appeared as incidental material in a full-page advertisement for the Rolls-Royce automobile. In one paragraph we read that the automatic gear selector is bored to a tolerance of 1/4000 of an inch, that it is then blasted by particles of ground coconut shell, and that it is polished with ground oat-husks. When Walt Whitman wrote an editorial against slavery for the *Daily Eagle*, he included a vivid description of life aboard a slave ship, and when he wrote against capital punishment, he described the scene at the hanging of a woman. Judicial opinions, particularly those of Supreme Court justices, often contain cogently reasoned discourse, but there is usually an exposition of the grounds for the decision. In such discourse the traditional distinction between exposition and argumentation is difficult to maintain. And how about philosophical argumentation? In Chapter II the point was made that a philosophical approach involves more exposition than persuasion in the usual sense. In fact, exposition may in some cases be much more than incidental material; it may be the dominant material. Finally, if school debating is viewed as an exercise in primarily "logical" persuasion, and if the traditional debate format is retained, explanation will continue to serve mainly in the presentation of affirmative plans, negative counterpropositions, and, less obviously, the causal hypothesis in the "need" argument which explains *why* the status quo is failing.

As a Persuasive Method

When explanation is the dominant material in persuasive discourse, the method is likely to be implicative rather than didactic. Instead of beginning with his proposition and supporting it with reasons and evidence, the implicative arguer starts with the background of the problem, narrates some relevant events, describes some conditions, explains the trend, and thereby builds up a pressure of facts and mental images which make the outcome seem inevitable. This is the method of implication, as Bosanquet named it, and it differs markedly from the method of linear inference such as we see in logical outlines.[1] Typically the implicative method delineates a problem, explains and disqualifies all solutions save one, and finally confronts the audience with a this-or-nothing disjunction. In this manner Woodrow Wilson discussed three choices: armed neutrality, submission, and declaration of war against Germany. Then he showed why choices one and two were out of the question, thereby leaving a choice between declaration of war and nothing.

There are both advantages and risks in this method. Theoretically, implication reduces the probability of a contrarient idea in a doubtful or a hostile audience, and it reasons from the *whole* situation rather than from the biased points of one side. As in a jig-saw puzzle, when all parts but one have been assembled, the place for the last one becomes inevitable. However, the risk is that if the audience prefers to deny the whole thought rather than to accept the implied conclusion, the case fails. This is why the "nothing" choice should be made factually or psychologically unacceptable to the audience.

A few illustrative applications of explanation as a persuasive method may serve to clarify the theory. Some years ago a student in a public speaking class met an informative speech assignment by explaining how frequency-modulation radio broadcasting works. After he finished, several members of the class charged that he had given a

[1] B. Bosanquet, *Implication and Linear Inference* (London: Macmillan and Company, 1920), pp. 1–30; also G. M. Graham, "The Natural Procedure in Argument," *Quarterly Journal of Speech Education*, XI, No. 4 (1925), 319–337.

persuasive speech. They were convinced, they reported, that all radio transmission should be done in the way he had explained. Without intending to do so, the student had used a form of implication. Another student used this method intentionally in an attempt to convince his audience that the United Nations could succeed where the League of Nations had failed. First he listed the reasons given by historians for the failure of the League. This was reporting, not linear inference. Then, after merely stating that another organization was trying to do better, he explained the organization and functions of the U.N., including the police force, the provisions for the studying of social and economic problems, and the work of the Secretariat. At no time did he directly argue that the U.N. would succeed because of these provisions. Through reporting and explaining he built the implication that the U.N. would succeed because it did not start with the shortcomings which had doomed the League. Finally, if school debating were occasionally conducted as an exercise in popular persuasion but without demagoguery, and if its stylized form were on those occasions abandoned, we might find that explanation in the implicative form had become a much more familiar method than before.

So much for the theory of implication and the examples of its utilization. The hypothesis that this theory will be proved experimentally has not been sufficiently tested. The theory seems plausible, and some practical applications have lent some confirmation to it, but a broad generalization concerning the persuasive impact of the implicative methods would not now be warranted. In the next chapter some instruction on the organization of persuasive explanation will be given.

ETHOS

The Concept Defined

Early in Chapter I this form of support was briefly defined as the persuasive impact of a speaker's personality, but brevity may result in the oversimpification of a complex, suggestive phenomenon. More than twenty centuries ago Aristotle wrote in his *Rhetoric* that the character of a speaker is a source of persuasion when it makes him seem worthy of belief. He explained that in general we trust persons of probity more than others, and in relation to uncertain or debatable matters we trust them almost absolutely. If we cannot judge what is true and what is false, or what is wise and what is unwise, we must place our trust in worthy advisers. They merit our trust because of their intelligence, character, and good will. In Book I, Chapter 2 of his *Rhetoric*, Aristotle went so far as to declare that the speaker's ethos is probably the most potent of all the means of persuasion. Despite this evaluation we are treating ethos as an ancilary form of support, because in general argumentation popular persuasion is not the main concern.

In ancient times ethos meant the impressions which the listeners formed of the speaker while he spoke. Nowadays this concept includes the original meaning plus reputation, status, and the like. In fact, one's prior reputation often accounts for the size of the audience which will assemble to hear him. In contemporary social science research, ethos is known as credibility of the source of the message, and it includes speakers, writers, and the media in which they operate.

Ethos is a cultural variable; its constituent elements are not the same in all times and places. Persons differ in what they value in others. The implication for an advocate is that he should so analyze his public that he may ascertain what traits its members value in a person. For instance, the general voting public is thought usually to prefer a Presidential candidate who has a solid American background, preferably humble; who looks moderately attractive on television and newsreels; who appears healthy and vigorous; who has an attractive family; who is successful in a private career; who is identified with popular and safe issues; who acts as if he were drafted; and who makes himself conspicuous.

An advocate's ethos, aside from any matters of antecedent reputation, is ultimately determined by the choices he makes—by the propositions he chooses, by his evidence and reasoning, by his attitudes, by his emotional reactions, by his language and general demeanor—indeed by all the cues or signs which are available to the listener or the reader. For example, a speaker who is reasonably confident and well poised exerts a positive suggestion upon his audience. Likewise a person's grasp of his subject indicates intellectual competence and personal integrity. Other signs of general competence are enthusiasm, adaptability, sincerity, fairness, courage, directness, good taste, some trace of a sense of humor, and perhaps a modest reference to some experiences which qualify him to write or speak on the proposition.

Its Importance

Estimates of the importance of ethos or "image" can be based upon rhetorical theory, personal observation, and the findings of experimental studies. An importance such as Aristotle attributed to ethos stems in part from the advocate's personal identification with his subject. Any writer or speaker has some of this identification, but one who seeks to influence others is much more closely identified with his message in the minds of his public. When he supports an idea or an action, he stands as a sponsor of that cause. In many minds the spokesman and his cause are one. For this reason we may say that the use or nonuse of ethical persuasion is not a matter of choice. Ethos is inevitable; an advocate will surely be judged for something he does or fails to do. These are the generalizations from rhetorical theory and empirical observation.

More specific conclusions can be drawn from experimental studies because each investigation has focused upon a small part of what we call ethos. However, the concept is so broad and each study is so narrow that we still do not have enough results to permit definitive generalizing about the operation of ethos in real-life contexts. Instead of noting dozens of studies individually, let us refer to one report which summarizes the experimental research in ethos.[2] Both expert opinion and an announcement of what the majority opinion is will exert prestige suggestion. The prestige of the source affects the impact of the communication, but this wears off in time and loses its initial advantage. Some persons are more susceptible to prestige suggestion than others, but this correlates more highly with initial attitude than with education, age, intelligence, or sex. Both oral and printed propaganda can alter public images of persons, but direct attacks may backfire because of sympathy for the victim. Democratic strategists in the Kennedy-Nixon campaign were advised against attacking Nixon personally for fear they would lose more than they could hope to gain.[3] The highest character ratings were given to speakers whom their listeners perceived as belonging to their social class; in fact, the greater the social distance between speaker and rater the lower the rating of the speaker's character. Some laudatory remarks by an introducer may

[2] K. Andersen and T. Clevenger, Jr., "A Summary of Experimental Research in Ethos," *Speech Monographs*, XXX, No. 2 (1963), 59–78.
[3] *The Wall Street Journal*, February 1, 1960, p. 1.

enhance a speaker's ethos, but the speaker's own expression of self-praise (direct ethos) usually does him no good. Attempts to appear broad-minded by presenting both sides of a controversy are better than one-sided presentations in few cases and under special conditions. As we noted in relation to evidence, documentation does not improve source credibility unless the qualifying comment becomes a "build-up" for the source. There is some effect which can be attributed to dress, voice, and manner, but this is indefinite. Finally, it appears that the typical listener is a poor judge of sincerity. Perhaps this is why some campaigners try to get away with calling each issue "vital," an opponent a "menace," a rival idea "Communist-inspired," and each election a "crisis."

MOTIVATION

The Concept Defined

We often hear that motivation accounts for as much of a superior student's performance as his intelligence does. Sometimes we speak of his being self-motivated, while in another case we say that a skillful teacher motivated him. But when we refer to motivation in relation to persuasion, we mean the process of inducing or of modifying a response by supplying attractive reasons for the desired behavior. It involves the use of supporting materials which are intended to identify the listeners' or readers' goals, values, etc., with the acceptance of the advocate's message. Motivation is selective in that it lowers the threshold of stimulation for one appeal while raising it for competing appeals. It is said to be reinforcing or inhibiting because it adds to or subtracts from the intensity of stimuli which lead to one reaction, or it induces a set or a habit which aids or hinders a response. In motivation as well as in persuasion generally, the objective is the modification of attitudes, and this modification may be as obvious as an overt act or as subtle as an internalized response which can be detected only by an attitude measuring procedure.

This definition suggests that motivation has an affective core of feeling tones such as likes, dislikes, interests, and preferences. These elements are not drives nor are they universal; they vary among cultures, and their intensity varies among individuals in a culture. When situations matter to us, we experience feelings; and when because of our attitudes they matter very much, we have strong emotional reactions. Thus our affective (emotional) states sometimes outweigh our objective thinking in determining our behavior. Whether these affective states produce good or harm depends upon the adjustments we make. It is only when adjustments are immature that emotional behavior is deporable.

Separate treatments of reasoning and motivation in this book do not imply mutual exclusiveness. No strict dichotomy of reason and emotion is intended. In other words, thoughtful and emotional reactions are interrelated and occur in varying proportions in different situations. It is a matter of emphasis or central tendency, not one of all this or all that. For example, if one urges that guns be handled in a certain way and supports his proposition by showing how persons may be hurt or killed, he is using an appeal which is both logically and psychologically sound. It is clear that all behavior has its motives; therefore, an advocate who relates certain desires or values to his proposition is *not necessarily* using illogical thinking, but he *may* be.

Its Importance

When motivation is the main form of support, as in popular persuasion, it is obviously important; but when it is ancilary, as in rational arguments to critical listeners or readers, it is less important. Questions concerning the importance of motivation in this lesser role will be answered with theories from the literature, some references to real-life applications thereof, and some findings of experimental research.

Not all speeches of advocacy require motivational support. There are instances in which the communicator's main concern is with material and logical validity, regardless of the desires of some listeners or readers. A less extreme case is one in which the communicator gives *some* consideration to his audience, but only to the extent of seeking a *thoughtful* response from the *critical* listeners or readers. Finally, it is possible, even when adapting to a popular audience, to base an argument on their attitudes or beliefs and to reason both cogently and persuasively in showing the consequences of those attitudes.

According to rhetorical theory, one of the significant functions of motivation as ancilary material is the gaining of attention. Introductory

paragraphs are supposed to attract attention, and they do so by showing how the subject matters to us or by arousing our curiosity, to
mention only two of several ways to motivate attention and interest.
This kind of supporting material which holds attention and facilitates
the reception of ideas has the additional advantage of neutralizing the
doubting, inhibiting, or objecting attitudes which lead to disagreement. The following introductory paragraphs were used in a speech
on the Hoover Report which was delivered to an audience of businessmen in 1949. This introduction was designed to motivate attention:

Fellow Businessmen:
How long could you stay in business if your unit cost were 2½ times
the selling price? The Post Office spends 2½ cents on each penny post-
card, and its current annual deficit is five hundred million dollars.
Would any of you retain a purchasing agent who set up such complicated procedures that he spent ten dollars to order less than ten dollars
worth of supplies? About half of the three million government purchase
orders issued each year are for ten dollars or less. The average cost of the
paper work and other red tape far exceeds ten dollars per order. Thus, if
you were an operating man in one of the government agencies and ordered
a dollar's worth of pencils, it would cost the government eleven dollars
to make delivery to you. You men would soon look for a new purchasing
agent if you found anything like this going on in your business. Let us
see how this problem affects us and what we can do about it.

A second function of motivational support as incidental or secondary material is to reinforce the logical argument with reassuring
evidence of a favorable majority opinion. After arguing the reasons for
our sooner or later joining the fight against the Axis powers in World
War II, James B. Conant cited an opinion poll which showed nearly
seventy-one per cent of the American people to be in favor of naval
belligerency rather than let the British lose.[4] Experimental studies have
been done on facets of this phenomenon.[5] One finding is that the effect of majority opinion will vary with the degree of value one places
on his membership in the group. Another is that the influence of
majority opinion is strongest when the majority is large. Of course,
those who have a streak of nonconformity in their personalities are
less influenced by disclosures of majority views. Some will, in fact,
take the opposite side after they hear what the majority thinks.

Already cogent arguments can be psychologically supported by

[4] "When Shall America Fight?" *Vital Speeches*, VII (1940–41), 518.
[5] C. I. Hovland, I. L. Janis, and H. H. Kelley, *Communication and Persuasion*
(New Haven: Yale University Press, 1953), Chap. 5.

citing corroborating opinions from respected persons, as we noted in the discussion of ethos. In relation to evidence, we would speak of this as the addition of audience acceptability to logical adequacy. The effect of this added material is similar to that of the disclosure of favorable majority opinion as explained above. For example, after developing a logical case for his side of a proposition, a debater may quote a supporting opinion from a high-prestige source such as a popular President or a beloved benefactor of humanity. Beginners sometimes express it awkwardly: "We have proved that foreign aid must be continued, and President Eisenhower agrees with us."

An advocate will often bolster his own ethos, credibility, or image before he introduces a cogent but unpopular argument. Minnick explains five methods of doing this: common-ground, yes-yes, yes-but, oblique, and implicative.[6] It is believed that an audience will react less unfavorably to an unpopular proposition if the introductory remarks serve to build up the advocate's acceptability. Certainly one of the striking instances of this occurred in the opening of Henry Ward Beecher's Liverpool Address: he reaffirmed the sincerity of his views; he explained that his opponents wished to silence him because their own case was weak; he said it mattered little to himself personally if he were not allowed to speak; he expressed courage and integrity ("You will not find a man—you will not find me to be a man who dared to speak about Great Britain 3,000 miles off, and then is afraid to speak to Great Britain when he stands on her shores"); he closed his introduction with a request for fair play, for which Englishmen were renowned.

A fifth incidental use of motivational material occurs when one inserts into an otherwise rational argument some words which he has chosen for their biasing effect. Words such as left-winger, fellow traveler, nigger lover, radical, agitator, reactionary, and alien are all-too-familiar examples.

Or one might argue that the acceptance of a logically adequate argument happens also to be in the best interests of the listeners or readers. Identification of their desires and values with the acceptance of the proposition is the persuasive device which is involved here. For instance, after developing a logical argument against the prior censorship of motion pictures, Jerry Wald closed with the assertion that only

---

[6] W. C. Minnick, The Art of Persuasion (Boston: Houghton Mifflin Company, 1957), pp. 126–131.

by preserving the freedoms of the First Amendment can we preserve our nation and our way of life.[7]

Finally, one can arrange his case in an order that is easier to follow and to accept. More will be said of this in the next chapter on the organization of cases. For the present, though, we might consider the possibility of using in actual presentation an outline which is more interesting and perhaps more persuasive than the formal, logical, "because-because-because" outline.

Methods of Motivation

Suggestion is a method by means of which a persuader tries to establish an idea more or less indirectly in another person's mind. While seemingly presenting one idea in the center of attention, the communicator subtly hints at another idea which may be perceived uncritically in the fringes of attention. This marginally perceived stimulus is intended to release habitual responses which require no intellectual effort. In this way Daniel Webster, as prosecutor in the Knapp-White murder trial, used what purported to be a narrative statement of the facts to dramatize the cunning and viciousness of the conspirators as contrasted with the innocence and helplessness of their sleeping victim. Webster not only narrated the facts; he made the jury want to exact the supreme penalty even before he called for it.

Several factors influence the efficacy of suggestion. One is, as we have seen, the prestige of the source. This being true, a speaker should either quote recognized authorities or establish his own ethos on the subject. A second factor is the speaker's ability to make his listeners see and feel the idea. Vividness of imagery and forcefulness of presentation are essential devices. Thirdly, a positive approach combined with an implied reward for agreement is often persuasive. This may be accomplished by calling for the acceptance of the desired idea rather than the rejection of its opposite, and the act of acceptance should be associated with a pleasant outcome. Polarization or unification of the audience is a fourth factor. Undivided attention to a speaker plus a unified response to his remarks may be achieved by means of (a) compact seating, (b) unison activities such as applauding, singing, and

[7] "Movie Censorship—The First Wedge," *Saturday Review*, April 8, 1961, p. 54.

raising hands, (c) the use of respected symbols such as banners, flags, pictures of respected persons, uniforms, and objects related to worship, (d) comfortable surroundings, and (e) the placing of the speaker in a dominant position on a raised platform. Repetition is a fifth factor in suggestion, but only if the style of composition produces a cumulative effect. Unskilled repetition is obvious, dull, and negatively suggestive. Sixth among the factors of suggestion is indirectness of approach. Through this approach a persuader may, by implication, induce his listeners to think the suggested idea was theirs. Finally, the avoidance of any suggestion of a rival idea is thought to be a significant principle in persuasion. For this reason we are advised not to repeat a rumor, even for the purpose of denying it.

Rationalization is a second method of motivation. This process of associating the persuadees' desires with the persuader's idea involves the use of an emotionally aroused conclusion which is made plausible on pseudological grounds. People prefer to believe that they are acting logically, even when they are influenced by emotional appeals. For instance, they often do what they desire to do, and then they invent plausible reasons for their impulsive behavior. Knowing this, some speakers and writers use emotional appeals coupled with pseudological "reasons" such as "Business is business," "You're young only once," or "If I don't get it, someone else will."

It is not suggested that students adopt the ethics of demagogues; they ought to feel more social responsibility than "rabble-rousers" do. But there are times when an audience, having been motivated by emotional appeals to accept an ethically sound proposition, still wants a seemingly rational justification for the action. Since some decisions are influenced more by desire than by evidence, an advocate can satisfy his audience and justify his own position by determining the motives in his public, associating those motives with his proposal, and finally presenting his logical support.

As listeners and readers, we need to understand the method of motivation by rationalization, even though we intend never to use it. Critical thinking is an important skill which involves the recognition of these characteristics of rationalization: it focuses attention on materials that merely *seem* relevant; its apparently clear ideas are actually vague; it disguises suggestion as deliberation; it treats plausible reasons as real ones; it masks subjective ideas as objective ones; it seemingly invites scrutiny while circumventing it; it capitalizes upon fallacies and strategems which thwart critical thinking.

Open statement or direct suggestion associates desires or values with a proposition by means of an open, frank statement or a demonstration of the connection. Instead of being subtle or devious, the persuader directly establishes the desired connection; he may explain how the acceptance of his ideas will result in certain satisfactions, he may demonstrate or give a sample, or he may do both. This method utilizes that principle of learning which holds that the proffered motive should be logically relevant to the desired goal.

Speech techniques are not exactly coordinate with the three preceding methods of motivation, but they are sufficiently related to warrant treatment here. Speakers may use motivation positively or negatively, and it may be speaker-centered or audience-centered. A positive approach facilitates the desired response, while a negative approach inhibits some undesirable response. A speaker-centered (subjective) approach urges others to follow the speaker's appraisal of the listeners' needs, but a listener-centered (objective) approach is based upon the listeners' conceptions of their own needs. For instance, a speaker using the objective, positive approach would facilitate the desired response by encouraging the listeners to analyze their own needs or interests, by helping them to analyze their needs as an aid in designing solutions, or by associating their "need" stimuli with those leading to the speaker's desired response instead of pressing the audience to fit the speaker's notion of their needs.

Effective persuaders draw attention to some value and show how it can be realized or how it is threatened. Often the appeal is to the common values of patriotism, local loyalties, truth, sportsmanship, and the like. These values are brought vividly into play by suggestion, rationalization, or open statement; the claim is made that these values are in jeopardy; and the audience is moved to block the threat. Some of the popular, vivid narratives for this purpose are those involving the exploitation of the "underdog" and other unjust acts. When the speaker thinks that the listeners at least temporarily favor his proposal as a remedy, he seeks to convert this impulse into a quick, overt action as in a vote, a show of hands, or the signing of a document. Such an overt expression of enthusiasm serves to prolong it and may lead to a more lasting expression.

QUESTIONS

1. Why are explanation, ethos, and motivation treated as ancilary forms of support? In what circumstances should they not be so classified?
2. Explain the differences between explanation as incidental material and as a persuasive method.
3. What is ethos? How important may it be in various situations?
4. Under what circumstances is it ethical to persuade others with motivation?
5. What are the functions of motivational support as ancilary material?
6. What does published research tell us about the effectiveness of ethos? Of motivation?

EXERCISES

1. Identify the motive appeals in selected advertisements.
2. Cite and evaluate some instances of explanation as incidental material in the Appendixes.
3. Point out some ethos-building clues in assigned items from Appendixes.
4. Look for examples of some of the seven incidental uses of motivational material in the discourses which are reprinted in the Appendixes.
5. Locate and evaluate some specimens (in Appendixes or elsewhere) which illustrate some of the methods of motivation.
6. Outline and deliver a short speech of advocacy in which the three ancilary forms of support are used in addition to the logical argument. Label them parenthetically in the outline.
7. Write an argumentative essay in which logical argument is supplemented by the three ancilary forms of support. Use marginal notes or footnotes to identify these three materials.

CHAPTER IX

CASE CONSTRUCTION

IN ARGUMENTATION, A CASE MAY BE DEFINED AS THE TOTAL REPRESENTA-
tion which one side makes on behalf of its stand on a proposition. A
total representation includes the evidence, reasoning, assumptions,
narration, exposition, description, motivation, and strategy upon which
one side elects to base its cause and upon which it will win or lose. The
"one side" which is referred to means either affirmative or negative,
and it may consist of one person, an organization, or a school debate
team.

When a case is expressed in full, it appears as a complete speech
or essay, or as a series of speeches or essays. An abridged case appears
as a case outline or a précis. Ideally, as has been shown in Chapter II,
a case should be the best statement that a side can make in relation
to its logical and ethical responsibilities. This implies that a case may
be adapted to the opposition, the audience, and the occasion so long as
the substance of the proof remains consistent with the evidence, a
reasonable interpretation of that evidence, and the social responsibility
of the advocate.

THE CONCEPT OF A PRIMA FACIE CASE

In Relation to Issues

A prima facie case is one which, on first view or on its face, is adequate
to prove its side until it is refuted. Such a case has probative force for

[163]

the reason that it is logically sufficient to establish a reasonably high degree of probability in its favor. An affirmative case is said to be logically adequate if it has evidence and reasoning to affirm all potential issues, as explained in Chapter IV, except those which the negative waived or admitted before the affirmative submitted its case. In practice, any affirmative must, except in the few special situations explained below, prepare as if every potential issue were to become actual. The negative, on the other hand, is expected to offer a case which will logically support a negative answer to *at least one* of the issues.

Even though issues are of crucial importance to a prima facie case, this does not mean that stock language such as "Is there a need for a change?" should be used. It is better to express an issue in a question such as this: "Are there important shortcomings in the present system of academic probation?" The principle is that an issue can be stated more meaningfully in terms of the subject matter of the proposition, the kind of proposition, and the type of argumentative situation (philosophical, legislative, etc.).

While constructing a case to affirm or negate the issues, an advocate is concerned with "talking points," otherwise known as points in partition. These are the main, declarative sentences which answer the issues. They appear as Roman-numeral topics in a case outline. Sometimes the issues and the points in partition differ only in that the former are interrogative while the latter are declarative. More often, however, the wording and the arrangement of points in partition differ from those of the issues. There need not be a one-to-one relationship between issues and points in partition. A difference in wording can be seen in these specimens: (issue) "Will compulsory arbitration prove to be an effective solution?"; (point) "Compulsory arbitration won't work."

When we think of argumentation as a critical apparatus, it is important to note that the requirements for a prima facie case serve to test an advocate's analysis as well as the completeness and the consistency of his case. Critical thinkers demand to know whether an advocate is developing all the essential ideas and doing so in a consistent fashion. In nonlegal situations "prima facie" need not apply to specific items of evidence in the same way that it does in court. In general argumentation we say that, if the evidence appears to support its point, it is prima facie. However, we usually apply the modifier "prima facie" to the whole case rather than to any small part such as an item of evidence.

In Relation to Presumption and Burden of Proof

It will be recalled that a correctly worded proposition gives the presumption to the negative and places the burden of proof upon the affirmative. In consequence of this, the affirmative has to make a prima facie case before the negative is under obligation to reply. To put this idea differently, one might say that a presumption favors the negative at the outset of the debate, and this temporary advantage can be overcome only by the presentation of a prima facie affirmative case. After such a case is presented, the negative has an obligation which will be discussed under "burden of rebuttal." A fruitful debate cannot take place unless the affirmative sets out a prima facie case to meet its burden of proof and the negative counters with a prima facie rejoinder.

Two situations, one involving a proposition of legal fact and the other a proposition of policy, will serve to illustrate the relationship between a prima facie case and the burden of proof. The government brought antitrust action against five drug manufacturers, charging criminal conspiracy to fix prices on polio vaccine. In dismissing the case, the judge opined that the government had not met its affirmative burden of proof because a prima facie case had not been made. It was not prima facie because the issue of intent had not been affirmed. Some facts had been established, but the inference that the actions were contrived was not proved. In school debates and orations on propositions of policy, many affirmative spokesmen fail to discharge their burden of proof. Their cases are not prima facie because in many instances they either fail to prove the causal connection in their "need" arguments, or they neglect to show how their plans will remedy the ills which they lament. The reader may wish to review Chapter II on this point.

In Relation to the Burden of Rebuttal

In the light of what has been explained thus far, we may conclude that the negative does not have a burden of rebuttal or any obligation to go forward with the debate until the affirmative makes a prima facie case. In other words, the affirmative proofs must justify the acceptance of the proposition on rational grounds before the negative has any obligation to reply. When the affirmative does complete a prima facie case, the burden of rebuttal falls on the negative. Then, if the negative makes an adequate rejoinder, the burden of rebuttal is shifted to the affirmative side. Thus it is that the burden of rebuttal, but not the burden of proof, may shift back and forth. In short, the presentation of a prima facie case by one side shifts the burden of rebuttal to the opponent. Thus if an affirmative spokesman who urges the cessation of financial aid to Slobovia shows that the money is not needed and that it is actually being used to aid the enemies of the donor, the defenders of aid for Slobovia have the burden of rebuttal. Methods of replying to cases which are prima facie as well as those which are not will be treated under "Attack and Defense."

When a Prima Facie Case Is Not Required

If one were to count the cases which are not prima facie, he might conclude that there are many situations in which a logically sound case is not required. He would probably be right if his criterion were audience acceptability in the context of popular persuasion. We know that many listeners and readers are gullible; countless unwarranted claims are accepted as if they were proved. But students of argumentation presumably hold higher standards. For them there should be fewer situations in which cases that are not prima facie are tolerable.

Three kinds of circumstances in which logically incomplete cases *might* be acceptable come to mind: when a time limit requires some abridgement of the content, when an audience is interested in fewer than all of the potential issues, and when the disputants waive some of the issues. The word "might" is intended to caution the lazy and the unprincipled advocates against the temptation to offer a shoddy case merely because some listeners or readers let it go unchallenged. The time element is familiar to classroom, radio, and television speakers. If a student has four minutes for an argumentative talk on the United Nations, he cannot do justice to all issues; he will be well advised to limit his scope to "Five Defects in the U.N.," for example. When school debaters have twenty-eight minutes of air time, they often agree in advance to limit the discussion to one issue such as "need." Limitations imposed by audience interest can be illustrated with the controversy over "Pay-TV." If the public is interested primarily in the comparative quality of programs under the subscription plan as compared with the commercial system, we should expect the rival advocates to speak to that issue almost exclusively. Finally, if the disputants are interested in only one issue, they are likely to waive all others. When many lawyers debated the proposed judicial amendment to the Illinois constitution in 1958, the popular issue concerned benefits versus disadvantages.

Frequently we receive incomplete cases when only one side is represented. Advocates tend to argue less cogently when they think it is safe to do so. Obviously the presence of a competent opponent motivates an advocate to make a case as best he can. Cases which are less than prima facie are frequently offered by campaigners, salesmen, propagandists, and writers of letters to editors, to list but a few of the sources. Those who would excuse this practice on the ground that the absence of opposition makes a prima facie case superfluous are giving an explanation but not a good excuse. Regardless of the presence or the absence of an opponent, an advocate has the ethical and the logical responsibilities which were expounded in Chapter II. Defective proof as we often perceive it in popular persuasion is successful when critical thinking is wanting in the audience. That is why this book stresses rationality in preference to popular belief as the major test of proof.

In this sense, a prima facie case is the *only* kind of case that can prove a proposition. In actual practice, particularly in school debates and in argumentative conversations, we deviate from the rule that the affirmative must complete a prima facie case before the negative has any burden of rebuttal. Typically the give-and-take of conversation is informal, and attack and defense occur on each fragment of a case as soon as it is stated. In school debate the time limits, the order of speeches, and the division of labor between teammates result in the first affirmative speaker's giving little more than half of the case before the negative has an opportunity to attack it. Following the first negative speech, the second affirmative speaker has an opportunity to finish the affirmative constructive case.

STEPS IN DEVELOPING A CASE

General Hints

At this stage in his preparation an advocate knows what his proposition is and presumably understands his responsibilities for it, he has analyzed and investigated it, he has assembled his evidence, he has reasoned about his evidence and the ancilary forms of support, and he is ready to build his case. If he has taken the steps listed above, he is now at the stage called "partitioning a case" in Chapter IV.

When a spokesman proceeds to build this "total representation of a position," as it was called at the beginning of this chapter, he will, it is hoped, be mindful of his logical and his ethical responsibilities to offer the strongest case which the available materials warrant. In other words, cogency is the first, ideal goal, while persuasiveness in a popular sense may have to be the second, practical goal.

In the process of achieving either or both of these goals, several time-tested hints will be found helpful: 1. Determine the philosophical assumptions upon which the case must stand, such as laissez-faire economics or the notion that human rights should always take precedence over property rights; 2. Select points that are necessary for a prima facie case, which means that they are *worth* proving; 3. Consider whether these points *can* be proved; 4. Use as few points as will fulfill your responsibilities; 5. Adapt to the demands of popular persuasion, if necessary, but without sacrificing sense or integrity; 6. Organize the *preparation* (case) outline rigorously; 7. Compose the final presentation attractively.

For Nonpolicy Propositions

This class of propositions is so constituted because the subtypes share a common analytical process, as has been shown. The crucial questions have to do with definition and classification or criteria and application. Following the pattern of Chapter IV on analysis, this section on nonpolicy propositions will begin with the first subgroup consisting of the propositions of legal fact, of past fact, of present fact, and of prediction.

Since all four varieties of propositions of fact have in common two analytical steps, as explained in Chapter IV, it is feasible to illustrate the process of case construction with one real-life specimen. To locate the proposition in the following letter requires, first, a determination of the status quo at that time. The prevailing situation was that the Chicago Transit Authority had banned the sale of certain publications in newsstands located at CTA stations, and it had done so on the ground that it had the "right to say what can be sold on CTA properties." The letter writer, being the dissatisfied party who challenged the status quo, has the burden of proof for his proposition of legal fact: "The position taken by the CTA is unwarranted and illegal." Actually, in the light of the case which follows, the word "unwarranted" should be deleted in the interest of limiting the proposition to a single idea.

Two issues are raised: Is the CTA a public, governmental agency? Has it failed to comply with the law concerning such bodies? In affirming the first issue, the writer first refutes the assumption that the CTA is a simple, private business which would have the right to control sales on its property. Then he argues that the CTA is a municipal governmental corporation created by state statute, and as a public agency it must respect certain constitutional guarantees. To affirm his second issue, the writer shows that the CTA resorted to an arbitrary, administrative fiat instead of seeking the enactment of an ordinance which would be subject to judicial scrutiny. Two lesser points were that the fiat contained no definition of "objectionable" literature, and it was enforced by threats to cancel leases to vendors. This case for a proposition of legal fact is much shorter than a lawyer would submit in court; it does not document evidence or cite statutes.[1]

Virgil E. Gunlock, chairman of the Chicago Transit Authority, in seeking to justify the CTA's ban on the sale of certain publications because of alleged lewdness and obscenity, has stated: "This is not censorship, but rather the exercise of our right to say what can be sold on CTA properties."

It would appear from Mr. Gunlock's statement that the CTA regards itself as a simple private business (which has indeed the right to control what may be sold on its property). The position taken by the CTA is unwarranted and illegal.

The CTA is a municipal governmental corporation created by state statute, and as such it is a public agency with the obligation to respect the guarantees of freedom of speech and press and due process of law contained in the Constitution of the United States.

The CTA has appointed itself as a public censor of the reading matter available to the public and has done so in the most arbitrary and capricious fashion—by administrative fiat—without the use of a standard or definition of what is objectionable material.

The issue here is not the literary value of a few unpleasant publications but rather the far more important issue of public governmental bodies abandoning their constitutional responsibilities and failing to act pursuant to statutory authority.

The CTA is granted by statute the right to pass ordinances regulating

[1] "Letters to the Editor," *Chicago Daily News*, April 13, 1960.

the use and operation of its property. By its refusal to adopt a valid ordinance the CTA has evidently sought to by-pass judicial scrutiny of the constitutionality of its actions.

The CTA's current policy is effectuated by the circulation of lists of banned publications and the utilization of the threat of cancellation of newsstand leases of dealers who do not comply with the CTA directives. These methods now being used by the CTA are clearly unconstitutional.

John L. McKnight.
Executive director,
Illinois Division, American
Civil Liberties Union.
Chicago.

The second subgroup of nonpolicy propositions consists of propositions of value. These are often used in the philosophical kind of debates. In this application of argumentation we encounter a greater risk of ambiguity because there are fewer standard definitions of terms and common interpretations of concepts such as "desirable," "out of place," "detrimental," "better than," "wrong in principle," etc. As we saw in Chapter IV, the basic and frequently implicit human values which underlie these disputes cannot be proved in the objective way that facts can be demonstrated. It often happens that the dispute turns on what the evaluative term means or should be taken to mean.

Let us take from Chapter IV the proposition that big-time football is out of place on a university campus. Assuming that an affirmative advocate were to start building his case by asking the three pairs of criteria-and-application questions, he could proceed in either of two ways: he could so define his proposition that the validity of the three criteria would be assumed, and then his constructive case would argue the application of those criteria to football; or he could argue in defense of both the criteria and their application. Taking the first option, the affirmative would include in his introduction a statement of this sort: "Before we can show that big-time football is out of place on a university campus, we must explain what 'out of place' means. In the light of what many prominent educators have said a university should be (quoting or paraphrasing some), we conclude that any activity is out of place if it is not academically relevant, if it becomes an end in itself, and if it exploits its participants. We shall proceed to show that big-time football is academically irrelevant, it has become an end in itself, and it exploits its participants." If the affirmative thought the criteria would be sharply contested, he probably would build a case in defense of them instead of briefly defining them and assuming their acceptability.

Taking the negative side for a moment, we can see that several positions are possible: challenge some of the criteria, show that other criteria have been overlooked, defend football against the unfavorable application of the affirmative's criteria, and show how football measures up favorably in terms of a revised set of criteria. Obviously two or more of these strategic options could be combined into one case.

For Propositions of Policy

In the next main section, "Types of Cases," there will be found more specific suggestions on the building of affirmative and negative cases. At this particular time we shall consider in general terms the relationship between analysis and case construction. Referring back to "Analysis Illustrated" in Chapter IV, we see an arrangement of issues and subissues for a proposition which calls for a change from the quarterly calendar to the semester plan at some college. If the affirmative side chose to affirm all of those potential issues and subissues, the preliminary sketch of the body of its case would look something like this:

  I. A quarterly calendar has serious defects, for
     A. Shorter courses sacrifice some comprehensiveness in the students' grasp of the subjects, and
     B. Shorter courses allow too little time for independent study between meetings, and
     C. Short terms aggravate the problems of academic adjustment, and
     D. The frequent starts and stops break the continuity of learning.
 II. A change to the semester plan would remedy these defects, for
     A. Longer courses would provide more comprehensive treatment of each subject, and
     B. It would allow for more independent work, and
     C. It would provide more time for academic adjustment, and
     D. It would provide more continuity of study.
III. The semester plan would be the best solution, for
     A. It would suit our purposes better than a trimester plan, and
     B. It would be better than some other scheme, and
     C. It could be adopted without serious inconvenience.

Three cautions need to be expressed concerning the tentative case plan sketched above: supporting materials must be supplied under the Roman-letter points; the affirmative might not elect to build such a traditional case; the arguments under point III might be modified in response to the type of case the negative uses.

Applications to School Debate

Since almost all school debates are based upon propositions of policy, the following sketch of case development for school debate will be limited to that kind. Preceding chapters have treated the processes which a debater needs to work on before he constructs a case: analysis, investigation, the testing of evidence, reasoning about the evidence, and perhaps some lesser processes. Consequently, this brief exposition will deal only with the typical duties of each speaker in a traditional-style school debate. Other kinds of affirmative and negative cases will be described in the next section of this chapter.

The first affirmative constructive speaker usually has ten minutes for his part of the case. Since there is no preceding speech, he does not have to adapt or refute. His speech can and should be well prepared without being "canned" (memorized). In approximately a minute and a half of introduction, the first speaker includes opening pleasantries, tries to arouse interest in the proposition, states the proposition, defines terms and the proposition as a whole, and sketches the affirmative approach. If the goal or the basic philosophy of the case were to be given as an assumption rather than an argument, it would be stated in the introduction. For instance, if the proposition called for a system of government scholarships to encourage young people to attend college, this assumption or goal might be stated in the introduction: "We want every youth in the United States to have the best education which his aptitude will permit." If the negative attacks the assumption, the next affirmative speaker will have to defend it. When the affirmative doubts that the negative will accept the assumption, the idea is incorporated into the body of the case as a part of the first point. After the goal is handled one way or the other, the traditional "need" argument is advanced by means of points, subpoints, and evidence: "Our present methods of financing higher education leave many young persons educated below their potential level of achievement." This speaker should make two points: that there are many who could have gone higher in school, and that one important reason for their failure to do so was financial.

Some teachers of school debating say that the first affirmative constructive speech may end here. Others would include the plan, and there are some who instruct the first speaker to give the prima facie case *in toto*. In this last situation, the second affirmative "constructive" speech becomes a rebuttal, and the series of eight speeches sometimes degenerates into one constructive speech and seven rebuttals. This "cannot but make the judicious grieve," as Hamlet said of another excess. However, if the plan is stated amply in the proposition, the first speaker may have time to go on with the point that the proposal would remedy the alleged ills. A debate on the abolition of capital punishment would be a case in point. Regardless of how far this speech goes into the case, it should close with a brief recapitulation and a forecast of the colleague's line of argument.

Appearing in second position is the first negative constructive speaker. He and the following two constructive speakers have the same time limit as the opening speaker. His introduction is usually shorter than the first affirmative's. It includes opening pleasantries and a response to the affirmative definitions and assumptions. Depending upon the kind of case the negative has chosen to use (see next section), this speech will take one of four actions with respect to the first affirmative speech: refute the cause for action and perhaps raise general objections to the affirmative plan, minimize the need for action and show how the present situation can be improved, defend the present situation, or admit the cause for action and offer a counterproposition. Close adaptation to the affirmative line of argument is required in any case. Finally, some first negatives pose a few questions for the second affirmative before closing with a recapitulation of the negative position and an estimate of the damage done to the affirmative case.

Third in the order of appearance is the second affirmative constructive speaker. He would do well to begin by countering the effect of the closing remarks of the preceding speaker. Sometimes this is called "taking one hot off the bat." Next he should rebuild the parts of the affirmative case which have been attacked (see Attack and Defense), stressing the language of the affirmative. Then he might show how some negative points do not pertain to the affirmative case, or how some affirmative points were missed by the negative. Before answering any questions posed by the first negative, he should request that their significance be shown, thereby nullifying any negative advantage from a time-wasting tactic. Next, if this has not been covered by his colleague, he will explain the plan and show how it will meet the needs expressed in the first speech. His last main point would very likely deal with the additional advantages of the affirmative plan or the contention that the plan is the best remedy. This speaker faces the danger of appearing to be on the defensive or of seeming to debate on the negative's terms instead of his own. In his closing recapitulation he should try to show that the affirmative case has thus far withstood assault.

The fourth and last constructive speech in the traditional format of school debating is that of the second negative. It comes immediately before the first negative rebuttal speech, and for this reason some coordination between them is essential. If the negative expects to get ahead, this is the time to do so. These two speakers have fifteen minutes in which to block the affirmative case. The duties of the second negative will vary in terms of the kind of case or approach that is used. If refutation were the negative approach, this speaker would attack the workability of the plan and perhaps argue that it would worsen the situation it was supposed to improve. If the negative chose to repair the status quo, this speaker might contrast the improved situation with the affirmative's plan, showing the former to be more efficacious, less expensive, etc. In case the negative were to defend the present situation, this speaker might either ignore the affirmative plan or contrast it with the present situation. Finally, if the negative were to offer a counterproposition, preferably in their first speech, the second negative would contrast the rival plans in order to show that the affirmative did not have the better solution. This would block the affirmative case.

TYPES OF CASES

In the immediately preceding section we have considered the traditional kinds of cases in terms of their general construction for use in school debates. Here we shall survey the varieties of affirmative cases and examine in greater detail the kinds of negative cases.

Affirmative Cases

A few general principles are basic to all kinds of affirmative cases. As has been explained, an affirmative case must affirm all issues if it is to be prima facie. In addition, it will be more difficult to defeat if it is based upon a sound interpretation of the proposition and is set forth in a clear and simple structure. In this connection it is wise to assume no more burden of proof than the proposition calls for and to limit the number of points and subpoints to be supported.

Under "school debate" the traditional type of affirmative case on a proposition of policy was sketched. Topics of need for a change, plan, and advantages were briefly illustrated. However, it is well to note that in some propositions of policy there is no necessity to explain a plan; the statement of the resolution says all that we need to know about the proposed action. A proposition calling for the diplomatic recognition of Red China would be a case in point. Simple definition would be sufficient. Perhaps for this reason the affirmative would prefer to offer a "principles" case as explained below.

A "principles" case can be made for a proposition of value as well as for one of policy. In effect, this approach minimizes the difference between these kinds of propositions; there is no "plan case" for the implementation of the policy. This is the customary sense of the term, "principles case." Four obvious applications of this approach come to mind: states' rights vs. federal authority in school desegregation cases, debates on lowering the voting age to 18, the moral issue in universal military training, and voluntarism vs. compulsion in medical care plans. One possible advantage in using this type of case is the reduced importance of card quoting and the encouragement of fundamental, philosophical debating. At the outset of the debate, any affirmative that intends to use the "principles" case on a proposition of policy ought to: 1. Make sure that it is suited to the situation; 2. Announce its intention; 3. State the principle or principles; 4. Define it or them; 5. Call upon the negative to respond to it or them.

Another deviation from the traditional affirmative case for a proposition of policy is the "comparative advantages" case. In the first part of the case the cause-for-action point may be played down, developed indirectly, or developed as fully as in the traditional case. In any event the general idea of this approach is the comparison of the status quo with the affirmative plan on the basis of results for the purpose of predicting improvements. This comparative testing is intended to arrive at greater probability of desirability on the side of the proposed change. The standard of desirability is, of course, the goal which the affirmative should announce early in the proceedings. That goal might be greater justice, efficiency, economy, or some other ideal. For instance, if an affirmative advocate were to urge the change from a quarterly calendar to a trimester plan, he could employ this kind of case to advantage. Topics of "need," "plan," and "advantages" could be covered either directly or indirectly in this kind of structure:

I. A longer period for the study of a subject would be provided, for
   A. A quarter is only 10 weeks, and
   B. A trimester would be 15 weeks.
II. There would be less frequent interruptions, for
   A. There are finals and registrations every three months or less under the quarter plan, and
   B. These breaks would be spaced much farther apart in trimesters.

There would be more points and evidence than this sketchy illustration contains, but the principle is that the goals are stated in the main points while the subpoints compare the two plans in terms of their achievement of those goals. In an editorial which urged the United States government to "tie strings on its aid to India," the writer made the point that American aid should be provided in ways that contribute to economic betterment rather than to economic retardation. His subpoints charged that unrestricted aid hurt the Indian economy, while a requirement that the recipient "put his economic and financial house in order" would make a real contribution to economic growth.

For nonpolicy propositions which involve criteria and application or definition and classification, the affirmative does not always establish the standards before applying them. Sometimes the criteria or definitions are assumed to be valid, and the advocate proceeds at once to their application. For instance, a literary critic wrote on the proposition that the elements that make up the traditional novel are worn out. He discussed the demise of character and story without first establishing that these are the essential elements of the traditional novel, but his *Saturday Review* audience probably did not need the first point that he omitted. Similarly some political campaigners made an historical evaluation of the New Deal, alleging that it was bad for the country for seven reasons: it centralized power in the executive; it encroached upon states' rights; it developed a bureaucracy; it subverted the Constitution; it redistributed wealth; it leaned toward socialism; it retarded recovery. These affirmatives assumed that each of the above actions or characteristics was bad, and their case dealt only with showing that the New Deal did those acts.

Negative Cases

Any choice which a negative spokesman makes among the possible cases is judged by its ability to raise at least one vital objection to the acceptance of the affirmative's proposition. Such a case might contain many points, or it might have only one: "It won't work," or "No change is needed," for example. Five strategic options which pertain mostly to propositions of policy will now be explained.

Pure refutation or denial involves attacking evidence and/or reasoning offered by the affirmative, and it may be used on one or more of the main arguments. The minimum requirement is the blocking of the affirmative on one issue. This strategy is risky when the affirmative is strong, because the confrontation takes place on the affirmative's chosen ground. Furthermore, when an audience is present, the negative suffers a psychological disadvantage if it does not stand *for* something. It seems merely to bedevil the affirmative. Two tactical points in its favor, though, are its adaptability to all kinds of affirmative cases and propositions and its ease of preparation. No set case is ever prepared; one readies several denials and selects appropriate items to suit the affirmative case as it develops. Although this is a theoretically legitimate negative approach, it is in general the least desirable choice. It gains in strength when it is combined with one of the other options. The president of an ethical pharmaceutical company used pure refutation against the "plan" case of the affirmative on the Kefauver-Celler bill in 1961: elaborate controls would hamper research; it would not reduce medical costs; it ignores the values of the patent system; it is based upon distorted facts.

Defense of the present situation, at least in principle, is a strong position if the status quo is defensible. This prepared case plus the refutation of the need-for-a-change point is theoretically sufficient to win for the negative. It has the advantages of a prepared position and of standing *for* something. Most propositions of policy and some of value offer opportunities for the use of this kind of negative case. "No serious problem exists" is the essence of this conservative position on a proposed change. In response to a demand for a change from school segregation to racial integration, the negative might say there is nothing seriously wrong with the present situation.

Adjustment or repair of the present situation is seemingly the most popular negative case on propositions of policy. Arguing that the status quo is basically sound, the negative minimizes the affirmative "need" argument with refutation and then explains how the present situation can be improved without going to the drastic extremes which the affirmative proposes. With this case the negative does not have to risk appearing ridiculous while denying any and all difficulties even though some are glaringly apparent. When an opponent of the administration's medical insurance plan (in 1960) based upon Social Security proposed an alternative in the form of Title VI of the Mills Bill (H.R. 12580, 86th Congress), which provided "a locally administered health aid program designed to help those who need help," this was not a counterproposition; the essential features of the status quo remained inviolate.

Counterproposition or counterplan is that kind of negative case which concedes the essence of the cause-for-action issue but offers a rival solution in an attempt to defeat the affirmative plan. Plan A *vs.* Plan N is what the clash boils down to, and each side has the responsibility to prove its own case. The theory is that, if the negative makes its plan seem desirable enough to cast doubt upon the wisdom of adopting the affirmative plan, the negative should win insofar as the *logic* of the situation is concerned. But this does not mean that in a legislative situation the negative plan should be adopted forthwith. A motion to adopt the counterproposition would first have to be debated. When we say that the counterproposition needs only to cast doubt upon the wisdom of adopting the afirmative plan, the implication is that the negative plan appears to be as good as the affirmative plan. Thus the negative plan need not be shown to be superior to the affirmative plan; it is the affirmative plan which must be the better if that side is to discharge its burden of proof.

Three cautions are worth noting in connection with the use of this negative case: it should be submitted in the first presentation by the negative; the counterproposition should be stated with utmost clarity; it must be fundamentally inconsistent with the affirmative plan. For instance, if the affirmative calls for a six-nation common market in the Western Hemisphere and the negative counters with a two-nation scheme, the affirmative can easily win by taking over the negative plan as a stage in the development of their own, broader program. Let us suppose that a school debate team speaks in favor of revising the United Nations into a federal world government. If their negative opponents propose the dissolution of all international organizations, this is a counterproposition.

Outside of school debating the situation is sometimes different and sometimes not. In a parliamentary situation the nearest equivalents of a counterproposition are amendments and substitute motions. In either case the debate is on the *new* proposition; the original motion is no more. In 1850 the Northern Abolitionists and Free Soilers favored the Wilmot Proviso, and the Southerners wanted to extend the Missouri Compromise line to include California, but the actual debate was on the Clay Compromise. In a public debate growing out of a hearing conducted by the Congressional Joint Economic Committee in 1958, Senator Paul Douglas proposed a tax cut as the most effective counter-recession program, while Professor John Galbraith argued for public works.[2] In this situation both solutions were before the public at the same time. In another economic debate a Treasury official proposed to hire the Lone Ranger to sell savings stamps to children via television, but the negative countered with a program of fiscal reform to "rescue the dollar."[3]

Combined approaches are, as the name indicates, mixtures of some of the other four. Note in the following case outline[4] a combination of minimized need, adjustment and repairs, and a new-and-greater-evils attack upon the affirmative plan:

I. The need for a new medical-care plan for the aged is exaggerated, for
   A. Most oldsters are healthy, and
   B. Most oldsters are not needy, and
   C. Oldsters are individuals like the rest of us, for
      1. They differ only in the number of birthdays.
   D. Only a minority cannot be properly covered by existing means
II. Title VI of the Mills Bill is the best solution, for
   A. The House approved it, and
   B. The A.M.A. approves it, and
   C. It would help the really needy, and
   D. It would allow the non-needy to maintain their independence, and
   E. It provides local, expert, personal administration, for
      1. Medical care cannot be mass-produced or administered at long range.
III. A compulsory scheme through Social Security threatens serious hazards, for
   A. The quality of medical care will decline from being the world's finest, for

[2] *Chicago Daily News*, March 15, 1958.
[3] *Wall Street Journal*, September 10, 1958.
[4] Based upon A.M.A. advertisement in *Chicago Daily News*, August 16, 1960.

1. Government will tell doctors how to practice, and
2. Government will tell nurses how to nurse, and
3. Government will tell hospitals how to handle the sick.
B. The cost would be staggering, for
   1. It would dent the pay envelopes of workers paying Social Security taxes.
C. Magnificent, private, voluntary plans would be destroyed in time, and
D. It would lead to complete regimentation in the health area, for
   1. This scheme is a beginning, and
   2. Eventually it would cover all ages, and
   3. More services would be added.

OUTLINING CASES

After an individual or a team has decided upon the kind of case to be used and what it will contain, the next step is the outlining of that case. The general purposes of this step are three in number: to aid in the preparation of a case, to aid in the presentation of a case, and to aid in the understanding of a case. A knowledge of correct outlining helps a speaker's preparation in that it guides his placement of material and enables him to see where he needs more or less of it. It goes without saying that a good outline enables an advocate to make a better presentation and that it makes for more efficient listening or reading by his audience.

Divisions of a Case Outline

There are three broad divisions of this as well as other kinds of outlines—introduction, discussion, and conclusion. The introduction comes first, is generally noncontroversial, and is topically outlined as explained below. It prepares the audience for the arguments by gaining attention, arousing interest, providing a context, defining terms, stating the issues, partitioning the case, and making a smooth transition to the first argument. Sometimes there is no need for one or more of these functions, but more advocates seem to err in omitting some which would have been helpful.

In the discussion section, which is by far the longest, the advocate outlines the case proper. This is the array of points, subpoints, evidence, explanations, and any other materials in support of the position. The outline is logical and its topics are sentences unless an indirect or an implicative pattern, as described below, is used instead of the traditional format.

The last, relatively short portion of a case outline is called the conclusion, as most readers know. There is no further development of any argument here. Some of the possible purposes of the closing portion of a case are to point up main ideas, make an ethical appeal, call for action, and provide a note of finality.

Principles of Case Outlining

In the process of building the framework of a case, an advocate has occasion to use some sort of arrangement, and the one which has been especially developed for this purpose is called a case outline. It shares some of the characteristics of outlines generally, but it has some special adaptations which are required by its purpose. These adaptations will be explained in terms of eight principles of case outlining.

Simpleness is the principle which requires that each unit in the outline contain only one idea or statement. Note the difference between the "right" and "wrong" specimens below.

(WRONG)
1. Married women should not be allowed to work for pay because their husbands support them and many of them have inheritances; besides, unemployed men and unmarried women need these jobs, and married women let their outside work interfere with their duties at home.

(RIGHT)
1. Married women should not be allowed to work for pay, for
   A. They do not need to earn money, for
      1. Their husbands support them, and
      2. Many of them have inheritances.
   B. Their jobs are needed by others, for
      1. Some men are unemployed, and
      2. Many unmarried women have to support themselves.
   C. Outside work interferes with their home duties.

Coordination means that a series of topics has a generic relationship, which means that the points have one or more important elements in common. The inclusion of a foreign or an unrelated idea in the otherwise homogeneous list is a violation of this principle. More will be said of coordination under the principle of symbolization. Observe the error in subpoint "C."

    I. Chronic illnesses make great financial burdens, for
        A. This kind costs more, and
        B. The costs continue longer, and
        C. Untreated contagious diseases are a threat to public health.

Subordination has to do with the relationship of inferior points to their superiors. Whenever we express the simplest unit of argument, as in "This is true because that," the "this" becomes the superior point, while the "that" becomes the inferior point. The inferior supports its superior, and this relationship is indicated by symbols and indentation.

    I. There is a need for civil service reform, for
        A. Abuses exist in the present method of appointing officials, for
           1. (Evidence here)

Discreteness requires each topic or point in an outline to be a separate and distinct idea. It is a mistake to allow points to overlap, merge, or otherwise become indistinct or confused. Subpoint "B" violates this principle.

    I. Collective bargaining has failed, for
        A. Management and labor are deadlocked in the railway dispute, and
        B. Some important disputes have not been settled by this procedure.

Sequence is more of a convenience than a requirement. It means the arrangement of coordinate points in some order of progression such as problem-solution, cause-effect, motivated sequence, and the like. Subpoint "C" deviates from the chronological order.

    I. Plans for international political organization have failed in the past, for
        A. This was true of the Cruce plan in 1623, and
        B. It was true of the League of Nations, and
        C. It was true of the Saint-Pierre plan in 1713.

Symbolization, as mentioned above, means that each topic in an outline requires a letter or a numeral which indicates its relative rank in terms of coordination and subordination. Points having similar symbols are expected to be of comparable importance in the hierarchy of speech materials. Common usage recommends Roman numerals for main points, capital letters for the principal subpoints, and Arabic numerals for lesser points, and so on. One symbol per item is the rule, and uniform indentation facilitates reading.

(WRONG)
I. A world government would solve the international peace problem, for
    1. A. It could succeed even if one country opposed it, for
        A. 1. The process of proposing it and the likely adoption of it would show up any recalcitrant as a potential aggressor.

(RIGHT)
I. A world government would solve the international peace problem, for
    A. It could succeed even if one country opposed it, for
        1. The process of proposing it and the likely adoption of it would show up any recalcitrant as a potential aggressor.

Logical relationships among ideas are indicated by the indentations, connectives, symbols, and other devices of case outlining. In logical outlining there is one relationship which is most important: each subpoint must support (assist in proving) the point to which it is immediately subordinated. Connectives *for* and *because* appear between main points and supporting points. Consecutive, coordinate points are connected by *and*. To test the logical adequacy of this type of outline, read it from top to bottom, stressing the connectives. Next, read the points in inverse order, substituting *therefore* for *because* (or *for*), but retaining *and's*. If both readings make sense, the outline is probably sound. Logical relationships apply to refutory as well as constructive arguments. These relationships may be seen in the following segment based upon a speech by Carl Schurz on civil service reform.

    I. There is a need for civil service reform, because
        A. Abuses exist in the present method of appointments to office, and
        B. The spoils system has an adverse effect upon the individual and the body-politic.

Declarative sentences are required by the nature and purpose of logical case outlines. As the preceding specimens and those in Appendix A show, the chains of reasoning in case outlines are intended as confirmatory enthymemes. This being the case, a series of words and phrases as in topical outlines would not serve as well as sentences in building a logically disciplined case outline.

Kinds of Outlines

One could list a dozen or more kinds of outlines if the several bases of definition and classification were considered as a unit. In the study of argumentation, however, there are three principal kinds which are distinguishable on the basis of length, completeness, and complexity. They are the brief, the case outline, and the speaker's notes. Subtypes of the last two will be treated in appropriate places.

A *brief* is the longest, most nearly complete, and certainly the most complex of the three outlines. Years ago when many students were required to draw briefs up to twenty-five or thirty pages in length, they often asked what was "brief" about the document. They received slight comfort from the explanation that the speeches or essays which could be made from the brief would run much longer. Today there appears to be less emphasis upon the brief in nonlegal argumentation; several case outlines can be made in the same time, and they afford a wider experience in the basic processes.

Consequently no complete brief will be presented here, but the principles of briefing will be stated tersely. First is the matter of definition. Some books distinguish among brief, full brief, traditional brief, and flexible brief, but this one does not. The nonlegal brief is here defined as a detailed, logical outline which holds in readiness the usable materials on one side of a proposition. It differs from a case outline, which is another variety of preparatory instrument, in that it contains enough material for more than one case outline. In a sense the brief is a survey of the potential proof for one side.

Most of these general principles of briefing have been explained and illustrated in the preceding section on principles of case outlining: 1. State the proposition at the top; 2. Divide the matter into introduction, discussion, and conclusion; 3. Use sentences in the discussion; 4. Use symbols consistently to show relationships; 5. Indent to indicate coordination and subordination; 6. Limit each point to one ideal; 7. If one point requires two or more lines, indent them the same; 8. Use impersonal language.

Rules governing the introduction of a brief have been partially covered earlier, but they will be expanded upon here. Include only those of the following eight items that may improve interest and understanding: statement of proposition, history of the problem, indications of present timeliness of subject, definitions, statement of excluded or admitted matter, list of issues, partitioning of the case. Use only non-controversial material, and state it in topical outline form.

Rules or principles pertaining to the discussion section have, in part, been mentioned above. They are listed here for emphasis: 1. Each point in partition is a Roman-numeral topic; 2. Each point should be supported with some kind of backing; 3. Logical outlining must be used; 4. Document the evidence and qualify the authorities; 5. Keep coordinate points free of overlapping; 6. Coordinate points should be all-inclusive; 7. Objections to be refuted should be put in where they relate to the case; 8. State clearly any point to be refuted and outline the reply under it ("The charge that this treaty will lead to war is unfounded because . . ."); 9. Any concession in connection with a point should be written in as a subordinate clause ("While it is true that treaties have often been violated, we maintain that this one will be kept.")

The conclusion of a brief is almost always a short summary of the points in partition, followed by a statement of the proposition to be affirmed or negated. There are none of the rhetorical flourishes which have embellished some presentation outlines. It might be as bald as this: "Therefore, since no inherent defect has been found in the present ordinance, and since the proposed ordinance could not be enforced equitably, the negative urges the rejection of Ordinance X."

A *case outline* is shorter than a brief, because it is a preparation outline for a specific occasion. When a case outline is merely an abridgement of a brief, it is bound to be formal, rigorous, and not very interesting to most persons. If a case outline is the only outline a speaker makes, it is at once a preparation and a presentation outline. When this document is intended for public presentation, the considerations of interest and persuasiveness are added to those of completeness and logical rigor. Such concessions to audience psychology are rare in case outlines for school debates, possibly because an audience is equally rare. There is some doubt as to which is the cause and which the effect here. Be that as it may, the case outline which resembles the brief in format may be called the enthymematic or the linear type. It will be demonstrated in Appendix A.

Indirect-order or so-called inductive case outlines have been recommended as having some advantage over the linear variety when used to persuade doubtful or hostile audiences. The hypothesis is that it is more effective to lead up to the conclusion than to begin with it. This is done with a series of examples followed by a proposition, or by an inverted enthymematic structure. Often the format is a mixture of logical and topical outlining. Note that in the partial outline below the inverted enthymematic structure is used. Note also that evidence, which has been omitted, should be used for each subpoint.

"DO WE NEED MORE REGULATION OF UNIONS?"

    (1) Evidence . . . , therefore

    a) There are serious problems in some union trusteeships, and

    b) There are serious problems in the handling of union funds, and

    c) Members can scarcely protest against ineffective or corrupt officials, and

    d) Compulsory membership presents problems, and

    e) Voting rights of union members are allegedly violated, therefore

  1. There are serious problems within unions.

    a) Big unions can affect the national economy, and

    b) Union-management collusion is a serious threat, and

    c) Some union leaders try to influence political matters, and

    d) Secondary boycotting is a menace, therefore

  2. There are serious problems which transcend internal union affairs, therefore

A. Serious problems stem from labor union activities

  1. National union leaders have been implicated in unlawful practices, and

  2. Local leaders in various places have been implicated in misdeeds, therefore

B. The problems related to labor unions are nation-wide in scope.

  1. Increased state regulation cannot end these problems, and

  2. Union self-regulation cannot do any better than it has, and

  3. Moderately increased federal regulation will not remedy the problems, therefore

C. The problems in the internal and external affairs of unions are inherent in the present pattern of federal regulation, therefore

I. There is a need substantially to increase the regulation of labor unions by the federal government.

Implicative arrangements of material are, like the indirect order, intended for situations characterized by doubtful or disbelieving audiences. The merit of a questionable point or proposition is implied by the acceptability of the related points which are offered as a context. In the most familiar adaptation of the implicative outline, a problem is stated and two or more possible solutions are offered. When all but one have been disqualified, the procedure is called the method of residues, because the conclusion confronts the audience with a this-or-nothing disjunction.

"WHICH COURSE IN SOUTH VIET NAM?"
I. There are four possible solutions:
   A. Continue to pour in aid to beat the Communists while keeping hands off the government, or
   B. Sponsor a coup d'etat, or
   C. Make continued military and economic aid contingent upon governmental reform, or
   D. Continue to aid the country while trying by gentle persuasion to effect some reforms in its government.
II. It is folly to pour in aid with no strings attached, for
   A. It would cost us too much, and
   B. We can't defeat the enemy that way.
III. Any scheme to promote a coup d'etat is unwise, for
   A. There are no interested leaders, and
   B. This is out of character for the U.S.A.
IV. Tying aid to governmental reform is too risky, for
   A. It is a bluff, and
   B. When it is called, the U.S.A. will have to back down.
V. Therefore, in the interest of winning the war without compromising our modern tradition, we should continue to aid South Viet Nam while using gentle persuasion on its government.

Attention-problem-solution-appeal patterns of various sorts appear in public speaking textbooks. Probably the most familiar scheme is the "motivated sequence," as Monroe calls it in *Principles and Types of Speech:* 1. Attention, 2. Need (for a solution), 3. Satisfaction (plan), 4. Visualization (dramatizes plan working), and 5. Action (what to do now).

Speaker's notes constitute the shortest and least formal kind of outline. This kind is strictly a guide to presentation. Its function is to remind a speaker of points, quotations, and the like. Words and key phrases are often used in lieu of the sentences which may have appeared in the brief or the case outline. In short, topical outlining is most often used in speaker's notes. Any functional abbreviation of one of the kinds of outlines explained above will serve as speaker's notes. In informal controversy the disputants seldom prepare anything more elaborate than sketchy topics, and often they are not even written.

QUESTIONS

1. Select a case which was made for one side in one of the Appendix items. Is it prima facie? Explain your decision.
2. Choose (or invent) a case which you think is not prima facie. Explain why it is not prima facie and why this defect is or is not acceptable.
3. In discussing the steps in developing a case, why differentiate between policy and nonpolicy propositions? In what important respects do they differ?
4. State some propositions (and situations in which they might be used) as follows: one for which a traditional case would be appropriate, one for a "principles" case, and one for "comparative advantages."
5. Describe a situation in which the negative's best choice would be: (a) a case of pure refutation, (b) defense of status quo, (c) counterproposition, (d) adjustment or repair, (e) combination of approaches.
6. Identify the kinds of affirmative and negative cases used in one or more debates, either in an Appendix or elsewhere.

EXERCISES

1. With either 2 or 4 students on each proposition, resulting in 1 or 2 on each side, a series of cases could be assigned as written work for one week and oral for the next. For oral clashes they could be matched as follows:
    a) Affirmative on proposition of prediction *vs.* pure-refutation negative
    b) Affirmative on proposition of value *vs.* defense of status quo (prevailing evaluation)
    c) Affirmative on proposition of policy *vs.* either adjustment or counterproposition.
2. After drawing up an affirmative or a negative case outline in the traditional pattern, write a second version in which the original is modified into an implicative or an indirect arrangement.
3. Using the appropriate doctrine in this chapter, report on the case which

the Speech Association of America addressed to the Federal Communications Commission (*Quarterly Journal of Speech*, February, 1960, pp. 83–84).

4. Discuss the types and the logical adequacy of the cases in the controversy over debating both sides. See *The Speech Teacher* for January, September, and November, 1957, January, 1958, and September, 1963. This may be an oral and/or written report.

5. The equivalent of Exercise 4 may be based upon a controversy in an Appendix or elsewhere. These two exercises may be extended later to include the tactics of attack and defense as explained in the next chapter.

CHAPTER X

ATTACK AND DEFENSE

INTRODUCTORY CONCEPTS

THREE TOPICS WILL BE TAKEN UP IN THIS CONNECTION: DEFINITIONS OF attack and defense, opportunities for and importance of these activities, and the requisite knowledge and attitudes. Attack is defined as the attempted destruction of opposing proof. Several methods will be explained, but for the moment let us say that attack involves the refutation of premises, evidence, reasoning, or other essential elements for the purpose of preventing an opponent from making good on one or more of the issues. Defense is defined as the attempted rebuilding of any proof which has been attacked. Its purpose is to re-establish a position on one or more issues. Sometimes this process is named rebuttal, but this intended synonym is potentially ambiguous in that it may also mean a second round of speeches in school debates. Attack and defense are explained separately for convenience, but in practice they are interdependent and complementary. Obviously the rebuilding of an argument implies an attack upon the objections which necessitated the defense. To put it differently, we know that one can justify his preference for one case over its rival either because of its own merits or because of the defects in the alternative. Sometimes it is much more effective to integrate these two. This is the essence of genuine debate in anyone's language.

Opportunities and Importance

When opportunities or openings for attack and defense are considered, the detection of faulty analysis and interpretation, flaws in evidence, and fallacious reasoning is implied. Faulty analysis appears as the lack of a prima facie case, the use of vulnerable assumptions, the use of questionable definitions, the giving of undue prominence to a minor point, and other defects in proof which will be explained. Flaws in evidence, fallacies in the structure of argument, and miscellaneous fallacies will also be defined and illustrated in this chapter.

Three typical instances of opportunities for rejoinder will be cited from real-life controversies. The first is a claim based upon poor evidence or, more accurately, a defective warrant. A workman sued his employer for substantial cash damages for a cancer which was allegedly caused by an injury incurred on the job. "I got hurt, and so I got a cancer," he claimed. The plaintiff did not have the support of experts on forensic pathology and medicine because, at that time, they did not believe that a blow could produce cancer. Experimentally, a single trauma had not been able to initiate a malignancy. At most there was merely a possible causal connection in six cases per one hundred thousand. Lack of supporting evidence and the existence of contradictory evidence offered an opportunity for attack. The second illustration involves an affirmative charge, a negative attack, and an affirmative defense. The opening for this affirmative defense was the allegedly partial reply by the negative. For the affirmative side a Democrat argued that the design and the size of the Eisenhower defense plan was inadequate to meet the possible events. Some Republicans answered that our nuclear striking power, mainly in manned bombers, was an effective deterrent because it was the world's strongest. While conceding that the bomber force was the strongest in the world, the affirmative countered with the idea that the negative had failed to consider the fact that a first-strike nuclear attack against us could destroy our bomber force before it could react. Finally, let us look at a possible inconsistency in a case as an opportunity for an attack. When the Republican strategists opened their 1958 campaign to regain control of Congress, "President Eisenhower took the high road" on the politics-in-defense issue, "Sherman Adams took the low road," and Vice President Nixon "trod" the middle road, as the Wall Street Journal reported (Jan. 24, 1958). While the leader seemingly was speaking of national defense as being outside of politics, his assistant was blaming Democrats for a missile lag, Pearl Harbor, and the Korean War. Whatever the tactical considerations may have been, the fact remains that the Republican case, taken as a whole, was vulnerable to the charge of inconsistency.

Most reasons for the importance of the principles of attack and defense are obvious, but some advantages and limitations of these procedures are less well known. One significant but little-known value of training in attack and defense of ideas has come from psychological research on "brainwashing." A shielded mind has been found easiest to change by propaganda, but one that has been exposed to the give-and-take of arguments is much more resistant. The resistant ones first heard arguments against their beliefs, then heard these refuted, and finally were given strong propaganda against their beliefs. William McGuire's experiment at the University of Illinois suggests that many persons hold to their beliefs simply by avoiding exposure to contrary views. However, it should be noted that the techniques of attack and defense are not designed to persuade rival advocates; they are intended to make one case appear the better in the judgment of those who are to decide. When Senators Fulbright and Russell spoke for opposite sides on the nuclear test ban treaty, each one was hoping to influence some undecided opinions, not his opponent. If one were to try to persuade his equal by means of a conversation, a Rogerian approach might be more fruitful: assure your opponent that he has been heard and understood, state the valid elements that you see in his position, and invite him to do likewise for yours.[1]

Attitudes and Knowledge

There is something to be said for the foregoing advice when applied to public situations, too. For instance, if one finds himself in a situation which offers occasions for attack or defense, he will do well to read or listen carefully in order to understand what is said and why. Some tolerance of others' views is an asset; at least it seems advisable to avoid equating difference and error or villainy. The analogy of the stopped clock that is correct twice a day may be instructive. Another suggestion is that the focus of an attack be upon ideas, not persons.

[1] Anatol Rapoport, *Fights, Games, and Debates* (Ann Arbor: University of Michigan Press, 1960.)

Of course a complete separation is too much to expect when there is ego involvement in the arguments, as there often is. However, a clear-cut violation of this ideal is both a personal affront and a fallacy. Finally, the attitudes of honesty, fairness, and courtesy in attack and defense are taken to be inherently related to any ethical conception of advocacy. This implies stating opposing points fairly, making requests or charges courteously, and being truthful.

Knowledge of many kinds and in ample amount is patently useful in preparation for attack and defense. Much of what was said of analysis and investigation (Chapters IV and V) applies here. In addition to those procedures a well planned rebuttal file is useful. It typically contains preconceived tactics and related notes on evidence. A rebuttal card differs from an evidence card or a bibliography card. For ready use in attack and defense, a rebuttal card should state the side that will use it, the opposing point to be met, the relevance of the item to an issue, the replies that are possible through two or more exchanges on the point, and possibly some cross-references to evidence cards. The importance of knowing what both sides can do with each point cannot easily be exaggerated. One-sided preparation is a poor protection against surprise attacks. Finally, in oral controversy, a command of the extemporaneous method is practically essential.

ORGANIZATION

Where to Place Refutation

Any advocatory speech or essay after the opening affirmative presentation, assuming that the one in question is in opposition to the one it follows, has opportunities for attack or defense. The problem at the moment concerns where to place that part. Some adaptations to the requirements of real-life confrontations as well as those of rebuttals in school debates will be suggested. In some circumstances there are conventions or rules which place constructive points, replies, and questions in specific locations.

When is it appropriate to start with refutation? If the other side makes a point which logically requires an answer before the following speaker or writer can safely continue with his own case, the situation clearly calls for refutation at the beginning of the rejoinder. Lodge does this in reply to Boothby when, in Appendix F, he retorts that the United Nations is "not the only point of contact" between the United States and Red China. In school debates on propositions of policy, the second affirmative constructive speaker typically begins with a defense against some attack which the first negative brought against the first affirmative.

When is it wise to follow up refutation with positive proof? "Generally but not always" is the best short answer. The reason is that most often an advocate tries to discredit one item and gain acceptance for its opposite. In this situation refutation is insufficient. Even though pure refutation proves to be sufficient throughout most of a negative speech, for example, it is better to end on a constructive note. The theory is that positive proof deserves the most emphatic place.

This leads to the question, "What are the emphatic positions in a message?" As with constructive proof, the strongest positions are the beginning and the end. Thus, if the answer is important and needs to be made as persuasive as possible, the beginning or the end of the speech would be the place for it. Lesser arguments, which are often shorter, can be placed between the major ones, which tend to run longer.

Finally, is it better to make the reply a separate point or to weave it into one of the constructive points? Its importance to an issue should be the controlling factor. If the reply is moderately important but not closely related to a point in one's own case, it should be made separately and prior to the continuation of the case. If it is moderately important and closely related to a constructive point, the two can be developed together. However, if the reply to an opponent's attack is of such importance that an issue is at stake, there need be no hesitation in making that reply a main point in the case and placing it where it fits best. Whichever choice one makes among these four, he should plan to conclude with a statement of his own position.

Steps in Attack and Defense

Even a sleepy reader (for reasons other than any soporific effect of this book, it is hoped) will notice parallels between the suggested steps in attack and those in defense. The reason is, as has been explained, the close relationship which makes them almost indistinguish-

196 · *Reason in Controversy*

able at times. "A good offense is the best defense" applies to more than football. These are the recommended steps in attack: 1. Select an item *worth* attacking, and show why it is so; 2. State it clearly and fairly; 3. Show how it will be attacked (methods below); 4. Evaluate the result in terms of issues. The affirmative tries to keep the clash on its own case, while the negative tries to lure the affirmative into a discussion of the negative case. In defense of a point these steps are to be taken: 1. Review your point which was attacked; 2. Sketch the essentials of the attack; 3. Show how that attack will be answered; 4. Launch a counter-attack or rebuild the point in the language of your case (methods below); 5. Evaluate the result in terms of issues. In the following condensation of segments from an extended written controversy, we can observe some instances of both good and poor tactics of attack and defense. Our readers are invited to examine the dialogue in its entirety.[2]

While commenting in generally favorable terms upon an English scientist's disarmament proposal, John Fischer remarks that Dr. Blackett's idea is based upon a questionable assumption. It is clear that Fischer is selecting a point which he deems worthy of attacking. Then he states it clearly and fairly, pointing out that Blackett assumes that Russia and the United States are essentially alike in their motivations. Fischer's third step consists in attacking this assumption on the ground that Russia is aggressive while the United States is defensive. The effect of this attack is to show that negotations such as those which take place between men of good will should not be expected to occur when we deal with the Russian government.

Later in this exchange of letters we observe the steps in defense as used by Lord Russell in replying to Mr. Fischer. But before the significance of this defense can be appreciated, it is necessary to trace the give-and-take on the issue in question. In his June *Harper's* article, Dr. Blackett questions the wisdom of the American missile build-up. In the "Easy Chair" essay in the same issue, Editor Fischer replies that the defense must be superior when facing an aggressor that is willing to launch the first blow. Entering the fray with a letter on March 4, Bertrand Russell contends that mankind is in danger of annihilation by an "apparatus of global butchery" which depends upon radar that cannot tell the difference between a missile and a meteorite.

[2] John Fischer, "A 'Scientific' Formula for Disarmament?" *Harper's*, January, 1963, 12–19; also "Bertrand Russell on the Sinful Americans . . . ," *Harper's*, June, 1963, 20–30.

Fischer's letter of March 10 attacks Russell's point by stating that it is factually demonstrable that our nuclear weapons do not rest upon short-warning systems and do not depend upon the kind of radar that Russell describes. The defensive tactic with which we are concerned may be seen in the Russell letter dated March 15. He does not specifically review his own point which has been attacked, but he quotes the language of that attack, thereby reminding us of its essentials. He says he will examine the facts and expose Fischer's ignorance of them. Then he goes about counter-attacking and thereby rebuilding his point about annihilation by radar error. If warning time is not crucial, did President Kennedy lie when he charged that Russian missiles in Cuba reduced the warning time? And why does the United States have the Distant Early Warning radar network and the North American Air Defense Command? These are designed to provide a fifteen-minute response. Experts are quoted indirectly as saying that radar cannot distinguish between natural phenomena and missiles. Further, there have been accidents due to radar failure, he claims. In this connection he alleges that the safeguards are inadequate. Russell does not specifically evaluate the effect of his defense upon the issue at hand.

While the tactics on the previous issue are moderately good, the same cannot be said for the exchange on the question of each other's expertness or ethos. Fischer starts the personal abuse (*ad personam*) with a gratuitous insult to the effect that Bertrand Russell "has been pathetically susceptible nearly all his life to neat but harebrained schemes for reforming everything from education to matrimony to international affairs." Replying in kind in his first letter, Russell refers to "an article by a Mr. J. Fischer" and characterizes it as being unworthy of examination. Nevertheless, he disavows the views which the Fischer article attributed to him. He will explain his views in language sufficiently simple for his opponent to understand, he promises. Fischer's retort is that Russell's reply clearly illustrates the man's incompetence outside his own field. Russell next reminds Fischer that an *ad hominem* argument is illogical, but he goes on to decry his adversary's "invincible ignorance." Finally, Fischer accuses Russell of spreading misinformation. Apparently tiring of this unsophisticated technique of controversy, both men reduce it sharply in the last exchange of letters.

EXPOSING DEFECTS IN PROOF

Why Fallacies Occur

How often does one admit that he has done some crooked thinking? The infrequency of such candid self-criticism might tempt us to define a fallacy as an error in reasoning committed by someone else. If we will avoid self-deception for a moment, we can see in ourselves some tendency to commit fallacies when the conditions are propitious. Perhaps an amateurish psychological explanation of this behavior will help us to cope with it in a constructive way. It is useful to know that rationalizing and straight thinking are similar except for the self-critical characteristic of cogent reasoning. Then comes the question, "How can I make my thinking self-critical?" Intelligence and education as commonly defined are not the complete answer, although stupidity and lack of information do account for much fallacious thinking. Barring the psychiatric problems for which this book has no answers, we may say that a functional grasp of the principles of argumentation plus an application of some psychological insights into the phenomenon of prejudice can be of significant value.

Those who are expert in such matters tell us that a closed mind has set notions about what is and what ought to be. It rejects and resents dissonant information and reasoning. In other words, selective perception is practiced. A bigot selects only the items which fit his preconceived framework, and he excludes any perceptions which fail to fit his preferred stereotype. He can be insensitive to some stimuli while being hypersensitive to others. A large-scale example of closed-mindedness occurred in the fall of 1957, when two young ladies returned from a trip to Russia with accounts of progress in housing, higher education, jet aircraft, etc. They found to their dismay that scarcely anyone would believe the Russians could do anything worthwhile. Some Americans took to calling the girls "pink" and "pro-Communist," while others scoffed at the possibility of fearing an atomic bomb attack from a country that couldn't even make a decent automobile. Needless to say, the young tourists soon quit talking about their trip. Maybe it is easy to dismiss the testimony of two young women as being inexpert, but what about the report of Charles Lindberg on the apparent power of the Nazi air force prior to 1940? He knew what he had seen, and subsequent events proved him right, but his countrymen refused to take his report seriously when he made it. There seems to be an abiding faith in ignorance as a form of protection.

In controversy a bigot uses supporting material (if any) from authority (persons of like views), faith, intuition, and special insight which seems not to be available to others. When pressed, he responds angrily, and this induces reckless reasoning. Perhaps he knows that an argument cannot be beaten without meeting it, but when his pet prejudice is questioned he responds irrationally with a stratagem like name-calling, imputing bad motives, or some equally irrelevant diversion. "The one thet fust gits mad's most ollers wrong," said Lowell in *The Bigelow Papers*. There are those who blame labor unions for almost everything but the weather, and there are others who label every legitimate criticism of union excesses as "labor baiting."

Questionable Analysis and Interpretation

First among the four general classes of defective proof is questionable analysis and interpretation of the proposition. It is placed first because it concerns the most fundamental process, and that process logically comes first in the order of events. One could say that any proof which violates the appropriate principles in Chapter IV is defective and consequently vulnerable to attack, but a discussion of some specific attacks and ways to meet them will be more instructive. Definitions of key terms are so vital to the controversy that any questionable one should be attacked on the ground that it is not recognized by experts in that field, that it has been applied in the wrong context, or that it is only partly true, for instance. In defense one might cite authoritative sources in the appropriate field instead of relying upon a general dictionary for definitions of highly specialized terms. If the negative attack on a proposition of policy tries to interpret "should" to mean "will," the affirmative should defend on the ground that these two verbs are not synonymous.

Analysis is often attacked for not producing a prima facie case, although this terminology is not often used outside of judicial and school debates. More likely the charge will be the omission of some vital point or the assumption of a questionable premise. During a debate on national Republican strategy in 1959, one side said the party must find out what the people want and promise to give it to them. The idea was to select a popular image and then find skilled politicians who could put over the program. The other side replied that salvation for the party must grow out of its men rather than being foisted upon them. "Let someone raise high a standard, and men will repair to it," editorialized the *Wall Street Journal* (Jan. 15, 1959). Possible defenses against attacks upon analysis are implied by the theory of analysis in Chapter IV. In reply to an attack upon a premise or an assumption, the soundest alternative is to explain and defend the philosophy of the case. Closely related to this would be the affirmative use of a "Principles" case when the proposition of policy apparently called for a program. If the proposition said California should change the district boundaries for election purposes, an affirmative advocate might discourse only upon the theory of redistricting, but the negative attack would probably demand a workable scheme for doing it. Then the affirmative would have some explaining to do. Finally, there is that affirmative defense which does not deny what the negative attack says, but it replies with a wholly different standard of judgment which it says is preferable. When the Wilderness Bill was before Congress, an opponent argued on materialistic grounds that the preservation of a wilderness would create a wasteland. The affirmative defense retorted that trees are not just for lumbering, that vegetation is not merely livestock feed, that mountains are not valuable solely for ores, and that money is not the only value worth serving.

Three general defenses against attacks which allege defects in proof will be indicated briefly. They apply to allegations of faulty analysis, deficient evidence, fallacious reasoning, and, indeed to all the kinds of defective proof. First, one might defend his proof against the charge that it is defective, either by showing that it was misinterpreted or by explaining its validity. Second, he might be able to show that the deficiency was overstated and that his proof still holds up. Finally, he might counterattack by showing defects in the opponent's argument which alleged the deficiency. The defense could score by pointing to a fallacy in the attacker's argument, for instance.

Flaws in Evidence

Unsupported assertion or a total lack of evidence is an inviting opening for attack. In the example referred to here, the lack of evidence is compounded with question begging. An editorial writer asked *why* President Roosevelt "gave away whole nations" (Poland, Czechoslovakia, Hungary, etc.) . . . to do a politeness to Stalin." The attack asked for factual support: "Where is the evidence that F.D.R. gave those nations away?" If the give-away were proved, then the *why* question would have been proper.

Insufficient evidence is generally a little less vulnerable to attack, but in this case it was a serious defect. Justice William O. Douglas, of all people, asserted in his 1954 book, *An Almanac of Liberty*, that in 1952 in New York City there were at least 58,000 orders issued for wiretapping. Asked by a Congressional committee to give his source, Justice Douglas named a Mr. Davis, who was then called to testify. His testimony indicated that he had conversed with some unidentified policemen and lawyers and that his investigation took "about a day or two." The district attorney of Kings County subsequently testified before the same committee, reporting on a careful investigation which turned up 480 cases—not 58,000—in New York City in 1952.[3]

Biased or unqualified evidence presents many opportunities for attack, but sometimes an arguer makes it easy for his opponent by undermining his own source. Such was the misadventure of Professor Bestor in his article, "We Are Less Educated Then 50 Years Ago." [4] His major sources of evidence were some publications of the U.S. Office of Education, which he branded as a propaganda outlet for professors of education who cling to the nonsense about education as life-adjustment.

Inaccurate and possibly careless reporting has occasionally led to embarrassment. One habitual writer of letters to editors complained that a newspaper story on transit fares neglected to explain why Chicago fares were forty per cent higher than New York fares. He went on to say that no newspaper had ever answered the question, although several of them had been asked repeatedly. The editor replied that the New York system was subsidized by taxes and that the explanation had been printed many times.

Using something less than the best evidence, or the habit of rushing to the attack without the latest and the best, gives the defense an easy opening. It seems that a magazine science editor wrote a feature on brain research in relation to President Eisenhower's stroke.[5] A physi-

---

[3] *Chicago Daily News*, June 15, 1963, p. 12.
[4] *U.S. News and World Report*, November 30, 1956, pp. 68–82.
[5] *Saturday Review*, December 14, 1957.

cian challenged a statement which the editor had attributed to a researcher, Dr. Penfield. The attacker charged that no documentation had been given, but that a Penfield paper in 1954 had given different information from that used by the editor. In defense the editor advised his critic to "do his own research more carefully before criticizing others." The editor *had* cited his source, which was a Penfield paper given in 1957—three years more recent than the one used in the attack.

Irrelevant evidence is as serious a weakness as too little if the persons who might reply are sufficiently alert to detect the defect. "So what?" is the blunt introduction to an attack upon this flaw in proof. An affirmative speaker on complete medical care for all citizens at public expense used three factual statements in support of his charge that our present system of medical care fails in preventive medicine: there is much preventable cancer, most cases are diagnosable, and most people do not have examinations. The negative attack was, in effect, "So what? There is no correlation shown between these facts and the number of visits to doctors." Attacks based upon failure to give relevant information occurred an estimated total of sixteen times in two final debates of West Point tournaments.

Boners in statistical methods make up a substantial group of flaws in evidence, just as misinterpretations of statistical data account for many fallacies in reasoning. Actually, it is often difficult to determine whether a given instance is one of method or of interpretation; an inference based upon an inadequate sample involves too little evidence and a hasty generalization. Be that as it may, here are a few flaws that provided openings for attack. President Kennedy told a business audience that the average age of equipment in U.S. factories was roughly nine years, while in West Germany the proportion of equipment under five years of age grew from one-sixth of the total in 1948 to two-fifths in 1957. The obvious criticism is that the figures are not comparable; one is an average figure, while the other is a percentage of a total. In Chicago the police statistics for 1955 showed an increase of 6.7 per cent in juvenile arrests over 1954. This was used to prove a worsening situation, but the defense pointed out that increasing police attention to this problem and a larger population, not a per capita rise in juvenile delinquency, comprised the factual situation. A trade paper crowed that Kuwait's purchase of some 10,000 air conditioners had given that state the world lead in units per capita (one per 16 inhabitants *vs.* one per 23 in the U.S.A.). The attack pointed out a ratio of 7,000,000 units to 10,000 in favor of this country and called the per capita figure meaningless. To a brokerage house announcement that 9,000,000 American families own shares of stock, a critic replied that eighty per cent of our families must therefore own none.

Defenses in response to attacks such as those above may be varied to fit the nature of the attacks. To the charge of too little evidence one might explain that in a matter of common knowledge that is no defect, or he should produce more evidence if the matter is not one of common knowledge. If a source is attacked, the defense might point out that this need not discredit the content, or he might defend his source, or he might add evidence. When evidence is attacked by overmatching rather than by impeaching it, the defense might add better evidence, but it may be wiser to reason more cogently from the evidence than the opponent did. There is little profit in a card-quoting contest. Finally, in case the validity of the evidence itself is attacked, the defense might add substantiating evidence or defend the content of the first evidence. He may be able to show that his opponent has taken a fact for an inference, or vice versa.

Fallacies in Structure of Argument

In this section the opportunities to expose defects in proof will be classified and explained in terms of the nine kinds of arguments which were set out in Chapter VII.

Example to descriptive generalization may go wrong in two ways: the generalization erroneously describes the pattern of the examples, as in "Most American collegians are mainly interested in fun," or else the examples are atypical of their class, as in citing selected "horrible examples" to prove the failure of education, public relief, or foreign aid.

Criteria to verbal classification likewise has two potential flaws; either the criteria are unsatisfactory, as in "You can judge a used car by its price tag and its paint job," or the characteristics fail to meet the criteria, as in justifying permanent academic dismissal for one D grade on the ground that it meets the test of reasonableness.

Cause-to-effect reasoning has four potential weaknesses which were mentioned earlier. One is that some component generalizations do not confirm the warrant. This can be expressed in the order of the Toulmin layout as follows: If we abolish fraternities and sororities, the academic climate will improve, because time and energy diverted from the former will naturally flow to the latter. A second defect occurs when examples disconfirm the warrant. An advertisement for jet aircraft claimed that they would increase warmth and understanding among peoples because of shrinking the distances between nations. Examples of terrible wars between close neighbors disconfirm the warrant. Third, the situation in the data is unlike that described by the warrant. Refer to the example of the difference between government regulation and government ownership of utilities in Chapter VII. Finally, other factors may alter the predicted effect, as in the illustration of the subsidy and the tariff reduction.

From literal comparison has two flaws to watch for; either part A of the literal comparison is untrue, as in the League of Nations example, or parts A and B are dissimilar, as in the example of Berlin and Korea. When an attorney for a chain grocery complained that the Meat Cutters' Union discriminated in favor of dogs and against people in allowing the night sale of meat for dogs but not for people, a union spokesman contended that the two situations were dissimilar in respect to the time and labor involved.

From testimony is often hard to distinguish from the evidence itself. Reasoning from testimony involves saying that, for instance, the treaty should not be approved because the eminent diplomat, Mr. X, says it should not, and he ought to know. If we are urged to believe an expert's conclusion without hearing his reasons, we cannot classify the argument according to his reasoning; we have only a kind of sign to go on, as some writers call it, but here it is called argument from testimony. The best way to attack inferences from testimony is to cite others "who ought to know" and who disagree with the conclusion in question.

From observed effect to unobserved cause, as in scapegoating, may involve a poor correlation of effect and cause, as in the example of the recognition of Red China, or other events may better account for the data, as in the Russo-British case.

Circumstantial evidence to hypothesis may be a scientific procedure, or it may be merely a jump to a conclusion, depending upon how carefully it is done. One of three possible flaws occurs when the hypothesis fails to explain the evidence: "Students must be studying harder nowadays; there's more mononucleosis around." A second weakness is insufficiency of evidence to justify the hypothesis, as we saw in the French disarmament case. Finally, another hypothesis may be at least as probable as the chosen one, as in the oligopoly example.

Definition to characteristics may have three vulnerable spots, as we saw in Chapter VII: the basic definition may be unacceptable, as in "Union means contract"; the conclusion may not be implied by the definition ("This is a democracy, so I can do as I please"); a qualification may change the warrant and negate the conclusion, as in the example of free speech in a national emergency.

Analogy or figurative comparison may not serve to establish a principle for one of three reasons: the patterns in the figure may be dissimilar; the patterns may be similar but fail to fit the facts; the figurative analogy may not conform with experience. Calvin Coolidge stated in "Government and Business" that government and business are like two parallel streams which always flow side by side but never touch. Hugh Johnson's speech on "Pied Pipers" referred to Huey Long and Father Coughlin who allegedly led people astray by emotional appeals. John Altgeld's "Unnecessary Imprisonment" speech compared the police-culprit relationship to the teacher-pupil relationship. For all three kinds of defective analogy the essential question is, "Is *one principle* common to both halves of the comparison?"

Miscellaneous Fallacies

Diversions can be attacked by showing their irrelevancy and the possibility of their being stratagems to change the subject or to stop debate on a losing proposition. In order to disprove the point that fraternities stereotype their members, it would be necessary to show that at least some do not do so, but the user of irrelevant conclusion argued instead that stereotyping is unfortunate. Another speaker tried to show that athletes on his campus had taken bribes, but his argument was that bribery must not be permitted. Diversions to other ideas beside the point occur when speakers ignore intellectual argument and resort to appeals to interests, motives, and prejudices. Student speakers have been known to urge the rejection of an innovation on one campus on the ground that it is in use on the campus of a disliked, rival institution. The merit of the idea is ignored. Attacks upon persons instead of ideas can be classified here.

Diversions may be made to other ideas, as above, or to stop argument on a losing point, as in the cases which follow. The use of abstruse statement, technical jargon, and other incomprehensible remarks is a means of escape for some bluffers. Improper use of expert opinion occurs when one lists allegedly favorable authorities without quoting them or reasoning about their supposed testimony. While speaking for an honor code a student said, "The administration, student leaders, and prominent alumni all favor this idea." Another version of this can be seen in a speaker's use of his own prestige or status in lieu of logical support. Or a speaker may appeal to tradition or custom in advising against a course of action because it has not been done that way before. In times of hysteria associated with wars, depressions, and witch hunts, demagogues play up nonrational and irrational appeals to fear, ignorance, anxiety, prejudice, and the like.

Substitution of nonrational matter or manner for a sensible treatment of a controversial point is a familiar sophism of the diversionary type. Intimidation, or appeal to force, ranges from threatening someone's job to international rocket rattling. Lesser bullies, having less power, must content themselves with ridicule, irony, bombast, and anger. They raise their voices instead of reinforcing their arguments.

Manipulations to confuse appear in several forms. They do not necessarily leave the point entirely, but they do distort it. An unfair extension of someone's argument to the point of absurdity is one form of manipulation. Some years ago the arguments for prison reform and the eight-hour day for labor were extended by the negative to mean "giving convicts and workers everything on a silver platter." Whenever we have a controversy which arouses strong feelings, we can expect *both* extremes to practice unfair extensions of arguments.

Special pleading is a manipulative tactic which involves using in one situation an argument which the same person would reject in another. The person who demands a police "crackdown" on traffic violators—until *he* gets a ticket—is a familiar instance. Omission of relevant but unfavorable evidence is akin to special pleading. We have observed it in spokesmen for certain states that boast of their low taxes but neglect to mention their low standard of public education.

A genetic fallacy occurs when an idea that is before us is judged solely on its source: "That ordinance must be a bad one for us tenants, because it was proposed by the real estate interests." Related to this is "poisoning the well," which involves discrediting a source even before the testimony has been received: "My opponent will no doubt quote from Mr. X, whom you can't believe even under oath."

Forcing ideas into arbitrary classes, as in saying that one must be a radical if he is not a reactionary, is a manipulation which some polemicists use. Those who habitually seek a middle-of-the-road position on any controversial subject on which they are asked for an opinion apparently think an idea is right if it lies half-way between the extremes.

Trick questions are intended to confuse ideas and persons by means of an apparently meaningless sequence of questions, a distortion of the respondent's answers, ambiguous questions, pseudo (unanswerable) questions, and complex questions ("Have you quit cheating in examinations?").

Inconsistency is here taken to mean either the appearance of irreconcilable statements in one message or the use of a conclusion which does not follow from its premise. Some persons quote Shakespeare in praise of consistency: "Consistency, thou art a jewel." Others prefer Emerson's dissent: "A foolish consistency is the hobgoblin of little minds, adored by little statesmen and philosophers and divines." An inconsistency in the traditional sense was found in a Beveridge speech on child labor. At one point he said new immigrants should be guaranteed job opportunities equal to those of older American groups because they are equal as citizens. A bit later he argued that child labor degraded the Anglo-Saxon race to a level which ought to be forced upon only the children of "foreigners." On September 11, 1958 President Eisenhower said in a broadcast that a loss of Quemoy to Red China would lead to the loss of Formosa and all free world positions in the western Pacific area. But on October 1 he told his press conference that Quemoy and Matsu were not vital to Formosa and that, as a military man, he felt that the Nationalist buildup of troops on those islands was unwise. The explanation is that a change in official policy occurred in the interim. In the case of Bertrand Russell's turnabout on the question of Russo-American relations, a period of thirteen years separated his allegedly inconsistent recommendations. In 1945 he felt that the West should threaten war against the Soviet Union, but in 1958 he urged the pursuit of agreements. He explained that it is absurd to continue to advocate a policy after all the circumstances have changed.[6] This is the best defense against an attack which alleges an inconsistency.

The simple nonsequitur (does not follow) occurs when someone uses an argument in which the conclusion does not follow. "There are some impoverished old persons, therefore the nation needs a system of compulsory, complete medical care at public expense." "Decent

[6] "Why I Changed My Mind," *Saturday Review*, May 31, 1958, p. 18.

housing is a basic need of every citizen; therefore the proposed national housing bill should be enacted." "The federal income tax deprives states and localities of some revenue; therefore it should be repealed." Some apparent nonsequiturs would become acceptable if missing links such as assumptions and implied premises were supplied.

Misuse of language may appear in many forms, three of which will be mentioned briefly here: ambiguity, loaded language, and tautology. Ambiguity formerly meant the use of words having two meanings, but now the usage seems to include vagueness. In this broader sense, ambiguity can be found in many places; in fact, it is frequently used intentionally. This is what the man in the street means when he complains about the "doubletalk" of his employer, some politicians, and diplomats. A study of the Kennedy-Nixon television series of 1960 [7] indicated some ambiguous passages in the speeches of both men. Their remarks on farm policy in the first program were among those designated as ambiguous.[8]

Loaded language is highly subjective in that expressions which presumably are meant to describe actually convey the attitude and feeling of the user toward the subject. Figurative language, often hyperbole, is the typical locution. "Slanted" expressions are familiar in political discourse, particularly at campaign time. In fact, it is easy to identify the party preference of many newspapers by noticing which way the language is loaded. This specimen left no doubt: "Millions of dollars were spent by New Deal propaganda mills to create and spread the myth that F.D.R. was an all-seeing, all-knowing, and all-honorable commander, philosopher, and philanthropist."

Tautology may be taken to include circular reasoning, question-begging words and definitions, and nonevident premise. This is a simple case of reasoning in a circle: "The story must be true, because I read it in a book, and it wouldn't have been published if it weren't true." Question-begging was explained in relation to propositions, but here is another specimen: "Un-American activities should be declared unpatriotic." An oversimplified instance of nonevident premise appears in this sentence: "Since the system of free enterprise has made this country what it is, we should preserve the system as it is."

In defending against the charge of fallacious thinking, two general

[7] L. A. Samovar, "Ambiguity and Unequivocation in the Kennedy-Nixon Television Debates," *Quarterly Journal of Speech*, XLVIII, No. 3 (1962), 279.

[8] S. Kraus, ed., *The Great Debates* (Bloomington: Indiana University Press, 1962), 355–356.

procedures are available; admit it if it is true, or explain why the inference is valid if interpreted as it was intended.

TACTICAL PROCEDURES

In addition to the foregoing methods of attack and defense which are predicated upon defects in analysis, evidence, and reasoning, there are tactical procedures, sometimes called special methods, which can be quite effective in particular situations. In other words, they do not have the broad applications that the preceding group has. Seven of the more specialized procedures will be explained.

Turn the Tables

Once in a while a debater will have an opportunity to turn an opponent's proof to his own advantage. In reply to the argument that parents who send children to private elementary and high schools bear a double burden (taxes plus tuition), Walter Lippmann wrote: "Whether it is fair to describe as 'discrimination' such double payments for education can best be tested by asking what would be the situation if private schools were supported by the taxpayer. In that case the parent whose child goes to the public school will be paying twice over—once to support the public schools which his child attends and once to support the private school which his child does not attend." [9] In a thoroughgoing refutation of the previously-cited Bestor argument (footnote 4), Professor Hand [10] turned the tables by using Bestor's own source to disprove the affirmative claim. After showing the statistical comparison between 1900 and 1950 to be fallacious because of an invalid base, Hand went on to cite other pamphlets from Bestor's favorite source which proved that the high schools offering no geometry, physics, or chemistry enroll only two per cent of American high school students.

Sometimes there is no good reply to the table-turning tactic, but the possibilities to consider include attacking the opponent's frame of

[9] "Opinion: Federal Aid to Education," *Presbyterian Life*, May 15, 1961, p. 23.
[10] H. C. Hand, "Black Horses Eat More Than White Horses," *A.A.U.P. Bulletin*, XLIII (1957), 266–279.

reference or his interpretation of the point, showing that he admits the point, or pointing out that he has shifted ground.

Reduce to Absurdity

As in table-turning, one uses the opponent's proof, but in this tactic he extends it to the absurd. It is simple, direct, and vastly entertaining to the "groundlings," as Shakespeare called them. An apocryphal story tells of a lawyer who contended that a corporation could make no oral contract because it had no tongue. The judge replied that it could not, by the same token, make a written contract because it had no hand. Combining irony, ridicule, and reducing to absurdity, a student wrote a letter to the campus paper to attack the proposal to delete questions on race and religious preference from the admission application forms. He argued that all these admissions questions and procedures could lead to discrimination: applicant's name, home address, name of high school, grade transcript, father's occupation, education of parents, age, sex, serial numbers, etc. On this last point he wrote: "If serial numbers are assigned, they must not be given in sequence as this would allow discrimination against applying later than others. Ridiculous, isn't it?" [11]

Some debaters have replied to such tactics by reaffirming the original point, attacking the analogy (if any), showing an irrelevancy, charging an unfair extension of the point, or pointing out that no substantive flaw was found in the argument which was ridiculed. An exchange in *Harper's* illustrates a *reductio ad absurdum* and two modes of reply. The first event was an "Easy Chair" (February, 1960) item which was critical of billboard advertising. The April reply said the critic's argument, if carried to its logical conclusion, would do away with store window displays, theater marquees, and all business signs. "Billboards are an integral part of the great system of free enterprise . . . ," it concluded. The editors replied that window displays are on the advertiser's own property, that abolition is the only constructive answer to billboards, and that such action has no more relevance to free enterprise than the abolition of slums. It should be noted that a charge of absurdity may either amuse or alienate an audience, and it can boomerang in the form of table-turning by the intended victim.

[11] *Daily Northwestern*, February 15, 1956, p. 2.

Match the Proof

Instead of discrediting the proof or its application, the person replying may choose to match or overmatch his opponent's proof. He can do so by using evidence and/or reasoning of the same or of a different kind. Two cautions need to be observed: quality is more important than quantity, and the user must make clear the fact that he is employing the tactic of outweighing proof. In a written controversy over the proper balance between police powers and civil liberties, the negative did not attempt to attack the affirmative's evidence directly; instead, he marshaled his evidence to show the opposite conclusion.[12]

One defense against the matching tactic is the argument that mere quotation counting is not enough. Another is the possibility of pointing out that the matcher has shifted ground. A third kind of reply was made in the 1961 final debate of the West Point tournament. The second negative constructive speaker proposed to match evidence on the distribution of medical facilities in the United States, but the affirmative replied that *interpretation* of evidence was more significant.

Pose a Dilemma

Two or more untenable consequences of a position are alleged to exist. Seeing a person drown, a nonswimming bystander may jump in and become a dead hero or stay out and be a live coward. The principle of the dilemma is that the choices (horns) cover the possibilities, and each one is damaging. Without foot soldiers we would either lose on the installment plan or resort to a suicidal nuclear holocaust, it is argued. In opposition to wage increases for steelworkers, an editorial [13] posed this dilemma: if the wage increase were to come out of profits, the firms would have difficulty in finding capital for expansion and replacement, and the resultant retarded growth would harm the nation and the workers themselves; but if the wage hike were passed on in higher prices, the workers would find their raises nullified by a price spiral.

In reply one might take an option which was not covered (tie the

[12] Inbau vs. Kamisar, *Journal of Criminal Law, Criminology and Police Science*, LIII, No. 1 (1962), 85–89, and No. 2 (1962), 171–193.
[13] *Wall Street Journal*, March 17, 1959.

wage rate to productivity or to the value of the dollar), break down one of the given options (different effect from the cause), or reduce the argument to an absurdity (permanent wage freeze apparently implied).

Apply Residues

Both sides can use this procedure. It consists of the division of a point into parts, as in a dilemma, but here one part is left intact after the others have been disqualified. The result is constructive proof for the refuter's side. Exhaustive division plus ample proof of the residue will make it work. In his renowned speech on conciliation with the American colonies, Edmund Burke treated three ways of proceeding: remove the causes of the stubborn spirit, prosecute it as criminal, or comply with it as necessary. After disqualifying the first two, he concluded by saying the only reasonable choice was to submit to the situation as a necessary evil.

Not all residues are as formidable as Burke's. The division may not be exhaustive, or the residue may be refuted, or one of the disqualifying arguments may be refuted. Sometimes two of these can be combined, as in denying the residue and supporting one of the disqualified choices. Defenses against the dilemma have some parallels here.

Force the Defense

Keeping the opponent on the defensive is the favorite sport of the negative side. This is accomplished by means of all the tactics which are discussed in this chapter. In general the idea is to get the affirmative to use the language of the negative case. There is no doubt that the negative side is the easier one for persons who wish to bedevil the opposition. One method which has not been discussed is the use of questions as exploratory refutation. It is called setting up a point for refutation, and it is accomplished by asking, for instance, how the affirmative plan would be financed, assuming that the negative has a devastating rejoinder to the likely affirmative answer.

In the management of his defense, an affirmative will find several hints most useful. When confronted by questions and objections, he can press the negative to explain each objection, to show the significance of each question, and to support every dire prediction. He will follow each answer to a negative attack with a reaffirmation of his own point. He will answer legitimate questions, but he will not react gullibly to "scatter gun" and "straw man" attacks. He will not allow the negative to narrow the whole thing down to one or two objections; instead, he will point up any negative failures to deal with some matters. Finally, he will keep the affirmative case in its own language before the audience, not by mere repetition but by adding support in each exchange on a point.

Argue a Fortiori

This tactic uses the idea of "all the more probable." If a conclusion is true in a less favorable case, so the argument goes, think how nearly inevitable it must be in a more favorable one. "If the head of an institution devoted to the training of engineers was thus misled . . . (by Bestor's statistics) the likelihood is very great that most of the readers . . . came to the same grossly erroneous conclusion . . ." [14]

DIALECTIC AND CROSS-EXAMINATION

In Chapter I dialectic was briefly defined and shown to be a forerunner of argumentation. Now, both in its original form and in the modern form of cross-examination, it will be discussed as an important procedure in attack and defense.

A Neglected Method of Argument

In 1921 Professor Hunt wrote on dialectic under this title.[15] He urged that interest in it be revived because of these values to be gained through practice in cross-examination: 1. It accustoms one to study

[14] See footnote 10.
[15] E. L. Hunt, "Dialectic: A Neglected Method of Argument," *Quarterly Journal of Speech Education*, VII (1921), 221–232.

both sides of a question; 2. In problem solving, the differing opinions serve as constant checks on each other by constantly clashing and adapting to each other; 3. It is more of a thinking together process than are long speeches by one individual; 4. It is a stimulating mental exercise; 5. It is excellent preparation for formal debate; 6. An audience listens more closely and with more interest to cross-examination than to one speech or even debate; 7. It has a wider range than debate. It may be used for stimulation and discussion as well as problem solving.

Socrates asked the disturbing question, "What do you mean?" In Plato's *Dialogues* we see the old master, as Plato would have us remember him, deflating humbug by testing ideas to see if they could stand honest, logical examination. In its original sense, dialectic could serve as a teaching-learning discipline to reduce the tendency toward dogmatism. The disputants were encouraged to achieve understanding, if not agreement, by placing their opposition within a common universe of discourse. Sophistication in the sense of poise, courtesy, and controlled temper was essential. These were some of the occasions in which this version of dialectic was used: 1. differing interpretations of the meaning of a statement, 2. differing assumptions, 3. differing consequences of assumptions, 4. a desire to reduce disagreement by focusing upon agreement first, 5. a desire to clarify the basis of disagreement, and 6. a desire to explore a point of agreement.

But not all evidence in support of the dialectical methods is ancient. Some is modern and scientific. Prediction and verification, as well as the method of multiple working hypotheses, involve some dialectical procedure. We say "some" because dialectic alone is inconclusive. Talk cannot determine what is a fact, but it can examine the meanings of facts. Another value has been discovered through psychological experimentation; it is that questioning, as in the Socratic method, increases the consistency of beliefs.[16]

At this point a discussion of how dialectical thinking functions may be helpful. In Aristotle's *Topics* (100^a 18) demonstrative reasoning, as in most advocacy, starts from premises which are true and primary, or are such that we know about them through primary, true premises. Dialectical reasoning, which is our present concern, starts from opinions

---

[16] C. I. Hovland and M. J. Rosenberg, eds., *Attitude Organization and Change* (New Haven: Yale University Press, 1960), p. 204.

that are generally believed on the strength of themselves alone. Hegel distinguished dialectic from induction and deduction within one mind and showed that its essence was opposition, conflict, and duality, whether within one mind or between two. Adler [17] says dialectic is the way in which opinions are placed in opposition and attacked, defended, combined, etc. It is intended to aid us in answering the question, "What does it mean to say thus-and-so?" The three stages in the process are definition, analysis, and synthesis. In the first two the opposition is clarified by setting out its systematic consequences. Originally and in an educational sense, the question-and-answer procedure was used for speculative inquiry, but when it is used in cross-examination, the purpose is to build a progression of dialectical syllogisms. How this is done in court, in school debate, in philosophical dialogue, in hearings, etc., will be explained and illustrated.

Cross-examination in Court

In the courtroom there are four possible aims of cross-examination: 1. To discredit the testimony of the witness, 2. To use this testimony to discredit unfavorable testimony of other witnesses, 3. To use this testimony to corroborate the favorable testimony of others, and 4. To use it to contribute independently to the favorable development of the questioner's case.[18]

What makes a good witness in this trying situation? The author of *The Art of Advocacy* [19] characterizes five difficult types in terms of responses to the psychological pressures: nervous, "wise guy," suspicious, fawning, and lying. His ideal witness has five traits: 1. He is conscientious about telling the truth; 2. He is well prepared, knows his facts, and can narrate them clearly; 3. He has courage, strong character, and toughness; 4. His vision, hearing, and memory are good; 5. In appearance he is healthy and wholesome.[20]

[17] M. J. Adler, *Dialectic* (N. Y.: Harcourt, Brace and Co., 1927).
[18] L. W. Lake, *How To Cross-Examine Witnesses Successfully* (Englewood Cliffs, N. J.: Prentice-Hall, 1957), p. 6.
[19] L. P. Stryker, "What Makes a Good Witness," New York *Times Magazine*, May 16, 1954, p. 13.
[20] See also A. Steuer, *Max D. Steuer, Trial Lawyer* (N. Y.: Random House, 1950).

Application to School Debating

Purposes of questions in cross-examination school debating are not quite the same as they are in judicial debating. In educational forensics there is typically less emphasis upon trapping witnesses in lies and badgering them to make damaging admissions. Instead, the stress is supposed to be on getting information, testing inferences, verifying sources, clarifying meanings of statements, and sharpening the contrasts in their cases. Instead of pressing for conclusions, the skillful practioners ask questions the answers to which may provide premises for further argument. This is what was meant by the earlier assertion that the purpose of cross-examination is to build a progression of dialectical syllogisms.

Preparation is the key to better cross-examining and answering. It includes attitude as well as knowledge. Both parties are expected to be reasonable, even-tempered, courteous, and interested in getting at the essentials. They are supposed to regard this period as a vital part of the debate. These attitudes should lead to thoughtful preparation of questions and answers. This means anticipating and adapting to the possible twists and turns that the dialectic may take.

Suggestions for questioners are not rules, but they are common-sense advice based upon considerable experience.[21] The interrogator should use the time for questions only. Instead of making interpretative or evaluative asides, he should bring out such inferences by asking follow-up questions. The questioner has control of the time; he may probe whatever matters he wishes, but he may prevent the respondent from wasting time in rambling or evasive replies. This does not mean that he may insist upon yes-or-no answers except on simple questions of fact. His questions, in turn, should be brief and to some point. He may very properly be aggressive in his interrogation, but obnoxious behavior as in personal abuse is out of bounds. Instead of trying to get an admission of defeat from a witness, he should start on common ground and probe deeper and deeper, looking for weak spots in assumptions, evidence, reasoning, omissions, etc. A planned but flexible order of questions is best for this purpose. Beginners err in slavishly running through a written list of questions regardless of the case they meet or the answers they get. The idea is to follow through to some point or basis for a premise and then to point up the unit by repeating the

[21] See R. P. Newman, *The Pittsburgh Code for Academic Debate* (Pittsburgh: University of Pittsburgh Press, 1962).

opening question. Audience interest can be improved by composing questions clearly and in other ways trying to keep them abreast of what is going on. These events become exceedingly complex at times. Questioners are advised to know the answers to most of their questions. There is to be no conferring between colleagues during the examination. Finally, it is poor technique to use "Isn't it a fact that . . ." and question-begging questions.

Suggestions for witnesses have been foreshadowed by the advice given on purposes of questions, preparation for dialectic, and questioning. An individual or a team should, through analysis, determine what positions must be maintained, how they may be attacked, and how to reply. Anticipation of traps is essential, because no conferring is permitted during the examination. It is equally important for this side to remember and use later the results of the questioning. Replies are to be brief and pointed, but the respondent should feel free to request clarification of ambiguous questions. Mere stalling for time is improper, but one need not let the examiner rush him unduly. This implies answering directly and fairly but with reasonable qualifications. One may, of course, decline to answer question-begging or unclear questions if the examiner refuses to amend them. In case a witness does not know an answer, he is advised to admit it. With respect to behavior, he should maintain good humor, speak so as to include the audience, and stay in his role as the witness. In some school tournaments there are rules governing appeals to the chair.

Standard formats of school debating which include some dialectical procedures may be seen in several textbooks [22] which have been designed to serve contest debaters. The familiar formats are designated by names such as Oregon Style, Montana Style, Heckling Debate, Mock Trial, and others. For classroom exercises this short form will serve the purpose:

First affirmative constructive	5 minutes
Second negative questions first affirmative	3 minutes
First negative constructive	5 minutes
Second affirmative questions first negative	3 minutes
Second negative rebuttal	3 minutes
Second affirmative rebuttal	3 minutes

[22] J. H. McBurney and G. E. Mills, *Argumentation and Debate*, rev. ed. (N. Y.: Macmillan Co., 1964), pp. 340–356; A. J. Freeley, *Argumentation and Debate* (San Francisco: Wadsworth Publishing Co., 1961), pp. 306–312; J. H. McBath, ed., *Argumentation and Debate*, rev. ed. (N. Y.: Holt, Rinehart and Winston, Inc., 1963), pp. 285–298; D. Ehninger and W. Brockriede, *Decision by Debate* (N. Y.: Dodd, Mead and Co., 1963), pp. 320–328.

Specimens

Printed records of dialectical jousts, including cross-examinations, vary in length from three terse remarks to dozens of pages. One attributed to Lincoln qualifies as possibly the shortest. He said to a campaign opponent,

> "Suppose I call the tail of a mule a leg, how many legs would the mule then have?"
> "Five," said his witness.
> "No," replied Lincoln, "he would still have four. Calling a tail a leg doesn't make it one."

The audience probably thought that Abe had made a fool of his rival, even though the dialectical situation would have permitted any of three answers: five legs, four legs, or one leg. The question actually implied, "What is meant by calling a mule's tail a leg?" Toward the other extreme in length we might place Senator Thurmond's questioning of Secretary of Defense McNamara, not because of its total length but because of its low yield in information per 100 words.[23]

Two interesting little exchanges took place when the Young Republican Club of Evanston, Illinois met to hear spokesmen for and against the city manager form of government. After one antimanager debater finished his prepared statement, a lawyer in the audience asked him the name of his home town. It happened to be Highland Park. Pressed further, the witness admitted that his home town had the manager form of government. The clincher came in this question: "Isn't it a fact that Highland Park last year was selected as an All-America City, best governed in its class?"

The second antimanager debater admitted under questioning his conviction that an alderman under the manager system might become too powerful in his ward. Asked why he thought so, he exclaimed, "My alderman wants more power. My alderman demands more power. My alderman needs more power to be effective." Asked if he really believed this, he answered emphatically in the affirmative. Asked if he were certain of his alderman's appearance and feelings, he again answered firmly in the affirmative. Then the questioner gave the coup de grace: "It hurts me and embarrasses me . . . but I must break the

[23] New Yorker, June 15, 1963, p. 82.

news to you that you live in the eighth ward and I am your alderman and I don't look and don't feel that way." [24]

Next is a short extract from the cross-examination of the plaintiff in a civil suit for damages. Notice how quickly his story comes apart:

> Q. After this occurrence, were you ever employed by them again?
> A. No.
> Q. Did you go back to your job with them?
> A. No, I didn't.
> Q. Did you seek to go back to your job with them?
> A. I knew that I couldn't stand on the floor no (sic) length of time so it was useless.
> Q. So the answer to my question is you didn't, is that correct?
> A. No, I didn't.
> . . .
> Q. When you worked at a lathe, that was at a bench, was it?
> A. Yes.
> Q. Did you work standing up or sitting down?
> A. Sitting down mostly.

The final specimen of dialectic in this collection is reported to have taken place at Oxford University. It is a philosophical-theological dialogue between logical positivists and Catholics.

Logical positivism (a close relative of American philosopher John Dewey's pragmatism) erects its system of thought on the premise that no statement (except in logic and mathematics) may be considered meaningful if it is not potentially verifiable by evidence of the senses. The idea of God is one of the first things that logical positivists throw overboard. Last week philosopher Tony Quinton of All Souls' College undertook to dispose of God in the heart of the enemy camp, the Roman Catholic undergraduate Aquinas Society.

Notice the Boop. To hear the assertion that God exists, declared handsome Tony Quinton, is like visiting a friend and having him ask: "Did you notice our boop when you came through the garden?"

"No, what is it—an animal of some sort?"

"Yes, it's a sort of dog; it guards the house."

"I didn't see anything like a dog."

"Oh, you wouldn't see it. It's invisible."

"Well, can you smell it, touch it, hear it?"

"Not exactly . . ."

"Anyway, I thought you'd been burgled recently; it can't be a very good guard."

"Ah, you wouldn't talk like that if you knew what it was to have a boop. Of course, it hasn't dealt with the burglars yet, but it knows who they are and is going to punish them."

[24] *Evanston* (Illinois) *Review*, March 19, 1959.

God, said Quinton, is just about as evident as a boop. Then he went on to draw a prestidigitator's "proof" of God's nonexistence from Christian dogma: "God created the world." "World" in this sense, said Philosopher Quinton, means not "earth" but "everything."

"God," he went on, "obviously didn't create Himself. The only thing outside of everything is nothing. Therefore, if God created everything except what is outside of everything, namely nothing, and if God is the only thing outside everything, then God is nothing."

I Believe. After 55 minutes of such fast-stepping talk, the Rev. Thomas Corbishley, chubby Jesuit Master of Oxford's Catholic Campion Hall, got to his feet. "Mr. Quinton," he began, "do you believe the statement that no statement is true unless it is verifiable?"

"Certainly," replied Quinton.

"How," asked Corbishley, "can you verify that statement?" Quinton admitted that this cornerstone of positivism is unverifiable.

"Then why do you believe it to be true?" asked the priest.

"I believe it to be true because it is true," Quinton answered.

"There!" shouted Father Corbishley triumphantly. "So I believe that God exists because He does exist. Now where are we?" [25]

REBUTTALS IN SCHOOL DEBATE

Extensive treatments of this subject can be found in textbooks and journal articles which are intended for school debaters and their directors. The brief discussion in this place is intended to show in a general way how the procedures of attack and defense apply here. This will be done by sketching some familiar flaws in rebuttal speeches, indicating some possible improvements, and outlining the work of each rebuttal speaker in the traditional format.

Familiar Flaws in Rebuttal

Poor organization and stereotyped style can be observed all too often in contest debates. A critical reading of some published debates which have not been edited will reveal occasional rebuttal speeches which seem to be composed of disconnected remarks. Failure to carry the main ideas beyond the point reached in constructive speeches accounts

[25] *Time,* June 3, 1950, p. 82. Courtesy of *Time,* copyright Time, Inc., 1950.

for the widespread complaint that nothing much happens in rebuttals. Perhaps some students do not know what a rebuttal period is for, or at least they fail to do what is needed. For instance, in a final debate for the "national championship," the first affirmative rebuttalist defended at length the "need" point which had not been hit very hard, but he almost neglected the negative "objections" point which had been pressed vigorously. These and other shortcomings stem from several causes, one of which is the trend toward moving the rebuttal type of activity closer to the beginning of the debate. Some adaptation is essential, but, as has been stated earlier, there is little sense in having one constructive speech followed by seven rebuttal-type speeches. Negative cases of pure refutation, at least in the way they are often handled, tend to aggravate this problem.

Suggested Remedies

Memorable rebuttal speeches have not been characterized by the attempt to attack or defend practically everything which was said previously. The skillful debaters selected important items in terms of positions and issues. Some were selected to be clarified, others to be attacked or defended. Attention was certain to be called to the points which the opponent had not attacked. Rebuilding of points which had been hit was done with new evidence and variations in the original strategy; it was no mere repetition. Effective summaries have pointed up the arguments handled, the significance of each, and how the crucial ones were resolved in the speaker's favor.

Duties of Each Speaker

What each of the four speakers should do in a school debate depends upon the type of proposition, the side, the kinds of cases, and the tactical situation at the moment. However, several general principles can be stated: 1. Try always to be honest, fair, and courteous in attacking and defending ideas; 2. Never bring up a new constructive point in the rebuttal series; 3. Tie all attack and defense to the crucial parts of each case as a whole; 4. Remember the previous advice to keep the other side on the defensive so far as possible.

Within the limits expressed above, each speaker's duties can be suggested. The first negative rebuttal speaker has five minutes immediately following the second negative constructive speaker's ten-minute period. This awkward situation results from the custom of having the affirmative side both open and close the debate. But since this convention is likely to persist, the best course for the negative teams is so to divide the responsibilities that each speaker knows what to do and can thereby avoid duplicating his colleague's efforts. The first rebuttal speaker should take up where the preceding constructive speaker stopped, and he should focus on a few topics, or at most the "need" issue. However, if the negative uses a counterproposition, there is no clash on "need." In any event this speaker points up the affirmative's duties and tries to keep that side on the defensive.

Following fifteen minutes of negative speaking, the first affirmative rebuttal speaker takes the floor. If the opponents have spent their time advantageously, this speaker faces a critical period. He must make every second count, not by speaking at a frantic rate, but by focusing upon a few matters and composing his remarks clearly and briefly. The "need" issue may or may not require attention, but the "plan" and "advantages" most likely will. Even while defending against negative objections, this speaker should keep the affirmative case in terms of its own language before the audience.

The last rebuttalist for the negative should try to make the main attacks on the affirmative case prevail; and if his side has a constructive case, he should try to make the negative points stand out in preference to those of the affirmative. This is the last opportunity to focus upon ("boil down to") major clashes. In anticipation of the final affirmative speech, the last negative speaker usually points out what the affirmative side has failed to do and why that is serious.

In closing the debate, the final affirmative rebuttal speaker tries to re-establish the main thrust of the affirmative case. A three-stage treatment of each vital element includes setting up an affirmative point, refuting the negative attack on it, and reaffirming the original point.

QUESTIONS

1. Why are attack and defense called the essence of genuine debate? Describe an imaginary or a real joint appearance of announced affirmative and negative spokesmen in which attack and defense did not occur.

2. Suppose someone were to say that attack is the negative's business while defense is the affirmative's. What would you reply?

3. Point out the opportunities for attack against one speech or essay in Appendix B or C or elsewhere.

4. Select an exchange in which one affirmative message has been followed by one negative. Point out the opportunities and obligations that would apply to any affirmative spokesman who might appear next. This does not assume a school debate.

5. Again using a debate as a specimen for analysis, point out where refutation was placed and explain how the steps in attack and defense were used. Use Appendix E or F or some other.

6. Using Section III (Exposing Defects in Proof) as a frame of reference, explain how each side in Appendix D, E, or F used these items in attack and defense.

7. Cite as many as possible of these tactics in Appendixes D, E, and F: a) turn the tables, b) reduce to absurdity, c) match the proof, d) pose a dilemma, e) apply residues, f) force the defense, and g) argue a fortiori.

EXERCISES

1. For at least a week, conduct a "fallacy hunt" in editorials, letters, speeches, advertising, conversations, etc. In reporting the findings, classify the items according to Section III (Exposing Defects in Proof).

2. After hearing or reading a school debate or an approved substitute, write a critique of the attack and defense.

3. Conduct a direct-clash exercise, using one clash point for each exchange. If four persons were in each exchange, the order might be as follows:

a) five minutes to set up a point (either affirmative or negative) from a previously announced proposition; b) four minutes for an attack upon that point; c) four minutes for defense; d) four minutes for attack. Suppose the announced proposition were "The sale of cigarettes to minors should be prohibited by law." This is one of several clash points on which the affirmative side could begin: "Cigarette smoking is a menace to health." Or a clash could begin with a negative point such as, "This prohibition would be less successful than the Volstead Act."

4. Conduct one or more cross-examination debates with four students in each. Use propositions that have served in earlier exercises. The 22-minute format near the end of Section V (Dialectic and Cross-Examination) is suggested.

5. Pairs of students might be assigned to edit and re-enact some noteworthy dialogues and debates such as Lincoln-Douglas (*The Rivalry*), Bryan-Darrow (*Inherit the Wind*), the trial of Socrates (*Barefoot in Athens*), the limited test-ban treaty (*Congressional Record*, Sept. 9–20, 1963).

6. Oral or written critiques based upon observations of the work of classmates on Exercises 3, 4, and 5 might be assigned to vary the experiences and to get at different aspects of the principles of attack and defense.

CHAPTER XI

PRESENTATION

OF ARGUMENT

BECAUSE ARGUMENTATION IS TAKEN TO INCLUDE BOTH ORAL AND WRITTEN discourse, it becomes necessary to discuss presentation in terms of oral composition, written composition, and delivery. The treatment will be brief, not because presentation is inconsequential, but because the proper place for a satisfactory treatment is a textbook on public speaking or writing.

If a student of argumentation has studied writing and speaking, as many have, he does not need to be told that the presentation of argument is an important part of the process. It may often be less important than the invention of the arguments and the willingness of persons to listen or read, but how much more or less we cannot say. At least we know from our own experiences that a poorly presented argument starts out at a disadvantage. That is probably an understatement of the importance of presentation, because we also know of persons who deplore the ability of skilled speakers and writers to mislead their publics, at least for a while. In the history of our subject there have been well-meaning critics who have deplored style as "mere rhetoric" and delivery as "elocution." The fact that presentation can be overemphasized does not prove that it is unworthy of study.

ORAL COMPOSITION

Significance of Style

As a constituent of rhetoric, style means choice of words, sentence structure and movement, paragraph development, literal and figurative expression, and like matters. "Proper words in proper places" was Jonathan Swift's over-simplified definition. Wilhelm Wackernagel, in an equally general remark, said the concern of style is the surface of linguistic expression, not its substance. Both definitions are acceptable as far as they go; their weakness is their lack of specificity. In the paragraphs which follow we shall see that style is more than a kind of mechanical knack or a lifeless mask placed upon the body of ideas. It is the manner of linguistic expression which has been conditioned by the speaker's background, the subject, the purpose, the audience, the occasion, and possibly other factors.

Oral and written discourses do not always differ in style, although they should have distinctive characteristics more often than they do. The general reason is that listening and reading involve perceptual processes which are somewhat dissimilar. We know that listeners have the greater need for instantaneous intelligibility of the material; they cannot go back over it as readers can and do. Then too, the oral situation is more intimate or personal, hence it calls for patterns of language that are more like those of conversation. In fact, this is precisely what directness in style means.

The observations of many teachers and the findings of a few empirical studies support several generalizations concerning the differences between oral and written styles. These are estimates of central tendencies; consequently, exceptions are to be expected. Oral style tends to use fewer complex sentences, fewer interrogative and imperative sentences, fewer uncommon words, and less formal English. But oral style has more simple sentences, shorter and more loosely structured sentences, more repetition and restatement, more simple words and contractions, more idioms, and vastly more devices of direct discourse. For these reasons someone has declared that a speech is not just an essay standing on its hind legs!

If we turn from the viewpoint of the listener to that of the speaker, we can understand another dimension of the differences between oral and written styles. The writer has more interest in permanence and artistry, while the speaker must be more concerned with immediate effect, as Wichelns has explained.[1] Thus the speaker cannot be as leisurely in his composition; he must quickly adapt to changing moods in his listeners if he would increase their involvement in what he is saying. Note the directness of real talk in this extract from a student's prepared speech:

"How do you explain the fact that you own an album of Paul Robeson records? Didn't you join a liberal club in college? Do you deny having debated in favor of United Nations membership for Communist China when you were in school? Your answers to questions such as these can cost you plenty some day."

Most of us could, with slight effort, cite passages from speeches or quote testimonials to indicate the importance of style. Daniel Webster said on this point, "For, depend upon it, it is with our thoughts as with our persons—their intrinsic value is mostly undervalued, unless outwardly expressed in an attractive garb." This does not imply one style for all persons and times. There must be adaptations to speakers, subjects, occasions, and audiences. A style which seems tactless, crude, dull, stilted, mechanical, humorless, or otherwise ill-suited will damage the ethos of the speaker. Students who give argumentative speeches in class or in contest debates need to stress the communication of ideas, attitudes, and feelings—not merely the jargon of the practice exercise or the game, however they view it. These and other expressions are frequently used to excess: *colleague, post hoc ergo propter hoc, burden of proof, so we see, need, plan, inconsistency,* and *proved beyond a doubt.*

Perhaps we would not use such poor oral composition if we took more time to plan our remarks and practiced extemporizing in the presence of critics who cared. This is not to say that the hazards of extemporaneous speaking can be eliminated. Spontaneity occasionally exacts a price: a sentence that goes nowhere, a grammatical error, a barbarism, and even an embarrassing double-entendre. The following are specimens of "The White House Syntax Problem"[2] with ad libbing in press conferences:

[1] H. A. Wichelns, "The Literary Criticism of Oratory," *Studies in Rhetoric and Public Speaking* (N. Y.: Century Co., 1925).
[2] *Time,* January 26, 1962, p. 18.

Eisenhower, April 9, 1958: "I have not had an official or exhaustive poll made of this thing, but my mail shows that; except for a number of people come in and they have a particular excise tax, but it is always applying to the particular business in which they are engaged. That seems to be a favorite point in the correspondence that comes to me, but I notice this: it's that *particular* tax, and they want to show how we can keep all the others off the books."

Kennedy, January 15, 1962: "We're talking about $2 billion a year which we are now, I think that we—I'm hopeful that we can use our productive power well in this field. But I think the question of the balance and I think that [the Presidential Assistant] and [the Secretary of Agriculture] in my judgment will be in balance by the time they go before the Congress."

In commenting upon this "sprawling syntax," *Time* said it was "a little hard to guess which President said what." The writer must not have noticed that *hopeful* and *judgment* were two of Kennedy's favorite words.

Desirable Qualities

Emphasis, force, and *vigor* can be grouped into one desirable quality of oral style. The opposite quality is weak, tame, drab, colorless, lifeless, or dull. Animated, colorful style suggests an active mind and responsive emotions behind it. It permits the listeners to hear, see, and feel what the speaker thinks and how he feels about it. In order to achieve emphasis through word choice, speakers use short and specific words, active voice, affective language, and short groupings of words. To get emphasis by the selection of supporting details, they use figures of speech, vivid experiences, quotations from highly regarded sources, dramatized ideas, striking facts, and emotive allusions to literature, etc. Achieving emphasis by means of sentence arrangement involves choices among these devices: suspense-order or climax-order of key ideas, anthithesis and balance in some sentences, varied sentence structures, placing strong words at beginnings and ends, and giving more space to important materials. It is well known that the principal emphatic devices are intensives (*profoundly, deeply,* etc.) repetition, position, and pause (in delivery).

Accuracy means grammatical correctness, precision of denotation and connotation, fidelity of sentence to idea, specificity of words, and the ability to express desired nuances of meaning. When this quality is lacking we get verbal atrocities: *enormity* misused to mean *enormousness*, *disinterested* for *uninterested*, *imply* for *infer*, *lion's share* for *larger part*, *American way* for *my way of doing things*, *un-American* or *socialistic* or *communistic* for *people, ideas, and practices I dislike intensely*. Some writers on semantics call these "blah" words.

How can accuracy in oral style be improved? One suggestion is to select simple, familiar, specific words which have relatively precise referents. An abridged dictionary, by the way, is of little value when words like *discrimination* and *reasonable* are at issue. Extremists on both sides avidly seize upon whichever one of several listed meanings suits their purposes, and in the case of *discrimination,* the choices could be *ability to make nice distinctions* (virtue word) or *unfair or injurious distinction* (bad word). A second suggestion is the use of apt illustration, which Beecher called "a window in an argument." Other means include the use of vivid description, the citation of specifics that constitute a generalization, and, best of all, a systematic program of personal vocabulary improvement.

Suggestiveness is the quality which enables a speaker's language to say more than the words explicitly state. For one thing, it says something about the speaker. As Buffon put it, "Style is the man himself." One implication of this is the individuality of style, which should warn us against imitating the styles of others. The charge of affectation is the imitator's reward. In some of the writings and speeches in the appendixes there are interesting specimens of suggestive style. Here are a few of the connotations a reader might notice concerning certain persons or ideas: that someone was naive, that someone felt his adversary to be inferior to himself, that a situation was intolerably bad, that there was a shameful motive behind an act, and that of course we want the United States to be ahead of all other countries in whatever one is discussing.

Directness in the mental sense is a function of style. The goal is a conversational quality but only in the best sense of the word. The sloppiness of much conversation is not being held up as a standard. What we do want is the spontaneity, genuineness, and intellectual crackle of the most stimulating conversation. Assuming that a speaker has something worth hearing, he can improve his directness by means of certain adaptive techniques. He can adapt his expressions to the experiences of his listeners, the purpose of his speech, and the occasion, for instance. A direct speaker senses what his listeners think and feel, and he adjusts to them, even though he does not intend to agree with their conclusions. He uses their experiences and talks their language. Devices of direct discourse—questions, answers, imaginary dialogue, personal pronouns—are specifically intended to increase directness. Observe the directness of Newton Minow's "Vast Wasteland" speech in Appendix C.

Unobtrusiveness or ease characterizes an oral style that does not call attention to itself, either because of its polish or because of its roughness. If there be ornament, it should be used without a suggestion of display or pomposity. The style should not "smell of the lamp," which is an ancient way of saying that one's style should not sound as if he had worked on it far into the night. Nor should it sound as if the total preparation had taken place in the few minutes between classes. Appropriate language cannot be precisely prescribed for all occasions, but at least one can avoid any superfluous "big" words, immoderate language, boners, and the like. Some speakers have achieved unobtrusiveness with figurative and rhythmic prose, others with rather plain styles. The test is the listeners' subjective appraisal; if they think a speaker is more concerned with his language than his ideas and his listeners, they will consider his style obtrusive.

Clearness is, from many points of view, the most important quality of oral and written discourse. Although we cannot literally convey our ideas to others, we can use audible and visible symbols which our audiences interpret in their own terms. Thus the clarity of our symbolization is of great importance. There must be a community of reference between a speaker and his audience if clearness is to be achieved. This implies the importance of audience analysis beforehand and some "feedback" during and after the speech. Two test questions are suggested: Will the typical listener understand the arguments? Will the best informed listeners find the arguments impossible to misunderstand?

If we may assume that a given speaker's thinking is clear, which is assuming a great deal, there are steps he can take to clarify his verbal expression. The use of specific and concrete language to clarify general and abstract concepts is one such step. Those who follow each abstraction with a "for instance" are using this procedure. Generalities have their place, but it is not to disguise shallow ideas. Specificity in language means closeness to reality, as in saying "a tall, slender, sharp-featured man" instead of just "a man." Concreteness refers to physical substance as in "Honest Joe," while the abstraction would be "honesty." Other aids to clearness are the minimal use of involved sentences, a serious attempt to use the language of the audience, the development of a smooth progression of ideas which make the "drift" of the speech clear, and the use of definition where needed for instantaneous intelligibility.

Variety or freshness implies originality and imagination as opposed to monotony and banality. Attention and interest are often captured and held by this quality of style. Two intercollegiate speech events have provided some negative instances of variety. A winning oration in 1961 opened with this trite sentence: "Picture, if you will, a jury room in one of our large Midwestern cities." Each speaker in the West Point final debate of 1962 seemed to have some favorite words which were used to excess. The unedited tape reveals the frequent use of these sentence openers: *and then, this then, but then, and then, then what, now, well, what about,* and *one, two, three.* There is a figure of speech, called anaphora, which involves the use of the same beginning in a series of clauses or sentences, but the repetition of *then* in the example above grew tiresome. However, it was no worse than "stranger than fiction," "better late than never," "it's a small world," "teeming millions," and "usually reliable sources."

Characteristic Figures

Any scholarly effort to distinguish between the characteristic figures of speech in oral discourse and those in written discourse would have to be based upon an extensive survey using the technique of content analysis. This would mean defining the figures, finding and counting them in a large number of speeches and essays, and determining in which mode of discourse each figure was more likely to appear. This has not been done. Instead, the familiar figures of speech will be discussed under "Oral Composition," even though they appear in written discourse as well.

Simile is a somewhat exact form of comparison, and it is identified by the presence of *like* or *as.* It seems to come to mind more readily than the subtler metaphor, and for that reason it is typically an oral device. When a likeness is developed at greater length and is used as a form of reasoning, we call it either an argument from comparison or an analogy, depending upon whether the parallel is literal or figurative. This simile appeared in a student's speech on a constitutional controversy: "Two of the basic principles of democracy are like two pillars which support the arch: one the principle that all men are equally entitled to life, liberty, and the pursuit of happiness, and the other the belief that such opportunity will best advance our civilization."

Contrast or antithesis means the juxtaposition of opposites to highlight differences. Advocates often use it to point up the differences between the present situation and a proposed change, or between affirmative and negative plans. A student speaker said, ". . . first in war, last in peace; talk big, but act little." Another student contrasted the sudden type of war we knew in 1917 and 1941 with the long, uncertain, smoldering kind of conflicts we have to cope with nowadays.

Direct discourse, which has been alluded to earlier, takes several forms, four of which are popular in speechmaking. They are pronouns of the first and second person, quotation or dialogue, rhetorical question, and questions and answers. The personal pronouns are *I, my, mine, me, we, our, ours, us, you, your,* and *yours.* They can increase the personal touch in a speech, but the first four can, if not used judiciously, suggest a speaker who is self-centered. Real or imaginary conversation can improve directness through creating the illusion of real talk, as in "I'd rather be found in the beam of an enemy searchlight than in the awful glare of an understanding woman." In the strict sense, a rhetorical question is interrogative in form but not intent. The speaker expects listeners to infer the desired response, as in this example: "Shall our mineral wealth sleep undeveloped in the soil? Shall our waterpower run idle, and the bustle of our factories cease? Shall our laborers go unemployed?" Sometimes a speaker leaves nothing to chance; he answers his own question. In that event the question is not rhetorical. Here is a combination of dialogue and question: "Joe, the Italian boy who worked next to me, wants to ask a question: 'What is more important— the tin can or the man.' To whom shall he go for the answer? To the foreman? . . ."

Exaggeration for emphasis rather than for deceit is called hyperbole. It is popular in political controversy. According to many campaigners, disaster looms just before each election, and it can be averted only by voting as the speaker requests. Rufus Choate's use of hyperbole in this specimen is less heavy-handed and much more fanciful than the average:

I would as soon think of bounding a sovereign state on the north by a dandelion, on the east by a bluejay, on the south by a hive of bees in swarming time, and on the west by three hundred foxes with firebrands tied to their tails, as of relying upon the loose and indefinite bounds of commissioners a century ago.

Sarcasm and ridicule should be marked "handle with care." Even if a speaker does not hesitate to hurt the feelings of his personal target, he should ponder the probability that his listeners will think less favorably of him for his unkind remark. Any unsportsman-like, ill-mannered, or intemperate remark may undermine a speaker's ethos. In sarcasm the distinguishing feature is its harshness; it has none of the playfulness of some satire and irony: "If your plan is so good, why don't you call up the President and tell him about it?" In the heat of a high school debate, one boy said with reference to his opponent's Western footwear: "He has to wear cowboy boots so he can wade away from the lectern after his speech." With reference to ridicule, a professor of philosophy once said, "If it's ridiculous, why not ridicule it?" The answer is that ridiculing a foolish idea is not so bad if one can resist the temptation to ridicule the person. True, the two are not easy to separate, but many of us do not even make an attempt to separate them.

Metaphor is a short, compact, and implied comparison. It serves to arouse images, gain attention, and enable persons to see significant resemblances. "Our present mode of making appointments is a blindfold game," said Carl Schurz. A student orator used this metaphor: "Without freedom of thought . . . we can blow out the light and fight it out in the dark . . ."

Metaphors are risky in extemporaneous speaking because of the probability of mixing them and producing boners: "We must bring this deadly viper (liquor traffic) to its knees"; "The administration has knifed the male students in the back once again. Maybe this time they've hit the straw that will break the camel's back."

Irony and satire are related but not identical. When a writer or a speaker implies something quite different from what he says, either to amuse or to hold up to disapproval, he is using irony. Thus a writer who intensely disliked the late publisher of the *Chicago Tribune* referred to him as "that eminent historian, learned military strategist, political philosopher, savior of America, and expert on revised spelling." Satire may include irony or sarcasm used for serious, playful, or malicious purposes. For example, when the English customs officers imposed a duty on some crates of snow which were imported from Norway for a ski-jumping contest, a satirist wrote, "Ready, men? Watch out for French air in the bicycle tires, Swiss mud on the ski boots, Italian sunburn, Continental *élan.*"

Lesser figures include alliteration, pun, onomatopoeia, interjection, and some others the names of which either amuse or astound. Alliteration means the use of the same letter or sound at the beginning of a series of words, as in "cunningly concocted," "only the bunting but not the blood," and "haughty, hating Tories." Imitative words suggest natural sounds, as in *buzz, whirr,* and *splash.* This interjection was written in a prepared speech: "The continued security of our country demands that we aid the enslaved millions of Europe—yes, even of Germany—to win back their liberty and independence." Amplification by climax order was used by Debs: "I said then, I say now, that while there is a lower class, I am in it; while there is a criminal element, I am of it; while there is a soul in prison, I am not free." Style like this is rarely an impromptu phenomenon; it takes practice and time.

WRITTEN COMPOSITION

What Is Involved

Written style is not merely a matter of avoiding the so-called mechanical errors; it involves word choice, sentence construction, paragraph development, the techniques of revision, and related matters. A brief reminder of some common errors to be avoided or corrected will serve to introduce the instructions on writing. Malformed invented words qualify as linguistic horrors: *academic-wise, escapees* for those who escape, *standees* for those who stand, etc. Why not *readees* for readers and *sitees* for sitters? Faulty repetition is a second type of error, as in "The modern Communist of today must not give his first loyalty to his own country." Misplaced modifier is a third type: "While attacking the United States and England, Acheson ruled Gromyko out of order." A fourth is shifted construction, and in the following specimen the shift is from active to passive voice: "The delegates were getting their work done rapidly in the morning session, but in the afternoon they were found wrangling and wasting time." Fifth in our list is the run-on sentence or comma fault: "The first meeting was a failure, the chairman became disgusted and left the room." Pronouns of the wrong case comprise the sixth error: "I hope you don't mind me sitting here." Wrong verb tense is seventh: "The old invasion route lays across the Middle East." Finally, there is lack of agreement: "If there is any one of us who cannot trust their own judgment, they ought to admit it now."

Some kind of training routine is called for when students do not write competently. The freshman English requirement has for many years been intended to serve that need, but its success in doing so has been a perennial proposition for debate. The kind of written composition that we are discussing here is not creative writing or fine writing; it is argumentative writing. It is the kind that takes place after one has assembled and outlined his material on one side of a proposition. Any program that is intended to improve this kind of writing should include these elements: 1. A procedure for determining who has the prerequisite intelligence and desire to learn; 2. Some experiences to make students more keenly aware of style; 3. Analytical-critical reading of specimens; 4. Writing argumentative discourses; 5. Thoroughgoing criticism by teacher and students; 6. Required revision of each manuscript that is returned to a student. This represents a considerable amount of work for students and teachers. Thus far we have not invented machines to do it for them.

Steps in Process

Sentence construction normally precedes paragraph development in the teaching of the writing process. The following sentence in a student's argumentative editorial was also a paragraph. Its construction exemplifies some of the problems we face in writing and in criticizing the writing of others:

To sneer on the small jobs that are being done toward this end and to suggest that there is no starting point is an advocation of an inert attitude that would hope for prejudice and discrimination to be eradicated by their own momentum.

One may say that a sentence is defective if it fails to represent the writer's purpose, his view of the subject matter, or if it does not improve the reader's grasp of the subject, or if it actually confuses him. A systematic study, including writing, of sentence elements, the ordering of the elements, and the relationships among those elements is the best way to effect the desired improvement.

Paragraph development is the second major step in the writing process. In argumentative writing one is concerned with logical paragraphs as distinguished from the chronological and the impressionistic. A logical paragraph begins with a topic sentence which was a point or a subpoint in the case outline. The rest of the paragraph supports the topic sentence with reasons, evidence, and kindred materials. Suppose a writer has a case outline in which the first point in partition is set up like this:

    I. —
       A. —
          1. —
          2. —
       B. —
          1. —
          2. —

How many paragraphs should he write? For a short essay he might write only one or two paragraphs, but for a longer case he might easily write four. Much of what has been written in this book pertains to the process of building such paragraphs.

Revision of the resulting manuscript can be accomplished by adding, deleting, and changing. Content, arrangement, and style—especially style at this stage—are possible candidates for revision. One writer should have done a bit of editing on this sentence: "My feelings in the matter are not alone, as I have many upright citizens who are friends of mine and of yours who agree with me that the present action of the city and Northwestern is uncalled for." The following paragraph was in the first draft of a written speech:

The second organization that I would consider this afternoon is the Rio Pact, the pact of defensive nature that exists between the nations of the Western Hemisphere. One major defect of this organization is its limited memebership, that is, it only concerns the Western Hemisphere. And aside from that, again, it does not provide for the economic bolstering of Europe. It does not provide a coordinated propaganda attack or approach to the Russian people.

Below is the revised draft of the above paragraph from a student's speech manuscript:

Thus it appears that the largest international organization, the United Nations, has some serious defects. "But," you may ask, "is there no other scheme that will help?" Perhaps there is. Let us consider a second attempt, the Rio Pact. As you probably know, this is a defense pact among the nations of this hemisphere. That is of some value, to be sure. But this regional defense pact has three weaknesses which may concern us seriously. It includes *only* the nations in *our* part of the world. It does not do anything about the economic bolstering of Europe. It provides no way to influence the captive peoples behind the "iron curtain."

DELIVERY

Scope of Treatment

Anyone who speaks to an audience becomes involved with delivery, the elements of which are voice, bodily action, platform behavior, and eye contact. This book merely reviews these main topics, because it is assumed that the fundamentals of public speaking have been studied elsewhere. No one should draw the inference that delivery is incidental or trivial. A little observation will convince most persons that delivery can make an argument sound worse than it is, which is regrettable, or better than it is, which is an ethical problem.

Expressive Voice

Vocal aspects of delivery add meaning to what is said. Listeners judge how a speaker means his remarks, and they derive impressions of his personality through the suggestive impact of his presentation. A voice that is to communicate and thereby influence others must be heard, be pleasant (or not unpleasant) to listen to, and not be so unusual as to distract attention from the message.

Melody, which is expressive modulation in pitch, is absent in monotonous voices. Dull, flat voices inadequately express ideas that require sincerity, animation, and intensity. Exercises for drill in vocal variety include questions and answers, dialogue between characters, and assertions which are to be given several meanings by changing the vocal melody.

Time or rate can be too fast or too slow. Tournament debaters as a class belong in the first category. However, a halting, *and-uh, well-er* rate can be even more annoying. Variety in pause, rhythm, and rate prevents the monorate form of indirectness and facilitates the communication of nuances of meaning.

Force or emphasis enables one to be heard without electronic augmentation, as the gadgeteers say. A speaker must make himself heard, and he should vary his loudness or his intensity to indicate the stress he wishes to place on each word or phrase. Vocal force in speech serves the same function as underlining and exclamation marks do in writing. While using force in this way, a speaker should maintain a reserve for use in moments of maximum emphasis.

Quality is suggestively related to the sincerity and intensity of a speaker's emotional reactions. Listeners are influenced by the clarity, purity, resonance, and general timbre of vocal sounds. A responsive vocal instrument can convey the emotional color that stems from genuine feeling. Voices that squeak, whine, whisper, wheeze, or rasp do not make oral argument sound impressive. We prefer a voice that suggests integrity, self-assurance, warmth, and other positive attributes.

Articulation is the process of shaping the consonants with the action of tongue, lips, jaw, and soft palate. Intelligibility and even social acceptability are impaired by slurred articulation, strange accents, mispronunciation, and some dialects or regional peculiarities. Some of the common faults are lisping, infantilism, tight jaw, and talking with a foreign substance in the mouth. Clinical attention is suggested for cases that do not respond to simple drills.

Visible Aspects

The visible code includes posture, movement, gesture (including facial expression), eye contact, and external visual aids. It is important because audiences look as well as listen, and because the *whole* person speaks. The visible part of delivery suggests something of the personality, aids in conveying meaning, provides emphasis, adds variety, helps to hold attention, serves as an outlet for nervous energy, and stirs up emphatic responses in the audience.

Mechanical directions on stance and movement are elocutionary and passé. This is not to disparage the use of general hints. First, effective movement is coordinated, meaning that all of the body must work as a unit. Second, the whole body should be animated and respond to what the voice and the language say. Third, all action is better when integrated with the ideas, inwardly motivated, and somewhat uninhibited. Fourth, there should be some reserve in a speaker's action, that is, action should be spontaneous yet controlled. But the reading of these general hints will not serve to modify the physical behavior of many student speakers. They need also to be observed and criticized by qualified teachers.

Meaning of Extempore

In the literature of public speaking, *extempore* does not mean offhand or without preparation, as some dictionaries have it. When speech people speak of completely unprepared or ad lib speaking, they call it *impromptu*. Extempore, extemporaneous, or "extemp." speaking is the kind of public address in which the speaker knows in advance what, in general, he is going to say, but in which the final composition takes place during the act of speaking. The speaking advocate knows his proposition; he has analyzed and investigated it; he has assembled his proof; he has outlined his case. It may be that he has also modified the outline into speaking notes and has learned his opening and closing paragraphs. There remains only the task of composing oral sentences and paragraphs while he speaks. *Only* is deceptively simple. The best extemporaneous speech has the desirable qualities of good conversation plus appropriate modifications in rate, sentence structure, and vocabulary. It is prepared yet flexible. It is not read, done from memory, or given without preparation; it is composed from notes by the speaker while he is speaking. Anyone who cannot learn from this exposition the nature of extemporaneous speaking can be assured that participation in the direct-clash assignment for Chapter X will remedy the deficiency.

QUESTIONS

1. In terms of your own observation, what would be a fair statement of the role of presentation in oral argument?
2. Comment upon the style of the obviously written messages in the appendixes.
3. Evaluate the oral styles in Appendixes C and F.
4. Identify and evaluate the figures of speech in designated speeches or essays.

EXERCISES

1. Recast an essay (Appendix B or another) into a speech as you would care to give it. Explain the differences you have seen fit to make.

2. Prepare a manuscript of a short argumentative speech. After someone else has read it and made comments, prepare a revision.

3. Compile critical notes on a round of extemporaneous argumentative speeches or a series of debate exercises. Note the matters of style which were treated in this chapter. A played-back tape would aid in the corrective procedure.

4. Discuss the kind and the qualities of style in a piece which is satirical or ironical. Might it have the effect of argument? One specimen is Harry Golden's "My P-T Plan" in *Saturday Review*, January 17, 1959.

APPENDIX A

CASE OUTLINES

AFFIRMATIVE AND NEGATIVE ON A PROPOSITION FOR SCHOOL DEBATING [1] (Resolved, that the federal government should provide complete medical care for all citizens at public expense).

AFFIRMATIVE

Introduction

Affirmative philosophy rests upon three assumptions: complete medical care is the right of all citizens; it is the responsibility of government to provide essential care which individuals cannot provide for themselves; all citizens should have equal health care opportunities.

Discussion

I. Significant harms result from failure to have complete medical care for all citizens, for
   A. Much loss could be prevented with adequate medical care if disease is detected early, because

[1] Adapted from materials prepared by students in the National High School Institute in Speech at Northwestern University, August, 1963.

[*241*]

    1. Many deaths and illnesses could be prevented with prompt and early treatment, for

        a) "At least 90,000 lives are lost needlessly each year because of chronic illness. If these diseases were caught in time, at least these 90,000 could have been saved." (E. E. Witte, *Social Security Perspectives*, 1963.)

    2. Many days of work and school are lost due to illness that could be prevented, for

        a) "A total of 250.3 million days were lost by workers during 1960. On an average day during that year, there were 1,050,000 employees absent from work." (Health Insurance Institute, *Source Book of Health Insurance Data*, 1962, p. 8.)

B. Many unnecessary deaths and illnesses occur because people are unable to pay for adequate medical care, for

    1. Income is the overwhelming determining factor of the ability to get needed medical care. (University of Michigan Study Appearing in the Report to the Senate Finance Committee, June, 1960.)

C. There is a great national injury suffered because of unnecessary death and illness, because

    1. National efficiency is hurt because of work days lost, for

        a) "Employed Americans lose millions of days of work each year because of acute illness, the U.S. National Health Survey reports. A total of 250.3 million days were lost by workers in 1960. On an average day during the year, there were 1,051,000 employees absent from work." (Department of Health, Education, and Welfare, U.S. Health Survey, 1962.)

    2. Contagious diseases are a threat to national health, for

        a) "Eight hundred thousand Americans with serious contagious diseases need medical supervision to protect the health of the general public, but four hundred thousand of these—that's one half—are receiving no supervision of any kind." (*Public Health Reports*, 1960.)

D. Certain groups of the population have particularly poor health, for

    1. The aged have poor health, for

        a) "While the aged constitute about 9 per cent of the

population, they make up more than 55 per cent of all persons with limitations due to chronic illness." (*Basic Facts on the Health and Economic Status of Older Americans,* June, 1961.)

2. The indigent have poor health, for

a) "Most forms of cancer, arthritis, asthma, respiratory infection, disorders of the genital organs, and skin diseases are more prevalent among the poor. Even heart disease, commonly regarded as the affliction of bankers and executives, occurs at higher rates among people of lower income." (A Committee of Physicians, *Monthly Review,* September, 1960.)

E. General health levels of the U.S. are not as high as needed or desirable, for

1. Infant death rates are lower in other countries, for

a) "Our infant mortality rate per 1,000 live births in 1958, was 26.9 which compares with 23.9 in the United Kingdom, 22.2 in Switzerland, and 15.8 in Sweden." (Marion B. Folsom, "Goals of a National Health Program for Meeting Needs," *Annals of the American Academy,* September, 1961.)

2. Life expectancy is higher in other countries, for

a) "Dr. O. L. Peterson, Assistant Director of the Rockefeller Foundation, reported that a dozen countries in the world have lower mortality rates than the United States, that Americans see a doctor more often (5.3 visits a year) than Britons (4.7) or Sweden (2.5) and that the citizens of the United States have the shortest life span of the three countries." (*New York Times,* August 30, 1962.)

II. The economic flaws in the present system are serious and inherent, for

A. The cost of medical care is high and rising, because

1. The cost of medical care is high and growing faster than the average consumer price index, for

a) ". . . we find that the cost of medical care has been increasing at a faster rate than any other part of the cost-of-living index. The overall increase in consumer prices from 1947 to December 1960 has been 27.5 per cent. The cost of medical care during that same period has increased 58 per cent or more than twice . . ." (M. B. Folsom, *Annals of the American Academy*, September, 1961.)

2. This trend will continue, and
3. The cost of medical care is rising faster than the per capita income, and
4. Hospital, doctor, and drug costs have risen greatly, for
   a) "The biggest increase has been in hospital rates, which have risen since 1947–9, 123 per cent. Other health costs have risen in this fashion: Physician's fees, 45 per cent; dental care, 37 per cent, eye care, 21 per cent, drugs, 23 per cent. Health Insurance premiums are up, too—for instance, hospitalization policies cost 74 per cent more now than in 1952." (*Changing Times*, "Budgeting for Medical Bills," June, 1961.)
5. People are spending a greater portion of their income on medicine, for
   a) "They put out close to $20 billion a year now—about 6 per cent of their disposable income. In 1950, it took about 4½ per cent of disposable income." (*Business Week*, "Health Insurance: Why Spending Is Soaring," June 24, 1961, p. 148.)

B. The causes of the cost increase are inherent in our medical system, for
1. In general, this cost increase is the result of medicine's being a private business, and
2. Some hospital cost increases are due to essential specialization and research for better equipment, and
3. Doctors' fees increase for inherent reasons, for
   a) Attempts to provide comprehensive medical care under a fee-for-service system have always resulted in progressive pyramiding of costs. (Dr. George Baehr, *Doctors, Patients and Government*, 1953.)
4. High drug costs are caused by tremendous mark-ups necessary to make a profit, support publicity campaigns, engage in research, and provide a profit for the several middlemen involved, for
   a) ". . . some prescription drugs have been marked up 7,000 per cent by the time they reach the sickroom table." (William Michelfelder, *It's Cheaper to Die*, 1960, p. 15.)

5. Cost increases result from the wasteful duplication of our medical facilities, for

a) ". . . another general problem needing urgent attention is the lack of proper coordination of health activities. There is far too much duplication of effort and far too little overall planning at local, state and national levels. Our resources of men and money could be employed more profitably if more wisely administered and more closely coordinated." (Marion B. Folsom, *Journal of Public Health*, June, 1963.)

C. Many groups cannot afford complete medical care, because

1. The aged cannot finance their medical care, for

a) Aged insurance policies are inadequate, for

(1) "Private health insurance doesn't meet the problem. Most insurance companies simply will not insure persons sixty-five or over, those that do charge premiums of seven dollars to ten dollars monthly which most older persons cannot afford. So more than half of the aged have no private insurance coverage at all, and those who do have limited protection." (*Nation*, "Which Bill Is Best," May 28, 1960.)

b) The aged need an excessive quantity of medical care, for

(1) ". . . more than half of these old people have yearly incomes of less than $1,000. One government study in 1958 showed that nearly half of them had less than $500 in liquid assets to their name, and nearly a third had no assets at all. And only 40 per cent have some kind of private medical insurance. On a per capita basis, people 65 or over spend twice as much time in hospitals, and pay out nearly twice as much in medical bills as those under 65." (*Newsweek*, August 29, 1960.)

c) The aged have higher health costs, for

(1) "People 65 and over have two to three times as much chronic illness as the rest of the population. . . . Their expenditure for health services is 90 per cent greater than expenditures on health by the rest of the public; for hospitals, it is 120 per cent higher and for drugs it is also 120 per cent higher." (Sena-

tor Wayne Morse, *Congressional Record*, October 26, 1961.)

2. The indigent are not provided medical care, because
   a) Indigent persons can afford very little of anything and must budget first more necessary items, and
   b) Welfare programs do not adequately provide care for the indigent for
      (1) "Seven million persons on public relief, and other low income families, have more than their share of illness and receive by ordinary standards inadequate health care." (Dr. James Dixon, stated in Congress, July, 1959.)
3. Youth cannot afford care because incomes are inadequate below the age of twenty-four, and
4. Middle-income groups cannot afford complete medical care, because
   a) They cannot withstand severe and prolonged major bills, and
   b) Constant drug treatment is too costly.
5. Rural groups cannot afford adequate medical care, for
   a) Generally, they have low incomes, for
      (1) "While private health insurance is inadequate for most city folk, farmers have even less; it is of poorer quality; it costs more; it pays less of the bill." (Pat McNamara, *Congressional Record*, May 17, 1962.)
   b) Most health insurance is associated with industrial salary plans.
      (1) "It is a sad fact that the individual commercial policies which give such a poor return in benefits are more prevalent among low income families, particularly rural ones, who tend to fall less obviously into some insurable groups. (*The Economist*, August 29, 1959.)
D. Private health insurance is an inadequate means of financing medical care, for
   1. Insurance rates are too high and are increasing, for
      a) "The charges made to subscribers and policy holders for hospital, medical, and surgical costs have been increasing sharply during recent years . . . they are justified and further increases might be expected." (National

Association of Insurance Commissioners, 93rd Annual Meeting, 1962 proceedings, Volume II, Conclusions of Blue Cross—Blue Shield Studies, p. 497.)

2. The aged cannot purchase insurance, for
   a) "Private health insurance programs are not meeting the special needs of aging, because such programs discriminate against the elderly through higher premiums and reduced benefits." (Senator McNamara, United States Senate Committee on Aging, July 11, 1961.)

3. National enrollment in insurance programs is insufficient, for
   a) "Allowing for duplication it appears that 44 per cent of the population at most were covered. Altogether less than one half of the population had any insurance against non-surgical doctor bills." (Herman M. Somers, *Doctors, Patients and Health Insurance*, 1961, p. 230.)

4. Much of the cost of private insurance policies goes into a profit margin for the company and middlemen, for
   a) "On some individually purchased policies, the broker gets 25 per cent, the general agent another 10, and the company itself charges more for its overhead." (Sidney Margolius, *A Consumers Guide to Health Insurance Plans*, p. 18.)

5. Low-income groups cannot afford insurance, for
   a) "Although they are the most in need of hospital insurance the poor have the least, since they can't afford the premiums: only 40 per cent of poor families have it, as against 63 per cent of all families." (Dwight MacDonald, *New Yorker*, January 19, 1963.)

6. Insurance policies are limited by maximum levels of benefits where no more will be paid to the insured, for
   a) "Because even in group policies there is frequently a maximum money limit leading to cancellation, the protection for many employees may prove at least partially illusory." (H. Somers, *Labor Law Journal*, July, 1958, p. 470.)

7. An unemployed person, who needs insurance most, cannot pay for it, for
   a) "A major problem with respect to group insurance coverage is its general dependence on the employment

status. Those who lose coverage at retirement or on being disabled or unemployed are in a poor position to
obtain any other health insurance." (Herman and Ann
Somers, "Doctor's Patient's and Health Insurance,"
Brookings Institute.)

8. An ill person cannot get insurance, for
   a) "Generally speaking, experience has indicated that serious inequities may arise if the insurance undertakes to
   pay benefits for conditions that existed at the time the
   policy was purchased. Hence, individual policies almost
   always exclude such pre-existing conditions from coverage." (Charles A. Siegfried, "Medical Expense Insure
   Group and Individual," *Life and Health Insurance Hand-
   book*, 1959, p. 551.)

9. Health insurance is the first budget item to be dropped in
   an economic depression although it is needed most, and

10. Insurance companies often enforce deductible clauses on
    the benefits they pay to the insured, for
    a) "Since most medical cost losses are small, a deductible
    provision eliminates the substantial claim payments and
    settlements associated with a great number of small
    losses. (O. D. Dickerson, *Health Insurance*, 1959, p. 96.)

E. Public aid is not adequate, for
   1. State welfare programs are inadequate, because
      a) Many indigent do not know what facilities are available,
      and
      b) The ability of states to support welfare programs is often
      inverse to the population's need for public welfare assist-
      ance, for
         (1) "Such thinking that all states are capable of adopting
         Kerr-Mills completely ignores the fact that many
         states are unable even with substantial help from
         the Federal Government to adequately finance the
         health needs or even the basic living requirements
         of the most indigent aged." (Special Committee on
         Aging, June 15, 1962.)
      c) Often no doctor choice is allowed the welfare recipient,
      for
         (1) "Even those relatively few aged persons who are de-
         clared eligible for some help under MAA frequently

find that they can't get care from doctor of their own choice." (Staff Report to Special Senate Committee on Aging, "Performance of the States," June 15, 1962.)

    d) Federal-state fund programs, such as Kerr-Mills, are inadequate, for

        (1) "As a result of 25 states not adopting the Kerr-Mills bill coverage and quality vary from state to state. Surely it would be far better and favorable to provide a universal approach instead of a needs test program which doesn't prevent idigency; but operates only after indigency is created." (Address by John F. Kennedy, January 21, 1963.)

2. Workmen's Compensation care is inadequate, for

    a) "Of the total premiums paid by insuring employers under workmen's compensation, it has been estimated by various authorities that only about 60 to 65 per cent reach the beneficiaries in the form of compensation payments or medical care . . . in contrast to between 95 to 98 per cent in such insurance as O.S.S.D.I. or Unemployment Insurance where the program is financed by governmentally collected taxes." (Dr. Burns, "Unemployment Insurance and the Workmen's Compensation," *Public Welfare*, January, 1962.)

3. The means test discourages the use of welfare, for

    a) "A major objection to the Kerr-Mills law . . . is that the patient must prove to a welfare interviewer that he can't pay his own medical bills. Many oldsters, the argument goes, are too proud to take the "means test." (*Newsweek*, April 12, 1962.)

4. Local control of welfare programs is often arbitrary and discriminatory, for

    a) "Arbitrary predetermined cutoffs, while simplifying somewhat the task of determining eligibility, do not take into account existing debts for medical care or anticipated medical costs. Thus, in a state with an income limit of $1200, an aged individual with an income of $1300 a year who has a heart condition which necessitates medical and nursing home care costing $3000 or $4000 a year is ineligible for medical assistance under the MAA program." (A Staff Report to the Special Senate Committee on Aging, "Performance of the States," June 15, 1962, p. 18.)

F. Private charity as a method for providing medical care is inadequate, for

   1. Charity pays only a small portion of medical bills, for

      a) "The charity load in all communities is rising, and the county and state pay only a portion of the cost of indigent care. The balance of this cost must be put on the private patient, the local charity, and the members of the prepayment program." (J. R. L. Johnson, Jr., "The Competitive Position of Blue Shield in Today's Market," *New York State Journal of Medicine*, Dec. 1, 1961.)

   2. Many needy persons avoid charity, for

      a) "The indigent often do without the care they need to avoid receiving medical charity." (Edward Chase, *Reporter*, May, 1961.)

III. The present system fails to provide adequate nationwide health care, for

  A. There are serious shortages of medical personnel and facilities in the United States, because

    1. There is a shortage of doctors, for

      a) There is a shortage of medical students, for

         (1) "Decisive federal action is necessary to stimulate and assist in the establishment and expansion of medical and dental schools and to help more talented but needy students to enter the health professions (while bolstering the quality of their training.)" (John F. Kennedy, Special Health Message to Congress, February 7, 1963.)

      b) The working conditions and income in general practice are unattractive, for

         (1) "Many GPs are disenchanted with long hours, night calls, etc. and leaving the field to specialize. As a result, medical students are reluctant to enter a "family doctor" career. This is supported by the fact that 70 per cent of physicians were GPs in 1930; five per cent are now." (*Science Digest*, May, 1963.)

    2. There is a lack of hospital facilities, for

a) "Complete medical care cannot be obtained today, because there is a lack of hospital accommodations. There is a shortage of beds. Over 40 per cent of the counties have no general hospitals to serve their 29,000,000 people." (*Nation's Health*, August 7, 1962, p. 34.)

3. There is a lack of nursing homes, for

a) "The Senate Subcommittee on Problems of the Aged and Aging reported that nearly one half of the 308,000 nursing homes were found nonacceptable because they failed to meet the fire and health standards. Even so, no beds at all were available for another 30,000 persons who need nursing home care."

B. There is a maldistribution of doctors and hospitals, because

1. Most facilities are located in urban areas, for

a) "The doctor has become preponderantly a city man. Today slightly more than one half of our people live in metropolitan areas but 70 per cent of the physicians are found here. Conversely, only 4 per cent of the physicians live in counties that have no larger than 2500 population whereas 8 per cent of the people live in such counties." (*Saturday Review*, February 26, 1955.)

2. Facilities tend to concentrate around the greater wealth found in urban areas, for

a) "The distribution of hospitals is far from equitable. Wealthy communities are better provided than those less endowed; and urban areas have many more hospital beds than the rural." (Avedis Donabedian, "Organizing Medicare Programs to Meet Health Needs," *Annals of American Academy*, September, 1961, p. 51.)

3. Some areas suffer from a harmful shortage of medical facilities, for

a) "There are urban centers with one physician per 600 population, while some towns have 1 per 2000–3000 . . . and some communities with 5000 have no physician at all." (*New York Times*, April 10, 1960.)

C. There is a harmful lack of preventive medicine in the U.S. today, for

1. A large portion of the population doesn't see a doctor even once a year, for

       a) "28 to 27 per cent of the population do *not* see a doctor even once a year." (*Doctors, Patients, and Health Insurance*, 1961, p. 156.)

  2. Economic factors deter persons from getting checkups, for

       a) "Under fee-for-service, consumers will tend to economize by seeking attention only when they are very ill. This discourages early diagnosis and treatment and extends cost and illness in the long run." (Jerome Rothenberg, "Welfare Implications of Alternate Methods of Financing Medical Care," *American Economic Review*, May, 1951.)

  3. Preventive and early treatment drugs are prohibitively expensive, for

       a) "Studies by economists, insurance carriers, and responsible cost analysts go as high as 200, 300, and 400 per cent increases since 1947 in the price of ethical (prescription) drugs." (William Michelfelder, *It's Cheaper to Die*, 1960, p. 10.)

  4. Because people wait until they are seriously ill before using medical facilities, our hospitals are overcrowded with people who would not have to be there if their illnesses were detected early.

  D. There is a harmful lack of coordination in our medical care system, for

    1. There is little planning for the system as a whole, and

    2. Wasteful duplication results, for

       a) "There is far too much duplication of effort and far too little overall planning at local, state, and national levels. Our resources of men and money could be employed far more profitably if more wisely administered and more closely coordinated." (Marion B. Folsom, *American Journal of Public Health*, June, 1963.)

IV. There is a program to provide complete medical care to all citizens at public expense, for

  A. Administrative control will be under the Department of Health, Education and Welfare, and

  B. Doctors and medical agencies will submit bills to local boards, and

  C. A federal board will be established to control abuses and set fee rates, and

    D. Financing can be done through one of several methods: income tax, employee tax, employer tax, or a combination of these, and

    E. Enforcement can take the form of suspension from the program or lesser fines.

V. Such a program is workable and will meet the affirmative need, because

    A. By paying the medical bill, the plan will eliminate the financial factor which bars the public from medical care, for

        1. "It is through some nationwide insurance program applicable to our entire population that the economic burden of illness can be met and a desirable degree of utilization attained of what medical science has to offer for the promotion and preservation of a healthy nation." (Subcommittee of the Aging, 86th Congress, April, 1960.)

    B. The plan will eliminate the financial factor to the individual, because it will strike at the cause of rising medical prices, the profit motive.

        1. "Although attention has been drawn to its manifest defects, the National Health Service has served the nation well. Year by year the chief medical officer of the Ministry of Health is able to report striking progress in the treatment of diseases. Medical and hospital facilities are more evenly distributed over the population and, with some exceptions, have shown notable improvements in quantity and quality. Over a wide range of care there is no barrier to anybody, whatever his position in society, obtaining treatment of the highest standard." (*New Statesman*, "Health Service Under Scrutiny," April 30, 1960, p. 632.)

    C. The plan will increase our supply of doctors by offering a greater financial opportunity to prospective doctors, and

    D. Doctors would distribute themselves more evenly because the paying abilities of the public would be more evenly distributed, for

        1. "In 1948, with private practice pulling doctors into more prosperous areas, 60 per cent of the people of Britain were living in . . . underdoctored areas. Today, only 18 per cent of the people now live in underdoctored areas . . . The total number of doctors in the United Kingdom has increased from 36,500 to over 49,000." (Don Cook, *Harper's*, May, 1959.)

E. The plan will encourage preventive medicine by paying the first costs of medical care and early treatment, for

   1. "It is surprising how much illness that used to remain undisclosed and unchecked, particularly among women, has come to light in the last six months. The period the doctor is speaking about was the total time in which the Health Service had been in effect. One can conclude that the Health Service encourages preventive medicine, since actually only the aged and the dependents of workers were ones not covered by the Health Service before 1948." (Dr. J. Leslie MacCallum, *New York Times Magazine*, June 9, 1949, p. 14.)

F. Because of its record abroad, a national health program would probably be successful here, for

   1. "Following countries have governmental health care programs: Argentina, Belgium, Brazil, France, West Germany, Great Britain, India, Italy, Japan, Mexico, Sweden." (House Interstate and Foreign Commerce Commission, *Congressional Digest*, March, 1955, p. 79.)

VI. The affirmative plan will not cause serious disadvantages, for

A. The cost of the program will not pose a serious problem, for

   1. It will not create a financial strain on the individual because

      a) The tax would not be an added burden, for

         (1) "Do not treat the taxes which support such a system as if they would be additional burdens on each American; most such taxes would merely replace what is now spent on medical care." (William DeMougeot, *Congressional Record*, February 15, 1962.)

      b) People would be relieved of the expense of paying medical or insurance costs out of pocket.

   2. The cost will not harm the national financial position, for

      a) It would relieve the tax program of the medical expense deduction, and

      b) Taxes would be adjusted upward to meet these new costs, and

      c) The cost of the program is not likely to be great, for

         (1) "The cost of administering a single nation-wide plan would be less than the administrative costs under many competing private insurance plans. The savings in administrative costs would make it possible to pay the same benefits as private insurance at less

cost, or more adequate benefits at the same cost."
(W. J. Cohen, *American Journal of Nursing*, April,
1960.)

3. The setting of fees will reduce the cost of health care, for
   a) "The basic answer to controlling unnecessary usage of
   services is not the imposition of fiscal controls upon the
   medically indigent . . . The answer lies in the use of
   medical controls whereby the person's physician and the
   physicians who comprise medical review boards are responsible for the decisions as to the necessity, appropriateness, and duration of medical care." (Special Committee on Aging, June 15, 1962.)
B. The quality of medical care would not deteriorate, because
   1. Facilities and services would not be overused, for
      a) ". . . it has been proved that the administrative over-
      head may be surprisingly low. The very limited number
      of surveys of the general practice in Europe does not offer
      evidence that the quality of medical care is lower in
      countries with prepaid medical systems." (Karl Evang,
      M.D., *American Journal of Public Health and the Na-
      tions Health*, April, 1958, Vol. 48, No. 4.)
   2. Removing financial barriers would improve the doctor-patient
      relationship, for
      a) "The absence of any financial barrier between doctor and
      patient must make the doctor-patient relationship easier
      and more satisfactory." (Dr. Guy H. Dain, *Harper's*,
      May, 1959, p. 33.)
C. There will be no shortage of doctors, because
   1. Doctors have no place to flee to; all other industrialized
      countries have similar systems, and
   2. Doctors in all other countries have eventually supported
      national health programs after they have been instituted, for
      a) "British doctors have their choice to join the National
      Health Service or not. Ninety-eight per cent have chosen
      to join." ("British Doctors and National Health Service,"
      Time, January 26, 1962.)
   3. The British experience reveals that the number of persons
      studying for the profession has not decreased because of
      government health activity, for
      a) "There has always been a certain flow of young English-

trained doctors to America as there is a traditional flow in the opposite direction of doctors seeking postgraduate experience in Britain. No evidence can be found of any change in this pattern attributable to the Health Service." (Kenneth Robinson, "Case for England's Health Service," *New York Times Magazine*, November 18, 1962.)

Conclusion

Therefore, since significant harms result from failure to have complete medical care for all citizens, since the economic flaws in the present system are serious and inherent, since the present system fails to provide nation-wide health care, since there is a program to provide complete medical care to all citizens at public expense, since such a program is workable and will meet the affirmative need, and since the affirmative plan will not cause serious disadvantages, we conclude that the federal government should provide complete medical care for all citizens at public expense.

NEGATIVE

Introduction

The philosophy of the negative is that the federal government should not be responsible for the medical care of all citizens, because it is not a federal obligation to provide medical care to *all* citizens, and a definite need should be shown before any person should expect to get free medical care from *any* source.

Discussion

I. The present situation in medical economics does not warrant drastic action, for
   A. Factors other than money deter many persons from using medical facilities, for

1. Lack of education is a factor, for
   a) "Educational attainment of the head of the family is directly related to the rate of physician visits among family members. The rates for the two-year period ending July, 1959, varied from a low of 4.3 visits per year for members of families whose head of family had had less than 5 years of education to a high of 6.0 visits for those whose head of family had attended college." (*Health Statistics*, from U.S. National Health Survey, U.S. Dept. of Health, Education, and Welfare, June, 1957–June, 1959.)

2. Fear is a factor, for
   a) "A survey of health needs and income revealed that in both low and high income groups unmet medical needs could be traced back to fear of treatment rather than to the amount of income." (E. G. Jaco, *Patients, Physicians and Illness*, 1958, p. 161.)

3. Religion is a factor, for
   a) "There are approximately forty religious denominations in the United States whose members number in the millions, believe in divine healing and who do not use medicine or medical treatment." (Dominco Gagliardo, *American Social Insurance*, Harper and Brothers, 1955, p. 513.)

4. No ill person will be denied care for financial reasons, for
   a) "The AMA, which represents 90 per cent of the practicing physicians in the country, has repeatedly affirmed its position that no one in America will be denied medical care solely because he cannot pay for it." (George M. Fister, *Saturday Evening Post*, February 23, 1963) and
   b) "We have an understanding among our members whereby anyone unable to pay or anyone without means of paying the regular fee is attended to without charge or at a fee based on inability to pay." (*Today's Health*, July, 1962.)

B. The financial barrier has been exaggerated, for
  1. Today we work fewer hours to pay for more medical care, for
   a) "The real cost of medical care in terms of hours of work to purchase it, is less today than it was 20 years ago. To pay for doctor's services required only 55 per cent as

as much working time in 1959 as in 1939. Surgeons—49 per cent; Dentists—56 per cent; Drugs—43 per cent; all care—61 per cent." (U.S. Bureau of Labor Statistics, *Today's Health,* April, 1961.)

2. Persons nowadays receive more for their health dollar, for

a) "From 1950 to 1960 medical science has made enormous strides. Lifesaving techniques and operations unheard of 10 years ago are widely available today. New diagnostic skills bring far earlier discovery and thus better chances for curing of disease. Drugs and equipment are available now to beat diseases and defects that only a decade ago were almost always fatal." (*Business Week,* June 24, 1961) and

b) "Eighty per cent of the drugs commonly prescribed today were unknown just 10 years ago. The United States had made more important drug discoveries in the last two decades than all the rest of the world combined, or seven times as many as the next leading country." (George Fister, *Today's Health,* February, 1963, p. 6.)

3. Private health insurance can meet most needs, for

a) Enrollment is high, for

(1) "Between 1960 and 1962 the number of private health insurance companies increased by 59.2 per cent from 1,147 to 1,739. Not only did the number increase but the benefits grew by 63 per cent. It is estimated that by 1972, 95 per cent of the nation's medical bills will be paid by private insurance companies." (*American Journal of Public Health,* March, 1963.)

b) Plans cover medical needs, for

(1) "In 1925, only 10 per cent of the cost of hospitalization was paid by insurance of one form or the other. The remainder was met by the individual from his own resources. Ten years ago, insurance paid 25 per cent of the hospital costs. Today it is 60 per cent. The prediction is that by 1970, 90 per cent of all private expenditures for hospital care will be paid for by some form of prepayment insurance." (Harry S. Salzstein, M.D., Detroit, Mich., *Journal of the Michigan Medical Association,* 1960.)

c) Rates are not prohibitive, for
  (1) During 1961 Blue Cross paid out $2,058,317,080 to hospitals for care of 11,621,550 members for 65,-108,910 days of care. This amount represents 92.36 per cent of total income, the remainder being devoted to total operating expenses, 4.98 per cent of total income and added 2.66 per cent to reserves. (1963 *World Almanac & Book of Facts*, p. 306.)
d) Limits on coverage are reasonable, for
  (1) "For total discharged patients, some 56 per cent of the male patients and 49 per cent of the female patients had ¾ or more of their hospital bills paid by health insurance. Of patients for whom health insurance paid some portion of their hospital bills, 79 per cent of the males and 73 per cent of the females had ¾ or more of the hospital bill paid (in 1961)." (Health Insurance Institute, "*Source Book of Health Insurance Data*," 1962, p. 65) and
  (2) "Even a $25 deductible would constitute a tremendous saving to insurance carriers through the elimination of a very considerable administrative cost, and through its effect in stimulating more efficient methods of care." (Walter Kidde, *Journal of the Medical Society of New Jersey*, March, 1960.)
e) The aged are covered, for
  (1) "3,500,000 over 65 now have Blue Cross-Blue Shield programs. The new programs will pay full cost of medical and surgical services for persons whose annual income is $2500 or less and couples whose income is below $4000. Surgery in office or hospital, 30–70 visits, anesthesia, radiation treatment, x-ray, and laboratory tests. Cost: $3.00 per month." (*New York Times*, January 19, 1962, p. 1.)
4. Public Assistance can cover the remainder, for
  a) Workmen's Compensation applies to many employed laborers, for
    (1) "In 1961 more than 43 million wage earners were protected by insurance or other formal arrangements against loss of income incurred during disability periods." (Health Insurance Council, 1963.)

   b) Veterans have Veterans' Administration benefits, and
   c) There are provisions for the indigent, for
      (1) "The Federal Government makes grants to the states
           to help them provide financial assistance, medical
           care, and other social services to the needy aged,
           blind or disabled, or to children dependent because
           of the death, disability, absence, or unemployment
           of a parent; and medical care for those aged per-
           sons who can provide for their maintenance, but are
           unable to pay for their medical care. In addition, in
           all the states some help is provided from state and/or
           local funds only to some other needy persons." (*In-
           formation Please Almanac*, 1963, p. 295.)
   d) The aged are being increasingly covered, for
      (1) "Probably close to 30 per cent of total public ex-
           penditures for patient care in hospitals goes for
           treatment of the aged who comprise only 9 per cent
           of the population." (*Health Care of the Aged*, U.S.
           Dept. of Health, Education and Welfare, 1962.)
   e) Unemployed persons are included, for
      (1) "It long has been the position of the members of
           the medical profession that no one needing medical
           attention should go without it because of inability
           to pay. This policy has been given greater publicity
           in recent years through special programs designed
           to inform the public of the medical profession's de-
           termination to see that no legitimate need for med-
           ical care goes begging." (*Today's Health*, March,
           1962.)
5. Title VI of the Mills Bill (or its equivalent) would remedy
   any minor flaws, for
   a) It would cover the gaps in existing programs for the
      needy, and
   b) It would exempt those who do not need help, and
   c) It would be locally administered
C. The place of medical bills in the family financial situation is
   often distorted, for
   1. Only a minority have great costs, for
      a) "A survey prepared for the Federal Reserve Board
         showed that 80 per cent—43 out of 53 million—of Amer-

ican families reported no medical debts whatsoever. Only 1.2 million families, a mere 3 per cent reported debts of over $200.00." (Walter B. Martin, House Committee on Interstate and Foreign Commerce, January 28, 1954.)

2. Tax deductions may be taken for medical bills, and
3. It is unreasonable to exempt health costs from inclusion in consumer credit, and
4. We spend as much on nonessentials as we do on medical care, for
    a) "Many so-called low-income families have cars, radios, TV's, and other once considered luxury goods. The concept of the bare American grubbing for a bare existence is becoming obsolete. (E. G. Jaco, *Patients, Physicians and Illness*, 1958, p. 69.)
5. Loans for paying bills are available.

D. The health situation in the U.S. is good, for
  1. Mortality rate is constantly declining, for
    a) "The general death rate has gone down steadily since the turn of the century. In 1900 there were 17.2 deaths per 1,000 people; in 1958 there were 9.5 deaths per thousand. This marked the tenth consecutive year in which the death rate was below 10 per thousand of population." (U.S. Dept. of Health, Education and Welfare, 1959.)
  2. Survival rates of mothers and infants has been increasing, for
    a) "The safety of mothers at childbirth has increased drastically from a mortality rate of 63.3 per 1000 live births in 1933–34 to a low of 4.5 in the 4 years ending in 1958. In the same period, the mortality of infants after their first week of life dropped from 33.9 per 100 live births to 9.6." (Dr. Austin Smith, "The Health of a Nation," *Vital Speeches*, January 15, 1960.)
  3. Life expectancy continues to improve, for
    a) "The life span of Americans has lengthened 20 years since 1900. In 1920, only 4.7 per cent of the population were 65 years of age or over. Today, this figure has risen to 9.2 per cent. This year there are almost 17 million Americans who are 65 or over." (*America*, June 9, 1962, p. 383.)
  4. The shortage of physicians is exaggerated, for
    a) "According to official estimates there are approximately

261,000 licensed physicians in the U.S. today. That works out to one physician for every 760 people, the lowest ratio in the world except for Israel." (*US News & World Report*, May 28, 1962) and

b) "Many diseases that once required prolonged medical treatment now can be cured quickly through the use of new drugs and antibiotics. In a pneumonia case a doctor once made about 36 visits. Now he makes about 5." (*US News & World Report*, May 9, 1958.)

5. Hospital building is provided for under Hill-Burton Act.
6. Nursing homes are increasing rapidly, for
 a) "The number of nursing homes in the U.S. has increased from 7000 to 9700 from 1954 to 1961 . . . but the bed capacity rose from 180,000 to 338,700." (*Chicago Daily News*, April 11, 1963) and
 b) "Nursing homes have now mushroomed to provide nearly as many beds in the nation as do general hospitals." ("The Health Care of the Aged," U.S. Social Security Administration, 1962.)

II. The proposed plan would not solve the alleged problems, for
 A. Comparisons with other countries are invalid, for
  1. "America cannot be strengthened by copying medical systems under which one country after another has lost leadership in the science and art of medicine. The strength of this nation does not lie in the direction of substituting medical failure for medical success." ("Case against Socialized Medicine," *American Medical Association Journal*, March, 1962.)
 B. It would not get at the important noneconomic factors, for
  1. The Los Angeles County Medical Association regularly advertises in local newspapers that free medical care is available to anyone who (A) needs it, and (B) phones in to numbers listed in the ad. The most recent ads ran within the last month. Not one person has phoned. (Emil E. Brill, "Why a 'Must' Now?" *Missouri Medicine*, October, 1960) and
  2. Healing is an integral part of some religions.
 C. It would not increase the number of physicians, for
  1. "Students by a margin of more than 5 to 1, say they would be less enthusiastic about entering the medical profession

if health services were eventually nationalized as they are in Great Britain. A majority of the students favor private rather than federal funds for assistance in financing medical education. Half of those who say they would accept federal help insist it would have to come without strings attached." ("Future Doctors Oppose Federal Medicine," *Nation's Business*, June, 1962, p. 34.)

D. Preventive medicine would not be improved, for

    1. "Compulsory health programs, wherever they operate always result in overcrowded waiting rooms and long waiting lists for admission to hospitals. Both conditions reduce the chance of early diagnosis of truly serious ailments—often billed as the most important aspect of government program." (Dr. Helmut Schoeck, "Why Socialized Health Schemes Fail," *Nation's Business*, March, 1963.)

III. Serious disadvantages would follow the adoption of the federalized health plan, for

A. It would prove to be costly, for

    1. "Expenditures under Sweden's compulsory health insurance plan have exceeded by far all expectations. The cost of the subsidy for prescriptions alone more than tripled in the first 6 years. Overall expenses for the NHS reached $545 million in 1960. A further increase to at least $900 million by 1970 now is anticipated." ("How Europe Deals With Medical Care," *U.S. News & World Report*, July 30, 1962) and

    2. "The British budget soared from 12 billion dollars in 1950 to an all time high of 18 billion in April, 1961. Two-fifths of this greatly increased sum now goes to the welfare state. And this is over and above local taxes for such social services as education, subsidized housing." (Graham Hutton, "America—Beware of the Welfare State," *Reader's Digest*, October, 1961.)

B. It would be inefficient, for

    1. "Under compulsory insurance, the government would become practically the sole buyer of the private practitioner's services. It could establish the rate of pay as surely as any monopoly can establish the price of a commodity. It has been estimated that about ¼ of our people don't adhere to or depend upon the services of medical institutions. The poor doctor would make about as much as the best. More pa-

tients, more annual medical visits, innumerable forms to be filled out, with no immediate increase in the number of doctors must . . . result in a rationed and degraded quality of medical care." (Haven Emerson, "Why Compulsory Medical Care Fails," *Christian Science Monitor*, March 8, 1963, p. 3) and

2. "The cost of medical care would presumably increase because of administrative expenses and the tendency of insured persons to make unnecessary and often unreasonable demands upon the medical care service." (*Business Week*, September 27, 1960.)

C. The shortage of doctors would be aggravated, for

1. Increasingly, England is relying on the general hospital staffing from doctors from overseas, particularly from the underdeveloped countries, from India and Pakistan. By 1960 they already had 41 per cent of all residents and interns born and trained outside England. (*U.S. News & World Report*, May 28, 1962, p. 72.)

D. The quality of medical care would deteriorate, for

1. "Concerning patient treatment, if the doctor must see as many patients as doctors under the British system do, the U.S. doctors will never have enough time. Doctors see 60 to 80 patients per day in England—can't spend a sufficient amount of time with any." (*New York Times Magazine*, February 18, 1962, p. 76.)

Conclusion

Therefore, since the present situation in medical economics does not warrant drastic action, since the proposed plan would not solve the alleged problems, and since serious disadvantages would follow the adoption of the federalized health plan, we conclude that the federal government should not provide complete medical care for all citizens at public expense.

APPENDIX B

AN ARGUMENTATIVE ESSAY

ISAAC STERN,
"WE'VE GOT TO MOVE FAST!"[1]

WE ARE LIVING IN A VERY IMPORTANT, DRAMATIC AND PERHAPS DAN-
gerous moment in our musical history. Western musical civilization as
we know it is going to be thoroughly tested and tried in the next ten
to fifteen years. Unless we are very alert to this and to the dangers involved we may be facing the end of the kind of culture we have known.
I don't think that the remedial actions can be delayed very long. They
have to be started now, not five years from now or ten years from now,
but now.

Over the last 30 years the center of standards has moved slowly
westward from Europe to the United States, via the great conductors,
the great performers, the teachers. We have inherited the best of traditions very much in the same way that we have inherited our mores and
our ethics from older civilizations. The war years, the oppressive years
in other areas, have forced people to come to us and to take root here.
They have taken root to the extent that today first and second generation Americans are the standard-setters. They are not students—they
are the teachers, because they have themselves been the children and
disciples of distinguished teachers of the past. But now they are old
enough to set their own standards.

[1] *Bravo! Magazine of the Lively Arts*, Vol. I, No. 2, 1961, pp. 8–10.

[265]

There may be arguments about this thesis. Some will say, "Look at the performances of certain musicians, orchestras, opera and ballet companies in Europe, both in Western and Eastern Europe!" And yet, in the main, I think that a cold look at the question has made it very clear that, if there is a residue of strength, it is *here*, in the United States.

The biggest proof is the quality of orchestral playing. The American orchestral standard is in itself a reflection of the American civilization. It is, again, an amalgam of many different styles. Its critics often criticize from a parochial viewpoint: A Frenchman does not like a German brass section; a German does not like French string playing; an Italian doesn't like Russian string playing, or a Russian doesn't like Italian brass playing. But we have had enough time, money and, I must say, taste to take the best of these and correlate them into what we call an orchestral or performing standard.

We are, then, to make a very big phrase, the standard-bearers of the best of Western civilization. Within the next two decades great, young and powerful forces will come into being: Asian and African cultural standard-bearers. Africa will take longer because it has a long way to go. But Asia will be soon. Red China particularly will make a very powerful advance.

The Chinese are accustomed to being world leaders. China was master of its world for 1,000 years and more, and its time out of world primacy has been, historically speaking, very short. It is anxious to regain that position, and no one can deny its right as a cultural entity to take a strong position. It has no connection with Western culture. Its roots are its own, and it is going to work first in an area where the people have roots close to its own.

I think that the world in which we live will not resort to war, but that cultural and economic penetration will be the first, and perhaps, in the long run, the most powerful weapons. That the Afro-Asian nations outnumber us physically, by far, goes without saying. Therefore, if we have any kind of faith in the traditions that nourished us, then it's up to us to take the responsibility to see that those traditions are not only nurtured, but expanded, and encouraged to become a potent force in our cultural and geo-political lives.

In the United States, this means certain things. In the first place we must, very quickly, accept the idea that we will be responsible for setting standards. The shoddy elements in our musical life must be removed.

Our conservatories have to take a good, hard look at themselves. If necessary, a new, call it "consortium" of teaching power has to be created. All those performers capable of giving direction, of setting standards, even though they may be unready or unwilling to do so, should be drafted. Somehow they must return to the public a part of the success, and loyalty, they have been given by that public.

We have been fortunate in our development in the last fifteen or 20 years in only one area—that of universities. The growth of university music schools has probably been the most encouraging sign of a musical coming-of-age in the United States.

There are certain schools today which have as good, and in some cases better, standards than some of our leading conservatories. What we lack lamentably is a standard of teachers and teaching in primary education. Here, we are criminally at fault.

This is perhaps a little difficult to establish on a national basis because under our Constitution we run smack into States' rights governing primary education. But it is one of our most glaring weaknesses and its result is apparent: when you compare the few students studying string instruments to those studying band instruments, you have your answer.

The fault lies in two things: First, the lack of recognition of the kind of life that a cultured society can live, not as an acquired social habit, but as a part of the dignity of a civilized country. The second fault lies in our economic setup: Why should parents encourage their youngsters to spend ten or fifteen years of very hard work to learn an instrument and enter a field where they *might* be able to earn three or four thousand dollars a year, when a plumber or an electrician or a stagehand or, in some cases, a taxi driver, earns a great deal more with more security?

If this sounds like a plea for Federal subsidy, it is not—at the present time. I believe subsidy of the arts is a necessity. But I don't believe it is either psychologically or politically possible now on a Federal basis, because we are not trained for it, we are not geared for it, we haven't been educated that way. Nor do the people whose responsibility this inevitably would be have any reason to feel this way because they haven't been educated for it at all.

We do have one of the most enormous governmental subsidies operating anywhere in the world, but in a peculiarly American form—it's called Foundations.

This is direct government subsidy via the tax route. But it is not enough. The point is, what can one say constructively, what can one do now?

Certain things *can* be done. (I do not want to be among those who merely say how terrible it all is.)

One of the first courses of action should be the accepting by the professional musicians of their responsibility. They have to realize that if they want to live in this field, and gain recompense and do something fruitful and leave a legacy, they have to face their responsibilities to the public generally, and especially to young people.

The most important group in this country is made up of the young people of college age. The kind of reaction you get when you play in a college town is unmatched anywhere. The students come with an enthusiasm, a warmth, a lack of predetermined bias, a willingness to be moved, a readiness to exult in an emotional experience that is refreshing and necessary. At the same time, they are an influenceable group. Within five to ten years they become an influential group. They become voters. How articulate they will be as voters depends on what kind of experience they have been given. They become parents, therefore they can begin, via their own experinces, to demand a beneficial kind of educational pattern for *their* children.

This means then, that the first attack must be made on the wall that has been built up around music and its process of work and development between the professionals on one side and listeners on the other. The listeners must be brought into the mainstream of the American cultural development. They must feel that they have a part in it, that they have a goal to reach, that they have a voice in it, that they belong to it. There must be outlets created and subsidized by local money—that is, state, municipal, foundation and labor union funds to develop a musical life to which youngsters can aspire, and in which they can begin to earn a living. Our youth can thus become a pool from which the major professional organizations can draw. They also can be the outlet for young performers, composers, conductors.

Through such subsidies, everyone can be involved in performances at popular prices. Thus, even after a family pays for a baby sitter, a parking lot, and has dinner, concert-going still can be within an average family budget.

If this is done at a local, municipal and state level, it is only a question of time until this habit becomes so ingrained that a national form of subsidy can be thought about. You cannot proselytize or harass or lobby into existence an acceptance of a cultural idea.

I don't say that anyone should stop lobbying for Federal subsidy—it should be continued—but I don't think it will be immediately successful, at least not in time to save the glorious kind of musical culture that I fear may die out if it isn't helped rapidly.

This then brings up the question of teaching standards. If we can enlist interest in and support of young people while, at the same time, we create a standard-setting machinery, the world will have to say: "If we want to find out how to do things properly, we must look to America."

Such status would mean that we would have an institute or series of institutes to set our standards. It would also mark our becoming the artistic center (as we are today the commercial center) of all musical activity. There is no reason why, with all the talents that we have in the United States, both foreign-born and American-born, we cannot have the same kind of standard-setting machinery in the arts (ballet, architecture, painting, music) that we have in the sciences or in medicine. We can just as well have music schools that are the equivalent of the Massachusetts Institute of Technology, and the Harvard and Yale Law Schools, and such great medical centers as Johns Hopkins. It's simply a question of having those qualified to transmit these ideas brought together in one area; then, realizing what can be done both politically and artistically, organizing all this into one driving force.

All of what I have said so far is the basis for a hope, for an ideal:

I hope that the next year or two can see the fruitful beginnings of a concrete plan to solve some of these problems. I hope that the great performers will find it possible, each in his own way, to do all they can, with their enormous influence, their names, their knowledge and their experience, to help realize such a plan and thus pass on their experience to those who will follow.

We've got to move fast.

Speedy action can help create, not only young performers, but far more importantly, an alert, efficient and dedicated group of young teachers to do what performers cannot do: take the time and trouble to develop a base upon which can be built what might be called a Golden Era in the Arts. I firmly believe that this can be done by the enthusiastic cooperation of America's best minds and talents.

APPENDIX C

AN ARGUMENTATIVE SPEECH

NEWTON MINOW,
THE "VAST WASTELAND"[1]

GOVERNOR COLLINS, DISTINGUISHED GUESTS, LADIES AND GENTLEMEN:

Thank you for this opportunity to meet with you today. This is my first public address since I took over my new job. When the New Frontiersmen rode into town, I locked myself in my office to do my homework and get my feet wet. But apparently I haven't managed to stay out of hot water. I seem to have detected a certain nervous apprehension about what I might say or do when I emerged from that locked office for this, my maiden station break.

First, let me begin by dispelling a rumor. I was not picked for this job because I regard myself as the fastest draw on the New Frontier.

Second, let me start a rumor. Like you, I have carefully read President Kennedy's messages about the regulatory agencies, conflict of interest, and the dangers of ex parte contacts. And of course, we at the Federal Communications Commission will do our part. Indeed, I may even suggest that we change the name of the FCC to The Seven Untouchables!

[1] Address by Newton N. Minow, Chairman, Federal Communications Commission, to the 39th Annual Convention of the National Association of Broadcasters, Washington, D.C., May 9, 1961.

It may also come as a surprise to some of you, but I want you to know that you have my admiration and respect. Yours is a most honorable profession. Anyone who is in the broadcasting business has a tough row to hoe. You earn your bread by using public property. When you work in broacasting you volunteer for public service, public pressure, and public regulation. You must compete with other attractions and other investments, and the only way you can do it is to prove to us every three years that you should have been in business in the first place.

I can think of easier ways to make a living.

But I cannot think of more satisfying ways.

I admire your courage—but that doesn't mean I would make life any easier for you. Your license lets you use the public's airwaves as Trustees for 180,000,000 Americans. The public is your beneficiary. If you want to stay on as Trustees, you must deliver a decent return to the public—not only to your stockholders. So, as a representative of the public, your health and your product are among my chief concerns.

As to your health: let's talk only of television today. 1960 gross broadcast revenues of the television industry were over $1,268,000,000; profit before taxes was $243,900,000, an average return on revenue of 19.2 per cent. Compared with 1959, gross broadcast revenues were $1,163,900,000, and profit before taxes was $222,300,000, an average return on revenue of 19.1 per cent. So, the percentage increase of total revenues from 1959 to 1960 was 9 per cent, and the percentage of increase of profit was 9.7 per cent. This, despite a recession. For your investors, the price has indeed been right.

I have confidence in your health.

But not in your product.

It is with this and much more in mind that I come before you today.

One editorialist in the trade press wrote that "the FCC of the New Frontier is going to be one of the toughest FCC's in the history of broadcast regulation." If he meant that we intend to enforce the law in the public interest, let me make it perfectly clear that he is right—we do.

If he meant that we intend to muzzle or censor broadcasting, he is dead wrong.

It would not surprise me if some of you had expected me to come here today and say in effect, "Clean up your own house or the government will do it for you."

Well, in a limited sense, you would be right—I've just said it.

But I want to say to you earnestly that it is not in that spirit that I come before you today, nor is it in that spirit that I intend to serve the FCC.

I am in Washington to help broadcasting, not to harm it; to strengthen it, not weaken it; to reward it, not punish it; to encourage it, not threaten it; to stimulate it, not censor it.

Above all, I am here to uphold and protect the public interest.

What do we mean by "the public interest"? Some say the public interest is merely what interests the public.

I disagree.

So does your distinguished president, Governor Collins. In a recent speech he said, "Broadcasting to serve the public interest, must have a soul and a conscience, a burning desire to excel, as well as to sell; the urge to build the character, citizenship and intellectual stature of people, as well as to expand the gross national product. . . . By no means do I imply that broadcasters disregard the public interest. . . . But a much better job can be done, and should be done."

I could not agree more.

And I would add that in today's world, with chaos in Laos and the Congo aflame, with Communist tyranny on our Caribbean doorstep and relentless pressure on our Atlantic alliance, with social and economic problems at home of the gravest nature, yes, and with technological knowledge that makes it possible, as our President has said, not only to destroy our world but to destroy poverty around the world—in a time of peril and opportunity, the old complacent, unbalanced fare of Action-Adventure and Situation Comedies is simply not good enough.

Your industry possesses the most powerful voice in America. It has an inescapable duty to make that voice ring with intelligence and with leadership. In a few years, this exciting industry has grown from a novelty to an instrument of overwhelming impact on the American people. It should be making ready for the kind of leadership that newspapers and magazines assumed years ago, to make our people aware of their world.

Ours has been called the jet age, the atomic age, the space age. It is also, I submit, the television age. And just as history will decide whether the leaders of today's world employed the atom to destroy the world or rebuild it for mankind's benefit, so will history decide whether today's broadcasters employed their powerful voice to enrich the people or debase them.

If I seem today to address myself chiefly to the problems of television, I don't want any of you radio broadcasters to think we've gone to sleep at your switch—we haven't. We still listen. But in recent years most of the controversies and cross-currents in broadcast programming have swirled around television. And so my subject today is the television industry and the public interest.

Like everybody, I wear more than one hat. I am the Chairman of the FCC. I am also a television viewer and the husband and father of other television viewers. I have seen a great many television programs that seemed to me eminently worthwhile, and I am not talking about the much bemoaned good old days of Playhouse 90 and Studio One.

I am talking about this past season. Some were wonderfully entertaining, such as The Fabulous Fifties, the Fred Astaire Show, and the Bing Crosby Special; some were dramatic and moving, such as Conrad's Victory and Twilight Zone; some were marvelously informative, such as The Nation's Future, CBS Reports, and The Valiant Years. I could list many more—programs that I am sure everyone here felt enriched his own life and that of his family. When television is good, nothing—not the theatre, not the magazines or newspapers—nothing is better.

But when television is bad, nothing is worse. I invite you to sit down in front of your television set when your station goes on the air and stay there without a book, magazine, newspaper, profit and loss sheet or rating book to distract you—and keep your eyes glued to that set until the station signs off. I can assure you that you will observe a vast wasteland.

You will see a procession of game shows, violence, audience participation shows, formula comedies about totally unbelievable families, blood and thunder, mayhem, violence, sadism, murder, western badmen, western good men, private eyes, gangsters, more violence, and cartoons. And, endlessly, commercials—many screaming, cajoling, and offending. And most of all, boredom. True, you will see a few things you will enjoy. But they will be very, very few. And if you think I exaggerate, try it.

Is there one person in this room who claims that broadcasting can't do better?

Well, a glance at next season's proposed programming can give us little heart. Of 73½ hours of prime evening time, the networks have tentatively scheduled 59 hours to categories of "action-adventure," situation comedy, variety, quiz, and movies.

Is there one network president in this room who claims he can't do better?

Well, is there at least one network president who believes that the other networks can't do better?

Gentlemen, your trust accounting with your beneficiaries is over-due.

Never have so few owed so much to so many.

Why is so much of television so bad? I have heard many answers: demands of your advertisers; competition for ever higher ratings; the need always to attract a mass audience; the high cost of television pro-grams; the insatiable appetite for programming material—these are some of them. Unquestionably, these are tough problems not susceptible to easy answers.

But I am not convinced that you have tried hard enough to solve them.

I do not accept the idea that the present over-all programming is aimed accurately at the public taste. The ratings tell us only that some people have their television sets turned on and of that number, so many are tuned to one channel and so many to another. They don't tell us what the public might watch if they were offered half a dozen addi-tional choices. A rating, at best, is an indication of how many people saw what you gave them. Unfortunately, it does not reveal the depth of the penetration, or the intensity of reaction, and it never reveals what the acceptance would have been if what you gave them had been better—if all the forces of art and creativity and daring and imagination had been unleashed. I believe in the people's good sense and good taste, and I am not convinced that the people's taste is as low as some of you assume.

My concern with the rating services is not with their accuracy. Perhaps they are accurate. I really don't know. What, then, is wrong with the ratings? It's not been their accuracy—it's been their use.

Certainly, I hope you will agree that ratings should have little influence where children are concerned. The best estimates indicate that during the hours of 5 to 6 p.m. 60 per cent of your audience is composed of children under 12. And most young children today, believe it or not, spend as much time watching television as they do in the schoolroom. I repeat—let that sink in—most young children today spend as much time watching television as they do in the schoolroom. It used to be said that there were three great influences on a child: home, school, and church. Today, there is a fourth great influence, and you ladies and gentlemen control it.

If parents, teachers, and ministers conducted their responsibilities by following the ratings, children would have a steady diet of ice cream, school holidays, and no Sunday School. What about your responsibilities? Is there no room on television to teach, to inform, to uplift, to stretch, to enlarge the capacities of our children? Is there no room for programs deepening their understanding of children in other lands? Is there no room for a children's news show explaining something about the world to them at their level of understanding? Is there no room for reading the great literature of the past, teaching them the great traditions of freedom? There are some fine children's shows, but they are drowned out in the massive doses of cartoons, violence, and more violence. Must these be your trademarks? Search your consciences and see if you cannot offer more to your young beneficaries whose future you guide so many hours each and every day.

What about adult programming and ratings? You know, newspaper publishers take popularity ratings too. The answers are pretty clear: it is almost always the comics, followed by the advice to the lovelorn columns. But, ladies and gentlemen, the news is still on the front page of all newspapers, the editorials are not replaced by more comics, the newspapers have not become one long collection of advice to the lovelorn. Yet newspapers do not need a license from the government to be in business—they do not use public property. But in television— where your responsibilities as public trustees are so plain, the moment that the ratings indicate that westerns are popular there are new imitations of westerns on the air faster than the old coaxial cable could take us from Hollywood to New York. Broadcasting cannot continue to live by the numbers. Ratings ought to be the slave of the broadcaster, not his master. And you and I both know that the rating services themselves would agree.

Let me make clear that what I am talking about is balance. I believe that the public interest is made up of many interests. There are many people in this great country and you must serve all of us. You will get no argument from me if you say that, given a choice between a western and a symphony, more people will watch the western. I like westerns and private eyes too—but a steady diet for the whole country is obviously not in the public interest. We all know that people would more often prefer to be entertained than stimulated or informed. But your obligations are not satisfied if you look only to popularity as a test of what to broadcast. You are not only in show business; you are free to communicate ideas as well as relaxation. You must provide a wider range of choices, more diversity, more alternatives. It is not enough to cater to the nation's whims—you must also serve the nation's needs.

And I would add this—that if some of you persist in a relentless search for the highest rating and the lowest common denominator, you may very well lose your audience. Because, to paraphrase a great American who was recently my law partner, the people are wise, wiser than some of the broadcasters—and politicians—think.

As you may have gathered, I would like to see television improved. But how is this to be brought about? By volunteering action by the broadcasters themselves? By direct government intervention? Or how?

Let me address myself now to my role not as a viewer but as Chairman of the FCC. I could not if I would, chart for you this afternoon in detail all of the actions I contemplate. Instead, I want to make clear some of the fundamental principles which guide me.

First: the people own the air. They own it as much in prime evening time as they do at 6 o'clock Sunday morning. For every hour that the people give you—you owe them something. I intend to see that your debt is paid with service.

Second: I think it would be foolish and wasteful for us to continue any worn-out wrangle over the problems of payola, rigged quiz shows, and other mistakes of the past. There are laws on the books which we will enforce. But there is no chip on my shoulder. We live together in perilous, uncertain times; we face together staggering problems; and we must not waste much time now by re-hashing the clichés of past controversy. To quarrel over the past is to lose the future.

Third: I believe in the free enterprise system. I want to see broadcasting improved and I want you to do the job. I am proud to champion your cause. It is not rare for American businessmen to serve a public trust. Yours is a special trust because it is imposed by law.

Fourth: I will do all I can to help educational television. There are still not enough educational stations, and major centers of the country still lack usable educational channels. If there were a limited number of printing presses in this country, you may be sure that a fair proportion of them would be put to educational use. Educational television has an enormous contribution to make to the future, and I intend to give it a hand along the way. If there is not a nation-wide educational television system in this country, it will not be the fault of the FCC.

Fifth: I am unalterably opposed to governmental censorship. There will be no suppression of programming which does not meet with bureaucratic tastes. Censorship strikes at the tap root of our free society.

Sixth: I did not come to Washington to idly observe the squandering of the public's airwaves. The squandering of our airwaves is no less important than the lavish waste of any precious natural resource. I intend to take the job of Chairman of the FCC very seriously. I believe in the gravity of my own particular sector of the New Frontier. There will be times perhaps when you will consider that I take myself or my job *too* seriously. Frankly, I don't care if you do. For I am convinced that either one takes this job seriously—or one can be seriously taken.

Now, how will these principles be applied? Clearly, at the heart of the FCC's authority lies its power to license, to renew or fail to renew, or to revoke a license. As you know, when your license comes up for renewal, your performance is compared with your promises. I understand that many people feel that in the past licenses were often renewed *pro forma*. I say to you now: renewal will not be *pro forma* in the future. There is nothing permanent or sacred about a broadcast license.

But simply matching promises and performance is not enough. I intend to do more. I intend to find out whether the people care. I intend to find out whether the community which each broadcaster serves believes he has been serving the public interest. When a renewal is set down for hearing, I intend—wherever possible—to hold a well-advertised public hearing, right in the community you have promised to serve. I want the people who own the air and the homes that television enters to tell you and the FCC what's been going on. I want the people—if they are truly interested in the service you give them—to make notes, document cases, tell us the facts. For those few of you who really believe that the public interest is merely what interests the public—I hope that these hearings will arouse no little interest.

The FCC has a fine reserve of monitors—almost 180 million Americans gathered around 56 million sets. If you want those monitors to be your friends at court—it's up to you.

Some of you may say,—"Yes, but I still do not know where the line is between a grant of a renewal and the hearing you just spoke of." My answer is: Why should you want to know how close you can come to the edge of the cliff? What the Commission asks of you is to make a conscientious, good faith effort to serve the public interest. Every one of you serves a community in which the people would benefit by educational, religious, instructive or other public service programming.

Every one of you serves an area which has local needs—as to local elections, controversial issues, local news, local talent. Make a serious, genuine effort to put on that programming. When you do, you will not be playing brinkmanship with the public interest.

What I've been saying applies to broadcast stations. Now a station break for the networks:

You know your importance in this great industry. Today, more than one-half of all hours of television station programming comes from the networks; in prime time, this rises to more than ¾ of the available hours.

You know that the FCC has been studying network operations for some time. I intend to press this to a speedy conclusion with useful results. I can tell you right now, however, that I am deeply concerned with concentration of power in the hands of the networks. As a result, too many local stations have foregone any efforts at local programming, with little use of live talent and local service. Too many local stations operate with one hand on the network switch and the other on a projector loaded with old movies. We want the individual stations to be free to meet their legal responsibilities to serve their communities.

I join Governor Collins in his views so well expressed to the advertisers who use the public air. I urge the networks to join him and undertake a very special mission on behalf of this industry: you can tell your advertisers, "This is the high quality we are going to serve—take it or other people will. If you think you can find a better place to move automobiles, cigarettes and soap—go ahead and try."

Tell your sponsors to be less concerned with costs per thousand and more concerned with understanding per millions. And remind your stockholders that an investment in broadcasting is buying a share in public responsibility.

The networks can start this industry on the road to freedom from the dictatorship of numbers.

But there is more to the problem than network influences on stations or advertiser influences on networks. I know the problems networks face in trying to clear some of their best programs—the informational programs that exemplify public service. They are your finest hours—whether sustaining or commercial, whether regularly scheduled or special—these are the signs that broadcasting knows the way to leadership. They make the public's trust in you a wise choice.

They should be seen. As you know, we are readying for use new forms by which broadcast stations will report their programming to the

Commission. You probably also know that special attention will be paid in these reports to public service programming. I believe that stations taking network service should also be required to report the extent of the local clearance of network public service programming, and when they fail to clear them, they should explain why. If it is to put on some outstanding local program, this is one reason. But, if it is simply to carry some old movie, that is an entirely different matter. The Commission should consider such clearance reports carefully when making up its mind about the licensee's over-all programming.

We intend to move—and as you know, indeed the FCC was rapidly moving in other new areas before the new administration arrived in Washington. And I want to pay my public respects to my very able predecessor, Fred Ford, and my colleagues on the Commission who have welcomed me to the FCC with warmth and cooperation.

We have approved an experiment with pay TV, and in New York we are testing the potential of UHF broadcasting. Either or both of these may revolutionize television. Only a foolish prophet would venture to guess the direction they will take, and their effect. But we intend that they shall be explored fully—for they are part of broadcasting's New Frontier.

The questions surrounding pay TV are largely economic. The questions surrounding UHF are largely technological. We are going to give the infant pay TV a chance to prove whether it can offer a useful service; we are going to protect it from those who would strangle it in its crib.

As for UHF, I'm sure you know about our test in the canyons of New York City. We will take every possible positive step to break through the allocations barrier into UHF. We will put this sleeping giant to use and in the years ahead we may have twice as many channels operating in cities where now there are only two or three. We may have a half dozen networks instead of three.

I have told you that I believe in the free enterprise system. I believe that most of television's problems stem from lack of competition. This is the importance of UHF to me: with more channels on the air, we will be able to provide every community with enough stations to offer service to all parts of the public. Programs with a mass market appeal required by mass product advertisers certainly will still be available. But other stations will recognize the need to appeal to more limited markets and to special tastes. In this way, we can all have a much wider range of programs.

Television should thrive on this competition—and the country should benefit from alternative sources of service to the public. And—Governor Collins—I hope the NAB will benefit from many new members.

Another and perhaps the most important frontier: television will rapidly join the parade into space. International television will be with us soon. No one knows how long it will be until a broadcast from a studio in New York will be viewed in India as well as in Indiana, will be seen in the Congo as it is seen in Chicago. But as surely as we are meeting here today, that day will come—and once again our world will shrink.

What will the people of other countries think of us when they see our western badmen and good men punching each other in the jaw in between the shooting? What will the Latin American or African child learn of America from our great communications industry? We cannot permit television in its present form to be our voice overseas.

There is your challenge to leadership. You must reexamine some fundamentals of your industry. You must open your minds and open your hearts to the limitless horizons of tomorrow.

I can suggest some words that should serve to guide you:

"Television and all who participate in it are jointly accountable to the American public for respect for the special needs of children, for community responsibility, for the advancement of education and culture, for the acceptability of the program materials chosen, for decency and decorum in production, and for propriety in advertising. This responsibility cannot be discharged by any given group of programs, but can be discharged only through the highest standards of respect for the American home, applied to every moment of every program presented by television.

"Program materials should enlarge the horizons of the viewer, provide him with wholesome entertainment, afford helpful stimulation, and remind him of the responsibilities which the citizen has towards his society."

These words are not mine. They are yours. They are taken literally for your own Television Code. They reflect the leadership and aspirations of your own great industry. I urge you to respect them as I do. And I urge you to respect the intelligent and farsighted leadership of Governor LeRoy Collins, and to make this meeting a creative act. I urge you at this meeting and, after you leave, back home, at your stations and your networks, to strive ceaselessly to improve your product and to better serve your viewers, the American people.

I hope that we at the FCC will not allow ourselves to become so bogged down in the mountain of papers, hearings, memoranda, orders, and the daily routine that we close our eyes to the wider view of the public interest. And I hope that you broadcasters will not permit yourselves to become so absorbed in the chase for ratings, sales, and profits that you lose this wider view. Now more than ever before in broadcasting's history the times demand the best of all of us.

We need imagination in programming, not sterility; creativity, not imitation; experimentation, not conformity; excellence, not mediocrity. Television is filled with creative, imaginative people. You must strive to set them free.

Television in its young life has had many hours of greatness—its Victory at Sea, its Army-McCarthy hearings, its Peter Pan, its Kraft Theaters, its See it Now, its Project 20, the World Series, its political conventions and campaigns, The Great Debates—and it has had its endless hours of mediocrity and its moments of public disgrace. There are estimates that today the average viewer spends about 200 minutes daily with television, while the average reader spends 38 minutes with magazines and 40 minutes with newspapers. Television has grown faster than a teen-ager, and now it is time to grow up.

What you gentlemen broadcast through the people's air affects the people's taste, their knowledge, their opinions, their understanding of themselves and of their world. And their future.

The power of instanteous sight and sound is without precedent in mankind's history. This is an awesome power. It has limitless capabilities for good—and for evil. And it carries with it awesome responsibilities, responsibilities which you and I cannot escape.

In his stirring Inaugural Address our President said, "And so, my fellow Americans: ask not what your country can do for you—ask what you can do for your country."

Ladies and Gentlemen:

Ask not what broadcasting can do for you. Ask what you can do for broadcasting.

I urge you to put the people's airways to the service of the people and the cause of freedom. You must help prepare a generation for great decisions. You must help a great nation fulfill its future.

Do this, and I pledge you our help.

APPENDIX D

A SHORT, WRITTEN DEBATE

*A NEWSPAPER AND TWO READERS
DEBATE A CHARGE*

**Bettag Pioneers in Mental Care: State Now Seeks a Cure
With Square-Leg Beds** [1]

There has been a good deal of criticism of the way the Stratton-Bettag regime runs the state's mental hospitals. We have expressed some of it ourselves.

It is time, however, to note a strikingly original contribution of this regime to hospital management and the treatment of mental illnesses. It is plain that these boys have pioneered in a new direction.

They have been criticized for not trying to get enough money out of the legislature to run their institutions properly.

Illinois is among the most backward, poorest states in its provision for the daily care of patients. This is bad in the state hospitals; it is worse in the institutions for the retarded.

The Bettag team has been criticized because something in its methods has repelled some of the ablest psychiatrists and administrators in the state's hospital service. Some such people left Illinois for other states.

It is true that Illinois has been criticized because the attitude of

[1] *Chicago Daily News*, May 27, 1959.

[283]

the administration in this field has made it difficult to recruit promising young doctors and other specialists.

But Dr. Bettag and his associates undertook to counter all this with a historic innovation in patient treatment. They decided to buy hospital beds with square legs instead of round ones.

To be sure, this turned out to be remarkably advantageous for Mr. Bettag's pet supplier of hospital equipment, because Bettag's pet was prepared to offer the state beds equipped with square legs. Competitors, stuck with round-legged beds, saw their bids on a recent order rejected even when this price was lower.

The department held that the round-legged ones were not "equivalent" to the square-legged.

The department is evidently run by dedicated men. Having apparently decided that patients get well faster in square-legged beds, price was no object to them. They only scrimp on doctors, psychiatrists, psychologists, social workers, nurses, and assorted aids.

Bettag Rips Editorial on Mental Care [2]

The *Daily News* editorial of Wednesday, May 27, relating to the Department of Public Welfare and the state's mental health services, shamefully misused editorial privilege and scorned journalistic responsibility.

It ridiculed and impugned the motivations and decisions of persons who have devoted their lives to public service. It serves no honorable purpose and is destructive of public confidence and personnel morale.

Decisions relating to hospital equipment are made by a group of professional and technical personnel who proudly qualify for the designation "career employes."

To imply, as the editorial so maliciously does, that such decisions are dishonestly motivated or unsoundly based is a bitter reward for their years of service to the people of Illinois.

The same snide and destructive treatment characterizes the balance of the editorial.

TODAY, every patient has a bed, hospital overcrowding during the period has been reduced from 45.7 per cent to 35.7 per cent, all pa-

2 *Chicago Daily News*, June 1, 1959.

tients and institutional personnel enjoy better food than ever before, and personnel in the mental institutions has increased by 2,081, or 22.1 per cent.

There is also more efficient use of personnel in all areas of the care, treatment and rehabilitation service than ever before, and the highest hospital discharge rate in history has been achieved.

During this period, there has been inaugurated the psychiatric research and training program which has already received international attention and acclaim. Its outstanding success is so pronounced that Governor Edmund G. Brown of California, obviously believing that progress in mental health services transcends politics, has invited us to help set up a similar program in that state.

Otto L. Bettag, M.D.
Director

Charges Bettag Failed to Answer Main Criticisms of His Department [3]

In a letter printed on this page on June 1, Dr. Otto L. Bettag, director of the Illinois State Department of Public Welfare, bitterly criticized your editorial calling attention to his department's decision to purchase hospital beds with square legs and to reject beds with round legs.

It may be noted, however, that Dr. Bettag failed to explain why round-legged beds were unacceptable even though cheaper.

In his reply Dr. Bettag espoused the principle of career service and was offended by what he took to be criticism of "career employes."

Dr. Bettag's desire to build a career service in the department is a laudable objective, but his concern comes too late to prevent the flight of numerous career employes in the professional services who have found it impossible, for one reason or another, to serve under him.

Dr. Bettag stated that the "highest hospital discharge rate in history has been achieved." But he did not state that Illinois' *readmission rate* has also soared to new heights.

Our readmission rate is considerably higher than that of other states with comparable numbers of patients.

Dr. Bettag reported not only higher discharge rates, but also lower patient populations.

[3] *Chicago Daily News*, June 8, 1959.

Dr. Bettag did not report that probably the most important reason has been the use of tranquilizing drugs which happened to come into popular use during his administration.

Nor did he report that the pattern is nationwide.

Dr. Bettag also pointed with pride to better food now said to be served to patients. He did not add that his nutrition program was financed from the Mental Health Fund, which consists of payments made by families of patients and which was established in 1951 under the leadership of his predecessor in office, Fred Hoehler.

The Mental Health Fund also pays for the research and training program for which Dr. Bettag takes credit.

But the saddest oversight in Dr. Bettag's reply was his failure to boast of greatly increased psychiatric care and treatment in hospitals.

With only 13 board-certified psychiatrists, many of them in administrative positions, to minister to almost 48,000 patients, and with a rank of 30th among all states in per patient expenditures, we can understand Dr. Bettag's silence.

Dawn Clark, Chairman,
Committee on Illinois Government, Chicago.

A LONGER, WRITTEN DEBATE

*FRED E. INBAU AND YALE KAMISAR ON
PUBLIC SAFETY v. INDIVIDUAL LIBERTIES.*[1]

PUBLIC SAFETY v. INDIVIDUAL CIVIL LIBERTIES:
THE PROSECUTOR'S STAND

FRED E. INBAU

The author is Professor of Law at Northwestern University. This address was
the keynote address at the 1961 Annual Conference of the National District Attorneys' Association in Portland, Oregon, July 26, 1961.

Today we are faced with a serious international threat to our national existence. This we all know and recognize; and we are taking
reasonable and appropriate measures to guard against any Communist
attack upon this country. We are also trying to hold back the threat
to the security of the free world generally. What many of us don't
realize, however, is that we are also faced with another serious threat
to our public safety and security from another kind of enemy right
within our own borders—unorganized as well as organized criminals.
Just yesterday the F.B.I. released a report which reveals that although

[1] *Journal of Criminal Law, Criminology and Police Science* (Northwestern
University), Vol. 53, Nos. 1–4 (1962), pp. 85–89, 171–193, 329–332, 453–462.
Reprinted by special permission.

the population in this country has increased 18 per cent since 1950, the crime rate has increased 98 per cent. Murder, rape, or assault to kill occurs every 3 minutes. A burglary is perpetrated every 39 seconds. Robberies and burglaries in 1960 were 18 per cent higher than in 1959.

We are not only neglecting to take adequate measures against the criminal element; we are actually facilitating their activities in the form of what I wish to refer to as "turn 'em loose" court decisions and legislation. To be sure, such decisions and legislation are not avowedly for the purpose of lending aid and comfort to the criminal element, but the effect is the same. It is all being done in the name of "individual civil liberties."

Danger Signs in Supreme Court Decisions

What particularly disturbs me, and I am sure many of you, is the dangerous attitude that has been assumed by the United States Supreme Court. The Court has taken it upon itself, without constitutional authorization, to police the police. It has also functioned at times as a super-legislative body. Moreover, even as regards its constitutionally authorized judicial function, the Court has gone far beyond all reasonable bounds in imposing its own divided concepts of due process upon the states. It has also gone much too far as regards its concepts of admissibility of evidence in criminal prosecutions in the federal courts.

These are harsh words, I know. But the time has come for some plain speaking with respect to what has been going on in the field of criminal law.

I propose to demonstrate to you the validity of every statement I have just made. Before doing so, may I make it clear at the outset that I am not opposed to the Bill of Rights. I believe in the Bill of Rights, which is so often shaken in the face of some of us by flag-waving civil libertarians when these critical issues of criminal law administration are under discussion and debate. I believe in due process, equal protection, free speech, and all else. But I also believe that we should not be unmindful of what is contained in the Preamble to the Constitution itself. The Preamble states that the purpose of the Constitution was "to establish justice, insure domestic tranquility, provide for the common defense, promote the general welfare, and secure the Blessings of Liberty to ourselves and our Posterity."

The Exclusionary Rule

To illustrate what I have in mind, let me start off with a recent United States Supreme Court decision, *Mapp v. Ohio*,[1] which imposed the exclusionary rule upon all the states as a requirement of due process, whereas previously it was only a rule of evidence applicable in about half the states and in the federal courts also.

For many years the United States Supreme Court held that state courts and state legislatures were at full liberty to accept or reject the exclusionary rule with respect to evidence obtained as a result of unreasonable search and seizure. The Court said so as recently as 1949 in *Wolf v. Colorado*.[2] In that case the Court held that although the Fourth Amendment unreasonable search and seizure provision was applicable to the states through the Fourteenth Amendment, the admissibility of evidence thus seized was a matter for each state to decide. Now, this June, the Court holds that if a state admits such evidence it is a violation of due process! All states, therefore, must follow the exclusionary rule.

Some eminent jurists of the past, including Justice Benjamin Cardozo, at the time when he sat on the New York Court of Appeals, were opposed to the exclusionary rule. In his celebrated opinion in *People v. Defore*[3] Justice Cardozo gave some clear cut, sensible reasons why New York chose not to follow the exclusionary rule. He adhered to the view that relevant evidence should not be brushed aside and ignored solely because of the methods the police used to obtain it. The great scholar, Dean John Henry Wigmore, was opposed to the rule, and in his monumental treatise on Evidence he pointed out the historically unfounded judicial reasoning that was used in the first federal case to adopt the exclusionary rule.[4]

In any discussion of the pros and cons of the exclusionary rule, consideration should also be given to the fact that the free, law abiding countries of England and Canada have always admitted evidence even though it may have been unreasonably seized.

After all these years of a general recognition of the exclusionary rule as a rule of evidence only, and after it was for so long proclaimed to be

[1] 81 S.Ct. 1684 (1961).
[2] 338 U.S. 25 (1949).
[3] 242 N.Y. 13, 150 N.E. 585 (1926).
[4] See 8 WIGMORE, EVIDENCE § 2184 (1940).

such by the Supreme Court itself, the Court in *Mapp v. Ohio* suddenly labels the rule to be a requirement of due process. Of little comfort is the fact that three of the nine justices (Frankfurter, Harlan, and Whittaker) adhered to the former viewpoint.

Why this change in the Court's attitude? The answer, in my opinion, is very simple. It's just another example of the Court's continuing efforts to police the police—and that is an executive, or at most a legislative function of government. It certainly is not the constitutional function of the judiciary.

One further word regarding *Mapp v. Ohio*, and this will be of concern to those of you who come from the states that have been admitting illegally seized evidence. What courts will decide whether the evidence has been unreasonably seized? Your state courts? And will their decisions be final? Or will the decisions be the subject of federal court review by an independent determination of unreasonableness? If the latter—and that has been the trend—you had better plan on enlarging your staff to keep up with the volume of business. And we'll need more federal judges. In fact, we'll need more justices on the Supreme Court itself.

Furthermore, you'll experience some real jolts if the same standards of "unreasonableness" are applied to your own cases as in many federal cases. You recall *Work v. United States,*[5] where looking into a narcotic peddler's garbage can was held to be an unreasonable search. There are also such cases as *Morrison v. United States,*[6] where the court suppressed as evidence the soiled handkerchief found in a sex pervert's shack, after it was pointed out by a child victim who led the police to the location and told them where they would find the handkerchief the offender used to clean himself off after the commission of his act. The Court held that the handkerchief was merely evidentiary material; that since it was not an instrument of the crime, or the fruits of the crime, or a weapon, or a contraband, it was not subject to seizure.

Confessions

Another recent Supreme Court decision, *Culombe v. Connecticut,*[7] further illustrates the Court's growing assumption of power over the

[5] 243 F.2d 660 (D.C. Cir. 1957).
[6] 262 F.2d 449 (D.C. Cir. 1958).
[7] 81 S.Ct. 1860 (1961).

states and their courts and police. The facts of the case need not concern us now. What is important is the Court's pronouncement that if it finds a criminal confession has been coerced, the state court conviction will be reversed even though it is "convincingly supported by other evidence."

If the present trend continues, the time is not far off when the Court will impose upon the state courts—as a due process requirement— the same kind of rule that now prevails in the federal courts by reason of the McNabb-Mallory decisions.[8] As you know, those two cases hold that if a confession is obtained by federal officers during a period of unnecessary delay in taking the arrestee before a committing magistrate, the confession is not usable as evidence, regardless of how voluntary or trustworthy it may be.

Even before the Supreme Court gets around to doing that, however, some of what the Court has already said and done as regards the federal law enforcement officers will have "rubbed off" on the state courts, and they will establish similar rules even though they are not required to do so by any United States Supreme Court decision. As an example of that, there is the 1960 decision of the Michigan Supreme Court in People v. Hamilton,[9] in which the Michigan Court adopted the McNabb-Mallory rule. It did so of its own volition, since the rule has not thus far been labeled as a requirement of due process. So now, in Michigan, if there is a delay in taking an arrested person before a committing magistrate, and the court finds that the delay was for the purpose of interrogating the arrestee with a view to obtaining a confession if he happens to be guilty, the confession is inadmissible as evidence.

Let me give you another example of state court activity along a similar line. The New York Court of Appeals recently held in People v. Waterman,[10] that law enforcement officers have no right to interrogate anyone after he has been indicted—or, to put it another way, after the "formal commencement of the criminal action." The reasoning back of the decision appears in the following excerpt from the court's opinion:

"An indictment is the 'first pleading on the part of the people' . . . and marks the formal commencement of the criminal action against the

[8] Mallory v. United States, 354 U.S. 449 (1957); McNabb v. United States, 318 U.S. 332 (1943).
[9] 357 Mich. 410, 102 N.W.2d 738 (1960).
[10] 9 N.Y.2d 561, 175 N.E.2d 445 (1961).

defendant. Since the finding of the indictment presumably imports that the People have legally sufficient evidence of the defendant's guilt of the crime charged . . . the necessities of appropriate police investigation 'to solve a crime, or even to absolve a suspect' cannot be urged as justification for any subsequent questioning of the defendant. . . . Any secret interrogation of the defendant, from and after the finding of the indictment, without the protection afforded by the presence of counsel, contravenes the basic dictates of fairness in the conduct of criminal causes and the fundamental rights of persons charged with crime."

If the Michigan Supreme Court adopts the same rule that the New York Court did in the *Waterman* case—and my guess is that it will—then the police of Michigan (or rather I should say, the people of Michigan) will be confronted with an intolerable situation. What the two rules put together will mean is this: after the judicial process has started there can be no interrogation of the accused; and after arrest there can be no interrogation of the arrestee, since he must be brought before a committing magistrate without unnecessary delay. In other words, police interrogations will be outlawed altogether.

The seriousness of this development can be fully appreciated only when consideration is given to the fact that under such restrictions most serious crimes will go unsolved, because the only way most of them can be solved is by the interrogation of persons under suspicion. This point I need not labor to you men. But it certainly needs hammering home to some judges and legislators.

I referred to the *Mallory* case earlier—the U. S. Supreme Court decision outlawing a confession obtained by federal officers during a delay in taking the arrestee before a federal commissioner for arraignment. I think you'll be interested in what Mallory, the rapist, did after the Supreme Court turned him loose. Shortly thereafter he assaulted the daughter of a woman who had befriended him. Later he was caught in Philadelphia while burglarizing the home of a woman who claimed he raped her. Mallory was convicted of burglary and aggravated assault.

Judicial Legislation

Earlier I referred to the Supreme Court's indulgence in judicial legislation. Let me illustrate what I had in mind.

In the famous (or infamous) case of *McNabb v. United States*,[11]

[11] *Supra* note 8.

you may recall that the Court relied upon an old federal statute which dealt with the arraignment of arrested persons, and the Court's opinion related how this statute was intended to guard against "the evil implication of secret interrogation of persons accused of crime." As a matter of fact the statutory provision had no such purpose back of it. It had been tacked onto an appropriation bill for the purpose of putting an end to a practice that existed about the 1890's whereby federal commissioners and marshals were cheating the government in the matter of fees and mileage expense charges. That's why they were thereafter required to take an arrested person before the nearest magistrate. Moreover, there was no reference at all to the time when this was to be done. The Court filled that in.

Furthermore, in the *McNabb* case you will also recall how the Court erroneously assumed that the defendants had not been promptly arraigned. And even when that fact had been called to the Court's attention in a petition for a rehearing, the petition was denied.

A further example of the Court's eagerness to ascribe to a statute a meaning which was not at all in the minds of the legislators concerns Section 605 of the Federal Communications Act. Section 605 was not aimed at law enforcement officers as a prohibition against wiretapping for law enforcement purposes. It was merely a 1934 re-enactment of a provision in the Radio Act of 1927, with an entirely different purpose in mind.

Another example of the Court's propensity to distort the meaning and purpose of a statutory provision in order to reach a result commensurate with the Court's own philosophy is *Carroll v. United States*.[12] That case held that the government had no right to appeal from a trial court order suppressing evidence on the ground of an unreasonable search and seizure. It viewed appeals by the Government to be "unusual, exceptional, not favored." And this is a case where it seems clear to many, including the Court of Appeals, that the Congress wanted to confer that right upon the government.

Legislative Restrictions

Not only have the courts been unduly restricting the police and prosecution, many legislatures have been doing the same thing. In Illinois

[12] 354 U.S. 448 (1957).

we now have a statute prohibiting any kind of electronic eavesdropping over the telephone, on the street, or anywhere else.[13] And mind you, this was not a piece of legislation engineered by the hoodlum element of Illinois; it was the work of some starry-eyed civil libertarians.

Anyone with law enforcement experience in metropolitan areas, or in the federal government, knows all too well that wiretapping and other electronic eavesdropping activities are indispensible to effective law enforcement. To be sure, there must be controls upon the police to prevent abuses. But there are all too many legislators and others who will not lift their heads out of the sand and face up to the practical realities of law enforcement.

I could go on with additional illustrations, but these few should serve to permit me to draw some conclusions for your consideration.

Conclusion

We can't have "domestic tranquility" and "promote the general welfare" as prescribed in the Preamble to the Constitution when all the concern is upon "individual civil liberties."

Individual rights and liberties cannot exist in a vacuum. Alongside of them we must have a stable society, a safe society; otherwise there will be no medium in which to exercise such rights and liberties. To have "rights" without safety of life, limb, and property is a meaningless thing. Individual civil liberties, considered apart from their relationship to public safety and security, are like labels on empty bottles.

This truism that we can't have unbridled individual liberties and at the same time have a safe, stable society is the first message that we must get across to the public.

I am fed up with such platitudes as "the right to be let alone"— when it is used as though it were an unconditional right. Sure, as individuals, we all would like to be let alone. You and I at times would like to do as we please. If we are in a hurry to go somewhere in our car, we might want to run a red light or to exceed the speed limit and be let alone after we do it. The burglar, the robber, the rapist would also like to be let alone. But in the interest of public safety and public welfare, there must be reasonable restraints upon the conduct and activities of all of us.

[13] ILL. REV. STAT. ch. 38, §§ 14-1–14-7 (1961).

And talking about wants, let us have these wants alongside the want to be let alone. I want to be able to walk along the street after dark and be relatively secure that someone will not crack my skull for the money in my wallet. I want my daughter to be able to walk home after dark and be relatively free from being dragged into an alley and raped. I want property owners to be reasonably free from racketeers, and from the thefts committed by burglars, robbers, and others.

The public must be made aware of the practicalities of law enforcement. They must be made to understand that law enforcement officers cannot offer the required protection demanded of them from within the strait-jacket placed upon them by present day court and legislative restrictions.

PUBLIC SAFETY v. INDIVIDUAL LIBERTIES: SOME "FACTS" AND "THEORIES"

YALE KAMISAR

The author is Professor of Law in the University of Minnesota Law School. He is also a member of the Advisory Committee on the Revision of the Minnesota Criminal Law. In 1960–1961, Professor Kamisar was a Social Science Research Council Fellow, studying the prosecutor's discretion in the State of Minnesota and the substantive criminal law "in practice." Prior to joining the faculty of the University of Minnesota in 1957, he was engaged in the practice of law in Washington, D. C.

In the following article, Professor Kamisar replies to an article by Professor Fred E. Inbau, entitled "Public Safety v. Individual Civil Liberties: The Prosecutor's Stand," which appeared in the March, 1962, issue of the *Journal* (Vol. 53, No. 1) at pp. 85–89. The author responds to Inbau's criticisms of criminal law decisions handed down by the United States Supreme Court in recent years, discussing in particular cases concerning the exclusion of confessions and illegally seized evidence. He then examines the effect of the exclusionary rules upon police attitudes and practices, weighs the value of these rules against possible alternatives, and analyzes the statistical evidence pertaining to the effect of the exclusionary rules upon crime rates.—EDITOR.

"The facts that we dislike we call theories; the theories that we cherish we call facts." [1]

[1] F. S. Cohen, *Field Theory and Judicial Logic*, in THE LEGAL CONSCIENCE 134 (L. K. Cohen ed. 1960).

Professor Inbau detects a certain irrationality, if not hysteria, in this business of excluding illegally seized evidence and unlawfully elicited confessions "all being done in the name of 'civil liberties.'" He pleads for temperateness. No emotive words, he begs. No shaking of the Bill of Rights in our faces by "flag-waving civil libertarians," please.[2] So, let us accompany him as he approaches these critical issues of criminal law administration calmly and dispassionately:

In order to maintain "public safety and security from another kind of enemy right within our borders," he asks, shouldn't we remove the "handcuffs" the courts have placed on the police? Do you want "unbridled individual liberties," he continues, or a "safe, stable society?" Do you believe in the "unconditional" "right to be let alone" or are you willing to impose "reasonable restraints" "in the interest of public safety and public welfare?" Are you for or against decisions and legislation which have the effect of "lending aid and comfort to the criminal element?" Whose side are you on, concludes Inbau, the side of law and order—or the side of "the burglar, the robber, the rapist?"[3]

Of course, Professor Inbau is scarcely the first opponent of the exclusionary rule to respond to the sound and fury of "starry-eyed civil libertarians" with the voice of reason. For example, a generation ago, at the New York Constitutional Convention of 1938, the District Attorney of New York County similarly resisted two proposals to exclude evidence obtained in violation of guarantees against unreasonable searches and seizures and unreasonable interception of telephone communications. Alarmed because sponsors of these proposals were submitting "something which is dangerous, and concealed by high sounding phrases,"[4] he felt compelled "to place on the record the facts about both":[5]

"Who are the people who would be protected by these proposals? Call the roll: Al Capone, Lucky Luciano, Waxie Gordon, Dutch

---

[2] See Inbau, *Public Safety v. Individual Civil Liberties: The Prosecutor's Stand,* 53 J. CRIM. L., C. & P.S. 85, 86 (1962) (hereinafter referred to as "Inbau").

[3] See Inbau 85–86, 89; Inbau, *The Social and Ethical Requirements of Criminal Investigation and Prosecution,* 3 CRIM. L. Q. (Canada) 329, 333, 350–51 (1960); Inbau, *Restrictions in the Law of Interrogation and Confessions,* 52 Nw. U.L. REV. 77, 79 (1957).

[4] 1 NEW YORK CONSTITUTIONAL CONVENTION, REVISED RECORD 369 (1938) (hereinafter referred to as "NEW YORK CONVENTION").

[5] *Ibid.*

Schultz, Tootsie Herbert, and all the others." [6]

Another delegate to the convention more or less threw Hitler, Mussolini, and Stalin into the fray:

"[I]f you vote for the [proposals] . . . you are not alone aiding and abetting the crooks but you are also aiding and abetting . . . the Communists and the Fascists and the Nazi . . . [T]he people of this State care if an armory is set up in our midst and that house or home becomes an armory of crooks or enemies from within and is loaded down with machine guns, and there are a hundred machine guns there, and bombs and grenades, and then we will prohibit our law enforcement agents: they are prohibited from using evidence obtained illegally against those enemies from within." [7]

As for the home-grown, garden-variety criminal, observed this same delegate,

"[I]f that proposition prevails there will be the greatest single celebration in the City of New York among the crooks and gangdom and racketeers that was ever known in that city, and from far and wide all the other racketeers and murderers and kidnappers and embezzlers will all collect into the City of New York to celebrate this famous victory of the forces of evil, so that they can be protected by the Constitution of the State of New York." [8]

Sooner or later, no doubt, someone will come up with the suggestion that the underlying purpose of the bizarre gathering of "underworld overlords" at Apalachin, New York, was to celebrate the recent

[6] *Id.* at 373.

[7] *Id.* at 564. *Cf.* ABA, SUMMARY OF PROCEEDINGS OF SECTION OF CRIMINAL LAW 57–58 (1956): "Of course [commented California prosecutor J. Francis Coakley], the agents of the international criminal conspiracy of communism who desire to undermine and destroy our government also like these [recent Supreme Court] decisions, because thereby the way is made easier for them to pursue their trade. . . . The pendulum has swung too far to the left and it would be a good thing for this country if the pendulum would swing back to the middle where it belongs. . . ."

[8] NEW YORK CONVENTION 562–63. *Cf.* the testimony of Edgar Scott, District of Columbia Deputy Chief of Police, that the *Mallory* decision "is going to encourage the criminals to come to Washington . . . to commit their crimes. If a remedy is not found, that is what is going to happen." *Hearings Before the Special Subcommittee To Study Decisions of the Supreme Court of the United States of the House Committee on the Judiciary*, 85th Cong., 2d Sess., pt. 1, at 47–48 (1957) (hereinafter referred to as the "*1957 House Committee Hearings*"). A "remedy," i.e., the repeal or relaxation of the *McNabb-Mallory* rule, was not found, but Chief Scott's due predictions have not been borne out. See text at notes 159–168, *infra*.

Benanti "victory" and/or to plot winning strategy in the forthcoming *Elkins* and *Mapp* cases.[9]

The "Innovations" of the Warren Court

It has become fashionable in some quarters to hail virtually every important decision handed down by the Warren Court as a radical departure from reason and precedent. According to these observers, whether or not—like the mule—recent Supreme Court decisions lack hope of posterity, they do lack pride of ancestry.

In this respect, Professor Inbau parts company with his fellow-critics of the *Mallory* case.[10] Most of his brethren assumed an absolutely, positively thunderstruck pose when *Mallory* was handed down. While Inbau shares their distress, he can hardly share their astonishment. His difficulty is that 14 years ago he roundly condemned the *McNabb* decision on the very grounds upon which the *Mallory* case is now being criticized. At that time he said of the *Upshaw* case, then pending in the Supreme Court, that since the unreasonable delay in taking the arrestee before a committing magistrate preceded Upshaw's confession, "if the Court really meant what it seemed to say in the *McNabb* case, a reversal of the [conviction] is in order." [11] The subsequent reversal in

[9] Benanti v. United States, 355 U.S. 97 (1957), barred use of wiretap evidence gathered by state officials in federal prosecutions. Elkins v. United States, 364 U.S. 206 (1960), wiped out the "silver platter" exception to the federal exclusionary rule, i.e., the doctrine that illegally seized evidence may be used in a federal prosecution if state officers present it to federal authorities on a "silver platter." Mapp v. Ohio, 367 U.S. 643 (1961), rendered all evidence obtained by unreasonable searches and seizures inadmissible in state courts.

It has been said that the Apalachin meeting "points up the need for strengthening law enforcement on a statewide basis by permitting them to use modern electronic devices to combat organized crime." NEW JERSEY JOINT LEGISLATIVE COMMITTEE, REPORT ON WIRETAPPING AND THE UNAUTHORIZED RECORDING OF SPEECH 31 (1958) (minority recommendations). The trouble with this conclusion is that for 13 years prior to the meeting, the host, one Joseph Barbara, Sr., had been pursued by a state trooper "in all ways possible (including tapping of his telephone) and [he] got no evidence of illegality, although he did get word of the meeting if not of its purpose." United States v. Bufalino, 285 F.2d 408, 419 (2d Cir. 1960) (Clark, J., concurring).

[10] Mallory v. United States, 354 U.S. 449 (1957), reaffirming McNabb v. United States, 318 U.S. 332 (1943), operates to exclude from federal prosecutions all confessions or admissions elicited during pre-commitment detention, whether or not they appear to be voluntarily made.

[11] Inbau, *The Confession Dilemma in the United States Supreme Court*, 43 ILL. L. REV. 442, 454-55 (1948).

Upshaw demonstrated that the Court did mean what it said.[12] So did the later *Mallory* reversal. Thus, Inbau's own writings on the subject amply demonstrate that it was the Stone Court, per Frankfurter, J., which departed from the conventional voluntary-trustworthy tests. The Vinson Court, per Black, J., reaffirmed this approach; the Warren Court, per Frankfurter, J., re-affirmed it.

Although Professor Inbau's prior writings have narrowed the fronts on which he can attack *Mallory*, he has more freedom of movement elsewhere. Thus he registers shock and dismay over the Court's "pronouncement" in *Culombe v. Connecticut* [13] "that if it finds a criminal confession has been coerced, the state court conviction will be reversed even though it is 'convincingly supported by other evidence.' " [14]

Inbau's fear that *Culombe* signifies an ominous trend is difficult to justify. Here, too, the Court is simply restating "the rule of automatic reversal" in coerced confession cases formulated by the Stone and Vinson Courts.[15] On at least two occasions, Mr. Justice Reed, perhaps

---

From the outset, the Department of Justice seemed to perfectly comprehend the meaning of *McNabb*. See, e.g., the Department's Circular No. 3793, dated April 1, 1943: "The attention of all United States Attorneys is directed to two recent decisions of the Supreme Court reversing convictions because of the admission of confessions made while the accused were illegally detained by enforcement officers. *McNabb v. United States; Anderson v. United States*, decided March 1, 1943. . . . Although the opinions refer to circumstances, e.g., ignorance of the accused, discomforts of place of detention, extended questioning, which might be regarded as bringing into question the voluntary character of the confessions, the decisions are expressly based upon *failure of the arresting officers to comply with statutory duty to bring arrested persons before a committing magistrate with reasonable promptness.*" (Emphasis in the original.)

[12] Upshaw v. United States, 335 U.S. 410 (1948).

[13] 367 U.S. 568, 621 (1961).

[14] Inbau 87.

[15] See Lyons v. Oklahoma, 322 U.S. 596, 597 n.1 (1944); Malinski v. New York, 324 U.S. 401, 404 (1945); Haley v. Ohio, 332 U.S. 596, 599 (1948); Stroble v. California, 343 U.S. 181, 190 (1952); Brown v. Allen, 344 U.S. 443, 475 (1953).

It is true that there is some language to the contrary in Stein v. New York, 346 U.S. 156 (1953), a confession case considerably complicated by the "unorthodox" New York trial procedures employed to resolve the voluntariness issue, see Meltzer, *Involuntary Confessions: The Allocation of Responsibility Between Judge and Jury*, 21 U. CHI. L. REV. 317, 319–39 (1954), and by the fact that the automatic reversal doctrine was "put to a distorted use by the defense," who unsuccessfully sought an instruction that if the jury found the confessions involuntary they must *acquit*, whereas the proper remedy is the granting of a new trial. McCORMICK, EVIDENCE 245–46 n.27 (1954). Most commentators concluded that Stein did not constitute an abandonment of "the rule of automatic reversal." See McCORMICK, *supra*; Meltzer, *supra* at 339–54; Miller, *The Supreme Court's Review of Hypo-*

this generation's most "conservative" justice in these matters,[16] made similar "pronouncements" on behalf of the Court. He noted as early as 1944 that "whether or not the other evidence in the record is sufficient to justify the general verdict of guilty is not necessary to consider" for if "admission of this confession denied a constitutional right to defendant the error requires reversal." [17]

The reason for the rule is not hard to find. As Mr. Justice Whittaker observed for the Court: "[The prosecution] suggests that, apart from the confession, there was adequate evidence before the jury to sustain the verdict. But where, as here, a coerced confession constitutes a part of the evidence before the jury and a general verdict is returned, no one can say what credit and weight the jury gave to the confession." [18]

As might be expected, Professor Inbau has some unkind things to say about *Mapp v. Ohio*,[19] although, since former U. S. Attorney General Tom Clark wrote the majority opinion he can hardly blame this one—as he has others—on the "ex-law professors." [20] Police and prose-

---

thetical Alternatives in a State Confession Case, 5 SYRACUSE L. REV. 53 (1953); Paulsen, *The Fourteenth Amendment and the Third Degree*, 6 STAN. L. REV. 411, 423–29 (1954). They did so largely for the reasons later advanced by the Court for adhering to the *Lyons-Malinski-Haley* rule: "In that case [*Stein*] this Court did not find that the confession was coerced. Indeed it was there recognized that when 'the ruling admitting the confession is found on review to be erroneous, the conviction, at least normally, should fall with the confession. . . .' " Payne v. Arkansas, 356 U.S. 560, 568 n.15 (1958).

[16] See, e.g., his dissenting opinions in McNabb v. United States, 318 U.S. 332, 347 (1943), and Upshaw v. United States, 335 U.S. 410, 414 (1948).

[17] Lyons v. Oklahoma, 322 U.S. 596, 597 n.1 (1944). To similar effect is his statement in Brown v. Allen, 344 U.S. 443, 475 (1953).

[18] Payne v. Arkansas, 356 U.S. 560, 567–68 (1958).

[19] Inbau 86–87.

[20] Thus, in recent testimony Professor Inbau (who stressed at the outset that he did not appear "just in that capacity" but as one with much "practical experience") explained how the *McNabb* "innovation" came about, *Hearings Before a Subcommittee of the Senate Committee on the Judiciary*, 85th Cong., 2d Sess., on H.R. 11477, S. 2970, S. 3325 and S. 3355, at 58, 65 (1958) (hereinafter referred to as the "1958 *Senate Committee Hearings*"):

"Unfortunately, the United States Supreme Court, and it was made up at that time of some even more sensitive souls than we see, perhaps, at the present time—there were some law professors on it, ex-law professors—and they assumed that those practices which were revealed in these [coerced confession] decisions were commonplace, they were universal, and the Court, acting in that feeling of resentment, laid down in the *McNabb* case its so-called civilized-standards rule."

Evidently Professor Inbau does not realize that prior to mounting the teacher's platform "ex-law professor" Frankfurter, author of the much-maligned *McNabb* opinion, served several years as an assistant U.S. attorney in the Southern District of New York, and, then, an additional year as a special assistant to the U.S. Attorney General.

cutors have been making grating noises about the exclusionary rule in search and seizure cases for a long time. For whatever questions may be raised about the reliability of illegally procured confessions, there is not likely to be much doubt about the evidentiary value of illegally seized narcotics or counterfeit money. Thus, down through the years the exclusion of illegally seized physical evidence has drawn the hottest fire from law enforcement officers.

Mapp v. Ohio was hardly the beginning. If anything, it was the culmination of a series of developments. Then, when *did* it begin? This is not an easy question to answer.

"All is fluid and changeable," observed Cardozo. "There is an endless 'becoming.' " [21] "In a sense," Lon Fuller has written, "the thing we call 'the story' is not something that is, but something that becomes; it is . . . as much directed by men's creative impulses, by their conception of the story as it ought to be, as it is by the original event which unlocked those impulses. . . . The statute or decision is not a segment of being, but, like the anecdote, a process of becoming. By being reinterpreted it becomes, by imperceptible degrees, something that it was not originally." [22]

Chief William H. Parker of the Los Angeles Police Department might well say it began with *Wolf v. Colorado*,[23] where "for the first time in the history of the Country the United States Supreme Court applied the fourth amendment . . . to the states by virtue of the fourteenth amendment, and thus began a whole new era." [24] This takes us back more than a decade.

Wigmore probably would point to "the heretical influence of *Weeks v. United States*" [25] which "creates a novel exception, where the Fourth Amendment is involved, to the fundamental principle that *an illegality in the mode of procuring evidence is no ground for excluding it.*" [26] But we have now travelled back a full half century. Back to Mr. Justice Day, speaking for the White Court,[27] and to Mr. Justice Holmes, steadfastly subscribing to and extending the "heretical" principle with the ruling that "the essence of a provision forbidding the acquisition of evidence in a certain way is that not merely evidence so

[21] CARDOZO, THE NATURE OF THE JUDICIAL PROCESS 28 (1921).
[22] FULLER, THE LAW IN QUEST OF ITSELF 9–10 (1940).
[23] 338 U.S. 25 (1949).
[24] *1957 House Committee Hearings* at 74.
[25] 8 WIGMORE, EVIDENCE § 2184, at 32 (3d ed. 1940) (hereinafter cited as "WIGMORE").
[26] *Id.* at 36. (Emphasis in the original.)
[27] Weeks v. United States, 232 U.S. 383 (1914).

acquired shall not be used before the court but that it shall not be used at all." [28]

Perhaps *Mapp's* beginnings go back still further, way back to the reign of Elizabeth I. At that time, Wigmore tells us, the attorney-client privilege—the oldest of the privileges for confidential communications—"already appears as unquestioned." [29]

The privilege which protects a witness against self-incrimination and the privileges which shield confidential communications between attorney and client, husband and wife, physician and patient, and priest and penitent "do not in any wise aid the ascertainment of truth, but rather they shut out the light. Their sole warrant is the protection of interests and relationships which, rightly or wrongly, are regarded as of sufficient social importance to justify some incidental sacrifice of sources of facts needed in the administration of justice." [30]

If the sentiment of loyalty which attaches to the attorney-client privilege, or the desire to promote full disclosure by the client, overrides the search for truth, what is so bizarre about regarding the fourth amendment values and policies as more important than this same search? If the search for truth may be obstructed in the name of a physician-patient or marital relationship, what is so "heretical" about doing so in the name of constitutional guarantees?

Whether or not the exclusionary rule in search and seizure cases is a late offshoot of the deeply-rooted rules of privilege, the *Mapp* case is the latest offshoot of the firmly-imbedded *Weeks* rule. Here, as elsewhere, Professor Inbau cannot attack *this* Supreme Court without scathing many predecessor Supreme Courts as well.

Some 30 years ago, Professor John Barker Waite, a long-time critic of the exclusionary rules, observed that "such an issue as that in the *Olmstead* case is the perfect illustration of the judicial function of evaluating conflicting interests." [31] Why can't the same be said for *Mapp* or *Culombe* or *Mallory*? I approve of the recent Supreme Court decisions, but surely even those who deem them unwise cannot have forgotten that "the right to choose is not destroyed by the unwisdom of the choice." [32]

---

[28] Silverthorne Lumber Co. v. United States, 251 U.S. 385, 392 (1920).
[29] 8 WIGMORE § 2290.
[30] McCORMICK, EVIDENCE 152 (1954).
[31] Comment, 27 MICH. L. REV. 78, 82 (1928).
[32] Cardozo, J., in Pallocco v. Lehigh Valley R.R., 236 N.Y. 110, 114, 140 N.E. 212, 213 (1923).

Evidently, Professor Inbau is an ardent exponent of states rights. He is noticeably disturbed that *Mapp* destroyed the "full liberty" of state courts and state legislatures to accept or reject the exclusionary rule.[33]

What is his reaction on learning that the Michigan Supreme Court chose to adopt the *McNabb-Mallory* rule? [34] This is cited as a sorry example of what the Supreme Court "has already said and done" "rubbing off" on the state courts, causing them to "establish similar rules *even though they are not required to do so* by any United States Supreme Court decision." [35] Professor Inbau reiterates this point a moment later: The Michigan Court *"did so of its own volition,* since the rule has not thus far been labeled as a requirement of due process." [36] Running through these comments on the Michigan scene is a certain astonishment: Don't those state judges realize they are not *supposed* to do anything above and beyond the *minimum* requirements of fourteenth amendment due process!

The Supreme Court, charges Inbau, has "functioned at times as a super-legislative body." [37] How does he take the news that the Illinois *legislature* has prohibited law enforcement electronic eavesdropping? This, he protests "was the work of some starry-eyed civil libertarians." [38] Of course, if legislation is passed or state constitutions are amended to achieve results desired by opponents of the exclusionary

[33] Inbau 86.
[34] People v. Hamilton, 357 Mich. 410, 102 N.W.2d 738 (1960). Professor Inbau tells us none of the facts about the *Hamilton* case nor does he suggest the decision might have been a response to local conditions. Consider Bailer & Quick, *Evidence and Criminal Law,* 7 WAYNE L. REV. 51, 60–61 (1960):

> "It is to be noted that the McNabb doctrine was deemed necessary in fact, because of the widespread official gutting of the remedy of habeas corpus, by failure to arraign. This is of a special significance in the City of Detroit where there is substantial evidence that the Recorders Court, in cooperation with the police and prosecuting officials had, before the Hamilton case, effectively debilitated the grand old remedy of habeas corpus by providing that on application for habeas corpus the police may still be allowed to hold a person not charged with a crime for up to seventy-two hours even though there is no evidence against the individual. Indeed, persons illegally arrested were permitted to be incarcerated for shocking periods of time, even though not suspected of committing a crime. It was done in the interest of practicality (a defense not available to defendants)."

Perhaps it is not amiss to note that Kermit Bailer, Esq., co-author of the above article, is not and never has been a law professor, but *was* a former assistant Wayne County prosecutor.
[35] Inbau 87. (Emphasis added.)
[36] *Ibid.* (Emphasis added.)
[37] Inbau 86.
[38] *Id.* at 88.

rules, they tell us this is because "the people . . . became sufficiently incensed." [39] Sheriffs and police and prosecutors' associations, they would have us believe, never pressure legislatures; only civil liberties groups do.[40]

Current talk about the courts' usurping legislative powers in the process of "policing the police" [41] is difficult to reconcile with the tactics of exclusionary rule opponents a generation ago. For example, at the 1938 New York State Constitutional Convention, those seeking to write the exclusionary rule into the state constitution were told to "leave it to the courts":

"If we are well advised we shall leave the construction of the language of Constitution and statute alike to our own courts, as we have done

[39] Waite, *Judges and the Crime Burden*, 54 MICH. L. REV. 169, 197 (1954), discussing the 1936 amendment to the Michigan Constitution which permitted the introduction into evidence of illegally seized firearms and blackjacks. Narcotic drugs were covered by further amendment in 1952.

[40] *But cf.* Samuel Dash, former trial attorney in the Criminal Division of the Department of Justice and former District Attorney of Philadelphia, commenting on the 1957 California scene, DASH, KNOWLTON & SCHWARTZ, THE EAVESDROPPERS 199–200 (1959):

"Because of these bills [prohibiting police use of bugging equipment] on the one hand and on the other the feeling of the police that additional laws were needed to aid them in their investigations, the Peace Officers Association of California joined with the District Attorneys Association and the Sheriffs Association of California to influence legislative action. They prepared an impressive booklet which set out in brief form all the proposed law-enforcement bills. Under each bill, they printed in bold type 'approved,' 'approved with amendment,' or 'disapproved.'

"A very active lobbying program was undertaken by the law-enforcement organizations in Sacramento. District attorneys and police chiefs were assigned to meet with legislators during the legislative session and to persuade them to vote against the bills the law-enforcement organizations disapproved and to vote for the bills they approved. One police chief admitted that he had told a senator on the judiciary committee investigating police wiretapping and bugging that if he wanted to get ahead politically, he had better stop interfering with law enforcement. The police chief indicated that he was speaking for the combined forces of the Peace Officers Association, the District Attorneys Association, and the Sheriffs Association of the state of California.

"The only bill that was finally enacted relating to police bugging was the bill which the law-enforcement organizations had marked 'approved.' Staff members of the Regan Committee privately admitted that they had censored their own report and had not pushed for police restrictions because of the powerful influence of the law-enforcement groups. The governor vetoed this bill on the ground that he did not believe it was sufficiently restrictive of police bugging activity. This maintained the status quo, with the 1941 law permitting police bugging."

[41] Inbau 86.

hitherto. That process supplies, in a constantly changing situation, the best and simplest protection the individual and the public can have." [42]

Following *Olmstead v. United States*,[43] permitting the use of wiretap evidence in federal courts, regardless of state laws on the subject, a number of attempts were made to prohibit or limit tapping. In 1931, one such effort was resisted by Congressman Oliver of Alabama on the ground that "the weight and effect" of wiretap evidence "under the charge of the court, may properly be left to the jury." [44] When pressed by Congressman LaGuardia as to where he would "draw the line in respect to lawful and unlawful use of the wires," Congressman Oliver replied: "I said a few moments ago that it is a matter that must largely address itself to the courts and to the juries, under proper instruction." [45]

If a transcendental principle pervades the camp of exclusionary rule opponents, it seems to be this: Whatever the arena in which civil liberties groups choose to do battle, tell them they belong in the *other* one!

The "Unconditional" Right To Be Let Alone

Professor Inbau, for one, is against "*unbridled* civil liberties" and "fed up with such platitudes as 'the right to be let alone'—when it is used as though it were an *unconditional* right." [46]

Just what *unbridled* liberties and *unconditional* rights does Professor Inbau have in mind? Certainly, Dolly Mapp wasn't asking for any when several policemen forcibly opened the door to her house, prevented her attorney from seeing her or even entering the house, pulled a fake "warrant" from her bosom after she grabbed it from one of the officers who showed it to her, then "handcuffed" her because she had been "belligerent" in resisting their "rescue" of the "warrant" from her person.[47] Mr. Culombe would have settled for a good deal less than an *unconditional* right of privacy, too. "A moron or an imbecile" who "spent six years in the third grade" and who "has twice been in

---

[42] NEW YORK CONVENTION 479–80.
[43] 277 U.S. 438 (1928).
[44] 74 CONG. REC. 2903 (1931).
[45] *Id.* at 2904.
[46] Inbau 89. (Emphasis added.)
[47] Mapp v. Ohio, 367 U.S. 643, 644–45 (1962).

state institutions for the feeble-minded," Mr. Culombe "did not see an attorney until six days after he was first arrested and after he had confessed to the police." [48]

In an article appearing in this *Journal* a year ago, Professor Inbau urged legislation authorizing "privately conducted police interrogation, covering a reasonable period of time, of suspects who are *not unwilling to be interviewed.*" [49] If the police presently lack such authority, this does evidence an era of "unbridled liberties" and "unconditional rights." But do they? If the suspect is "not unwilling," what's the problem? Why do the police have to *arrest him at all*, let alone bring him before a committing magistrate? "It would be absurd to suggest that police must arrest a person before they can ask him questions." [50]

Evidently, Professor Inbau does not share the Supreme Court's view that "while individual cases have sometimes evoked 'fluctuating differences of view,' . . . it can hardly be said that in the over-all pattern of Fourth Amendment decisions this Court has been either unrealistic or visionary." [51] But he cannot quarrel with the proposition that "what the Constitution forbids is not all searches and seizures, but unreasonable ones." [52]

For example, in the recent *Draper* case,[53] the Court upheld an arrest (and accompanying search) without a warrant, but based on a tip from a known and "reliable" informer that petitioner was peddling narcotics. The information was corroborated only to the extent that the

---

[48] Culombe v. Connecticut, 367 U.S. 568, 639 (1961) (Douglas, J., concurring).

[49] Inbau, *Police Interrogation—A Practical Necessity*, 52 J. Crim. L., C. & P.S. 16, 20 (1961). See also *id.* at 19.

[50] Goldsmith v. United States, 277 F.2d 335, 344 (D.C. Cir. 1960). "Interrogation of suspects prior to arrest is a valuable technique," recently observed the U.S. Attorney for the District of Columbia, "and it is widely utilized by the F. B. I." Memorandum From Oliver Gasch to Maj. Robert V. Murray, Chief of the Metropolitan Police, in *Hearings on District of Columbia Appropriations for 1961 Before a Subcommittee of the House Committee on Appropriations*, 86th Cong., 2d Sess., at 621 (1960) (hereinafter referred to as "*Hearings on District of Columbia Appropriations for 1961*"). "Of course," added Mr. Gasch, "it should be emphasized that following arraignment [commitment] it is possible to interrogate the individual concerned." *Id.* at 622. Only last year, in this *Journal*, a commentator with prior police experience of his own maintained that "interviewing of a possibly concerned person has legal and psychological advantages over interrogation of an arrestee." Mueller, *The Law Relating to Police Interrogation Privileges and Limitations*, 52 J. Crim. L., C. & P.S. 2, 12 (1961).

[51] Elkins v. United States, 364 U.S. 206, 222 (1960).

[52] *Ibid.*

[53] Draper v. United States, 358 U.S. 307 (1959).

informer's detailed description of petitioner and report of his where-abouts on a certain morning squared with the arresting officer's ob-servations. The Court underscored the "large difference" between "what is required to prove guilt in a criminal case and what is required to show probable cause for arrest or search." [54] In rejecting petitioner's contention that the arresting officer's "hearsay" information was insuffi-cient to show probable cause or constitute reasonable grounds, the Court recalled that "in dealing with probable cause . . . we deal with probabilities. These are not technical; they are the factual and practical considerations of everyday life on which reasonable and prudent men, not legal technicians, act." [55]

Similarly, in the still more recent *Jones* case,[56] the Court sustained a search warrant based on a tip (corroborated by "other sources" and by the fact that the persons implicated were known to be addicts) from an unnamed but "reliable" informer that petitioner and another were engaged in illicit narcotic traffic and kept a ready supply on hand. *Jones* reaffirms that with or without a warrant the arresting officer may "rely upon information received through an informant, rather than upon his direct observations, so long as the informant's statement is reasonably corroborated." [57]

Professor Inbau, no doubt, disagrees that *Draper* and *Jones* illus-trate the general principle. He points to the rule first articulated in *Gouled v. United States* [58] some 40 years ago that objects of "eviden-tiary value only" are beyond the reach of an otherwise valid warrant or police officers acting on "probable cause." [59]

I share Inbau's view that the *Gouled* rule is unsound and unde-siderable.[60] So, it seems, does just about everybody else—"liberal" or

[54] *Id.* at 312–13.
[55] *Id.* at 313, quoting with approval from Brinegar v. United States, 338 U.S. 160, 175 (1949).
[56] Jones v. United States, 362 U.S. 257 (1960).
[57] *Id.* at 269.
[58] 255 U.S. 298, 309–11 (1921). See also, e.g., Abel v. United States, 362 U.S. 217, 237–38 (1960); Harris v. United States, 331 U.S. 145, 154 (1947); United States v. Lefkowitz, 285 U.S. 452, 464–66 (1932).
[59] Inbau 87. Actually, Professor Inbau points to the recent (and questionable) application of the *Gouled* rule in Morrison v. United States, 262 F.2d 449 (D.C. Cir. 1958).
[60] See Kamisar, *The Wiretapping-Eavesdropping Problem: A Professor's View*, 44 MINN. L. REV. 891, 914–18 (1960). The rule has far more often been pro-fessed in terms than followed in practice; "while 'a search for an object of purely evidentiary significance' may be taboo, objects have been and will continue to be found to possess a bit more than 'purely evidentiary significance' just about when-

"conservative"—who has written on the subject.[61] *Gouled* is wrong *because* it departs from the fundamental principles pervading search and seizure law. But how does it follow that the fundamental principles are also unsound?

To demonstrate the invalidity of a particular application of a general rule is hardly to destroy the general rule itself. If it were, neither the parol evidence rule nor the hearsay rule nor the rule against perpetuities *nor any other familiar rule* could survive attack.[62]

---

ever a resourceful judge wants to so find." *Id.* at 917. See also Broeder, *The Decline and Fall of Wolf v. Colorado*, 41 NEB. L. REV. 185, 211–13 (1961)

In any event, Professor Inbau's fears that "mere evidence"—non-documentary in nature—must now be excluded from state courts seem unfounded. For one thing, it is by no means clear that even in the federal courts the rule extends to *non-documentary* objects of purely evidentiary significance. See generally Comment, 20 U. CHI. L. REV. 319 (1953). For another, "whatever *Gouled's* contemporary vitality in the federal system, the point is that it rests both on the fourth as well as the fifth amendment, and that it is the fifth rather than the fourth which precludes the admission of the purely evidentiary items. *Mapp's* exclusionary doctrine on the other hand rests solely on the fourth amendment so far as the states are concerned. Thus, if *Gouled* depends both on the fourth and fifth, the doctrine would appear inapplicable to the states." Broeder, *supra* at 212. See also Weinstein, *Local Responsibility for Improvement of Search and Seizure Practice*, 34 ROCKY MT. L. REV. 150, 161, 174 n.122 (1960).

[61] See, e.g., MAGUIRE, EVIDENCE OF GUILT 183 (1959); 8 WIGMORE, EVIDENCE § 2184a, at 45 (McNaughton rev. 1961); Paulsen, *Safeguards in the Law of Search and Seizure*, 52 Nw. U. L. REV. 65, 66 (1957).

[62] Of course, over the years, opponents of the exclusionary rule have worked *both* sides of the street. They have sought to invalidate the basic principle not only by pointing to the *Gouled* doctrine, which goes too far, but also by citing the late "silver platter" doctrine—*which did not go far enough*. Thus, at the 1938 New York Constitutional Convention, opponents of the *Weeks* rule turned again and again to the "silver platter" doctrine as proof that "the Federal courts have been compelled to depart from their own rule in order that the guilty may not escape," NEW YORK CONVENTION 372; that "these exceptions to the rule illustrate its basic unsoundness," *ibid.*; that "they [the Supreme Court] found in individual cases that the rule had to be limited, and they limited it so that it was ridiculous," *id.* at 467; that there is "no great fundamental principle involved in this debate . . . because if there was, then the judges of the Supreme Court of the United States are also unprincipled because . . . they also say . . . and have allowed in our Federal courts down through the years evidence to be used that is procured by officers connected with the local political bodies," *id.* at 527.

No sooner was *Elkins* handed down, than opponents of the exclusionary rule hastened to the *other* side of the street. *Elkins* became support for the view that the Court is "willing to serve as a super-censor and super-jury over state practices. . . . Apparently improper searches and seizures carried out by state officers now are deemed to violate the fourteenth amendment due process clause, without regard to the constitutional and statutory provisions provided by the states themselves to govern conduct of their own law enforcement officers." George, *"The Potent, The Omnipresent Teacher": The Supreme Court and Wire-tapping*, 47 VA. L. REV. 751, 782 (1961).

At this point, Professor Inbau would probably trot out a decision which has nothing to do with the *Gouled* rule—*Work v. United States*,[63] the famous (or infamous) "garbage can" case. This case, Inbau tells us, establishes "the sanctity of the garbage can." [64] This case, Inbau insists, "illustrates the general principle." [65]

The facts in *Work*, according to Inbau, are quite simple: "Looking into a narcotic peddler's garbage can was held to be an unreasonable search." [66] "That particular case is an outrage, the case where, because the police rooted in somebody's garbage can and found evidence of narcotics . . . the narcotics peddler went free." [67] Can it really be that that's all there is to the *Work* case? Let's take a closer look.

Without a warrant, and admittedly without cause to make a search or arrest absent a warrant, two police officers entered petitioner's dwelling place. *Then*, petitioner walked past the officers and out of the house to an area under the porch. The officers followed her and saw

---

Would it not be more appropriate for Professor George to direct his attack at the scope of the substantive right rather than the *Elkins* decision implementing it? Improper state searches and seizures had been deemed to violate fourteenth amendment *more than a decade earlier*—in Wolf v. Colorado, 338 U.S. 25 (1949). From that date (with the probable exception of the fifth amendment-oriented *Gouled* rule), any state provision purporting to narrow the *substantive* protection afforded by the federal constitution against unreasonable search and seizure was invalid. See Allen, *The Wolf Case: Search and Seizure, Federalism, and the Civil Liberties*, 45 ILL. L. REV. 1, 6–11 (1950); Kamisar, *Wolf and Lustig Ten Years Later: Illegal State Evidence in State and Federal Courts*, 43 MINN. L. REV. 1083, 1101–08 (1959); cf. Foote, *Safeguards in the Law of Arrest*, 52 NW. U. L. REV. 16, 36–44 (1957).

Professor George is distressed that *Elkins* showed little regard for state law governing local officers. He is not disturbed at all, however, over what the "silver platter" doctrine might have been doing to *federal law governing federal officers*. Consider, e.g., the remarks of Delegate T. J. Curran, an opponent of the exclusionary rule: "I was for four years an assistant United States attorney in the Southern District of New York. As a matter of fact, there is no Federal rule, if we mean by 'Federal rule' an inviolate principle of law that the Federal courts always enforce. . . . For instance, Federal officers always work with local police officers. And what happens? . . . They then say to the local police officers, 'We will now leave you to conduct the illegal search . . . and when you get the evidence, you will go to the court and submit the evidence,' and that evidence is accepted. And there are thousands of cases in the Southern District of New York in which convictions were obtained by that method, and the same rule applies throughout this country." NEW YORK CONVENTION 527. See generally Kamisar, *supra* at 1177–90.

[63] 243 F.2d 660 (D.C. Cir. 1957).

[64] 1958 *Senate Committee Hearings* at 74.

[65] *Ibid.*

[66] Inbau 87.

[67] 1958 *Senate Committee Hearings* at 74. To the same effect is Peterson, *The Crooks Get All the Breaks*, Sat. Eve. Post, Sept. 23, 1961, pp. 10, 13.

her put something (which turned out to be narcotics) into a trash can located in the porch area, within the "curtilage" of her home.[68] "It would be unacceptably naive," declared the court, "to conclude that this attempt by her to hide [the phial] immediately following the presence of the officers in the hall, and that the finding of the phial by the officers, were not direct consequences of their unlawful entry." [69]

Work does not establish the "sanctity of the garbage can" any more than does *Williams v. United States* [70] the "sanctity of the precinct station corridor." In the *Williams* case, defendant was illegally arrested on the street, ordered into a police car, and driven to a precinct building. As he was being marched through the corridor leading to "the desk" where suspects are booked and searched, he dropped a cigarette package (containing narcotics) in an unsuccessful attempt to rid himself of the incriminating evidence before he reached "the desk." The evidence was suppressed as the "product" of a fourth amendment violation; the "throwing away" occurred as the result of and only because of the unlawful arrest.[71]

If *Work* and *Williams* do illustrate a "general principle," it is one that Professor Inbau appears to have missed: The courts will look at the totality of the circumstances and when they conclude that the proffered evidence was the "product" or "fruit" of an unreasonable search or seizure they will do the same thing in off-beat cases that they do in routine ones—they will exclude it.

An Exercise in Futility?

Whatever may be said for the courts "preserving the judicial process from contamination" [72] or against the government playing "an ignoble part" [73] or about it being the "omnipresent teacher," [74] I, for one,

[68] 243 F.2d at 661–62.

[69] *Id.* at 662.

[70] 237 F.2d 789 (D.C. Cir. 1956).

[71] See Kamisar, *Illegal Searches or Seizures and Contemporaneous Incriminating Statements: A Dialogue on a Neglected Area of Criminal Procedure,* 1961 U. ILL. L.F. 78, 126–28, especially n.224.

[72] Olmstead v. United States, 277 U.S. 438, 484 (1928) (Brandeis, H., dissenting).

[73] *Id.* at 470 (Holmes, J., dissenting).

[74] *Id.* at 485 (Brandeis, J., dissenting). *Compare* Paulsen, *The Exclusionary Rule and Misconduct by the Police,* 52 J. CRIM. L., C. & P.S. 255, 257–58 (1961), with George, *supra* note 62, at 785–93, *and* McGarr, *The Exclusionary Rule: An Ill-Conceived and Ineffective Remedy,* 52 J. CRIM. L., C. & P.S. 266, 267 (1961).

would hate to have to justify throwing out homicide and narcotic and labor racket cases if I did not believe that such action significantly affected police attitudes and practices.[75] At this point, however, I run smack up against Professor Inbau's grim, gray "facts":

"Although a trial judge or prosecutor may well be sensitive to a reversal on appeal, and consequently the reversal may serve to discipline him to avoid error and misconduct in the future, such a reaction cannot reasonably be expected from the police. They are generally insensitive to a court's rejection of evidence merely because of the impropriety of the methods used to obtain it." [76]

*   *   *

"[T]he average police officer whose confession [and presumably whose search] is declared invalid suffers no embarrassment or loss of prestige. . . . The clearance of a case by arrest . . . is all that really matters so far as the average policeman is concerned; what happens thereafter is the responsibility of the prosecutor and the courts." [77]

Coming from one with Professor Inbau's practical experience, these are telling blows. But more impressive, I submit, are the recent words and deeds of high law enforcement officials to the contrary. Evidently, there are jurisdictions where *somebody up there*—the attorney general or the district attorney or the chief of police—cares enough to make the average policeman care too.

Consider the post-*Cahan* observations of the Attorney General of the State of California:

[75] "[I]t would seem that the ultimate test of the exclusionary rules is whether they deter police officials from engaging in the objectionable practices. For if, as some assert, reversals of convictions in this area have had no substantial effect on police conduct, then the consequent gains even in terms of popular respect for law are tenuous, indeed." Allen, *Due Process and State Criminal Procedures: Another Look*, 48 Nw. U. L. Rev. 16, 34 (1953).

[76] Inbau, *Restrictions in the Law of Interrogation and Confessions*, 52 Nw. U. L. Rev. 77, 78 (1957).

[77] Inbau, *The Confession Dilemma in the United States Supreme Court*, 43 Ill. L. Rev. 442, 461–62 (1948). *But cf.* Inbau & Reid, Lie Detection and Criminal Interrogation 198 (3d ed. 1953) ("a practical and useful manual for criminal interrogators," according to p. ix): "A criminal interrogator should always remember that it his function not only to obtain a confession from a guilty subject, but also to obtain one which meets all the necessary legal requirements—*so that it can be used as evidence at the trial of the accused. For this reason*, familiarity with the law concerning criminal interrogations is in many respects equally as important as a mastery of the psychological tactics and techniques employed in eliciting the confession." (Emphasis added.) This passage opens a 35 page discussion of "The Law Concerning Criminal Confessions."

"I believe . . . that because of this decision the police are doing better work. Their investigations are more thorough and within American constitutional concepts. More guilty pleas have resulted because of the intensive pre-arrest work. For example, District Attorney Tom Lynch of San Francisco has advised me that in gambling and narcotic raids, as well as in other cases, the police discuss the facts with him and he is able to advise in advance just what is necessary in order to make a good case.

"In a great many instances, prior to the Cahan decision the police were satisfied with an arrest. They were not too concerned with conviction because the apprehension of the individual was sufficient in their minds. In these cases the defendant, upon his dismissal, would feel that the State was an equal violator of the law.

"In the field of narcotics, much more intensive work is being done with the peddler, the wholesaler and the seller. Prior to the Cahan case, the officers, in order to justify their existence, felt it necessary to make a certain number of arrests. It was always easy to arrest a known addict upon mere suspicion rather than do the tough, thorough work of getting to the wholesaler and peddler.

"I believe the over-all effects of the Cahan decision, particularly in view of the rules now worked out by the Supreme Court, have been excellent. A much greater education is called for on the part of all peace officers of California. As a result, I am confident they will be much better police officers. I think there is more cooperation with the District Attorneys and this will make for better administration of criminal justice." [78]

[78] Excerpts from letter from Governor Edmund G. Brown, then Attorney General of the State of California, to the *Stanford Law Review*, Dec. 7, 1956, on file with the *Stanford Law Review*, quoted in part in Elkins v. United States, 364 U.S. 206, 220–21 (1960), and in part in Note, 9 STAN. L. REV. 515, 538 (1957). I am indebted to the editors of the *Stanford Law Review* for sending me a photostatic copy of the letter, which is on file in the Minnesota Law Library. The *Cahan* reference is to *People v. Cahan*, 44 Cal. 2d 434, 282 P.2d 905 (1955), which saw the California Supreme Court overturn precedents of more than 30 years standing to adopt the exclusionary rule.

As Professor Barrett has pointed out, Barrett, *Exclusion of Evidence Obtained by Illegal Searches—A Comment on People vs. Cahan*, 43 CALIF. L. REV. 565, 587 (1955), prior to the *Cahan* decision, "the California situation was most unsatisfactory. . . .

"The rules were ill-defined. There was little direct pressure upon the police to conform to the rules. In practice, police discretion in determining the reasonableness of searches was rarely subject to check. The possibilities of the situation improving appeared slight. Law enforcement groups preferred the ambiguity of seldom-litigated rules and had no real incentive to take the risks involved in seeking legislative action."

The *Cahan* case led to the appointment of an Attorney General's Committee, whose recommendations in turn led to extensive new legislation, in many respects clarifying and codifying the case law on arrest and search and seizure, although not without raising some new problems. See 32 CALIF. STATE B.J. 607–10 (1957). Furthermore, as Professor Weinstein has recently noted, the state has compiled applicable California decisions in "a simple but well-written training publication for California peace officers that makes clear by hypothetical and rule what the police can and cannot do." Weinstein, *supra* note 60, at 169–70.

What of the experience in the District of Columbia, site of the *McNabb-Mallory* rule, as well as the W*eeks* doctrine? In large measure, the hopes and expectations of exponents of the exclusionary rule have been fulfilled on two counts.[79] Listen to Oliver Gasch, in his fifth year as United States Attorney for the District of Columbia at the time:

"In view of the widely divergent views concerning the meaning and effect of the *Mallory* decision, we felt that it was highly desirable to initiate a series of lectures to which supervisory officials of the Police Department and the detective force would be invited. These lectures were given about two years ago and in substance they have been repeated on a number of occasions both to the retraining classes of policemen as well as to the new men. We have encouraged questions both during the lectures and at the

[79] I am indebted to Bernard Weisberg, a member of the Chicago Bar and General Counsel of the Illinois Division of the American Civil Liberties Union, for alerting me to much found in the succeeding text by his careful summary of the District police's adaption to the *McNabb-Mallory* rule in Weisberg, *Police Interrogation of Arrested Persons: A Skeptical View*, 52 J. Crim. L., C. & P.S. 21, 33–34 (1961).

I want to make it quite clear that my reliance on the striking District of Columbia experience does not mean that I quarrel with the proposition that the desire to obtain convictions (as opposed to police "harassment") and "the policeman's remediable ignorance of the law" "constitute only a part of the explanation for American police misconduct." Allen, *Federalism and the Fourth Amendment: A Requiem for Wolf*, 1961 Sup. Ct. Rev. 1, 37. See also Barrett, *Personal Rights, Property Rights, and the Fourth Amendment*, 1960 Sup. Ct. Rev. 46, 54–55. But to concede that the exclusionary rule is not always decisive is hardly to agree it is never significant.

Professor Allen has pointed to "a large middle-western city in a jurisdiction which for almost forty years has applied the exclusionary rule" where—until recently—the police department did little to inform itself of current search and seizure law. See Allen, *supra* at 39. What does this necessarily prove other than that the exclusionary rule *per se* is not a "cure-all"? Other than that the exclusionary rule *ipso facto* cannot override the ill effects of poor leadership and tradition and/or low general quality and inadequate general training? That the exclusionary rule is wasted on some police departments scarcely establishes that it fails significantly to affect the work of better ones.

Is there any doubt that prior to *Mapp* the police departments of *many more* exclusionary states than admissibility states (if any) did demand extensive training in the rules of arrest and search and seizure? See, e.g., the late Justice Murphy's mail questionnaire study of police practices in Wolf v. Colorado, 338 U.S. 25, 44–46 (1949) (dissenting opinion). Denver is the only specific example given of a city in an *admissibility* jurisdiction providing fairly comprehensive instructions on search and seizure, *id.* at 46. But the Denver instruction manuals Justice Murphy evidently referred to do not bear him out. As was recently observed in Weinstein, *supra* note 60, at 159 n.45, "the second edition of Melville, Manual of Criminal Evidence in Colorado (1954) [written for Denver Police Academy] contains an extensive discussion of how confessions should be obtained in order to make them admissible (pp. 16–21); it ignores the search and seizure problem, thus furnishing striking evidence of the impact of an exclusionary rule on police training programs."

conclusion thereof. Our *Mallory* lectures have been printed by the congressional committee studying this subject.

* * *

"At the present time, due largely to the conscientious cooperation of our Chief of Police and in accordance with the teaching of the decisions and our lectures on it, the police are making better cases from the evidentiary standpoint. Extensive investigation prior to arrest of suspects has resulted. The accumulation of other evidentiary material has become standard operating procedure. It has been emphasized to the force that they may arrest only on probable cause and that persons arrested should be given a preliminary hearing without unnecessary delay. Even though a panel of our Appellate Court decided . . . that the Mallory decision does not require a preliminary hearing in the middle of the night, we have followed the practice of having preliminary hearings in the middle of the night in those cases in which question may arise as to the imposition of a sanction because of failure to comply with Rule 5a of the Federal Rules of Criminal Procedure.

* * *

"With respect to search and seizure . . . about two years ago, it became very evident to me that the time had come for training and retraining in the field of search and seizure. . . . This project was one of the most useful activities of our office in my judgment. These four lectures were recorded, carefully annotated, and have recently upon order of the Attorney General been distributed to all Federal law enforcement officers. You may be interested in how we set up these lectures. We asked the Chief of Police to circularize his entire force and to solicit from them questions in the field of search and seizure which gave them difficulty. We broke these questions down into three groups. Searches and seizures with warrants, searches and seizures incident to lawful arrests, and emergency situations. Using entirely for problem material the questions of the police force, we developed this series of four lectures. We in the prosecutor's office benefitted greatly by the need to go to the books and to analyze the rationale of the decisions for answering the questions presented.

"I am sufficiently optimistic to report to you that most of the policemen benefitted as well by these lectures. My men have given me a number of examples which indicate quite clearly that our policemen are thinking in terms of these decisions and our lectures, and to that extent their work has materially improved. Searches and seizures as far as possible are now bottomed upon a search warrant. The police realize that it renders more effective their work to check out the legal basis for the warrant with legally trained persons before attempting to accomplish a search or seizure." [80]

[80] Gasch, "Law Enforcement in the District of Columbia and Civil Rights" pp. 2, 3, 5, unpublished address of March 25, 1960, to Twelfth Annual Conference, National Civil Liberties Clearing House, in Washington, D. C., reported in the Washington Post, March 26, 1960, p. D1, col. 7 (hereinafter referred to as "Gasch"). I am indebted to Bernard Weisberg of the Chicago Bar for sending me a copy of this address, which is now on file in the Minnesota Law Library.

I am hardly in a position to appraise the general effect *Mapp v. Ohio* has had in those jurisdictions which used to admit illegally seized evidence. I think I do know that in at least one such jurisdiction, my home state of Minnesota, law enforcement training has already been substantially affected by the exclusionary rule and will continue to be so. Witness the attitude of the Attorney General of the State of Minnesota at one of several post-*Mapp* conferences on police procedures relating to the law of arrest and seizure:

"It is my personal opinion that the *Mapp* case is sound law. Years of experience demonstrate that the only way in which the Fourth Amendment can be made meaningful is to declare illegally-obtained evidence inadmissible—in short, to remove the incentive for obtaining evidence through illegal means and to make it essential for police officials to become skilled in the proper legal methods by which their cases can be built. The very fact that these institutes are being held is eloquent testimony, it seems to me, of the basic wisdom of the Court's decision. We are doing today, because of the Court's ruling, what we should have done all along. We are studying ways in which we can bring our police methods and procedures into harmony with the constitutional rights of the people we serve.

* * *

"Some persons claim the Supreme Court has gone too far. Others claim to know how constitutional protections may be avoided by tricky indirection. Both viewpoints are wrong—this Institute was called to assist us in better fulfilling our sworn duty to uphold the Constitution. It was not called to second guess the Supreme Court.

"For those who seek techniques to circumvent the constitutional rights of the people, I say that it is not only illegal, but contrary to our oath and destructive of the basic principles of a free society to do so. As Attorney General of this state, I do not propose to permit our Constitution to be circumvented and I serve notice upon anyone so inclined." [81]

To observe that the deterrent effect of the exclusionary rules has fallen far short of expectations in jurisdictions other than those mentioned above is hardly to condemn. So—for millenia—has the deterrent effect of the laws against murder, rape, and robbery.

The recent experience in the State of California and the District of Columbia, and the post-*Mapp* prospects in Minnesota, by no means constitute conclusive evidence of the efficacy of the exclusionary rules. But they do, I think, rudely dislodge the notion that these rules are merely an exercise in futility.

[81] Mondale, *The Problem of Search and Seizure*, 19 BENCH & BAR OF MINN. 16, 19 (Feb. 1962).

Might There Be a Better Way?

If the jaded debate over the exclusionary rules has accomplished any-thing, it has illustrated once again that "answers are not obtained by putting the wrong question and thereby begging the real one." [82] What are the *real questions*? One of them, surely, turns on what we should appraise the exclusionary rule *against*.

The fact that there is disagreement and inconclusive evidence that the exclusionary rule substantially deters police lawlessness is a good deal less significant, I think, than the fact that there is much agreement and abundant evidence that all other *existing* alternatives do not.[83] Thus, proponents of the rule are in good position if one major question is whether or not the exclusionary rule is the best *presently available, politically feasible* means of effectuating the constitutional safeguards. Evidently, this is not good enough for opponents of the rule. The ques-tion they like to ask is whether the exclusionary rule is the very best approach to police misconduct that man ever conceived, or ever will! Why does it have to be?

Suppose it can be shown that the present system of criminal law administration is irrational and illogical. That "punishment for a period of time and then letting him go free is like imprisoning a diphtheria-carrier for awhile and then permitting him to comingle with his fellows and spread the germ of diphtheria?" [84] If so, it is imperative that we strive for improvement, but does it follow we should burn up the statute books *in the meantime—before* we have attained the requisite number of trained "social physicians" who can determine and remove the cause of crime with the same degree of accuracy that the surgeon finds and cuts out an inflamed appendix? [85]

Suppose it can be demonstrated that "fiendish perpetrators of

[82] Frankfurter, J., dissenting in Priebe & Sons, Inc. v. United States, 332 U.S. 407, 420 (1947).

[83] A number of vigorous *opponents* of the exclusionary rules have recognized the futility of *existing* alternatives. See, e.g., remarks of former federal prosecutor T. J. Curran, NEW YORK CONVENTION 529; McGarr, *The Exclusionary Rule: An Ill-Conceived and Ineffective Remedy*, 52 J. CRIM. L., C. & P.S. 266, 268 (1961) (another former federal prosecutor); Plumb, *Illegal Enforcement of the Law*, 24 CORNELL L.Q. 337, 386–88 (1939).

[84] A criticism quoted in Cardozo, *What Medicine Can Do for Law*, in LAW AND LITERATURE 90 (1931).

[85] See M. R. Cohen, *Moral Aspects of the Criminal Law*, in REASON AND LAW 45 (1950).

horrible crimes on children could be reformed by being sent first for several years to a special hospital" and that "a certain social environment or . . . an elaborate college course will reform a burglar or gunman?" [86] Suppose, further, all hands agree that *logically, theoretically, ideally,* this sort of "treatment" and "re-education" is much to be preferred over "punishment?" Does it follow that we scrap what we have *now* in exchange for the hope or promise that ten or twenty or fifty years from now we might have the community support, the large funds, and the necessary psychiatric know-how to make the theoretically superior alternative a reality? [87]

I share Wigmore's view that the *Weeks* rule is "illogical." [88] I agree, too, that "the natural way to do justice here would be to enforce the healthy principle of the Fourth Amendment directly, *i.e.,* by sending for the high-handed . . . marshal who had searched without a warrant, imposing a thirty-day imprisonment for his contempt of the Constitution, and then proceeding to affirm the sentence of the convicted criminal." [89] But what does all this mean? It means, I take it, that we are afforded the opportunity to repeal the exclusionary rule *now*.[90] But *when—if ever—*do we get the chance to vote for legislation authorizing courts to send for the transgressing marshal and imprison him for his "contempt of the Constitution?" And what do we use to effectuate the Fourth Amendment *in the meantime?*

Those seeking the repeal of the exclusionary rule have often conceded the inadequacy of *existing* alternative remedies.[91] As a *quid pro quo* for the abolition of the rule, they have proposed, e.g., the establishment of a civil rights office, independent of the regular prosecutor, "charged solely with the responsibility of investigating and prosecuting alleged violations of the Constitution by law enforcement officials"; [92]

---

[86] *Id.* at 45–46.

[87] See *id.* at 46; Dession, *Psychiatry and the Conditioning of Criminal Justice,* 47 YALE L.J. 319, 332–35 (1938).

[88] 8 WIGMORE 35.

[89] *Id.* at 40.

[90] The debate has long been bottomed on the premise that the exclusionary rule is a rule of evidence which the Congress or the state legislatures could "repeal." *Mapp* changed all that. See Weinstein, *supra* note 60, at 155. For purposes of discussion, however, I am assuming that either a constitutional amendment or judicial overruling has occurred, so that we are still "free" to "repeal" the rule.

[91] See note 83 *supra.*

[92] Peterson, *Restrictions in the Law of Search and Seizure,* 52 Nw. U.L. Rev. 46, 62 (1957). The disadvantages of this proposal are considered in Paulsen, *The Exclusionary Rule and Misconduct by the Police,* 52 J. CRIM. L., C. & P.S. 255, 261 (1961).

"shifting the financial responsibility for improper conduct of policemen, on a *respondent superior* basis, to the municipality or sovereign which employs them." [93]

Have we ever known an opponent of the exclusionary rule to introduce a bill spelling out such proposals? Have we ever heard of a peace officers or sheriffs or district attorneys association "lobbying" for such a proposal? When—if ever—they do, the case for the exclusionary rule will be much weakened. I ask again, what do we do in the meantime?

I am sure that Professor Inbau and many people in law enforcement work would guffaw at the suggestion that adoption of the "British System" of narcotics control (permitting doctors to furnish narcotics to addicts in certain cases) is the way to eliminate *our* narcotics problem. Inbau, no doubt, would share the view that the "British System" is inapplicable to the United States. No doubt, he would retort, as others have, that the favorable narcotic situation in England is not the result of the "British System" at all but "the British people themselves. . . . [They] have a definite abhorrence of narcotic drugs, which has become incorporated into their mores and culture." [94]

Fine. But why, then, does Professor Inbau so blithely point to the fact that "the free, law abiding countries of England and Canada have always admitted evidence even though it may have been unreasonably seized?" [95] Why does he not touch on "the speed and certainty with

---

[93] McGarr, *supra* note 83, at 268. See also Plumb, *supra* note 83, at 387.

[94] See CALIF. SPECIAL STUDY COM'N ON NARCOTICS, FINAL REPORT 101 (1961).

[95] Inbau 86. To say that England has "always" admitted unreasonably seized evidence is to be somewhat misleading. As late as 1955, there was only one modern case bearing on the point, Elias v. Pasmore, [1934] 2 K.B. 164, 173 (a decision of a judge of first instance at that) and a survey of Commonwealth authority at that time revealed no uniform rule on the admissibility of evidence procured through illegal searches and seizures. See Cowen & Carter, *The Admissibility of Evidence Procured Through Illegal Searches and Seizures*, in ESSAYS ON THE LAW OF EVIDENCE 82–83, 100 (1956). That year, when, according to one commentator, "the lower courts in the United Kingdom seemed ready to revise [the rule of admissibility] if not to reject it," Franck, Comment, 33 CAN. B. REV. 721, 722 (1955), a decision of the Privy Council in Kuruma v. The Queen, [1955] 1 All E.R. 236, sanctioned the admissibility of evidence illegally obtained.

Professor Glanville Williams, the English participant in the Northwestern Law School's recent International Conference on Criminal Law Administration, criticized *Kuruma* on numerous counts: the opinion indicates that evidence obtained by "trickery" should be ruled out, but not that obtained by unlawful force—seemingly a "more flagrant breach of the law"; one of the possible reasons for excluding induced confessions—"to hold the police and prosecution to proper behaviour"—"would equally suggest the exclusion of evidence obtained by an illegal search"; American decisions to the contrary were omitted and "quite possibly misunderstood"

which the slightest invasion of British individual freedom or minority rights by officials of the government is picked up in Parliament, not merely by the opposition but by the party in power, and made the subject of persistent questioning, criticism, and sometimes rebuke?" [96] Why does he not allude to recent observations that—

"It must be surprising to any student who is not thoroughly immersed in English ways of thought to find that in a country where so much importance is attached to the liberty of the subject, the power of search is left so vague and unregulated. But as always the preference is for the unwritten law. The police are expected to act reasonably; and so long as they do so, the accused is as unlikely to insist upon his right to immunity from search as he is on his constitutional right to silence. The absence of judicial regulation suggests the lack of need for it; no situation has yet arisen in which anything corresponding to the Judges' Rules has been called for.

"Cases in which the right of search has been considered are from the lawyer's point of view lamentably few." [97]

It may well be that at this time the imposition of the exclusionary rule is neither necessary nor proper in certain other lands. How does this resolve *our* problem? I concede that we are *intellectually* capable of formulating better alternatives; I merely doubt that at the moment we are *politically* capable of effectuating them. I confess, further, that I am not enthused about scrapping the exclusionary rule *today* in exchange for assurances that these other potentially superior alternatives will undergo further study *next year* or the year after.

[only *Olmstead* was cited; not, for example, the earlier *Weeks* case nor the later *Nardone* cases]; Scottish decisions to the contrary "were misinterpreted and misstated." Williams, *The Exclusionary Rule Under Foreign Law: England*, 52 J. CRIM. L., C. & P.S. 272, 273 (1961). Professor Williams notes wistfully that "since decisions of the Privy Council are not absolutely binding in future cases even upon the Privy Council itself, this important question of public policy cannot be regarded as finally settled." *Ibid.* Most English and Canadian writers share Williams' dissatisfaction with the *Kuruma* result. See, e.g., Cowen & Carter, *supra* at 103–05; DEVLIN, THE CRIMINAL PROSECUTION IN ENGLAND 64–65 (1958) (criticizing the earlier *Passmore* case); Franck, *supra* at 723–31.

[96] JACKSON, THE SUPREME COURT IN THE AMERICAN SYSTEM OF GOVERNMENT 81–82 (1955).

See also Martin, *The Exclusionary Rule Under Foreign Law: Canada*, 52 J. CRIM. L., C. & P.S. 271, 272 (1961): "The problem of deliberate violation of the rights of the citizen by the police in their efforts to obtain evidence has not been as pressing in Canada as in some other countries. . . . In addition, the remedy in tort has proved reasonably effective; Canadian juries are quick to resent illegal activity on the part of the police and to express that resentment by a proportionate judgment for damages."

[97] DEVLIN, *op. cit. supra* note 95, at 64.

I agree that the exclusionary rule is not the best of all possible approaches in the best of all worlds, but is there a real alternative in the present state of affairs? After all, as Reinhold Niebuhr has put it, "democracy is a method of finding proximate solutions for insoluble problems." [98]

As Niebuhr has also observed, however, "any definition of a proper balance between freedom and order must always be at least slightly colored by the exigencies of the moment which may make the peril of the one seem greater and the security of the other therefore preferable." [99] Thus, to establish that the exclusionary rule is the best means at hand for effectuating liberty and privacy is to make a point, but hardly to win the debate. A host of questions—*real* questions, I admit—remain to be answered. In one way or another, they ask: *What price, exclusionary rule?*

"Crime Waves" and Rules of Evidence

Professor Inbau implies, if he does not assert, that the 98 per cent increase in the crime rate since 1950—five times the increase in population—is the product of recent " 'turn 'em loose' court decisions and legislation." [100] He hints, none too gently, that his and his daughter's freedom to walk home after dark turns on whether or not we rid law enforcement officers of "the strait jacket placed upon them by present day court and legislative restrictions." [101]

Chief William Parker of the Los Angeles Police Department, another vigorous critic of the exclusionary rule, is not content with innuendo:

"Following the Cahan decision, there was a departure from the trend of an accelerating nature with such a skyrocketing effect that December 1955 reflected the worst crime experience in the history of Los Angeles. In attempting to determine cause, it must be concluded that the greatest

[98] NIEBUHR, THE CHILDREN OF LIGHT AND THE CHILDREN OF DARKNESS 118 (1944).
[99] *Id.* at 78.
[100] Inbau 86. Professor Inbau is referring to FBI, UNIFORM CRIME REPORTS FOR THE UNITED STATES 1 (1960) (hereinafter referred to as "UNIFORM CRIME REPORTS" for given year). In 1960, the crime rate for seven major offenses—murder, forcible rape, robbery, aggravated assault, larceny ($50 and over), and auto theft—"was 24 per cent above the average for the past 5 years; 66 per cent over 1950; and 96 per cent higher than 1940." *Id.* at 2.
[101] Inbau 99.

single factor representing a change in the current situation was the imposition of the exclusionary rule at the close of April 1955. As the criminal army became familiar with the new safeguards provided to them, the acceleration in crime was an inevitable result." [102]

*   *   *

"[I]n Los Angeles during 1956 there was a 30 per cent increase over the year before, after we had experienced a downward trend. The Cahan decision reversed the trend, and the 1957 rate is 14 per cent over 1956. . . . .

"They are the facts. These are the things they don't like to talk about. That is what is happening throughout America.

"Q. Do you think the *Mallory* decision will have a similar impact?

"Yes. I will show you how the *Mallory* decision will put the *Cahan* decision to shame, as far as effect upon serious crimes is concerned." [103]

Professor Inbau, Chief Parker, and others in their camp raise real *questions*, all right. But do they supply real *answers*? It may be my own shortcoming, but I find so much so wrong with their reasoning that I am not quite sure where to begin.

Perhaps the way to begin is to ask some questions of my own. What was the increase in the crime rate from 1940 to 1950, when fewer jurisdictions utilized the exclusionary rule? From 1930 to 1940? Rises in crime, Chief Parker tells us, are "happening throughout America." But until the summer of 1961, the courts of half our states let in illegally seized evidence. Were these admissibility jurisdictions undergoing "crime waves" too? Or were the exclusionary states running well ahead of the national average?

Take, for example, the District of Columbia and its surrounding Maryland and Virginia suburbs. Until *Mapp* was handed down in the summer of 1961, Maryland admitted illegally seized evidence in all felony prosecutions; Virginia, in all cases. On the other hand, the District's law enforcement officers are not only "handcuffed" by the federal exclusionary rule in search and seizure cases but weighed down, too, by the *McNabb-Mallory* rule—the dread "ball and chain" which hampered no other police force during the 1950–1960 period. One would expect the District, then, to set the pace in crime acceleration, certainly far to outdistance Virginia and Maryland.

The "facts" that fellows like me are not supposed to want to talk about reveal that *the District's incidence of rapes, aggravated assaults and grand larency was lower in 1960 than in 1950.*[104] On a per 100,000

---

[102] Parker, Police 120 (Wilson ed. 1957).

[103] 1957 *House Committee Hearings* at 76.

[104] See Mintz, *Serious Crime Rate Down Here Despite Furor Raised by Congress,* Washington Post, July 5, 1961, p. B1, col. 6.

population basis, the overall felony rate increased a puny one per cent in the District, but a redoubtable 69 per cent in the three major Maryland and Virginia suburbs for which generally complete figures were available.[105]

No, I am not suggesting that the way to diminish crime is to *adopt* exclusionary rules of evidence. I only suggest that to point to a spectacular rise in national crime or in a particular state's crime is hardly to prove that restrictive rules of evidence have "caused" this increase.

Opponents of the exclusionary rules will hasten to point out, no doubt, that the above figures do not tell the whole story. Of course they don't. But why do they overlook the point when they trot out the figures on California and Illinois crime?

The explanation for the disparity in the crime acceleration between the District and its suburbs may lie in the explosive growth of the suburbs and the concomitant slight decline in the District's population. Or in the superior training of the District police. Or in the undermanned suburban police forces. Perhaps the key to the disparity is that the suburbs compile more complete records of crime than does the District, or better records than they did back in 1950.

I must confess, therefore, that I don't think these figures are decisive. Evidently, the critics of the *Weeks* and *McNabb-Mallory* rules don't either. For they have never had a word to say about them. If I may be permitted to ask, what dark inferences would Inbau, Parker & Co. draw if these statistical disparities had been *reversed*? If the District's crime had shot up 69 per cent and the suburbs but one per cent. Can you hear those trumpets now?

Perhaps the peremptory answer to this "numbers game" may be found in a masterful, critical analysis of the current sad state of criminal statistics appearing in this very *Journal* a short time ago. On that occasion, Ronald H. Beattie, long-time Chief of the California Bureau of Criminal Statistics, made an impressive showing that various cities in

---

[105] *Ibid.* Nation-wide, the crime rate for seven major offenses rose 66 per cent during this period. See note 100 *supra*. Preliminary figures compiled by the police departments of the District and surrounding suburbs for the 1961 calendar year indicate that the incidence of serious crime in the suburbs is continuing to rise at a greater rate than in the District. The seven-category felony increase in the District from 1960 to 1961 was 9 per cent; suburban increases for that period were: Fairfax, 21 per cent; Prince Georges, 20 per cent; Arlington, 15 per cent; Montgomery, 14 per cent; and Alexandria, 6 per cent. See Goshko, *Major Crime Rate Growing Faster in Suburbs Than D. C.*, Washington Post, Mar. 11, 1962, p. B5, col. 1.

the *same* state, to say nothing of different states, are using such disparate methods in crime reporting that "the differences observed in *Uniform Crime Reports* simply cannot be accepted as possessing any degree of reliability for showing true differences in crime rates among the states." [106]

Though I believe Mr. Beattie's critical analysis makes the "real facts" about the impact of rules of evidence on crime somewhat fanciful, Chief Parker has a right to be proud of Beattie's comments:

"California, in particular, has a history of police development over the past forty years, stemming from the leadership of August Vollmer, which means not only high levels of police efficiency and professional performance but also better and more complete records. This latter fact in itself causes California to appear to have a high crime rate. States where in general there are many police agencies with poor record systems, incomplete reporting, and lower standards of police proficiency should not be accredited as having less crime simply because the statistical data reported show less crime." [107]

* * *

"Los Angeles showed an over-all crime rate two and one-half times as great as San Jose, and this difference appears in all offenses. The widest difference occurs in aggravated assault, where the rates reported were 13 times greater for Los Angeles than for San Jose.

"Sacramento and Fresno, which represent valley metropolitan areas presumably not too different in general composition, showed rather strange differences in crimes reported. . . .

"This kind of comparison vividly demonstrates the wide differences in reporting from departments and areas within the same state. Actually, no conclusions about crime rates can possibly be made with any certainty from this kind of information. The Los Angeles area in particular has been named in public releases as having the highest crime rate in the country. The Los Angeles Police Department has been an outstanding department for many years. It has been recognized as one of the most effective and efficient large metropolitan police agencies in the country. It would appear that because this department is effective and efficient, and has complete records, the area is being identified as one with a high crime rate in comparison with other cities that do not have police departments of the standard and quality that Los Angeles possesses and do not keep as efficient and complete records of the incidence of crime." [108]

Mr. Beattie *could* be wrong; the statistics may truly reflect the extent of crime in various cities and states. However, I fail to see how this possibility aids the critics of the exclusionary rules.

[106] Beattie, *Criminal Statistics in the United States*, 51 J. Crim. L., C. & P.S. 49, 54 (1960).
[107] *Id.* at 53–54.
[108] *Id.* at 55.

Suppose Los Angeles really does have 1300 per cent the aggravated assault San Jose has? *Why?* They are both in the state of California and both subject to the same rules of evidence. What if the crime rates in the comparable cities of Sacramento and Fresno vary as much as the published figures indicate? Suppose Sacramento does have nearly twice the forcible rape rate of Fresno, and Fresno a much higher aggravated assault rate than Sacramento. Whatever the reason, how can it be the *Cahan* decision?

Similar questions can be raised about the state of crime in Illinois. Why is Chicago's burglary rate less than twice that of Champaign-Urbana, Peoria, and Rockford, but its robbery rate about five times that of Champaign-Urbana and Peoria and more than *twenty* times that of Rockford? Why is it that Peoria and Champaign-Urbana are about the same in total offense rate, but Champaign-Urbana has about three times the murder-voluntary manslaughter and aggravated assault rates of Peoria? [109] If these striking intrastate statistical disparities at all approximate the "real facts," don't they serve to illumine the insignificance, if not irrelevance, of the state-wide exclusionary rule?

The 98 per cent crime rise which Professor Inbau glibly tosses into the fray is a familiar figure. This is how J. Edgar Hoover opened an interview early this year.[110] Perhaps this is the place to begin. Midway in this interview, the Director of the FBI was asked to account for the sharp rise in crime. He spoke of the "steady decline of parental authority," the disintegration of "moral standards in home and community," the "highly suggestive, and, at times, offensive, scenes" on TV and in the movies, "public indifference to organized vice," the number of people who "lack the courage to aid the victim personally, or the interest to summon help," and the "abuse and maladministration of the systems of parole and probation." [111] *Nary a word about rules of evidence.*

Mr. Hoover's discussion of the problem was comprehensive, but hardly exhaustive. Other "causes" of crime and "crime waves" advanced from time to time are "tensions" from two world wars and/or the "cold war," the "strain" of modern living; the crowding of rural people unaccustomed to urban ways into the big cities; the population movement of the Negroes, the demise of the billy club, the displacement

---

[109] Based on Table 4—Index of Crime, 1960, Standard Metropolitan Statistical Areas, UNIFORM CRIME REPORTS for 1960 at 53–77.

[110] U.S. News & World Rep., Jan. 1, 1962, p. 34.

[111] *Id.* at 35–36.

of the foot patrolman with the squad car, more laws, better crime reporting, comic books, cigarette smoking, poor housing, overcrowded schools, "bad blood," *ad infinitum.*

While crime in the District of Columbia is still down from the peak years in the early 1950's it is up from the ten-year low set in 1957.[112] What "caused" *this* increase? The U.S. Attorney pointed to the "woefully and demonstratively understaffed" Juvenile Court, ill-equipped to "win away from a life of crime those border-line juvenile delinquents."[113] One District Commissioner found the "main reason" in "more probations," "earlier paroles" and the fact that "drunks are sometimes sent home rather than to jail."[114] This was immediately disputed by another Commissioner, who suggested "the cutback in the activities of the Metropolitan Police Boys Club [from 17,000 boys served, down to 5,000 in two years] may have contributed."[115]

He who links "crime waves" with rules of evidence is a bold man. Bolder than Oliver Gasch, former U.S. Attorney for the District of Columbia, who after wrestling with the *McNabb-Mallory* rule and the *Weeks* rule for six years, dismissed this suggestion as "much too speculative."[116] "He must be a bold man indeed who is confident that he knows what causes crime. Those whose lives are devoted to an understanding of the problem are certain only that they are uncertain regarding the role of the various 'alleged' 'causes' of crime."[117]

Perhaps this is not the way to start answering the "crime wave" argument. Perhaps we should begin further back, by asking: *What* "crime wave"?

[112] See Mintz, *supra* note 104, at p. B2.

[113] Gasch, *supra* note 80, at 6.

[114] Washington Post, Mar. 27, 1960, p. A27, col. 6 (Comm'r Robert F. McLaughlin).

[115] *Ibid.* (Comm'r David P. Karrick).

[116] Gasch, *supra* note 80, at 7, quoted in MacKenzie, *Mallory Ruling Held Blameless in Crime Rise,* Washington Post, Mar. 26, 1960, p. D1, col. 7. But more recently Deputy Police Chief Edgar E. Scott blamed the "rise" in District "street crimes" (as against the ten-year low-point of 1957) partly on "civil libertarians who scream about the Constitution, due process and the Bill of Rights," centering his criticism of the Courts on the *Mallory* decision. At the same time, Scott insisted that "the fight to maintain moral standards and good law enforcement is tied with the fight against communism, because . . . nations fall from weakness and corruption from within, rather than power from without." MacKenzie, *Scott Blames 'Civil Libertarians' for Street Crime,* Washington Post, Mar. 27, 1962, p. B1, col. 2. Chief Scott did not explain why crime is increasing more rapidly in the suburbs of Virginia and Maryland—which have no *McNabb-Mallory* rule.

[117] Frankfurter, J., dissenting in Winters v. New York, 333 U.S. 507, 526–27 (1948).

As Professor Herbert Wechsler, Chief Reporter for the Model Penal Code, and a former state and federal assistant attorney general, observed awhile back: "We cannot even be certain that the statistics on crimes 'known to the police' actually indicate an increase in the amount of crime." [118] For "better attention to complaints, more careful and systematic efforts to record and count offenses, more arrests, will make your crime rate go up higher on paper than in actual fact."

This is not mere speculation. There are striking examples of "crime waves" which turned out to be nothing more than "statistical reporting waves." When a Philadelphia reform mayor's police commissioner assumed office in 1952, he discovered that for years records had been distorted in order to "minimize" crime, e.g., one center-city district in one month handled 5,000 more complaints than it had recorded. When a new central reporting system was installed, the number of "crimes" went up from 16,800 in 1951 to 28,600 in 1953—"for the record" a staggering climb of over 70 per cent.[119] In New York City, similar faking had gone on for years. Following a survey by police expert Bruce Smith, a new system of central recording was established for 1952. Assaults immediately jumped 47 per cent, robberies 73 per cent, and burglaries 118 per cent! [120]

I have little doubt that Superintendent Orlando W. Wilson, if he were not the careful student of crime he is, could contrive an enormous increase in the amount of Chicago's crime. For shortly after he became head of the Chicago force he undertook a drastic revamping of the department's methods of reporting crime and maintaining records. For the first time, a crime analysis section at police headquarters now works from complete records on all crimes, big or small.[121] Common practices of the pre-Wilson era, it seems, were not to report stolen cars as stolen in statistical records if they were recovered within three days, and for a commander to "follow a practice of ignoring a lot of the little stuff to save work and make the district look better on paper." [122]

---

[118] U.S. News & World Rep., Sept. 26, 1960, p. 64.
[119] Bell, *What Crime Wave?* Fortune, Jan., 1955, pp. 96, 99. See also Bell, *The Myth of Crime Waves*, in THE END OF IDEOLOGY 138–39 (1960).
[120] *Ibid.*
[121] See Gowran, *Wilson Plea: More Radios, More Records*, Chicago Daily Tribune, Nov. 8, 1961, pt. 1, p. 8, col. 1.
[122] *Ibid.*

Did the Cahan Case "Cripple" California Law Enforcement?

Not only do critics of the exclusionary rule in search and seizure cases argue that its imposition swells the ranks of the "criminal army" but they also indicate that it has "rendered the people powerless to adequately protect themselves against the criminal army." The two contentions can be separated and distinguished. The first contention—the rule breeds more crime—may not be true, but the second contention—the rule seriously diminishes the capacity of law enforcement to cope with whatever crime is bred—may nevertheless be true.

Chief Parker found evidence of the severe blow dealt to efficient law enforcement by the *Cahan* decision in the reduction of narcotic arrests: "During 1954 the comparative [seasonal] periods reflected a 15.7 per cent increase in [narcotic] arrests, while a 4.5 per cent decrease followed the *Cahan* decision." [123]

Again, I venture to suggest that the chief has skipped a premise or two. For example, what are the comparative figures on narcotic offenses reported? On suspects released after arrest? On narcotic offenders formally charged? Convicted?

In any event, assuming Chief Parker's reliance on the arrest data is well placed, what *does* the "record" show? Adult felony arrests for narcotic law violations in California did drop slightly in 1955, from 7,457 to 7,313, but they were over 9,000 in 1956, over 10,000 in 1957, and, rising steadily and substantially every post-*Cahan* year, passed the 14,000 mark in 1960.[124] True, California's population has boomed, but the rate of adult felony arrests for narcotics per 1,000,000 population, which dipped from 60 to 56 in 1955, rose to 67 and 73.1 in 1956 and 1957, respectively, and reached 89.2 in 1960.[125] If the 1955 decline in narcotic arrests illustrates the blow *Cahan* dealt law enforcement, what do these more recent figures evidence?

J. Francis Coakley, District Attorney for Alameda County, California, also sounded the alarm in the summer of 1956 by reporting that "the *Cahan* decision establishing the Exclusionary Rule in California

---

[123] PARKER, POLICE 121 (Wilson ed. 1957).
[124] See CALIF. SPECIAL STUDY COM'N ON NARCOTICS, FINAL REPORT 53 (1961) (hereinafter referred to as "FINAL NARCOTICS REPORT"); CALIF. DEPT. OF JUSTICE, BUREAU OF CRIMINAL STATISTICS, CRIME IN CALIFORNIA 1960, at 47 (hereinafter referred to as "CRIME IN CALIFORNIA" for given year).
[125] CRIME IN CALIFORNIA 1956, at 35; 1957, at 32; 1960, at 45.

has broken the very backbone of narcotics enforcement." [126] The only statistical support I can find for this sweeping statement is that the rate of felony narcotic complaints per 100,000 population filed in California Superior Court fell from 22 to 18 in 1955 [127] and the percentage of narcotics convictions in California Superior Courts dropped from 86.6 to 77.6 in 1955, and to a still lower 76.8 in 1956.[128]

In 1957 the rate of narcotic complaints reached 23 per 100,000,[129] passing the pre-*Cahan* rate, and climbed to 25 in 1959, where it has remained.[130] But critics of the exclusionary rule can find some solace in the percentage of convictions in narcotics cases. Following the *Cahan* case, this percentage dropped for three successive years to a low of 74.3 in 1957.[131] While it has climbed back slowly to 77.5 in 1960,[132] this is still considerably short of the pre-*Cahan* figures of 82.5 (1952) 84.4 (1953) and 86.6 (1954).[133] Why?

In 1957, looking at the narcotics and bookmaking, the two offenses whose conviction percentage had dropped substantially since the *Cahan* case, the California Bureau of Criminal Statistics suggested the obvious: "Evidently, the adoption of the exclusionary rule has had some effect on these two offense groups." [134] Two years later, however, the Bureau was more cautious. Indeed, it balked at linking the *Cahan* rule with these lowered conviction rates, noting that "the large number of cases in Los Angeles County often distorts the picture for the rest of the State." [135]

The 1954 Los Angeles 85 per cent conviction rate in narcotic offenses fell to 67 per cent in 1957, before it rose somewhat to 70 in 1958 and 73 in 1959, but there was "very little change in other areas of the state." [136] From 1954 to 1959, for example, "the nine other Southern California counties in contrast varied only between a high and a low of 88 and 85 per cent convicted, respectively." [137] The same patterns

[126] ABA, Summary of Proceedings of Section of Criminal Law 58 (1956).
 [127] Crime in California 1955, at 42.
 [128] Crime in California 1954, at 60; 1955, at 60; 1956, at 61.
 [129] Crime in California 1957, at 53.
 [130] Crime in California 1960, at 95.
 [131] Crime in California 1957, at 66.
 [132] Crime in California 1958, at 62 (75.1 per cent); 1959, at 67 (77.3 per cent); 1960, at 104 (77.5 per cent).
 [133] Crime in California 1952, at 38; 1953, at 47; 1954, at 60.
 [134] Crime in California 1957, at 66–67.
 [135] Crime in California 1959, at 68.
 [136] *Id.* at 68–69.
 [137] *Ibid.*

held for bookmaking. The only conclusion the Bureau could reach was:

"Many things, other than the *Cahan* decision may be affecting the statistics on narcotics and bookmaking convictions in Los Angeles County. What has just been reported does not, in itself, prove or disprove any aspect of the multifaceted problem. All that can be said, with validity, is that convictions for narcotics and bookmaking in Los Angeles County have decreased since 1954 and that they continue to remain at a relatively low level." [138]

Further illumination is furnished by a six month study (Aug. 1, 1960, through January 31, 1961) made by the District Attorney's Office, County of Los Angeles, to determine the effect of the *Cahan* and *Priestly* decisions on narcotic cases. Of the total processed 1,420 narcotic cases which came to the attention of the District Attorney's Office during this period, those rejected by the District Attorney or dismissed by the Court because of *Cahan* or *Priestly* and those which resulted in an acquittal for the same reason came to a grand total of 128—"approximately eight per cent." [139]

During this same period, another 615 Los Angeles cases (140 in Superior Court) were dismissed, rejected, or otherwise "lost" for non-exclusionary rule reasons.[140] How does this compare with the pre-*Cahan* Los Angeles experience? If the California Attorney General's impression that *Cahan* led to "much more intensive [pre-arrest] work" in the field of narcotics is accurate,[141] and these observations hold for Los Angeles as well as the rest of the state, shouldn't *Cahan* be credited with a few narcotic conviction "assists," too? And shouldn't these offset the "losses" a bit?

If not, let me suggest another reason for supposing the "true figure" is probably lower than eight per cent. Some 439 other Los Angeles felony narcotic cases processed during the study period were

[138] *Id.* at 69.

[139] FINAL NARCOTICS REPORT 112. Eleven of the exclusionary rule releases were said to be due to the requirement established by Priestly v. Superior Court, 50 Cal. 2d 812, 330 P.2d 39 (1958), that an informant's identity must be disclosed where this information is the only evidence to establish "probable cause." This rule was cut down significantly in May of 1961 when the California Supreme Court held that where a search is made pursuant to a warrant valid on its face, the informer's identity need not be revealed in order to establish the legality of the search. People v. Keener, 55 Cal. 2d 714, 12 Cal. Rep. 859, 361 P.2d 587 (1961).

[140] FINAL NARCOTICS REPORT 112.

[141] See text at note 78 *supra*.

not considered in the calculations because they had not yet reached "final disposition." [142] According to the study, however, the *Cahan-Priestly* factor looms largest at the initial stages of a case. Thus, of the 128 "losses" due to the exclusionary rule, only 38 occurred after the cases were brought to Superior Court.[143] To look at it another way, the exclusionary rule was a factor in only 4.4 per cent of the 866 cases which reached Superior Court. There is reason to believe, therefore, that if the other 439 cases were followed up and taken into account the eight per cent figure would be appreciably lower.

Furthermore, whatever the true figure in Los Angeles, there is good cause for supposing the exclusionary rule is a significantly smaller factor in other California narcotic cases. For, as already noted, the narcotics conviction percentage runs about ten points higher outside Los Angeles. In any event, this much is *not* speculation: *ruling out* the exclusionary rule factor, the Los Angeles felony narcotics conviction percentage is still lower than most other California areas, *taking into account* the exclusionary factor.

This, too, must be said about the narcotics situation in California. When we stop thinking about narcotic offenses in lump form and start viewing the matter in terms of specific types of narcotic offenses we discover that while the 1960 statewide overall narcotics conviction percentage in California Superior Courts was 77.5, the state-wide figures for both *sales* of marijuana and *sales* of narcotics other than marijuana were 88.2 and 88.7, respectively.[144] To look at it another way, of the 460 narcotic cases dismissed in 1960, "approximately four-fifths were possession cases"; "there were only a total of 33 sale cases and 9 sale to minor cases dismissed." [145]

Finally, it should not be forgotten that while the overall narcotics conviction percentage is down substantially, from 85.5 in the 1953–1954 pre-*Cahan* years to 77.4 for the years 1959–1960, the rate of arrests as well as felony complaints filed in narcotic cases has risen appreciably. Thus, in 1959–1960, which experienced a substantially lower conviction *percentage*, some 5,696 were convicted of narcotic offenses in California Superior Courts [146] as against 4,419 for the record conviction percentage years of 1953–1954.[147]

---

142 FINAL NARCOTICS REPORT 112.
143 *Ibid.*
144 CRIME IN CALIFORNIA 1960, at 122.
145 *Id.* at 77.
146 CRIME IN CALIFORNIA 1959, at 67; 1960, at 104.
147 CRIME IN CALIFORNIA 1953, at 47; 1954, at 60.

I think I have demonstrated that the predictions and descriptions of near-disaster in narcotics law enforcement which greeted and followed the *Cahan* decision find precious little support in the available data. Until now, however, we have been dwelling on narcotic offenses— *the major category of crime most likely to be affected by the exclusionary rule.* But opponents of the rule have proclaimed its adverse effects on crime and law enforcement *generally.* Chief Parker reported its effect "catastrophic as far as efficient law enforcement is concerned"; [148] he considered it "conceivable that the imposition of the exclusionary rule has rendered the people powerless to adequately protect themselves against the criminal army." [149] An assistant attorney general for the State of California called the *Cahan* rule "the 'Magna Carta' for the criminals." [150] "Crime statistics indicate he is right," declared Chief Carl Hansson of the Dallas Police Department. "Many states," he tells us, "have adopted the Exclusionary Rule to the joy of the criminal and the detriment of society." [151] What can be gleaned from the records about the effect *Cahan* has had on California conviction rates generally?

The conviction percentage for murder, 67.1 in 1953, and 61.2 in 1954, was up to 69.8 in 1960; manslaughter, 81.1 and 90.2 in 1953 and 1954, respectively, is now at 93.2; felony assault, under 77.5 for the two pre-*Cahan* years, was 81.3 in 1960; rape, 76.5 and 79.3 in the two years immediately preceding *Cahan*, is now at 81.4.[152] Variances in conviction percentages relating to robbery and burglary are barely discernible. Robbery, 84.8 in 1953 and 85.8 the following year, rose to 86.3 the year of the *Cahan* decision, and is now at 85.4. The conviction percentage for burglary, which increased four-tenths of one per cent from 1953 to the 1954 figure of 90.8, *decreased the same four-tenths* to 90.4 in the *Cahan* year and is now at 89.6.[153]

The overall felony conviction percentage averaged 84.5 for the three years immediately preceding Cahan,[154] registered 85.4 for the *Cahan* year,[155] and has been at 86.4 (*including* the aforementioned

---

[148] PARKER, POLICE 114 (Wilson ed. 1957).

[149] *Id.* at 118.

[150] Reported in ABA, SUMMARY OF PROCEEDINGS OF SECTION OF CRIMINAL LAW 54 (1956).

[151] *Ibid.*

[152] CRIME IN CALIFORNIA 1953, at 47; 1954, at 60; 1960, at 104.

[153] *Ibid.*

[154] CRIME IN CALIFORNIA 1955, at 44.

[155] *Ibid.*

lower narcotic percentage) for the last three years.[156] Of course, the *number* of felony defendants convicted in California Superior Courts has risen substantially; for example, from 17,359 in the last pre-*Cahan* year [157] to the 1960 total of 24,816.[158]

Did the Mallory Case "Cripple" Law Enforcement in the District of Columbia?

Four years ago, in his testimony before a Senate subcommittee, Professor Inbau "suggested" that "we are paying a great price for the *Mallory* rule." [159] Last year, in the pages of this *Journal*, he was less cautious: "In the federal jurisdiction of Washington, D. C., which must cope with a variety of criminal offenses and problems similar to any other city of comparable size, this federal court rule has had a very crippling effect on police investigations." [160] Of course, Professor Inbau's voice has been but one of many raised in alarm. And the voices have been shrill indeed.

Thus, in his 1957 testimony before a House subcommittee, Robert Murray, Chief of the District's Police Department, stated flatly that "if the *Mallory* decision stands, it will result in complete breakdown in law enforcement in the District of Columbia." [161] Chief Murray claimed, then, that "an overwhelming majority of these major crime cases, and maybe as much as 90 per cent, are solved after the subject has been brought in and questioned." [162]

Deputy Chief of Police Edgar Scott picked up and amplified his superior's 90 per cent figure:

"The application of the Mallory rule would prevent the clearance of a majority of the planned crimes and serious crimes and those committed by professionals.

"I wish to emphasize that a little bit more because I think what the Chief meant on the 90 per cent was that 90 per cent of these types of crimes by professionals are planned crimes and could not be cleared.

[156] CRIME IN CALIFORNIA 1958, at 62 (86.6 per cent); 1959, at 67 (86.4 per cent); 1960, at 104 (86.3 per cent).
[157] CRIME IN CALIFORNIA 1954, at 60.
[158] CRIME IN CALIFORNIA 1960, at 104.
[159] 1958 Senate Committee Hearings at 73.
[160] Inbau, *Police Interrogation—A Practical Necessity*, 52 J. CRIM. L., C. & P.S. 16, 20 (1961).
[161] 1957 House Committee Hearings at 42.
[162] *Id.* at 43.

"There's another type of crime [unplanned] that would bring the overall clearance to a better figure, and I would say it would still be a majority of the crimes that could not be cleared, but of the ones committed which are planned by professionals and that had planned them ahead of time, I think the figure of 90 per cent is all right." [163]

* * *

"Mr. Cramer. As to that figure that Chief Scott indicated, that about 90 per cent of the cases require investigation, and fairly lengthy investigation, and a majority of the 90 per cent would require investigation within the lengthy period of time ruled out in the Mallory case, what you are saying is that of the planned crimes, planned by the professional criminal, 90 per cent would probably go free as a result of their knowledge of the Mallory case and their unwillingness to cooperate.

"Mr. Scott. Under the application of the Mallory case; yes, sir." [164]

The 1957 *Mallory* decision *did* stand. Consider the testimony some time later of Howard Covell, Deputy Chief Executive Officer of the District Police Department:

"First, those tables will show that, viewed in its relationship to the long-term trend in this city and nationwide, the present rate of crime in the District of Columbia is not excessive and, in fact, is favorably low.

"In brief, the calendar year 1958 crime rate of the District is only 6.7 per cent above the all-time low rate of the fiscal year 1957, is 31.5 per cent below the peak rate of calendar year 1952, and is 20.4 per cent below the rate of calendar year 1949, while the nationwide crime rate, as estimated by the Federal Bureau of Investigation, has increased steadily and by more than 50 per cent since 1949." [165]

* * *

"Mr. Santangelo. As a matter of fact, it appears to me that the percentage of solutions of the major crimes has increased down through the years?

"Chief Covell. I would say yes.

"Mr. Santangelo. For the last 3 years let us say, the homicides, rapes, and aggravated assaults, your percentage of solutions has increased, has it not?

"Chief Covell. I would say yes, but that also comes from, and I say this with modesty, from an increased efficiency of the Police Department and better coordination of the law enforcement agencies throughout the entire metropolitan area. I think that the cooperation of all departments in this area reflects in each other's department to some extent. . . . During the fiscal year 1958 there was a total of 51 per cent of all part 1 crimes [major offenses] solved as compared with 49.5 during 1957. The rate of clearance in 1958 is second to the highest; that was 55.6 attained by the

[163] *Id.* at 45.
[164] *Id.* at 46.
[165] *Hearings on District of Columbia Appropriations for 1960* at 419.

Department since the installation of the present system of reporting, which was made in 1948." [166]

Consider, too, the testimony of Chief Murray the following year:

"Mr. Santangelo. . . . Can you tell us what your experience in 1959 was with respect to the solution of crimes of criminal homicide and the other major crimes?"

*   *   *

"Chief Murray. . . . The average is 52.5, which I think is perhaps about double or nearly double the national average. I think the national average on clearance of cases is about 27 per cent. It runs consistently about 27 per cent.

"Mr. Santangelo. Last year, in 1958, the percentage of solution of crimes was 51 per cent, and in the year 1959 it was 52.5 per cent. So your percentage of efficiency has increased to that extent. Is that a correct statement?

"Chief Murray. Yes, sir; plus the fact that we have had a few more men to help us clear it. . . ."

*   *   *

"Mr. Santangelo. Your percentage of solutions has increased in the cases of robbery.

"Chief Murray. Yes, sir; we have, I think, a very good record in the clearance of robberies, 65 per cent.

"Mr. Santangelo. That rose from 61.3.

"Chief Murray. Yes, sir."

*   *   *

"Mr. Santangelo. In aggravated assault, you also have gone up from 84.3 to 88 per cent. In housebreaking, which is another difficult thing to solve, you have gone up from 50.5 to 54 per cent. Is that correct?

"Chief Murray. Yes, sir.

"Mr. Santangelo. For which I commend you, Chief Murray." [167]

Remember the 90 per cent figure the District's police officials tossed out back in 1957? Listen to United States District Attorney Oliver Gasch three years later:

"Another point I should like to emphasize concerning this issue is that while *Mallory* questions are well publicized they do not occur in every case. In fact, *Mallory* questions, that is to say, confessions or admissions, are of controlling importance in probably less than 5 per cent of our criminal prosecutions. At the present time, due largely to the conscientious cooperation of our Chief of Police and in accordance with the teaching of the decisions and our lectures on it, the police are making better cases from the evidentiary standpoint. Extensive investigation prior to arrest of suspects

---

[166] *Id.* at 440–41.
[167] *Hearings on District of Columbia Appropriations for 1961* at 619–20.

has resulted. The accumulation of other evidentiary material has become standard operating procedure."

* * *

"On the affirmative side, it can be said that police work generally is more thorough and exact. Reliance upon confessions generally has been minimized. It must be mentioned, however, that in some instances we have been unable to go forward with cases wherein we felt that we were largely dependent upon a confession and the confession was inadmissible under the *Mallory Doctrine*. Pleas to lesser included offenses have been accepted; and from the police standpoint, their ability to clear through interrogation other offenses of which the individual was believed involved has been reduced. The recovery of stolen property from such individuals has been hampered by reason of the need for arraignment without unnecessary delay. In short, the emphasis has been on according persons arrested a preliminary hearing with the utmost dispatch."

* * *

"To me, one of the important aspects of our local law enforcement pictures is this: Prior to the *Mallory* decision our police had an outstandingly high rate with reference to solving crimes. That rate is still outstandingly high. This is a great tribute to Chief Murray and his men. They have worked hard and effectively. Lesser men would have thrown up their hands in despair." [168]

Conclusion

It is true that the immediate effect of the *McNabb-Mallory* rule or the *Weeks* rule is often to free the "obviously guilty," but the rationale is these "hospital cases" have much more far reaching and much more salutary effects. This is neither a new nor a novel theory. The late Karl Llewellyn expressed it well a generation ago, talking about, of all things, the law of contracts:

"[M]y guess is . . . that the real major effect of law will be found not so much in the cases in which law officials actually intervene, nor yet in those in which such intervention is consciously contemplated as a possibility, but rather in contributing to, strengthening, stiffening attitudes toward performance as what is to be expected and what 'is done'. If the contract dodger *cannot* be bothered, if all he needs is a rhinoceros hide to thumb his nose at his creditor with impunity, more and more men will become contract dodgers . . . [I]n this aspect each hospital case is a case with significance for the hundreds of thousands of normal cases." [169]

[168] Gasch *supra* note 80, at 3, 4, 7.
[169] Llewellyn, *What Price Contract?—An Essay in Perspective*, 40 YALE L. J. 704, 725 n.47 (1931).

How well this theory works—in the form of the *McNabb-Mallory* and *Weeks* rules—remains to be seen. At the moment it appears to be doing quite nicely in the District of Columbia, the jurisdiction which has felt the brunt of what Inbau calls "turn 'em loose" court decisions.

The work of the District police "generally is more thorough and exact," "reliance upon confessions generally has been minimized," "the accumulation of other evidentiary material has become standard operating procedure," "extensive investigation prior to arrest of suspects has resulted." [170] This, as the song goes, is the whole idea.

If you are against the exclusionary rules it is helpful to think they exact an exorbitant price in increased crime and diminished law enforcement. This makes resolution of the issue easy. But in the two jurisdictions which have held the spotlight in recent years, the District of Columbia and the State of California, there is no tangible evidence that the rules have done anything of the kind. Of course, if you are for the exclusionary rules, it is comforting to believe that their cost in "letting alone" or "freeing" criminals is *de minimis*. This also makes resolution of the debate easy.

I do not know (and I doubt) that the cost is or will be *de minimis*. I do think I know that opponents of the rule have not established the contrary. They have made loud noises about the "disasterous" and "catastrophic" prices we are paying to effectuate constitutional liberties, but they have yet to furnish convicing evidence that the price is even substantial.

Even if by some miracle we could cleanly disentangle the exclusionary rule from the many other factors which "cause" crime or reduce the efficiency of police and prosecutors, I suspect Professor Inbau and I would still disagree. I suspect he would contend the data proves "we can't afford" the rule and I would maintain—unless the data greatly surprises me—that "it's cheap at the price." For we would still differ over the *value* of the commodity purchased.[171] It makes a lot of difference whether one views the fourth amendment as a fundamental safeguard against serious abuses or whether one thinks of it as merely a provision dealing with a formality.[172]

I am for the exclusionary rule as the best means available or pres-

---

[170] Gasch *supra* note 80, at 3–4.

[171] And, no doubt, as to the objective standards by which "police efficiency" can be judged. See Weisberg, *Police Interrogation of Arrested Persons: A Skeptical View*, 52 J. CRIM. L., C. & P.S. 21, 37 (1961).

[172] See Frankfurter, J., dissenting in United States v. Rabinowitz, 339 U.S. 56, 69 (1950).

ently feasible for enforcing guarantees of liberty and privacy. Professor Inbau tells us he believes in these rights, too.[173] How does he propose to effectuate them?

He suggests that in the *McNabb* case the Court might have "contented itself with an incidental reprimand to federal officers for failing to comply with statutory requirements regarding arraignment." [174] As for illegal search or seizure, he feels that "an effective way to teach a policeman a lesson is by bringing a civil suit directly against him." [175]

I leave it to the reader to decide which of us is "starry-eyed."

MORE ABOUT PUBLIC SAFETY v. INDIVIDUAL CIVIL LIBERTIES

FRED E. INBAU *

An article by Professor Inbau entitled "Public Safety v. Individual Civil Liberties: The Prosecutor's Stand" was published in the March, 1962, issue of the *Journal* (Vol. 53, No. 1) at pp. 85–89. Professor Inbau's paper evoked a detailed response from Professor Yale Kamisar of the University of Minnesota, which appeared in the June, 1962, number of the *Journal* (Vol. 53, No. 2) at pp. 171–93. The Inbau article also brought forth strong criticisms from two *Journal* readers; their comments appeared in the June, 1962, number (Vol. 53, No. 2) at pp. 231–32. In the comment which follows, Professor Inbau replies to his critics. A concluding comment by Professor Kamisar is scheduled to appear in the December number of the *Journal*.—EDITOR.

Whenever a champion of individual civil liberties is branded as anti-American or as a fellow traveler of the Communists he becomes highly incensed. And rightly so, because there is nothing un-American about being a civil libertarian, even of the starry-eyed variety; and a

---

* The author is a Professor of Law in Northwestern University. Long active in the field of scientific evidence, he served from 1933 to 1938 as a member of the staff of the Scientific Crime Detection Laboratory of Northwestern University School of Law, and from 1938 to 1941 as Director of the Chicago Police Scientific Crime Detection Laboratory. Professor Inbau has been the Managing Director of this *Journal* since 1945 and is the author of *Cases and Comments on Criminal Justice* (with Claude R. Sowle); *Lie Detection and Criminal Interrogation* (3d ed. 1953) (with John E. Reid); and *Self-Incrimination: What Can an Accused Person Be Compelled To Do?* (1950).

173 See Inbau 86.
174 Inbau, *The Confession Dilemma in the United States Supreme Court*, 43 ILL. L. REV. 442, 451 (1948).
175 ABA, SUMMARY OF PROCEEDINGS OF SECTION OF CRIMINAL LAW 60 (1956).

person can be an avid civil libertarian without embracing Communism. But many civil libertarians are themselves subject to the same fallacious reasoning with which their critics are sometimes afflicted. They assume that when a person criticizes court decisions which he considers too restrictive of police functions, that critic must be in favor of a "police state"; he must be of a Fascist bent of mind; he must be interested in allowing the police to do anything they please; he must favor the use of the "third degree," illegal searches and seizures, and all other police practices that the courts have condemned.[1]

It is high time that we shed ourselves of the kind of intolerance and misconceptions that prevail on both sides.

The police will have to accept the fact that in any democratic society police efficiency must necessarily incur a considerable measure of sacrifice in deference to the rights and liberties of the individual. They must realize that the public at large has made that decision and the police have no right to change it. On the other hand, the civil libertarian must appreciate the fact that some sacrifice of individual rights and liberties has to be made in order to achieve and maintain a safe, stable society in which the individual may exercise those rights and liberties. They cannot be exercised in a vacuum. In the recent words of a federal district court judge, "Pure liberty with no restraints produces anarchy, while pure discipline brings in the police state." [2]

In Professor Yale Kamisar's 23 page article in the last issue of this *Journal,* replying to the four page reproduction of a speech I had delivered at a meeting of the National District Attorneys' Association, he quotes with approval Reinhold Niebuhr's statement that "democracy is a method of finding proximate solutions for insoluble problems." [3] Let me apply that fine statement to the differing viewpoints which Professor Kamisar and I have expressed with reference to the United States Supreme Court's decision in *Mapp v. Ohio*—the 1961 case which imposed the exclusionary rule upon all the states as a requirement of due process.[4]

For many years the people of the State of Michigan sought to find a "proximate solution" to the "insoluble problem" of illegal search and

[1] See particularly the criticism aimed at my views in the letters published in the "Notes and Announcements" section of the June, 1962, number of this *Journal* (53 J. CRIM. L., C. & P.S. 231 (1962)).

[2] Comment of Judge Wade H. McCree, Jr., quoted in the Detroit News of Feb. 25, 1962.

[3] Kamisar, *Public Safety v. Individual Liberties: Some "Facts" and "Theories,"* 53 CRIM. L., C. & P.S. 171, 184 (1962).

[4] 367 U.S. 643 (1961).

seizure, and they were struggling with the problem during the time when the Supreme Court was holding that the exclusionary rule was only a rule of evidence which the states were at liberty to accept or reject.

By constitutional amendments in 1936 and 1952, the *people* of the State of Michigan—not just their representatives in the legislature—worked out what they thought to be a "proximate solution" to this "insoluble problem." They decided that the exclusionary rule was a good rule except as regards its application to narcotics and dangerous instrumentalities such as firearms and explosives. As to these various articles, the prosecution could use them as evidence regardless of the illegality of their seizure, provided the seizure did not involve an invasion of a person's home.[5] Here, then, was a democratic effort to arrive at a "proximate solution" to a very difficult problem—a problem that all the states had wrestled with from time to time, and, as we know, they were about evenly divided at the time of the 1961 *Mapp* decision; half of the states accepted and half rejected the exclusionary rule.

What right, I again ask, did the Supreme Court have to tell the people of Michigan, in its 6 to 3 decision in *Mapp v. Ohio*, that they were in gross error as regards the "proximate solution" they were seeking in their 1936 and 1952 amendments to the Michigan constitution? Let us remember that here was a state that had not ignored the problem. To the contrary, it was earnestly seeking a solution, and once again I call attention to the fact that at the time when the people of Michigan were making that effort they were privileged to do so insofar as the United States Supreme Court was concerned, because all along the Court had considered the exclusionary rule to be only a rule of evidence; it did not evolve into a due process requirement until the 6 to 3 decision in *Mapp v. Ohio* on June 19, 1961.

I do not think that the Court was justified in holding that its judgment (or rather that of six of the nine Justices) was superior to that exercised by the people of Michigan and the many other states that did not consider the exclusionary rule to be the solution to the problem of illegal searches and seizures. And if I am to be looked upon as a legal heretic for thinking so, then I have the company of some respectable fellow heretics—the three Justices who dissented in the *Mapp* case.[6]

---

[5] MICH. CONST. 1908, art. II, §10 (as amended in 1936 and 1952).

[6] In this connection, I should also like to point out that when I say that the Supreme Court has no right to police the police, I have some company in the person of Mr. Justice Harlan. See his dissent in Rea v. United States, 350 U.S. 214, 218 (1956).

Also among my fellow heretics may be added the majority of the members of Michigan's 1962 Constitutional Convention. They decided to include in the proposed revised constitution a provision which perpetuates the Michigan viewpoint as expressed by the people of that state in their 1936 and 1952 amendments to their present constitution. Moreover, the Convention did this while fully aware of *Mapp v. Ohio* and all its implications. They were sufficiently convinced of the merits of their own "proximate solution" to again declare—in rather specific defiance to the *Mapp* decision—that the provisions of the constitution regarding searches and seizures "shall not be construed to bar from evidence in any criminal proceeding any narcotic drug, firearm, bomb, explosive or any other dangerous weapon, seized by a peace officer outside the curtilage of any dwelling house in this state." [7]

What the Supreme Court did in *Mapp* it is also likely to do someday with respect to confessions obtained by state law enforcement officers who have interrogated arrestees while delaying in taking them before a committing magistrate or while they were without counsel during their police detention. The Court may tell the states that they must adopt the same rules and standards that the Court has prescribed for federal courts and federal law enforcement officers. And that possibility disturbs me more than what the Court did in *Mapp v. Ohio*. I think the effect would be disastrous to law enforcement and to the public's welfare and safety. State law enforcement officers can live with the exclusionary rule a lot easier than they could with a *McNabb-Mallory* rule that would, in effect, prohibit local law enforcement officers from interrogating criminal suspects.[8] By modernizing the laws of arrest and search and seizure, either by legislative enactment or court decisions (as the California and Illinois courts have done), there will be far fewer occasions for the police to violate the law as a matter of practical necessity; and there will be less need for the courts to reject incriminating evidence. But to deprive the police of an opportunity to conduct criminal interrogations—by a Supreme Court decision founded upon constitutional considerations—would produce consequences that cannot be modified in the same way as is possible with respect to arrests, searches and seizures.

[7] MICH. CONST., art. I, §11, as finally adopted by the Convention on May 11, 1962. See No. 136A, State of Michigan Journal of the Constitutional Convention.

[8] For details of the *McNabb-Mallory* rule and its application see Inbau, *The Confession Dilemma in the United States Supreme Court*, 43 ILL. L. REV. 442 (1948), and Inbau, *Police Interrogation—A Practical Necessity*, 52 J. CRIM. L., C. & P.S. 16 (1961).

Contrary to what Professor Kamisar implies,[9] I am not one of those who attributes the rise in the national crime rate, or even a substantial part of it, to the "turn 'em loose" court decisions of the past several years. There are other factors of considerably greater significance. However, I am convinced that some of the increase in crime is due to such decisions, and this factor will enlarge in significance if the present "turn 'em loose" trend continues.

Critics of the view I expressed regarding decision in *Mallory v. United States* [10] charge that there is no statistical proof that the *McNabb-Mallory* rule seriously hampers the police of Washington, D. C., or that the rule seriously affects the rate of convictions or of crime itself. They also state that the FBI gets along very well with the *McNabb-Mallory* rule. I cannot answer the first point with any statistics of my own—and I do not think statistics can support the opposite viewpoint either—but some simple logic is available to support the proposition that the *McNabb-Mallory* rule does, and is bound to have, a crippling effect upon law enforcement in any metropolitan jurisdiction saddled with the rule. But before developing this point I first wish to state that the FBI and the other national law enforcement agencies are not confronted by the same crime problems that are encountered by a metropolitan police department such as that in Washington, D. C. For instance, when the FBI is investigating cases like those involving the interstate transportation of stolen automobiles or of women for purposes of prostitution, or even cases of suspected espionage, there are many investigative procedures that may be employed and relatively little need exists for the interrogation of suspects themselves. Moreover, time is usually not a critical factor, and manpower and funds are ample for the volume of federal cases to be investigated. But a vastly different situation confronts the police of a city such as Washington, D. C., with its high incidence of robberies, burglaries, rapes, etc.— crimes that ordinarily cannot be solved except by the interrogation of the suspects themselves, since physical clues or any other evidence of guilt are seldom available.

In communities such as Washington, D. C., most serious crimes will remain unsolved if the police are not permitted to interrogate criminal suspects. To prohibit police interrogation—which, in effect, is what the *McNabb-Mallory* rule does—means, therefore, that fewer crimes will be solved and successfully prosecuted. More criminals will

[9] Kamisar, *supra* note 3, at 184.
[10] 354 U.S. 449 (1957).

remain at large, to commit other offenses. At the same time the deterrent effect of apprehension and conviction will be lost insofar as other potential offenders are concerned. The crime rate is bound to be greater under such circumstances, and I do not feel the need of statistics to support that conclusion.

One of my critics, Professor Alfred R. Lindesmith,[11] states that "in England police handling of suspects is guided by the Judges' Rules which, incidentally, forbid interrogation of the defendant after arrest." The implication is that the police in the United States could get by without interrogation opportunities. But I call Professor Lindesmith's attention to the fact that the police in England, out of practical necessity, have circumvented the rules out of existence; the Judges' Rules are now dead letters in England. In support of this statement I refer Professor Lindesmith to the published statements of two outstanding police officials and also to one of England's most respected legal scholars, Professor Glanville Williams.[12] Moreover, in England the courts will admit a confession obtained in violation of the Judges' Rules if it is otherwise voluntary.

By way of some further answers to my critics, I wish to repeat again several of my viewpoints which have been stated publicly by me on many previous occasions:

I am unalterably opposed to the "third degree" and to any other interrogation tactics or techniques that are apt to make an innocent person confess. I am opposed, therefore, to the use of force, threats, or promises of leniency—all of which might make an innocent person confess; but I do approve of other types of psychological tactics and techniques that are necessary in order to secure incriminating information from the guilty, or investigative leads from otherwise uncooperative witnesses or prospective informants.

I am opposed to illegal police searches and seizures, but I do not believe that the United States Supreme Court had the right to order

[11] See Lindesmith, Letter to the Editor, 53 J. Crim. L., C. & P.S. 231 (1962).

[12] One such acknowledgment was made by the Chief Constable of County Durham, England: St. Johnston, *The Legal Limitations of the Interrogation of Suspects and Prisoners in England and Wales*, 39 J. Crim. L. & C. 89 (1948). Another such acknowledgment was made by the Commander of the Criminal Investigation Department, New Scotland Yard, London, England: Hatherill, *Practical Problems in Interrogation*, in International Lectures on Police Science (Western Reserve Univ., 1956). And see Williams, *Police Interrogation Privileges and Limitations Under Foreign Law—England*, 52 J. Crim. L., C. & P.S. 51 (1961), republished in Sowle, Police Power and Individual Freedom: The Quest for Balance 185 (1962).

the states to free guilty persons merely because the police had acted illegally in obtaining the evidence of guilt. I also feel that there are other ways to guard against police lawlessness, and again I wish to repeat what I have said many times before: The only real, practically attainable protection we can afford ourselves against police abuses of individual rights and liberties is to see to it that our police are selected and promoted on a merit basis, that they are properly trained, adequately compensated, and that they are permitted to remain substantially free from politically inspired interference. Along with these requirements I also add the necessity for realistic laws and rules governing arrest, search and seizure, and criminal interrogations, so that there will be no practical necessity for evasion of the law by the police in their efforts to furnish the protection and safety that the public demands of them. Individual civil liberties can survive in such an atmosphere, alongside the protective security of the public.

One further point: I am not one of those persons who feels that *all* criminals have to be caught and sent to jail. I am perfectly willing to settle for the apprehension and conviction of only enough of them to discourage criminal conduct. What I do object to is the present day trend on the part of some courts and legislatures to lay down rules and regulations which are making it almost impossible to apprehend and convict anybody! It is time that a balance be struck between individual civil liberties and public protection.

SOME REFLECTIONS ON CRITICIZING THE COURTS AND "POLICING THE POLICE"

YALE KAMISAR *

This comment is a concluding paper by Professor Kamisar concerning an article by Professor Fred E. Inbau of the Northwestern University School of Law entitled "Public Safety v. Individual Civil Liberties: The Prosecutor's Stand," which appeared in the March, 1962, issue of the *Journal* (Vol. 53, No. 1) at pp. 85–89. Professor Kamisar replied to the Inbau article of the June, 1962, num-

* The author is Professor of Law in the University of Minnesota Law School. He is also a member of the Advisory Committee on the Revision of the Minnesota Criminal Law. In 1960–1961, Professor Kamisar was a Social Science Research Council Fellow, studying the prosecutor's discretion in the State of Minnesota and the substantive criminal law "in practice." Prior to joining the faculty of the University of Minnesota in 1957, he was engaged in the practice of law in Washington, D. C.

ber of the *Journal* (Vol. 53, No. 2) at pp. 171–93. Professor Inbau's rebuttal to the Kamisar response appeared in the September, 1962, number of the *Journal* (Vol. 53, No. 3) at pp. 329–32. Comments from readers concerning these articles appeared in the June, 1962, number (Vol. 53, No. 2) at pp. 231–32; further letters concerning this exchange of views appear in the "Reader Comments" section of the present issue.—EDITOR.

"[R]ecent years have seen a recurrence of that old storm of criticism of the Supreme Court which seems to renew itself in our history every twenty years or so. The main lines of the attack, whether by lawman or layman, have had a quiet consistency. The underlying beat is always: 'I don't like these *results!*' And that underlying drumbeat is commonly, though not always, masked by noise about how the Supreme Court (or the members thereof) are abandoning their Constitutional function, usurping legislative power, disrupting our commonwealth, and this or that in addition. Marshall's court got this treatment; Taney . . . And here we are again." †

"We say we believe in law. We dedicate a day to its honor, by formal proclamation of our President. . . . Yet, day by day, we hear many voices that seem to be subversive of law. . . . We have, in America, given a new exaltation to the power of the judiciary. We have accorded to our courts the power to invalidate the acts of those who are more directly responsible to the people's will. Both de Toqueville and Bryce have remarked that in our polity scarcely a question arises which does not become, sooner or later, a subject of judicial debate. . . . What is important is that we recognize the additional stresses to which our system subjects our courts, and, in the sense in which we now use it, our law. Our judges personify law and the rule of law. We owe them the same honor we owe the law itself." ††

We need the relatively few professors we have with Fred Inbau's rich background in law enforcement work and tough, earthy approach to problems of criminal procedure and constitutional law.

I don't think Professor Inbau would deny that he is "prosecution minded," but surely more of his teaching brethren are "defense minded." If he finds it difficult to set aside the question of the guilt

---

† LLEWELLYN, THE COMMON LAW TRADITION: DECIDING APPEALS 384 (1960). For a brief but incisive discussion of the passions roused by Marbury v. Madison, 5 U.S. (1 Cranch) 137 (1803); McCulloch v. Maryland, 17 U.S. (4 Wheat.) 316 (1819); and *Exparte* Milligan, 71 U.S. (4 Wall.) 2 (1866); "but a few of the violent controversies which swirled about the heads of the Justices of the Supreme Court during the first century of its existence," see McGowan, *The Supreme Court in the American Constitutional System: The Problem in Historical Perspective*, 33 NOTRE DAME LAW, 527, 532–43 (1958).

†† Horsky, *Law Day: Some Reflections on Current Proposals to Curtail the Supreme Court*, 42 MINN. L. REV. 1105, 1106–08 (1958). See also McGowan, *supra*, at 540–43.

or innocence of a particular individual and focus solely upon the procedural and constitutional features of the case, others sometimes find it difficult to take into account considerations of police efficiency and public security. If he dwells too long on the "needs" of the policeman —virtually to the exclusion of all other values and policies—others sometimes forget that constitutional guarantees "ought not to be an obstacle in a game but only a protection against arbitrary and capricious police action," that "if the rules make sense in the light of a policeman's task, we will be in a stronger position to insist that he obey them." [1]

Professor Inbau's law enforcement background and police-prosecution perspective were put to good use in his famous 1948 article, "The Confession Dilemma in the Supreme Court." [2] It has deservedly been called an "important" contribution to the literature.[3] But 1948 was a long time ago—in this business.

Then the *McNabb* rule looked as if it might be tottering; it has since been twice reaffirmed.[4] By then, the Court had already banned "dry run" hangings, beatings, and other crude practices on the part of state officers, but as torture and terror became outmoded and were displaced by more subtle interrogation pressures, the area was marked by uncertainty. There is little uncertainty now; for a number of recent state confession cases has seen a vigilant Court outlaw much "psychological coercion," as well as physical violence.[5]

Back in 1948, the Supreme Court had not yet ruled that the security of one's privacy against unreasonable search and seizure was binding on the states through the due process clause;[6] it has since held that not only are these guarantees applicable to the states but that they must be enforced against them by means of the same sanction used against the federal government—exclusion of the illegally seized evidence.[7] If more examples of the imposition of national stand-

---

[1] Paulsen, *Safeguards in the Law of Search and Seizure*, 52 Nw. U.L. Rev. 65, 66 (1957).

[2] 43 Ill. L. Rev. 442.

[3] McCormick, Evidence 241 n.1 (1954).

[4] Upshaw v. United States, 335 U.S. 410 (1948) (decided after the Inbau article); Mallory v. United States, 354 U.S. 449 (1957).

[5] E.g., Culombe v. Connecticut, 367 U.S. 568 (1961); Spano v. New York, 360 U.S. 315 (1959); Fikes v. Alabama, 352 U.S. 191 (1957).

[6] Of course, it was to do so the following year, in Wolf v. Colorado, 338 U.S. 25 (1949).

[7] Mapp v. Ohio, 367 U.S. 643 (1961).

ards on state criminal proceedings are needed, in certain situations the states are now required to furnish *all* indigent prisoners with a free trial transcript or an adequate substitute.[8]

Today, the course of the Court is clear. Once concerned with property rights much more than human liberty, "it is now the keeper, not of the nation's property, but of its conscience." [9] Whether or not this was always so, in the past decade a majority of the Court has heeded the warning that "federalism should not be raised to the plane of an absolute, nor the Bill of Rights . . . reduced to a precatory trust." [10] More and more, the Court has come to realize that to the peoples of the world "the criminal procedure sanctioned by any of our states is the procedure sanctioned by the United States." [11] Surely and steadily, "the national ideal is prevailing over state orientation." [12]

In the meantime, how has Professor Inbau reacted to all this?

I regret to say that his voice has grown louder and harsher. This is understandable, if not excusable. It has always been easier for winners to be more gracious than losers. And Inbau must have realized some time ago that he is taking a "somewhat lonely position," [13] that he is fighting a losing—if not a lost—cause. Convinced that a major factor accounting for the stream of decisions against his views is "the neglect or failure of the police and prosecution to present adequately . . . [their] side of the issue," [14] and evidently determined to remedy the matter, it is not too surprising that Professor Inbau has mistaken intemperateness for articulateness.

Criticizing the Court

Of course, I find nothing unprofessional or unlawyerlike in anybody's criticism of the Court for having overruled *Wolf v. Colorado*.[15] How

---

[8] Griffin v. Illinois, 351 U.S. 12 (1956).

[9] Lewis, "Historic Change in the Supreme Court," *New York Times Magazine,* June 17, 1962, p. 7.

[10] Brennan, *The Bill of Rights and the States,* 36 N.Y.U.L. Rev. 761, 774 (1961).

[11] Schaefer, *Federalism and State Criminal Procedure,* 70 Harv. L. Rev. 1, 26 (1956).

[12] Lewis, *supra* note 9, at 7.

[13] *Cf.* McGarr, *The Exclusionary Rule: An Ill-Conceived and Ineffective Remedy,* 52 J. Crim. L., C. & P.S. 266 (1961).

[14] Inbau, *The Social and Ethical Requirements of Criminal Investigation and Prosecution,* 3 Crim. L. Q. (Canada) 329, 350 (1960).

[15] 338 U.S. 25 (1949).

could I? I was one of the many who criticized the Court for *not* over-ruling the *Wolf* case.[16] But criticism comes in different sizes and varieties.

It is one thing to differ with the Court about what the law is or ought to be; it is quite another thing to *deny that the Court has the power or the right to say what the law is.* The court needs and welcomes criticism possessing "that quality of judiciousness which is demanded of the Court itself"; [17] the profession and the public can get along quite nicely without the kind that "fans the fires of lawlessness and cynicism . . . ignited in the wake of the school desegregation cases," [18] and without the kind that "offers comfort to anyone who claims legitimacy in defiance of the courts." [19] I leave it to the reader to label Professor Inbau's brand of criticism. Here are some samples:

"We are not only neglecting to take adequate measures against the criminal element; we are actually facilitating their activities in the form of what I wish to refer to as 'turn 'em loose' court decisions and legislation. To be sure, such decisions and legislation are not avowedly for the purpose of lending aid and comfort to the criminal element, but the effect is the same. . . .

"What particularly disturbs me, and I am sure many of you, is the dangerous attitude that has been assumed by the United States Supreme Court. *The Court has taken it upon itself, without constitutional authorization, to police the police.*" [20]

"[The overruling of *Wolf v. Colorado* is] just another example of the Court's continuing efforts to police the police—and that is an executive, or at most a legislative function of government. It certainly is not the constitutional function of the judiciary." [21]

"[T]he reason is perhaps more disturbing than the individual case decisions themselves.

"It has become all too fashionable in judicial circles to line up 'on the liberal side.' In their zeal to become 'great judges' the formula seems to be, with some who harbour that aspiration, either adopt a 'turn 'em loose' policy or count yourself out as a great judge." [22]

[16] Kamisar, *Wolf and Lustig Ten Years Later: Illegal State Evidence in State and Federal Courts*, 43 MINN. L. REV. 1083 (1959).

[17] FREUND, *The Court and Its Critics*, in THE SUPREME COURT OF THE UNITED STATES 177 (1961).

[18] *Id.* at 172.

[19] WECHSLER, *Toward Neutral Principles of Constitutional Law*, in PRINCIPLES, POLITICS AND FUNDAMENTAL LAW 47 (1961).

[20] Inbau, *Public Safety v. Individual Civil Liberties: The Prosecutor's Stand*, 53 J. CRIM. L., C. & P.S. 85 (1962). (Keynote address at the 1961 Annual Conference of the National District Attorneys' Association.) (Emphasis added.)

[21] *Id.* at 86–87.

[22] Inbau, *The Social and Ethical Requirements of Criminal Investigation and Prosecution*, 3 CRIM. L. Q. (Canada) 329 (1960). (Emphasis added.)

"The courts have no right to police the police. . . . Furthermore, the courts have enough troubles of their own. Witness what goes on in some of the municipal or magistrate courts of our large cities. In my opinion there are, in such courts, more hurts to the innocent and more trampling over of the basic individual civil liberties and ethical considerations than you will find in most police departments. *Much of the concern, energy, and efforts that the courts expend with respect to police conduct could be better spent on getting their own house in order."* [23]

In his "reply," appearing in the preceding issue of the *Journal*, Professor Inbau is a good deal more restrained than he has been in other recent writings. But he still cannot resist challenging, once again, the right of the High Court to tell the people of Michigan that the "proximate solution" they worked out for the search and seizure problem must be set aside, the *right* of the Court to tell the people of that state that their judgment must be overridden.[24]

I am not sure I fully understand such talk. If the Supreme Court lacks such a right, how does it ever declare state executive and legislative action or state constitutional provisions in violation of the federal constitution? Can it be that Inbau still resists the idea of constitutional review by an independent judiciary? Can it be that he still insists that "no society is democratic unless it has a government of unlimited powers, and that no government is democratic unless its legislature [or its citizenry] has unlimited powers"? [25] Can it be that he still disputes the proposition that "there are some phases of American life which should be beyond the reach of any majority, save by [federal] constitutional amendment"? [26] That due process rights "depend on the outcome of no elections"? [27] Can it be—at this late date—that Inbau is petitioning for rehearing in *Marbury v. Madison* [28] and *Fletcher v. Peck?* [29]

In his "reply," Professor Inbau tells us: "I am opposed to illegal police searches and seizures, but I do not believe that the United States Supreme Court had the right to order the states to free guilty persons

23 *Id.* at 350–51.

24 Inbau, *More About Public Safety v. Individual Liberties,* 53 J. Crim. L., C. & P.S. 329, 329–30 (1962).

25 An argument disposed of in Rostow, *The Democratic Character of Judicial Review,* 66 Harv. L. Rev. 193, 199 (1952).

26 *Id.* at 197.

27 Jackson, J., in West Virginia State Board of Education v. Barnette, 319 U.S. 624, 638 (1943).

28 5 U.S. (1 Cranch) 137 (1803).

29 10 U.S. (6 Cranch) 87 (1810).

merely because the police had acted illegally in obtaining the evidence of guilt." [30]

I realize you put a certain "punch" into your criticism when you phrase it in terms of the Court *ordering the states to free* the guilty. But the Court issues no such orders. Exclusion of the evidence, of course, does not necessarily free a particular defendant. On remand, he can still be—and he has been—convicted on properly obtained evidence, if there is such evidence and it is sufficient.

I am aware, too, that a complaint carries an extra "wallop" when you talk about the Court overturning state convictions *"merely be-cause* the police . . . acted *illegally."* The only trouble is that the Court doesn't upset state convictions unless the police acted *uncon-stitutionally, i.e.,* in violation of due process. There *is* a difference. For example, despite the "impressively pervasive [state] requirement" that arrested persons be promptly arraigned,[31] "the majority of the Court have steadily rejected the argument that the securing of the confession during a period when the prisoner's detention was illegal because of failure to produce him promptly for a preliminary hearing is of it-self a sufficient basis for overturning the conviction on due process grounds." [32]

As I translate Professor Inbau, then, what he is saying is this: I am opposed to unreasonable searches and seizures, but I do not be-lieve the Supreme Court has the right to reverse a state conviction and remand for a new trial merely because the first conviction was based on evidence obtained by the police in violation of the federal con-stitution. Somehow, when you put it that way, his position seems to lose some of its appeal, doesn't it?

The next time Professor Inbau feels the need to warn the courts

[30] Inbau, *supra* note 24, at 332.

[31] McNabb v. United States, 318 U.S. 332, 343 (1943).

[32] McCormick, Evidence 245 (1954). For more recent discussions of the problem see Mueller, *The Law Relating to Police Interrogation Privileges and Limitations,* 52 J. Crim. L., C. & P.S. 2, 7–8 (1961); Weisberg, *Police Interroga-tion of Arrested Persons: A Skeptical View,* 52 J. Crim. L., C. & P.S. 21, 28–31 (1961).

As an astute commentator has recently observed, "in most instances the [state] courts have not even discussed whether in-custody investigation by the police is legal"; they "have not needed to mark out the boundaries of proper police con-duct short of that extreme characterized as coercion." Barrett, *Police Practices and the Law—From Arrest to Release or Charge,* 50 Calif. L. Rev. 11, 22 (1962). This article, unfortunately not yet in print when I wrote my first "reply" to Pro-fessor Inbau, is an extraordinarily thoughtful, careful, and dispassionate treatment of a very explosive subject.

—and even the legislatures [33]—to leave the police alone, he should consider that "the root idea of the Constitution" has been said to be "that man can be free because the state is not." [34] The next time he feels the urge to protest that the Court has gone beyond its constitutionally authorized functions he should consider the post-*Baker v. Carr* [35] remarks of the U.S. Attorney General: "When people criticize the courts for invading spheres of action which supposedly belong to other parts of our constitutional system, they often overlook the fact that the courts must act precisely because the other organs of government have failed to fulfill their own responsibilities." [36] The next time he feels compelled to lash out at the Court for its indulgence in judicial legislation, he should consider the observation of Chief Justice Walter Schaefer of the Illinois Supreme Court: "That [U.S. Supreme Court] decisions are creative seems to me unavoidable, particularly in a developing area of the law. To a court the common denominator of all cases is that they must be decided. *The decision that lets a conviction stand may be quite as creative as that which strikes one down.* It, too, becomes a precedent, and so shapes the law of the future." [37]

"Policing the Police"

Professor Inbau insists that decisions dealing with the problems of arrest, search and seizure, and interrogation constitute "policing the police." [38] I prefer to call it *enforcing the Constitution.* Of course, here

[33] See, *e.g.*, Inbau, *supra* note 20, at 88–89.

[34] Rostow, *supra* note 25, at 195.

[35] 369 U.S. 186 (1962) (holding that the federal judiciary can hear cases involving the apportionment of state legislative seats).

[36] Remarks of Attorney General Robert F. Kennedy, quoted in Lewis, *Historic Change in the Supreme Court*, New York Times Magazine, June 17, 1962, pp. 7, 38.

[37] Schaefer, *supra* note 13, at 6. (Emphasis added.) The author also points out, *id.* at 4, that "the problems which are vital today were not presented to the Court until recently," *e.g.*, the right to counsel in 1932, the admissibility of a coerced confession in 1936. He observes, too, that "the lateness of these decisions cannot be explained on the theory that the Court was originally reluctant to decide such cases. Apparently the question simply did not reach the Court." *Ibid.*

[38] In a footnote supporting his criticism of *Mapp v. Ohio*, Professor Inbau assures us, Inbau, *supra* note 24, at 330n.6: "In this connection, I should also like to point out that when I say that the Supreme Court has no right to police the police, I have some company in the person of Mr. Justice Harlan. See his dissent in *Rea v. United States*, 350 U.S. 214, 218 (1956)."

I submit that the reference to Justice Harlan "in this connection" is, at the

as elsewhere, the question of the Court's power and responsibility cannot be resolved by "little more than a play upon words." [39] *Whatever one calls it, I think judicial intervention in these troublesome areas is more justifiable, more appropriate,* than in most other fields. For here "the Court has put its emphasis on procedure, on due process in the primary meaning of the concept, for which the judiciary has special competence and responsibility." [40]

A close student of the man and his work has observed that a main characteristic of Justice Brandeis was "an insistence on jurisdictional and procedural observances" and a "respect for the spheres of competence of other organs of authority." [41] Thus, in the celebrated case of *International News Service v. Associated Press,*[42] Brandeis "had been willing, indeed insistent, that the inequities of the competitive struggle be left for resolution by the legislature, lest the Court do an ill-considered job." [43] Yet, the Brandeis dissent in the *Olmstead* case [44] has well been called "a *locus classicus* on the theme of the dynamism of the law." [45] Why this apparent departure from his general philosophy?

---

very least, misleading. *Rea* was an extraordinary case which found a majority of the Court voting to *enjoin* a federal agent from giving, in a state prosecution, evidence which he had obtained in the course of an illegal federal search. Justice Harlan voiced doubts that "the federal courts share with the executive branch of the Government responsibility for supervising law enforcement activities *as such,*" 350 U.S. at 218. (Emphasis added.) He pointed to and relied on this language in *McNabb* (a case that has dismayed Inbau, but which Harlan voted to reaffirm in *Mallory*): "We are not concerned with law enforcement practices *except in so far as courts themselves become instruments of law enforcement,*" 350 U.S. at 218–29, quoting from 318 U.S. at 347. (Emphasis added.) How, then, does the *Rea* dissent give aid and comfort to Professor Inbau? He denies the right of the judiciary to "police the police" in cases such as *McNabb* and *Mapp* where the courts *were* instruments of law enforcement.

[39] *Cf.* Baker v. Carr, 369 U.S. 186, 209 (1962).

[40] FREUND, *op. cit. supra* note 17, at 180. See also Newman, *The Process of Prescribing "Due Process,"* 49 CALIF. L. REV. 215, 236 (1961): "Procedure (the kind of procedure that is used to deprive people of life, liberty, and property) is peculiarly a lawyer's topic. In other fields there are businessmen and churchmen and doctors and engineers for whom lawyers speak."

[41] FREUND, *Portrait of a Liberal Judge: Mr. Justice Brandeis,* in THE SUPREME COURT OF THE UNITED STATES 119–20, 126–27 (1961).

[42] 248 U.S. 215 (1918). The majority held that a company which gathers news has a *quasi* property in the results of its enterprise, as against a competitor.

[43] FREUND, *op. cit. supra* note 41, at 134.

[44] Olmstead v. United States, 277 U.S. 438, 471 (1928). The majority held that telephone wires and messages passing over them are not within the constitutional protection against unreasonable search and seizure.

[45] FREUND, *op. cit. supra* note 41, at 133.

Those who deny that the Court has the power or the responsibility to "police the police" would do well to consider the reasons advanced for Brandeis's activism in *Olmstead*:

"In this case the responsibility of the Court was inescapable. The issue involved the basic processes of government as they impinge on the individual against whom the forces of the law are brought to bear . . . [T]he processes of the criminal law had been applied to the individual, and no agency of government more appropriate than the Court could be expected to resolve the contest between public power and personal immunity." [46]

In his "reply," Professor Inbau once again comes out bravely for better police selection and training and more pay.[47] As if this were really an issue! Of course, I agree with him. We need these things badly.

But why must better methods of selection and promotion and proper training and compensation afford "the *only* real, practically attainable protection . . . against police abuses of individual rights and liberties"? [48] Why does the issue have to be framed in terms of better pay and training *versus* the exclusionary rules? Why can't we have both?

There is impressive evidence—which Inbau does not attempt to refute—that we *can* and we *should*. There is impressive evidence in the two jurisdictions which have held the spotlight in recent years— the State of California and the District of Columbia—that the exclusionary rules have stimulated intensive police training in the law of arrest, interrogation, and search and seizure and led to more thorough and exact police work generally.[49] In California, the *Cahan* decision has also evoked extensive new legislation, in many respects codifying,

[46] *Id.* at 133–34. For a similar conclusion about Justice Brandeis, based on *other* Brandeis opinions, see FELLMAN, THE DEFENDANT'S RIGHTS 5–6 (1958).

[47] Inbau, *supra* note 24, at 332.

[48] *Ibid.* (Emphasis added.)

[49] See the testimony of law enforcement officers collected in Kamisar, *Public Safety v. Individual Liberties: Some "Facts" and "Theories,"* 53 J. CRIM. L., C. & P.S. 171, 179–81, 191–92 (1962).

As the author of the *Cahan* opinion recently observed, the exclusionary rule has not "engendered the problems" about lawful and unlawful police conduct in search and seizure, but merely "tardily excavated them from the oubliettes where lie the stifled problems of the law. So long as illegally obtained evidence remained admissible in many states there was little motivation for full-scale inquiry." Traynor, *Mapp v. Ohio at Large in the Fifty States*, 1962 DUKE L. J. 319, 321.

clarifying, and streamlining the laws of arrest and search and seizure [50] —another Inbau objective.

I can see how improvements in police selection, training, leadership and tradition would *strengthen* the case for judicial review. Court opinions are more likely to be "wasted" on indifferent, insensitive police departments; more apt to exert a constructive influence on good departments, more apt to stir thought and action when quality and training are high. But I fail to see how better pay, selection, and training would *eliminate* the need for judicial review.

As an astute commentator has observed:

> "Order is not to be exalted at the cost of liberty, and so even the best selected and best trained and best disciplined police forces must be subjected to incessant scrutiny, exacting criticism, and rigorous control. . . . It is quite true, of course, that eternal vigilance is the price of liberty. But it is imperative to remember that the vigilance demanded by this maxim means vigilance against duly constituted authority—against the forces of order." [51]

Stare Decisis in Particular and "Neutral Principles" in General

In his "reply," Professor Inbau emphasizes that "*all along* the Court had considered the exclusionary rule to be only a rule of evidence; it did not evolve into a due process requirement until the 6 to 3 decision in *Mapp v. Ohio* on June 19, 1961." [52] He dwelt at some length on this point in his earlier commentary this year:

> "*For many years* the United States Supreme Court held that state courts and state legislatures were at full liberty to accept or reject the exclusionary rule. . . . The Court said so *as recently as* 1949 in *Wolf v. Colorado.* . . . Now . . . the Court holds that if a state admits such evidence it is a violation of due process!
> " . . . .
> "*After all these years* . . . the Court . . . suddenly labels the rule to be a requirement of due process. Of little comfort is the fact that *three of the nine justices . . . adhered to the former* viewpoint." [53]

This I am afraid, is another example of Inbau's soapboxmanship. *Not until* 1949 did the issue squarely face the Court—and badly

[50] See Kamisar, *supra* note 49, at 180 n. 78.
[51] BARTH, THE PRICE OF LIBERTY 193 (1961).
[52] Inbau, *supra* note 24, at 330. (Emphasis added.)
[53] Inbau, *supra* note 20, at 86–87. (Emphasis added.)

split it. (Professor Inbau neglects to point out that only *five* of the nine justices "adhered to the former viewpoint" in the first place.) *Not until* 1949 did a bare majority of the Court perform the remarkable feat of "simultaneously creating a constitutional right and denying the most effective remedy for violation of that right." [54] *Not until* 1949 did the Court hold that one may be executed or imprisoned on the basis of evidence *obtained* in violation of due process and yet, somehow, *not be deprived* of life or liberty without due process.[55]

The *Wolf* case and Professor Inbau's shock and dismay at its overruling a decade later well illustrate, I think, how "today's new and startling decision quickly becomes a coveted anchorage for new vested interests." [56]

In bemoaning the fate of *Wolf*, Professor Inbau exudes a considerable reverence for the principle of *stare decisis*. He has not always felt this way. There was a time when he urged the Court to overrule the *McNabb* case, adding that "in any event, the least the Court should do short of an abandonment of the *McNabb* rule itself is to . . . establish a new rule somewhat midway between . . . [the federal rule] and the conventional voluntary-trustworthy test of admissibility." [57] On the same occasion, he implored the Court "at the earliest opportunity, [to] *reconsider* the 'inherent coercion' rule [formulated and applied in the famous Fourteenth Amendment Due Process confession

[54] Perlman, *Due Process and the Admissibility of Evidence*, 64 HARV. L. REV. 1304 (1951).

[55] One federal district judge tried hard to explain *Wolf* this way: "An unreasonable search by a state agent or official is not *such a violation* of the Fourteenth Amendment as will invoke operation of that Amendment." Mackey v. Chandler, 152 F. Supp. 579, 581 (W.D.S.C. 1957). (Emphasis added.)

Mr. Justice Frankfurter was badly plagued by his own *Wolf* opinion when he dissented from the 5-4 majority opinion in Irvine v. California, 347 U.S. 128 (1954) (affirming a conviction based on evidence obtained as a result of Los Angeles police planting microphones in petitioner's hall, bedroom, and bedroom closet). (As Professor Francis Allen has observed: "[T]he Court has apparently treated the police behavior in *Wolf* as violating the defendant's Fourteenth Amendment rights; that is to say, rights 'basic to a free society.' . . . To label a right 'basic to a free society' is to say about as much as can be said. Yet *Wolf* refused to vindicate these rights by reversal of the conviction. Given *Wolf*, how are the rights flouted by the Los Angeles police in *Irvine* to be characterized? There is a certain inelegance in speaking of rights 'very basic to a free society' or in indulging in what appears to be almost a comparison of superlatives." Allen, *Federalism and the Fourth Amendment: A Requiem for Wolf*, 1961 SUP. CT. REV. 1, 9.

[56] Douglas, *Stare Decisis*, 49 COLUM. L. REV. 735, 737 (1949).

[57] Inbau, *The Confession Dilemma in the United States Supreme Court*, 43 ILL. L. REV. 442, 463 (1948).

case of *Ashcraft v. Tennessee* [58] . . . and *substitute* a rule which will be more intelligible and administratively practicable." [59]

Indeed, at the very time he laments the Court's departure from precedent in *Mapp*, Professor Inbau cannot resist trotting out the standard arguments for overruling the *Weeks* rule of exclusion in federal search and seizure cases [60]—and that goes back a full half century! I am sure Professor Inbau would not suppress his glee if *Weeks* were overturned, or if the "rule of automatic reversal" in coerced confession cases, first formulated by the Stone Court, met a similar fate.[61] Or the rule articulated in *Gouled v. United States*,[62] some 40 years ago, that objects of "evidentiary value only" are beyond the reach of an otherwise valid warrant.[63] Or *Rochin*, the famous "stomach pumping" case.[64]

Only when he likes a decided case, *e.g., Wolf v. Colorado*, does Professor Inbau manage to "acquire an acute conservatism" in the *status quo*.[65] When he is *unhappy* about the way a case was decided, Inbau, it seems, *does* agree that after all "it is the Constitution which [a Supreme Court Justice] swore to support and defend, not the gloss which his precedessors may have put on it." [66] When he *dislikes* a particular precedent, Inbau, it seems, *does* recognize that a Justice formulating his view cannot do otherwise but "reject some earlier ones as false . . . unless he lets men long dead and unaware of the problems of the age in which he lives do his thinking for him." [67]

In short, Professor Inbau's notion of *stare decisis* appears to run along these lines: It is more important that the applicable rule of law be settled than it be settled right (1) *especially* when you think it was "settled right," *e.g., Wolf*; (2) *except* when you think it was "settled wrong," *e.g., McNabb, Ashcraft, Gouled*. Of course, once the decision to invoke the principle of *stare decisis* turns on whether the case to

---

[58] 322 U.S. 143 (1944).

[59] Inbau, *supra* note 57, at 463. (Emphasis added.) See also *id.* at 447.

[60] Inbau, *supra* note 20, at 86.

[61] *Id.* at 87. See the commentary on Inbau's criticism of this rule in Kamisar, *supra* note 49, at 173.

[62] 255 U.S. 298, 309–11 (1921).

[63] Inbau, *supra* note 20, at 87. See the commentary on Inbau's criticism in Kamisar, *supra* note 49, at 177.

[64] Rochin v. California, 342 U.S. 165 (1952). For a critical view of this case, see Inbau, *The Perversion of Science in Criminal and Personnel Investigations*, 43 J. CRIM. L., C & P.S. 128 (1952).

[65] Douglas, *supra* note 56, at 737.

[66] *Id.* at 736.

[67] *Ibid.*

be overruled "seems to hinder or advance the interests or values" you support, you *no longer* have a principle—it has been "reduced to a manipulative tool." [68]

Mapp and *Wolf* deal with Fourteenth Amendment Due Process cases. This is hardly the battleground to make a brave stand for *stare decisis*. The Justice who told us that "*in most matters* it is more important that the applicable rule of law be settled than that it be settled right," [69] also told us:

"But in cases involving the Federal Constitution, where correction through legislative action is practically impossible, this Court has often overruled its earlier decisions. The Court bows to the lessons of experience and the force of better reasoning. . . ." [70]

I think the post-*Wolf* years contained some valuable lessons of experience.

For a long, long time opponents of the exclusionary rule have been telling us that the criminal should not go free merely because "the constable has blundered." [71] But this argument loses a good deal of its force when we are confronted with the *Chief of Police-approved* illegality that characterized the recent cases of *Irvine v. California* [72]

---

[68] WECHSLER, *Toward Neutral Principles of Constitutional Law*, in PRINCIPLES, POLITICS AND FUNDAMENTAL LAW 17, 21 (1961).

[69] Brandeis, J., dissenting in Burnet v. Colorado, 285 U.S. 393, 406 (1932). (Emphasis added.)

[70] *Id.* at 406–08. See also Davis, *The Future of Judge-Made Public Law in England: A Problem of Practical Jurisprudence*, 61 COLUM. L. REV. 201, 215 (1961): "[T]he need for logical symmetry and consistency is a variable. In real property law and in many portions of commercial law, certainty and predictability are primary needs. . . . But on problems of public law, which at any given time are especially difficult, creating law that will benefit living people is far more important than that the law be settled. Therefore, on most matters of public law, being governed by the ideas of men long dead is unsatisfactory and may be even abominable."

[71] E.g., Cardozo, J., in People v. Defore, 242 N.Y. 13, 21, 150 N.E. 585, 587 (1926).

[72] 347 U.S. 128 (1954). The Chief Justice and Justice Jackson took the position that a copy of the *Irvine* opinion—setting forth the "almost incredible" invasions of petitioner's privacy—should be sent to the United States Attorney General for his attention, *id.* at 138. The Attorney General did conduct an investigation, the results of which disclosed that "the police officers who placed the detectograph or microphone in Irvine's home were acting under orders of the Chief of Police, who in turn was acting with the full knowledge of the local District Attorney." Letter of Feb. 15, 1955, from Warren Olney III, then Assistant United States Attorney General, on file with the *Stanford Law Review*, reprinted in part in Comment, 7 STAN. L. REV. 76, 94 n.75 (1954).

and *People v. Cahan;* [73] and the deliberate, calculated illegality that accounts for systematic police raids and round-ups.[74]

In the course of overruling precedents of more than thirty years standing to adopt the exclusionary rule of 1955, the California Supreme Court, per Traynor, J., observed:

> "[W]ithout fear of criminal punishment or other discipline, law enforcement officers, sworn to support the Constitution of the United States and the Constitution of California, frankly admit their deliberate flagrant acts in violation of both Constitutions. . . . It is clearly apparent from their testimony that they casually regard such acts as nothing more than the performance of their ordinary duties for which the city employs and pays them.
> "
> . . . .

[73] 44 Cal. 2d 434, 282 P.2d 905 (1955). See Paulsen, *Safeguards in the Law of Search and Seizure,* 52 Nw. U.L. Rev. 65, 75–76 (1957).

Professor John Barker Waite, a sharp critic of the exclusionary rule for at least 30 years, has adapted remarkably to new events. Thus, in his latest writing, he expresses annoyance at the *Cahan* court *because* it "disapproved use of the dictaphones *despite* . . . the authorization by the police chief." Waite, *The Legal Approach to Crime and Correction,* 23 Law & Contemp. Prob. 594, 601 (1958). (Emphasis added.) This is not the first time opponents of the exclusionary rule have worked *both* sides of the street. See Kamisar, *supra* note 49, at 175–76, 177 n.62.

[74] See, *e.g.,* Foote, *The Fourth Amendment: Obstacle or Necessity in the Law of Arrest?* 51 J. Crim. L., C. & P.S. 402, 406 (1960); Note, *Philadelphia Police Practice and the Law of Arrest,* 100 U. Pa. L. Rev. 1182, 1195, 1197–98, 1201–02, 1205–06 (1952).

If Illinois had adopted the *McNabb-Mallory* rule, criticism to the effect that the rule regards the "overzealous officer" or the "blundering constable" as a greater danger than the unpunished criminal would have been likely, but, until quite recently, most inappropriate. Until it came to the attention of the courts a short time ago, Chicago Police Department Rule No. 465 baldly asserted that the requirement of promptly bringing an arrestee before a judge or magistrate "does not apply when the offender is a well-known criminal who is held pending investigation." "Thus an officer of the executive branch—a policeman—was authorized by police regulations to perform a judicial function and decide whether the suspect was a 'good guy' and therefore should receive the benefits of the law, or he could decide the suspect was a 'bad guy' . . . and make an exception and suspend the operation of the Constitution and laws of Illinois." Caldwell, *Police Efficiency in Law Enforcement as a Foundation of American Life,* 48 A.B.A.J. 130, 132–33 (1962). Mr. Caldwell also notes that the *former* Police Commissioner of Chicao reportedly told the city council's committee investigating crime that his "policy has always been . . . to pick up criminals, simply because they are criminals" even though "it may be illegal, and I have received some complaints from the civil liberties group." *Id.* at 132. Incidentally, the author of the aforementioned article, Arthur B. Caldwell, is not a "sensitive soul" (Professor Inbau's term for *other* law professors; see Kamisar, *supra* note 49, at 173 n.20), but a former federal prosecutor for many years who is currently Chief of the Trial Staff of the Civil Rights Division, U.S. Department of Justice.

"We have been compelled to [exclude illegally seized evidence] . . . because other remedies have completely failed to secure compliance with the Constitutional provisions on the part of police officers." [75]

The reaction of Chief William Parker of the Los Angeles Police Department to the adoption of the exclusionary rule is, I think, typical and most illuminating:

"It now appears that the Court will approve the introduction of evidence seized without a warrant only when the officer had probable cause. . . . Authority to search the person is apparently limited to the individual for whom there is probable cause . . . and does not include companions that may be with him.

" . . . .

"The actual commission of a serious criminal offense will not justify affirmative police action until such time as the police have armed themselves with sufficient information to constitute 'probable cause'. . . .

" . . . .

"As long as the Exclusionary Rule is the law of California, your police will respect it and operate to the best of their ability within the framework of limitations imposed by that rule." [76]

Of course, the "framework of limitations" was imposed by the state and federal constitutional guarantees, not the exclusionary rule. Of course, so long as the state and federal constitutions were operative, a criminal offense *never* justified "affirmative police action" *unless and until* there was "sufficient information to constitute 'probable cause.'" The police react to the adoption of the exclusionary rule as if the guarantees against unreasonable search and seizure had *just been written!*

[75] People v. Cahan, 44 Cal. 2d 434, 437–38, 445, 282 P.2d 905, 907, 911 (1955). Judge Traynor, author of the *Cahan* opinion, had earlier written an opinion rejecting the exclusionary rule, People v. Gonzales, 20 Cal. 2d 165, 124 P.2d 44 (1942). He has recently shed further light on "the education that leads a judge to overrule himself," Traynor, *Mapp v. Ohio at Large in the Fifty States*, 1961 DUKE L. J. 319, 321–22: "My misgivings . . . grew as I observed that time after time [illegally seized evidence] was being offered as a routine procedure. It became impossible to ignore the corollary that illegal searches and seizures were also a routine procedure, subject to no effective deterrent; else how could illegally obtained evidence come into court with such regularity? It was one thing to condone an occasional constable's blunder. . . . It was quite another to condone a steady course of illegal police procedures. . . . It is a large assumption that the police have invariably exhausted the possibilities of obtaining evidence legally when they have relied upon illegally obtained evidence. It is more rational to assume the opposite when the offer of illegally obtained evidence becomes routine."

[76] PARKER, POLICE 115–16, 117, 131 (Wilson ed. 1957). See the discussion in Kamisar, *Wolf and Lustig Ten Years Later: Illegal State Evidence in State and Federal Courts*, 43 MINN. L. REV. 1083, 1153–54 (1959); Paulsen, *The Exclusionary Rule and Misconduct by the Police*, 52 J. CRIM. L., C. & P.S. 255 (1961).

They talk as if and act as if the exclusionary rule *were* the guaranty against unreasonable search and seizure. *Why shouldn't the courts?*

Statistics, Testimony and the Force of "Simple Logic"

In my earlier article in this *Journal*, I dwelt at considerable length on statistics and law enforcement testimony regarding the impact of rules of evidence on crime rates and police-prosecution efficiency. I did so in response to the charge that proponents of the exclusionary rules do not like to look at and talk about these "facts." [77] Consequently, as Professor Inbau has observed, my article turned out to be a good deal longer than his speech which brought it into being. Perhaps it was too long. For I must confess that when I read Professor Inbau's "reply" to me, I sometimes had the uncomfortable feeling that he hadn't quite read the whole article.

For example, I pointed out that three years after *Mallory* was handed down, United States Attorney Oliver Gasch reported "*Mallory* questions, that is to say, confessions or admissions, are of controlling importance in probably less than 5 per cent of our criminal prosecutions," that "reliance upon confessions generally has been minimized" and "the accumulation of other evidentiary material . . . become standard operating procedure," [78] that the Washington, D.C., Police Department had testified that since *Mallory* was decided: (a) the District's solution rate had remained "nearly double" the national average; (b) indeed, the District's overall percentage of major crime solutions had *increased*; (c) specifically, the percentage had risen in cases of aggravated assault from 84.3 to 88; in robbery from 61.3 to 65; in housebreaking, from 50.5 to 54 per cent.[79] *How does Professor Inbau reply to all this?*

He tells us: "In communities such as Washington, D.C., most serious crimes will remain unsolved if the police are not permitted to interrogate criminal suspects. To prohibit police interrogation—which, in effect, is what the *McNabb-Mallory* rule does—means, therefore, that fewer crimes will be solved and successfully prosecuted." [80] No

[77] See Kamisar, *supra* note 49, at 184. (The charge was made by Chief William Parker of the Los Angeles Police Department.)
[78] Kamisar, *supra* note 49, at 192.
[79] *Id.* at 191–92.
[80] Inbau, *supra* note 24, at 331.

documentation. No attempt to refute the testimony of the high ranking law enforcement officers I quoted. No attempt to explain away the statistics they presented.

Take another example. After wrestling with the problem for several years, the United States Attorney for the District of Columbia dismissed the suggestion that the *McNabb-Mallory* rule affected the crime rate as "much too speculative." [81] Indeed, the District's incidence of rapes, aggravated assaults, and grand larceny was *lower* in 1960 than in 1950. During this period, Maryland and Virginia had neither the *McNabb-Mallory* rule nor the exclusionary rule in search and seizure cases; District law enforcement officers, of course, were "handcuffed" by both. Nevertheless, on a per 100,000 population basis, the District's overall felony rate increased a mere one per cent *as against* 69 per cent for the three Maryland and Virginia suburbs for which generally complete figures were available, and *as against* a nation-wide increase for the seven major offenses of 66 per cent.[82] *How does Professor Inbau reply to all this?*

As a result of the *McNabb-Mallory* rule, he informs us, "More criminals will remain at large, to commit other offenses. At the same time the deterrent effect of apprehension and conviction will be lost insofar as other potential offenders are concerned. The crime rate is bound to be greater under such circumstances, and I do not feel the need of staistics to support that conclusion." [83] Once again, Professor Inbau is unburdened by documentation and untroubled by the need to explain away the other fellow's.

Professor Inbau, it develops, need not deal with statistics or police-prosecution testimony because he has "simple logic" on his side. "[S]imple logic, he points out, "is available to support the proposition that the *McNabb-Mallory* rule *does, and is bound to have a crippling effect upon law enforcement* in any metropolitan jurisdiction saddled with the rule." [84] Again, no attempt to square this view with the Washington, D.C., experience.

Doesn't "simple logic" end, or stand in need of considerable revision, when experience to the contrary begins? Isn't *this* "simple logic"?

I think Professor Inbau has stymied me at last. I mean, when somebody issues a warning in 1957 that a bloody revolution or widespread

[81] Kamisar, *supra* note 49, at 187.
[82] *Id.* at 185.
[83] Inbau, *supra* note 49, at 331.
[84] *Id.* at 331. (Emphasis added.)

depression is going to occur in 1958 or 1959, he may or may not be right. His logic may or may not be sound. You can argue about it. But if this same person insists in the year 1962 that these events *did take place* in 1958 or 1959 and turns his back on you and walks off in a huff— chanting "simple logic, simple logic"—when you try to establish that they *never happened,* what do you do then? Where do you go from there?

APPENDIX F

AN ORAL DEBATE

*HENRY CABOT LODGE AND LORD BOOTHBY
ON "SHOULD RED CHINA BE ADMITTED
TO THE UNITED NATIONS NOW?"* [1]

INTRODUCTION BY HOWARD K. SMITH: Since that filmed report [2] was made about two years ago China has been at the center of great world events that are very hard to interpret. For example, Russia and China have launched a public debate over which has the best means of subverting the rest of the world. And there is talk of a serious split between the two. The commune system inside China, of which you have just seen a portrayal, appears to be in crisis and a condition of famine prevails in the country. Diplomatically at the UN the vote to refuse to consider Red China's entry into the UN has turned into a minority vote. Our side is now in a minority against the abstainers and those who would like to consider bringing Red China in. And allies of ours like Britain and Brazil and Pakistan have expressed the wish to see China in the United Nations. I would like now to ask for the opening statements of our two debaters: First, Lord Boothby, should China be admitted to the UN now?

[1] From transcript of Henry Cabot Lodge and Lord Boothby on "Face the Nation" Debate: "Should Red China Be Admitted to the United Nations Now?" Broadcast over CBS Television Network March 23, 1961.
[2] From "The Face of Red China," CBS News Report broadcast, Dec. 28, 1958.

LORD BOOTHBY: Well I think so and I know very well that some of the things I am going to say—must say—are bound to be unpopular tonight. I would therefore like to make it quite clear at the very beginning—first of all—that I have got nothing at all to do with the British government. I am not expressing their views. I seldom have. I nearly always express my own. Secondly, I am no defender of communism, and certainly not of Chinese communism, which is the toughest kind of communism in the world today.

But the two things I'd like to say at the outset, and there are just two points I'd like to make: First of all, in a very dangerous world I think it is extremely dangerous to base any part of your foreign policy upon illusion. And I think that this country does suffer from one illusion and that is that the government of China is somehow or other in Formosa. Now, that is not true. These 700 million people occupying 4 million square miles of territory are governed by the Chinese Peoples Republic in Peking. And I don't think it's any good pretending that they're governed by Chiang Kai-shek and Madame Chiang Kai-shek in Formosa because they aren't.

And the second point I'd like to make is that I think it's equally dangerous to have a neurosis, especially about a foreign issue.

Now, I think this country—and this is where I'm going to get into trouble, but I am just expressing my own views—I think that you have got a neurosis about China. I don't know why. Somehow or other I think many people in this country feel that they are responsible for the revolution in China. I don't believe that that was the case. I don't believe even Stalin was responsible for it, still less General Marshall. The people who were responsible for the Chinese revolution were the Chinese, not the United States of America. And one of the reasons was that China after the war was riddled with corruption.

MR. SMITH: Now, Mr. Lodge, can we have your opening statement. Should Red China be admitted to the United Nations now?

MR. LODGE: I'm against admitting Red China to the United Nations now, and I do not say forever. In fact, I will say this; that if Red China showed convincing signs of changing her aggressive and piratical ways against Korea, against Tibet, against India, against Laos, against Vietnam, against Formosa and against her own people, if it released our prisoners and dropped its fanaticisms and blind hatred of the United States, if in a word it ceased to act in ways which are contrary to the letter and to the spirit of the United Nations Charter then I think that the world, including the United States, would look very differently on the proposal to admit her to the United Nations.

Now, I also stress the fact that absence from the United Nations does not mean absence from our minds and it does not mean absence from the world. Admission of Red China to the United Nations is a very special question to which very special considerations apply. The United States has had 103 meetings with the Red Chinese on the subject of prisoners. Admission to the UN, when you consider that Red China has declared war on the UN, is a very special thing and would, I am sure, defeat its own purpose. What we ought to be after is not the admission of Red China to the UN. It is a change in the attitude of Red China so that she would conform to the Charter of the UN.

MR. SMITH: Can we now have a discussion on the points you have made. Lord Boothby, do you think that Mr. Lodge's conditions are the right ones for letting Red China in—

LORD BOOTHBY: No, I don't honestly think that they are. You see admission to the United Nations of Red China doesn't imply to my mind at all approval in any shape or form of Red China or of their policies. And nearly all the charges that Mr. Lodge brought against Red China can be brought equally against Russia, against the Soviet Union, practically all. I was listing them. The aggression, the attacks on the United States, the attacks on their own people, that form of government of which we heartily disapprove. I don't see how you could ostracize China on moral grounds and not ostracize the whole Communist world if you like—with the possible exception of Yugoslavia. I don't, therefore, see how Mr. Lodge can draw a logical distinction on moral grounds between China and Russia. I do, on the other hand, think that it's going to be almost impossible to conduct important negotiations with China at any level until she is seated in the United Nations, until in fact we face them face-to-face and have direct contact with them, which seems to me to be the point of the United Nations.

The United Nations, of course, belies its name as Mr. Lodge well knows with his experience. There is nothing united about the United Nations. But it is a point of contact and the only point of contact between the Communist and the democratic world and I think as such it has immense potential value. But if it is to go on being a point of contact we got to have them in. Otherwise we might as well pack up the United Nations altogether and have done with it and try something else.

MR. LODGE: With great respect to Lord Boothby, it's not the only point of contact. As I said, we have contacts with the Chinese Communist representatives now in Warsaw on the subject of prisoners. You don't need to be in the United Nations in order to conduct business with another government.

The United Nations Charter prescribes that members shall be and I quote, "peace-loving." They had a big debate in San Francisco at the time the United Nations Charter was being drafted as to whether it should be a cockpit in which the criminal and the law-abiding would be indiscriminately scrambled up or whether it should have a moral standard, and after a long debate it was decided to require that they be peace-loving, and I will say in passing that if the behavior of the Soviet Union in 1946 had been what it has been since then I do not doubt that the Soviet Union would not have been admitted. Of course, now it is quite impossible to expel the Soviet Union because they would veto their own expulsion.

So you would stultify the United Nations if you admitted a government which has done all these things and which, let us be fair to them, obviously does not want to get into the United Nations.

Now, Mrs. Roosevelt I notice said that the other day. Mrs. Roosevelt said, I don't believe she wants membership, because if she did she wouldn't act the way she does. And I started doing a little research and I found that Chou En-lai, the Prime Minister, said no later than January 1961 that he was opposed to Communist China coming into the United Nations unless she had jurisdiction over the island of Formosa.

I notice that Marshall Chen Yi told a CBS correspondent on March 18th, last Saturday, that not only must they have control over Formosa but the United States must take its fleet out of the western Pacific.

Now your esteemed colleagues in Westminster, Lord Boothby, don't agree with the Chinese Communists. I'd like to quote something that Mr. Godber—I'm sure you know him, he's Under Secretary of State for Foreign Affairs—and here's what he said: "A nation which advocates that world war is necessary and inevitable can scarcely complain if some of those who are trying to organize peace are lukewarm about her admission to the United Nations. The attitude of China toward the United States, towards the whole free world has been more inflexible than that of any of her opponents. A principal motive of Communist China is the banishment of the United States, and indeed if one follows the argument logically, all of the free world from the whole area of the Far East and the western Pacific." This is Mr. Godber, Under Secretary of State for Foreign Affairs of the United Kingdom, talking.

They demand that the United States completely withdraw from the Formosa area and leave that island with its 10 million inhabitants, 8 million of whom are indigenous Formosans, to be dealt with by the Chinese government as they choose.

The government—this is the British government—has no evidence whatsoever to show that the 8 million Formosans to say nothing of the 2 million mainland Chinese on the island have any desire to cast their lot with that of the mainland.

Now even Mr. Donnally, who is the author of the motion to censure the British government for not doing enough to get the Red Chinese into the UN said this: "I am not suggesting for a moment that Formosa should be handed over lock, stock and barrel to the Chinese Communists."

And Mr. Gilbert Langdon, who I am sure you know, who was—

LORD BOOTHBY: I know them all.

MR. LODGE: —over here, a charming man. He said this: "The invitation must be absolutely conditional on Peking's renouncing all claims to the island of Taiwan."

So British support of the proposition to admit the Red Chinese to the UN is conditional on a number of things but none of them say how you're going to get those conditions enforced.

LORD BOOTHBY: Well, I'm not absolutely convinced, you know, that the Chinese don't want to get into the United Nations. As long as we keep them out, as long as we ostracize them they're bound to put up a very belligerent attitude but certainly I'd like to put this to the test. I'm no more in favor of handing over Formosa to Red China than anybody else. I'm still less in favor of removing the Pacific fleet from the western Pacific waters. I'm not in favor of making that kind of concession at all. I'm not as convinced about the off-shore islands as I think you are, but that's another story. But I don't think we've ever really tested China's real wishes on this question. We've never said, "Will you come in?"

Now you, Mr. Lodge, talked about peace-loving nations, so that you've got to be a peace-loving nation to be a satisfactory member of the United Nations organization. This is a speech of Mr.—Dr. Chen Cheng, the Prime Minister of Taiwan and deputy to Chiang Kai-shek, quite recently: "There is no question of our not returning to the mainland. We are merely waiting for an opportunity to support a rising against the Communists. When we consider the moment right, we will land and establish a wide bridgehead. We must go back to the main-land. Communism must be destroyed. We know that some people in the West fear we shall start a global war."

Well, I don't call that exactly peace-loving. Whatever else it may be doesn't seem to me to exude peace and harmony. I am perfectly ready to see that Formosa is protected by the power of the United States, especially as you can get at them and there are a lot of other places in the world that are not so easily got at as Formosa. I'm all for that until a satisfactory arrangement can be reached which might be ultimately the neutrality of Formosa—under the protection of both sides. But I do say that this sort of talk about invading the mainland of China, the implication being, of course, that it would be with United States sup-port—because nobody imagines that Formosa alone could take on the invasion of the mainland of China—is not peace-loving, is provocative, can't do any good, and in a highly inflammable and dangerous world could do a great deal of damage.

MR. LODGE: I'm glad that Lord Boothby is not in favor of handing Formosa over to the Chinese Communists—

LORD BOOTHBY: Certainly not.

MR. LODGE: I'm glad Lord Boothby is not in favor of removing the Seventh Fleet from the western Pacific. In fact I'm getting to the con-clusion that Lord Boothby is much closer to my point of view than he is to that of the Chinese Communists, which doesn't surprise me.

LORD BOOTHBY: Not at all.

MR. LODGE: And—but I'm delighted to have him confirm it and all these estimable British statesmen whom I've quoted are also much closer to my point of view than they are to that of the Chinese Com-munists. Now, when Lord Boothby says in effect that—that no nation is really peace-loving; and when he takes the belligerent speech that some character made in Formosa to prove his point—

LORD BOOTHBY: The Prime Minister—it's a little more than "some character."

MR. LODGE: Well, it's just a speech and you and I have been making speeches a long time and you know that speeches are different from actually going in there with the guns and the tanks. When Lord Boothby makes that point, and I'm always glad to have him interrupt me when he feels the need, I simply say this: Let us admit that no nation is completely peace-loving. But certainly a nation which has been officially denounced as an aggressor by the United Nations itself is not peace-loving within the terminology of the United Nations. It seems to me that is an unassailable proposition and that's what—what's happened to the Chinese Communist regime and it hasn't happened to any other.

In 1954, when I was at the United Nations, the Chinese Communists were invited to come to the Security Council to discuss the question of the Straits of Formosa. They never came. I think it's when they do things like that that it gives color to Mrs. Roosevelt's statement that she doesn't think that they really want to come in. Here is a nation which is a member of the Soviet bloc which overtly wants to conquer the world. They don't—they don't hesitate to say so. A nation with a record of tremendous cruelty in Korea where—where we had—the United States had 142,000 casualties. A nation which has killed 15 million of its own people, which is certainly a violation of the declaration of human rights, if nothing else. Here is a nation that solemnly accused the United States of practicing germ warfare, which is certainly not a good thing to do. Here is a nation which practices an extortion racket against the overseas Chinese; which actively promotes drug addiction so as to destroy the—the—the character and the fiber, moral fiber of peoples in the free world and if we voted to admit this— this clique, the regime, to the United Nations the effect on the overseas Chinese communities in Southeast Asia would be absolutely catastrophic. They would lose confidence in the free world. It is impossible to predict what would happen. The results would be very serious for New Zealand. The results would be very serious for Australia. It would be building the kind of world that you don't like, Lord Boothby. I've only known you two days but I feel I know you well enough to say that this would be a step towards building the kind of world that the United Kingdom doesn't like, the United States doesn't like, and I don't think we ought to do it.

LORD BOOTHBY: Well, do you really feel, Mr. Lodge, that, that we can keep this vast nation, a quarter of the people of the world, ostracized out beyond the pale, indefinitely without far—

MR. LODGE: No, I do not.

LORD BOOTHBY: —greater danger than if—

MR. LODGE: No, I do not, and the question is keeping them out of the United Nations now. That word is there. And I—at the beginning I didn't say forever. I say 1961 is not the year to do it. And it is clear to me that they don't want to get in now.

LORD BOOTHBY: Well—now—you said "now."

MR. LODGE: Yes.

LORD BOOTHBY: Now that gives away something because they did want to get in and we kept them out for ten years and I think every year that passes that we keep them out with the danger of their becoming a nuclear power coming closer and closer, makes it more dangerous for the world as a whole. You quoted a lot of—of junior—respectable but junior—ministers in Britain and members of Parliament, expressing views about China's admission to the United Nations but our Secretary of State himself did say quite authoritatively the other day on behalf of the government, Lord Home, that he thought and we, the British government, thought that China should be now seated in the United Nations and I don't think he would have made a statement of that kind unless he'd—he'd meant it.

MR. LODGE: Now may I just ask you—

LORD BOOTHBY: Yes.

MR. LODGE: Lord Home doesn't favor it does he, turning Formosa over to—

LORD BOOTHBY: No, no.

MR. LODGE: —Red China. He doesn't favor removing the Seventh Fleet from the western Pacific?

LORD BOOTHBY: Certainly not. Nobody does, but we think—

MR. LODGE: Well then that's a condition, you see, that's a condition that the Chinese Communists don't want to meet.

LORD BOOTHBY: Well you say that but I just don't believe it. I believe that they're having to put up a bluff now because they're being held up and told they'll be handled on no terms whatever. But I believe that China would come into the United Nations any day now and negotiate subsequently about Formosa or anything else, but certainly not make it a condition of coming in.

MR. LODGE: That's what Chou En-lai said in January.

LORD BOOTHBY: Well, let's—let's try them out. What's the harm of that?

Now, I was listening to the President this evening at his press conference on the subject of Laos. I do think another danger which confronts the West is the danger of overextension of our commitments and responsibilities. I notice that Mr. Lippmann this morning described Laos as a classic example. He said the President faced defeat, or a meaningless diplomatic defeat, or a meaningless war. Now I don't, myself, accept that. I'm not so sure that Walter Lippmann is right on that. But this I did hear the President say this evening. He said we must have constructive negotiation among the nations concerned following a cease-fire.

Well, now, you would admit, I'm sure, Mr. Lodge, that the main aggressor in the last few weeks has not been Red China, it's been Soviet Russia. It's Soviet planes that have been flying in there and mounting this airlift. You must also admit that China, which actually borders Laos, is directly concerned, and therefore if we are going to have negotiations round the table it's no use pretending that Red China must not come into those negotiations.

MR. LODGE: We had negotiations after the war in Korea. The Red Chinese and the North Koreans were there. That doesn't mean membership in the United Nations.

LORD BOOTHBY: Yes, but don't you think—

MR. LODGE: If you wish to have—I think you can make a case for having Red China present at the proper time on talks for the suspension of nuclear tests, but I would be very much opposed to having Red China present at those talks now, because in her present fanatic state of mind she would try to sabotage the talks. I believe in bringing about a certain measure of understanding between the United States and our Allies and the Soviet Union before you bring the Red Chinese into it.

MR. SMITH: Early on, Lord Boothby said that the basis of America's policy was a neurosis, a sense of guilt, and many people think it is emotional, rather than serving some national interest. Does our policy serve a national interest?

MR. LODGE: I think our policy serves our national interests. I think every government has a right, if not a duty, to protect its people against things that are going to obviously be harmful to them, and we admit the right of every other government to do that, and naturally we expect other governments to admit our right to do that. I noticed Lord Boothby made quite a point about that neurosis and about illusions, said we were victim of illusions, and urged us to be realistic. I know there's a man that Lord Boothby admires as much as I do, Sir Winston Churchill, and when Hitler was devastating Europe and was in control of all of Europe, to the eternal glory of the United Kingdom, Sir Winston Churchill chose not to be, and I quote, "realistic." Unquote. He chose to take a stand on principle, a stand for what was right, even though it didn't look at the time as though it would prevail. I noticed that Great Britain extended recognition to a number of governments-in-exile, who had their headquarters in London, all through the war, and their writ did not run on the European mainland any more than the writ of the government of Nationalist China runs on the Chinese mainland. And yet I would be surprised if Lord Boothby were to say that Winston Churchill had made a mistake in allowing all those governments-in-exile to have their headquarters in the United Kingdom. There is more to life and there's more to the conduct of international affairs than a transient realism.

LORD BOOTHBY: Yes, but after the war Sir Winston Churchill said that we should arm to parley. And how are we going to get Red China to the conference table, on Laos, on disarmament, or anywhere else, when we exclude her from the one great world international organization that exists.

MR. SMITH: May I ask you a question—

MR. LODGE: With great respect, there is a nonsequitur there, between arming to parley, and I agree with you about that, we should arm to parley, and belonging to the United Nations. They are two entirely different things.

LORD BOOTHBY: The United Nations is for parley. It's all it is for, alas, at the present time.

MR. LODGE: Yes, but the United Nations—

LORD BOOTHBY: But you, yourself, were telling me only the day before yesterday how interesting it was, that parley that went on—in the United Nations.

MR. LODGE: It was very, very interesting, and I—to add one more nation that is going to act the way the Soviet Union acts; that is going to come in there and bang their shoes on the desk; that is going to come in there and try to destroy the Secretary-General; that is going to come in there and welch and refuse to pay their honest debts as members of the organization; that is not going to do the United Nations any good, and it's not going to do the world any good, or the United Kingdom any good.

LORD BOOTHBY: I thought it was Mr. Khrushchev who was trying to destroy the Secretary-General.

MR. LODGE: Yes, it is. And if you get the Chinese Communists, there'll be two of them trying to do it, and you've got to assume that they would act as a member of the Soviet bloc, which they are. Lord Boothby, I'd have been glad to sit down with Communists when there was some hope of working something out, and with Soviet representatives on one occasion we did work out a resolution on the question of outer space. But when they tell you to your face that they don't want to have anything to do with you; when they tell you to your face that they want to kick you out of the western Pacific; that they regard you as lower than the low; then there is nothing to be gained by talking with them until this present psychosis—you talk about neurosis, I say they have a psychosis—then we ought to wait until that psychosis blows over.

LORD BOOTHBY: It's a general universal psychosis. But there's one thing, Mr. Lodge, I really cannot allow you to get away with, if you don't mind, and that is comparing the position of the Formosan government in China today with the position of the European governments who were kicked out of Europe by Hitler during the war, and recognized by the British government. After all is said and done, the Chinese are at least, however much we may disapprove of the regime—the Peking government is Chinese. The European countries were under the heel of the Nazis. They were being governed by Hitler, and recognizing their governments-in-exile was another situation.

MR. LODGE: They were Quislings. Hitler had people who were French and who were Danish and who were Dutch. They were of the same nationhood—the—

LORD BOOTHBY: It was the Commanders-in-Chief who governed those countries. France, Belgium, Holland, always it's the Nazi Generals who did it.

MR. LODGE: Communist China—these were—Communist China was taken over by a tightly disciplined Communist gang. There isn't a broad public support for this government, and I don't believe anybody claims that there is.

LORD BOOTHBY: Well, was there for Chiang Kai-shek's government in China at the end of the war, after the war?

MR. LODGE: I don't think so.

LORD BOOTHBY: If so—what—no, I don't think so, either. If so, why did the Communists win? That's what I—

MR. LODGE: They won by force, by strength.

LORD BOOTHBY: To a large extent with arms supplied by you.

MR. LODGE: Correct.

LORD BOOTHBY: Which was given to them by Chiang Kai-shek's armies.

MR. LODGE: Correct.

LORD BOOTHBY: Sold to them. That's why—the main thing I think that you forget.

MR. LODGE: That does not constitute a valid election, and I'm sure you don't contend it does.

LORD BOOTHBY: No, I don't, but I think you should get rid of your neurosis that somehow or other you were responsible for the Chinese Revolution. You weren't. It's not your fault. You do have a sense of guilt about it. I'm absolutely certain of that, and I think it clouds, distorts your clear vision—

MR. LODGE: Well, I'm not going to indulge in personalities.

LORD BOOTHBY: Not at all.

MR. LODGE: I'm not going to do that.

LORD BOOTHBY: No, I'm not indulging in personalities, but I do—

MR. LODGE: You said I have a neurosis. That's what you said.

LORD BOOTHBY: Oh, oh, I think the whole United States has a neurosis—

MR. SMITH: Lord Boothby, essentially we're discussing whether a policy of conciliation or at least of opening gates to the Red Chinese will help produce constructive results. Now, Great Britain recognized Red China. Has that produced any constructive result?

LORD BOOTHBY: No, not very much. Not very much. I don't think that's good enough. You see, I happen to believe that in the modern world it's absolutely essential for the West to act together, and above all, for Great Britain and the United States to act together, and I think as long as we pursue differing policies we always come to grief. The classic examples were Suez and the Congo. Now, I believe that in both these cases it was the disunity of the West that brought about these particular crises. And I would just say, when Mr. Lodge talks about aggression, and Chinese aggression in Korea, at the time that he was slanging us for Suez, and, mind you, I was on his side over that, because I think we made a great mistake over Suez, he had hardly time to spare regardless of what was going on in Hungary, which was just as ruthless an aggression on the part of the Soviet Union as China has ever indulged in. And that was because of disunity. And I think we ought to sit down now, the West as a whole, under the leadership of Great Britain and the United States, and decide what our policy should be about China, and about a lot of other things as well, settle it, and have common policies for the first time since the war, because we haven't really had policies in common, and that's been the cause of nearly all the trouble.

MR. LODGE: Well, Lord Boothby, I certainly agree with that. I've been an advocate of closer consultation, of more frequent consultation, of a more rapid process of reaching decisions. I must very courteously differ when you say I didn't give a passing glance to the Hungarian crisis. I remember calling meetings of the Security Council for 3 o'clock Sunday morning. We had the two things going on at the same time, and I went 17 nights with just a nap or two on the sofa in the office, which I didn't think I'd ever have to do at my age. So I gave as much time to the Hungarian thing as to the Suez thing. But I certainly agree with you that we must have a much quicker process of consultation and of reaching decisions between our two countries. We must. We must do that.

MR. SMITH: Well, can we hypothesize about this question. Suppose the Red Chinese were admitted to the United Nations tomorrow, here in New York, at a time when the Soviet Union and the Communist bloc are engaged in a campaign that sounds like a campaign to rule or to wreck the UN. How do you think the Red Chinese would behave? Would they behave constructively or—

LORD BOOTHBY: They might come out passionately on the side of Mr. Hammarskjold. You can't be sure. You never know. They don't necessarily agree about everything. There's no doubt about that—Red China. They present a common front which we too seldom do. But I think the arguments behind the scenes are pretty fierce. That would be my imagination.

But what I would like to put to Mr. Lodge is this point about having them in as soon as the present crisis is over. You can't have them in the middle of a crisis, of course. But as soon as it's over. I am worried about disarmament. Now you yourself, Mr. Lodge, said disarmament is a problem that concerns all nations, large and small. And the point I want to put is: can we afford to permit China to develop the capability to destroy humanity without any control, without any direct contact within the United Nations, which she can do over the next ten years? I mean she might even do it in opposition to the wishes of the Kremlin —to Moscow. I really am—I think we must look ahead for a moment on this question of disarmament and I'm frightened of what—there's been no real danger of nuclear rearmament in China in recent years, but now it's coming. It may be no more than a cloud on the horizon the size of a man's hand, but it's there. And Mr. Lodge would probably admit that within the next decade it's quite possible to imagine that China will be a nuclear power. Now that fills me with apprehension if she's still ostracized—if she's still out in the wilderness—if she's under no kind of control, under no negotiation, and negotiations for disarmament must be conducted within the United Nations. That's the prospect that frightens me.

MR. LODGE: I was glad to note, and I made a careful note of it while Lord Boothby was talking, that he did say he did not think Red China should be admitted to the United Nations—and I wrote down his words—until the present crisis is over—

LORD BOOTHBY: In Laos.

MR. LODGE: —I think that sentiment does you credit, sir. I think that means that in effect you do not favor admitting Red China into the United Nations in 1961. That is the only point that I was making tonight and I am obliged to you for that. Now, I agree with you that disarmament is one of the big important questions that affects large and small states, and that assuming we can ever get a system of inspection that the Soviets and the West can agree on, that we cannot have effective disarmament agreement ultimately without having the Communist Chinese in it. I think that's true. That does not need to mean membership in the United Nations. This is not a simple thing. This is a—membership in the United Nations is a specialized thing. It's distinct from diplomatic recognition. It's distinct from talking to them about prisoners. It's distinct from dealing with them about the situation in Korea. The membership in the United Nations is a special thing. If the time ever comes that they are indispensable to a disarmament agreement, the fact of their being or not being in the United Nations won't be material as far as their accession to a disarmament agreement is concerned.

LORD BOOTHBY: May I, Mr. Chairman, make one point absolutely clear. When I referred to not having them in during the present crisis I wasn't referring, as Mr. Lodge well knows, to the year 1961. I was referring to the whizzing crisis we are in tonight which the President himself has told us must be resolved in a matter of days rather than weeks. Now I think that is true and I think that we must get a conference going to establish the neutrality of the State of Laos and I believe we—there's some reason for grounds for optimism that we may get Russian support. I believe that Red China must be at that conference because she's obviously directly concerned and I believe if that came off, then immediately after that was over, that would be the moment to invite China in. But I was merely referring to the terrific crisis we're undergoing at this moment. Obviously you can't make a tremendous move like accepting—inviting Red China to join the United Nations until this particular crisis is resolved. But I think it really is a matter of days rather than weeks and I certainly wouldn't cover it until the end of 1961. I would want to make that point clear—

MR. LODGE: I'm sorry if I misunderstood. I thought you meant the present world crisis that's going on now.

LORD BOOTHBY: I was referring to Laos.

MR. LODGE: I think on a matter of this kind when it is proposed that the present order of things be changed, that the burden of proof is on those who advocate the change to show that it would be demonstrably better. And it also seems to me evident that the prudent man must assume that the Chinese Communists, if they were in the United

Nations, would act like a member of the Soviet bloc. They would act the way they've been acting, and the way they've been talking. And with the United Nations in one of the greatest crises in its history, with the whole free world having to struggle with every muscle to prevent the Soviet Union from bringing the whole structure down, it is hard for me to see why someone who might favor it under more sanguine circumstances and who might well favor it if the attitude of the Chinese Communist regime was different, can really advocate doing such a thing now with the Chinese Communists in their present state of mind and with the world in its present state. I don't only mean Laos; I mean the situation in the Congo. How one can think it would help with the Chinese Communists in here sniping away at the Secretary General—doing everything possible to harass the United Nations' presence in the Congo is something I must admit that defeats me.

LORD BOOTHBY: Well, that does seem to me to be a gospel of despair, really you know, and I don't think we need take a wholly black view —after all, certain things have been going a bit better with the Soviet Union lately. There has been a very considerable extension of cultural exchange between the Western World and the Soviet Union in every field, in books, in opera, in music, in ballet, all the rest of it that's going. There has been a considerable extension of trade. There has been a relaxation of the censorship announced within the last day or so. And things are beginning to move. Now I believe passionately, that by far the best start off for some form of coexistence which we must surely all aim at if the whole planet is not to be blown to pieces, is to start in the fields of trade and culture and all the rest of it, and through UNESCO, and I believe that you can't really make any real headway in those fields unless the country concerned is a member of the United Nations. As long as you ostracize it, tell it, "Keep out. You're no good, we're going to have nothing to do with you," you're not going to make any progress at all in any field.

MR. LODGE: I agree that it's much easier at the present time to make progress in cultural fields and the relaxation of censorship and cultural exchanges and all that. That is much easier to do than in the political and the diplomatic fields and that's why I think your argument leads me to the conclusion that we ought to work on those cultural things which are feasible and which are possible and not knock our heads against a stone wall on these political and diplomatic questions. Don't take my word for it. Look and see what Mr. Stevenson, my successor at the United Nations, has had to say to Mr. Gromyko—just in the last week. There's never been anything more brutal, more tendentious, more calculated to create world tensions than what Mr. Gromyko has been saying here in the General Assembly. And nothing is to be gained by pretending he doesn't say it when he does.

LORD BOOTHBY: And I expect that he means it. But at the same time I recognize certain practical evidence of improvement and I think you make a great mistake in not trying to expand trade a bit further with China. Now there's famine in large parts of China. I have a feeling myself that some gesture on the part of the Western World on behalf—on the part, for example, of North America, Canada, and the United States, possibly Australia—in the direction of relieving that famine might in the long run have a very considerable psychological effect. You see it's this more or less shrugging the shoulders and saying, "Well it's no good, it's no good trying, we can't get it," because that's what frightens me, because I believe that in the end with this mounting armament all the time, the attitude of saying, "Well they're too bloody-minded, (if I may put it crudely like that) to be dealt with at all," may ultimately lead to that explosion which surely everybody on earth, including China and Russia, must wish to avoid.

MR. LODGE: Well, I agree with that and I'm sure you'll find, Lord Boothby, that in this country there would be no disagreement with the proposition of providing food for starving people, medicines for people who are sick. But I would also wager that the Chinese Communists would refuse to take food from this country, so great is their hatred of the United States.

LORD BOOTHBY: Well, I—

MR. LODGE: It's a sad thing when you think of the good relations we had for so many generations with China that they should be in this state of mind now. But I don't believe they'd take food from us, even though their people are now starving, largely because of the policies of the Chinese Communist government.

MR. SMITH: May I ask you something about the practical questions involved in bringing Red China into the United Nations. We could not throw the Nationalist Chinese out so there would have to be a two-China policy; would Red China come in on those conditions?

LORD BOOTHBY: I would hope that Red China—my view is that she would come in. I think so. But I think she would demand and I think she would have to be given a seat in the Security Council. I really think it is rather silly to seat the Formosan government on the Security Council. It shouldn't be on the ground that it's not big enough, or important enough, and nobody can deny that Red China is big and important, with—with 700—nearly 700 million people you can't just laugh that one off. I think they ought to be in the United Nations and they ought to be in the Security Council. And I think that in the meanwhile Formosa should be seated in the United Nations, too, and protected by the United States Fleet until a satisfactory negotiation—

MR. LODGE: Well, I'm not—

LORD BOOTHBY: —can be achieved.

MR. LODGE: —I'm not pretending China isn't there. I know China's there. And I've just quoted Chou En-lai and Marshall Chen Yi and Mrs. Roosevelt and I could quote a great many others to the effect that they do not want to come in unless they've—they've gobbled up Formosa, which these British statesmen do not want to see happen, and unless they've driven the United States out of the western Pacific—

MR. SMITH: Gentlemen—

MR. LODGE: —which you don't want to see happen either.

MR. SMITH: —Gentlemen, we've come to the point were I must ask you to sum up your arguments. You have two minutes each. Mr. Lodge, will you give your summary?

MR. LODGE: Well my—I have many arguments which I've tried to express tonight. But the—the basic argument is that the United Nations is not a cockpit where the law abiding and the criminal are indiscriminately scrambled up. The United Nations, under the Charter, is a place where nations must be, and I quote, "peace-loving." Now a regime that has done the violent and brutal things that the—that Communist China has done, which has violated the letter and the spirit of the Charter as regards Korea, as regards Tibet, as regards India, as regards Laos, as regards Formosa, as regards the overseas Chinese, as regards the drug traffic and many other things is not "peace-loving" within the definition of the United Nations Charter. To admit her to the United Nations, therefore, would stultify the United

Nations and I believe would result in the destruction of the United Nations. And the destruction of the United Nations would be one of the greatest single blows that you could take against the peace of the world. Now that doesn't mean that I wouldn't take another look at the whole thing the moment that Red Chinese behavior changed. The—the—I think Lord Boothby is a little confused. The question is not of admitting Red China. The question is of bringing about a change in attitude on the part of Red China. Once you do that then you can start solving the problems.

MR. SMITH: Robert Boothby, your summary.

LORD BOOTHBY: I think Mr. Lodge is still inclined to look back too much instead of looking forward. I think the record of Russia, the Soviet Union, is just about as bad over the last 30 years or 25 years, or whichever it is as the record of China since the war. And I think if one is always looking back, seeing what they did here is what they did then, and saying there is nothing to be done now because they behaved so badly in the past, you don't get anywhere. Now I believe that we got—humanity has got about 25 years at the outside to build some kind of a world order which will maintain peace or that this planet is going to be blown up, completely, and that will be a sticky and rather—and rather poor and miserable end to the human race. And I think that it is absolutely essential that if we are to avoid that you've got to have all the powerful nations in the world and Red China in particular, in the United Nations and try. Mr. Lodge himself said it would be a tragedy if the United Nations collapsed. If he means that, and believes it, then I think you've got to have the largest nation on earth within the United Nations and set down to the grim and difficult task of building some kind of a world government, some kind of a world order with some kind of an international police force ultimately to keep the peace of the world. Otherwise we'd all be blown to smithereens. Now that's why I want—that's the real reason why I want Red China in. Not because I love the Communists or Red China. Because I feel that the dangers involved in excluding her altogether from the only world organization that exists are too great to risk.

MR. SMITH: Well thank you very much, gentlemen, for an extremely well and tightly argued debate and thank you especially, Lord Boothby, for the understatement, I think, of the time when you said that for the planet to be blown up would be a sticky end.

INDEX